D1764767

A HISTORY

OF

THE CHURCH

FROM

𝕿𝖍𝖊 𝕰𝖆𝖗𝖑𝖎𝖊𝖘𝖙 𝕬𝖌𝖊𝖘

TO

THE REFORMATION.

BY

THE REV. GEORGE WADDINGTON,

Vicar of Masham, and Prebendary of Chichester.

PUBLISHED UNDER THE SUPERINTENDENCE OF THE SOCIETY FOR THE
DIFFUSION OF USEFUL KNOWLEDGE.

SECOND EDITION, REVISED:

IN THREE VOLUMES.

VOL. III.

LONDON: BALDWIN AND CRADOCK,

PATERNOSTER-ROW.

1835.

LONDON:
Printed by W. Clowes and Sons,
Stamford Street.

CONTENTS

OF

THE THIRD VOLUME.

a 2

CHAPTER XXIII.—*The Grand Schism of the Roman Catholic Church.*

Chapter XXIV.—*Attempts of the Church at Self-reformation.*

Chapter XXVIII.

PRELIMINARIES OF THE REFORMATION.

Section I.—*On the Power and Constitution of the Roman Catholic Church.*

Section II.—*On the Spiritual Character, Discipline, and Morals of the Church.*

HISTORY OF THE CHURCH.

PART V.

CHAPTER XXII.

Residence at Avignon.

(I.) *History of the Popes.*—Clement V.—conditions imposed on him by Philip—
he fixes his residence in France—Charges against the Templars—their seizure
—Council General of Vienne—its three professed objects—Condemnation and
punishment of the Templars—Remarks—Question on the orthodoxy of Boniface VIII.—Ecclesiastical abuses—Attempt at reform—Elevation and character
of John XXII.—his avarice—the apostolical chancery—his contest with Louis
of Bavaria—The emperor advances to Rome—creates a rival pope—fruitless
issue of the struggle—appeals from Pope to a General Council—charges of
heresy against John—his opinion respecting the intermediate state—commotion
in the Church—his dying confession—Remarks—Benedict XII.—his virtues
and endeavours to reform the Church—Clement VI.—Deputation from Rome—
its three objects—the Jubilee—multitude of pilgrims—conduct of the Romans
—Temporal prerogatives exercised by this Pope—Restrictions imposed in conclave on the future Pope, Innocent VI., and instantly broken by him—his
character and objects—disputes with the German Church—Urban V.—passed
some time at Rome—but returned to Avignon—Gregory XI.—deputation from
Rome—Catharine of Sienna—her pretensions—Embassy to Avignon—interview with the Pope—he goes to Rome and dies there—Observations—(II.) *General History of the Church, its heresies, &c.*—(1.) Decline of the papal power—
Intestine convulsions of the ecclesiastical states—consequent deficiencies in
papal revenues—means employed to replenish them—profligacy of the court of
Avignon—surpassing that of Rome—Temporal weakness and dependence of
the Avignon Popes—Growing contempt for spiritual censures—Appeals to
General Council—Disputes between the Pope and the Franciscans—Diffusion
of knowledge among the laity—(2.) Attempts at reform feeble and ineffectual
—(3.) The character of the rigid Franciscans—Schism in that order—The
Spirituals and Brethren of the Community—Their treatment by Clement V.—
by John XXII.—The Bull *Gloriosam Ecclesiam*—Some Spirituals burnt for
heresy—their consequent increase—they unite with Louis of Bavaria—the
Pope aided by the Dominicans—Remarks—Charles IV.—Change in the imperial policy—Triumph of the Pope and Inquisitors—Final division of the

Franciscans—The Beghards—The Lollards—their origin and character—their alleged opinions and mysticism—Some contemporary institutions of the Church —Heresy and persecution of Dulcinus—The Flagellants—their origin—progress—practice and sufferings—Concluding observations.

SECTION I.

History of the Popes.

Conditions of the election of Clement V.
WHEN Philip undertook to raise the archbishop of Bourdeaux to the pontifical chair, six conditions are believed to have been imposed by the monarch, and accepted by the subject. Five of them stipulated for the entire forgiveness of all the insults which had been offered to Boniface and the Roman See; for the restoration of the friends of Philip to communion and favour; for the power of exacting tenths for the five following years; for the condemnation of the memory of Boniface; for restitution of dignity to two degraded cardinals, and the creation of some others, friends of the king. The sixth was not then specified—the mention of it was reserved for a more convenient season *; and we may remark, that the others were obviously not suggested by any long-sighted policy aiming at the permanent humiliation of the Roman See, but rather by passion and temporary expediency. If we except the nomination of new cardinals, who would probably be French, there is not one among the conditions dictated, under the most favourable circumstances, by the great enemy of the see, which tended in effect to reduce it to dependence on his own throne, or even materially to weaken any one of the foundations of its power. Nor should this surprise us; since the violence which Philip exhibited throughout the contest, and the provocations which he received, make it probable that his animosity was rather

---

* Bzovius, Contin. of Baron. Annal. Ann. 1305, i. Fleury, liv. xc. s. xlix. Giannone, lib. xxii. cap. viii. Historians are not agreed what the sixth condition was—some assert that it was to heap additional anathemas on Boniface, and burn his bones; others suppose it to have been fulfilled by the condemnation of the Templars, others by the transfer of the papal residence to France. The violence of Philip's character, and the mere temporary character of most of his other stipulations, make the first, perhaps, the most probable conjecture.

personal against Boniface, than political against the Church, or even court, of Rome.

The first act of the pope elect was to assemble his reluctant cardinals at Lyons, to officiate at his coronation *; and his reign, which began in 1305 and lasted for nine years, was entirely passed in the country where it commenced. Clement V. was alternately resident at Bourdeaux, Lyons, and Avignon; and he was the first among the spiritual descendants of St. Peter who insulted the chair and tomb of the apostle by continual and voluntary absence : his example was followed by his successors until the year 1376. Thus, for a period of about seventy years, the mighty pontifical authority, which was united by so many ties to the name of Rome, which in its nature was essentially Italian, and which claimed a boundless extent of despotism, was exercised by foreigners, in a foreign land, under the sceptre of a foreign prince. This humiliation, and, as it were, exile of the Holy See†, has been compared by Italian writers to the Babylonian captivity; and this notion, which may have originated in the accidental time of its duration, has been recommended by other points of similarity. French authors have regarded the secession to Avignon in a very different light—but we shall venture no remarks on the general character of this singular period, until we have described the leading occurrences which distinguished it.

Clement V. immediately fulfilled most of the stipulated conditions—he restored the partizans of the French king to their honours; he created several new cardinals, Gascons or Frenchmen; he revoked the various decrees made by Boniface VIII. against France, even to the Bull *Unam Sanctam*—at least he so qualified its operation, as not to extend it to a country which had merited that exception by its faithful attachment to the

The secession to Avignon.

---

* King Philip officiated also, and condescended to lead the pope's horse by the bridle, according to the ancient fashion of imperial humiliation. Lyons boasted to be a free city, and the bishop had, in fact, gained the principal authority there, to the exclusion of that of the king of France.

† The popes who reigned at Avignon, and who were all French, were—Clement V.—John XXII.—Benedict XII.—Clement VI.—Innocent VI.—Urban V.—Gregory XI.

Roman See;—but when called upon to publish a formal condemnation of the memory of that pontiff, he receded from his
engagement, with the direct avowal that such an act exceeded
the limits of his authority, unless fortified by the sanction of a
General Council.

Very soon afterwards rumours were propagated respecting
various abominations, both religious and moral, perpetrated by
the Order of the Knights Templars—not in occasional licentiousness, but by the rule and practice of the society. Information of these offences was first communicated to Philip, afterwards to the pope; both parties attached, or affected to attach,
infinite importance to it; and at length it was determined to
refer that question also to a general council. The pope issued
orders for such an assembly, and appointed Vienne, in Dau-
phiny, as the place of its meeting. In the meantime, Philip
caused all the Templars in his dominions to be seized in one
day (October 30, 1307); and Clement exerted himself with
various, but very general, success to engage the other sovereigns of Europe to the same measure.

Council of
Vienne,
1311, A.D.
On October 1, 1311, the council assembled. Its professed
objects were three:—1. To examine the charges against the
Templars and secure the purity of the catholic faith. 2. To
consult for the relief of the Holy Land. 3. To reform the
manners of the clergy and the system of the Church *. The
first of these terminated in the entire suppression of the order;
their property† was transferred to the Knights of the Hospital,
who were considered a more faithful bulwark against the progress of the infidel—(it was thus that the *second* purpose of
the assembly was also supposed to be effected), while their
persons were consigned to the justice of provincial councils, to
be guided by the character, confession, or contumacy of the
individual accused. By these means the greater part unques-

---

* Bzov. Ann. 311, s. i. Fleury, l. xci. sect. xxvi.

† Excepting that in Spain and Portugal, which was consecrated to the formation
of a new order with the prospect of a Moorish Crusade, under the especial superintendence of the pope. We find it, moreover, affirmed by Dupin, Nouv. Biblioth.
Cent. XIV. chap. ii., that the publication of the Bull for the dissolution of the order
was prevented in Germany, nd that the Templars were there acquitted by a provincial council.

tionably escaped with their lives; but several were executed, and among these the Grand Master and the Commander of Normandy suffered under singular circumstances. They had confessed their guilt, and were consequently condemned by the bishops, to whom that office had been assigned by the pope, to the mitigated punishment of perpetual imprisonment. On hearing this sentence, they retracted their confession and inflexibly protested their entire innocence. The cardinals remanded them for further trial on the morrow, but in the meantime Philip, having learnt what had passed, and not brooking even so trifling a delay in the prosecution of his vengeance, caused them to be burnt alive in a small island in the Seine, on the same evening. They endured their torments with great constancy; and the assembled crowd, as it believed their guilt, was astounded by their firmness.

On the reality of their guilt or innocence depends the cha- *Probable* racter of Clement V.; for it is not probable that he was deceived *innocence* in a matter so important, involving the lives and property of so *of the* *Templars.* numerous and powerful a body, and to a certain extent the interests and honour of so many kings and nations. It is true that it was by Philip that the first attack was made both upon their character and their persons; but the blast which he sounded was presently repeated by the pope, and reiterated in every quarter of Europe. Again, the Templars were rich; and notwithstanding the nominal disposal of their property which was made at Vienne, there were few princes who entirely lost so favourable an opportunity for spoliation*. It is admitted, indeed, that Philip continually disclaimed any avaricious motive for his aggression; and he does not appear in fact to have turned his success to those ends; but he was irritated by their opposition to some former schemes, and against the Grand Master, in particular, he was known to entertain a personal and implacable animosity. As to the proofs of their guilt— the confessions, which several are affirmed to have made, do

---

* As the princes enjoyed the rents of the landed estates, until the commissioners of the Knights of Rhodes had made out their claims, there arose great delays in resigning them. Philip himself retained a certain sum for the expenses of the prosecution; but not sufficient to justify any suspicion of rapacity.

not rest on any satisfactory evidence, though it seems probable that some did really acknowledge all that was imputed to them. But of these some may have been driven into weakness by torment or terror; while others, individually guilty, may have imputed to the society their private crimes. At any rate, their confessions are confronted by the firmness of many others, who repelled, under every risk and torture, the detestable accusations. Indeed many of the charges were of a nature so very monstrous*, so very remote from reason or nature, as almost to carry with them their own confutation—at least, the most explicit and un-suspicious evidence was necessary to establish their truth; and none such was offered.

Philip was more successful in his efforts to destroy an ancient and powerful military order, than to disgrace the memory of an insolent pontiff; and the council, which suppressed the Templars with such little show of justice or humanity, con-tended with invincible eagerness for the reputation of Boniface. It was perseveringly attempted to attach the stain of heresy to his name; but though the king pursued this design with all the vehemence of malignity and revenge, the prelates assembled at Vienne, three hundred in number†, unanimously proclaimed his spotless orthodoxy—that he died, as he had lived, in the bosom of the Catholic faith. Disappointed in this favourite hope, the king was compelled to seek consolation in an edict published at the same time by the pope, which accorded a gracious pardon to the enemies and calumniators of Boniface.

---

* They are contained (see Bzovius. Ann. 1308, s. iii.) in six charges and four-teen questions—involving infidelity, blasphemy, and the most abominable im-purities. That which the sufferers appear most generally to have confessed under the torture, was the public denial of Christ, as a condition of admission into the order, attended with insults to the cross. We need scarcely refer the reader to the excellent remarks of Voltaire and Sismondi on this subject. The latter espe-cially confirms his opinion, that the Templars were *sacrificed*, by contemporary authority and substantial reasons. Ital. Rep., ch. xix.

† Bzov. ad ann. 1312, i. A very tedious process against the orthodoxy of Boniface had been carried on in 1310, before the pope at Avignon, where Nogaret appeared as his principal accuser, and the agent of Philip. But Clement, un-willing on the one hand to offend the king, and not daring on the other to scan-dalize the Church, interposed so many delays, that Philip at length decided to await the decision of the General Council. See Fleury, l. xci. s. xliii.

For the third and worthiest object of the labour of the The abuses of the Church. council, an abundant harvest was provided by the multiplied abuses of the church.   It was complained that (in France at least) the Lord's day was more generally devoted to business or to pleasure than to divine worship; that the ecclesiastical jurisdiction was frequently delegated to improper persons, and by them so scandalously perverted, that the censures of the church had lost their power and their terrors; that many contemptible individuals, defective alike in learning and in morals, were admitted to the priesthood; that prebends and other dignities, being now in most cases filled up by the pope, seldom by the bishop, were usually presented to strangers and even foreigners, men of dissolute morals, elevated by successful intrigues at the Court of Rome; and that thus the young and deserving aspirants for ecclesiastical promotion were frequently compelled to abandon the profession with disgust, and invariably became the bitterest and most dangerous enemies of the church.   Another abuse was, the immoderate indulgence of pluralities; many held at the same time four or five, some not fewer than a dozen benefices.   Another evil mentioned, is the non-residence of many of the higher clergy, occasioned by the necessity of personally watching their interests at the Vatican. The sumptuous luxury in which they lived, and the negligence and indecency with which the divine services were performed, constituted another charge against the beneficed clergy.   The profligacy and simony, publicly practised at the Roman Court, swelled the long list of its acknowledged deformities*.   On the

---

* The pope ordered all the bishops to bring with them to the Council expositions of all which seemed to demand correction.   Two of these memoirs are still extant, and from them the abuses here briefly enumerated are taken. See Fleury, liv. cxi. s. li., liii.   Semler, sec. xiv. cap. ii.   "Infinita fere sunt quæ reformari deberent; ignorantur quasi totaliter a Christianis articuli fidei et alia quæ ad religionem et salutem animarum pertinent . . .   Monachi non vivunt in suo monasterio; sicut equus effrenis discurrunt, mercantur, et alia enormia faciunt, de quibus loqui verecundum est et turpe . . prælati non possunt bonis personis hodie providere obstante multitudine Clericorum apud Curiam Romanam impetrantium, qui quidem nunquam Ecclesiam intrarunt . . etiam pueri obtinent dignitates . .   Utinam *Cardinales*, qui sunt animalia pennata, plena oculis ante et retro, talia perspiciant . . similes sibi similes eligunt . . bene dico opus esse in *Capite* etiam et in membris reformatione."   The author of this bold appeal to

dissolution of the council, Clement published, in 1313, its canons, which were fifty-six in number. Most of these were, indeed, nominally directed to the reformation of the Church: the progress of heresy was vigorously opposed; and attempts were made to prevent or heal some divisions now beginning to spring up *within* the Church—subjects to which we shall presently recur. Some constitutions likewise regulated the relation of the bishops to the monastic orders; and others imposed greater decency* on the *lower* orders of the clergy; but the grand and vital disorders of the Church, those from which its real danger proceeded, and which were in fact the roots whence the others started into life and notice, these were left to flourish unviolated, and to spread more and more deeply into the bosom of the communion.

Election of John XXII.

Clement V. died very soon afterwards; and so great was the fame of his wealth, acquired through the sale of benefices and other such traffic, that, as soon as he was known to have expired, all the inmates of his palace are stated to have rushed with one consent to his treasury; not a single servant remained to watch the body of his master, insomuch that the lights which were blazing round fell down and set fire to the bed. The flames were extinguished; but not till they had consumed half the body of the richest pope who had yet governed the Church. His death was followed by an obstinate difference between the French and Italian cardinals respecting the *nation* of his successor. This was prolonged by the impatient interference of the populace†, excited, as it would seem, by some Gascon soldiers, who proposed to terminate the dispute by seizing the persons of the Italians. Accordingly, they set fire

the head, which was not itself excepted from the general censure, is not known to posterity—the document is given by Raynaldus E *Cod. Vaticano*. Bzovius (ann. 1310, sec. vi.) enumerates, at great length, fifteen of the principal abuses with which the Church was charged on this occasion.

* The following is the Twenty-second Canon. "Clerici conjugati carnificum seu macellariorum aut tabernariorum officium publicè et personaliter exercentes, vestes virgatas, partitas, neque statui suo conducentes, portantes severius puniantur." See Bzovius, Contin. Ann. Baron., ann. 1313, sec. i.

† The conclave was held at Carpentras, a place on the banks of the Rhone, not far from Avignon. It happened that the court was assembled there when the Pope died; it therefore became the legal place for the new election.

to the conclave; but the terrified cardinals escaped by another exit, and immediately dispersed and concealed themselves in various places of refuge. Such, indeed, was their panic, or at least their disinclination, that two years elapsed before they could be reassembled. At length, after a second deliberation, which lasted forty days, they elected James of Euse, a native of Cahors, cardinal bishop of Porto—such long delay and repeated consultation did it require to add to the list of pontifical delinquents the name of John XXII.! That pope was of very low origin, the son of a shoemaker or a tapster*; but he had natural talents and a taste for letters, which were early discovered and encouraged, and his gradual rise to dignity in the Church was not disgraced by any notorious scandals.   It is admitted† that he was modest in his manner of life, sober, not luxurious, nor profuse in his personal expenditure.   In the course of almost every night he rose to say his office and to study; he celebrated mass almost every day; was easy of access and rapid in the performance of business.   Though hasty in temper, he was of an informed and penetrating mind; and an enlarged understanding qualified him for affairs of importance. But he had not long been in possession of the highest eminence, before he abandoned himself, without scruple or shame, to his predominant passion, avarice.   He was not, indeed, exempt from the ambitious arrogance without the Church, and the vexatious intolerance within it, which seem at this time to have been communicated by the chair of St. Peter to its successive possessors—in a greater or less degree to each, according to his previous disposition to those qualities; but avarice was the vice by which John was individually and peculiarly characterized, and to which he gave, during his long

* Giovanni Villani, lib. ix. c. lxxix.   Giannone, lib. xxii. cap. viii.
† By Giovanni Villani. See Fleury, l. xciv. s. xxxix.   The violent party writers of the day, Franciscans and Ghibelines, who heaped every epithet of abuse on the hostile name of John XXII., have been too hastily credited by some modern writers.   The qualities and habits mentioned in the text at least repel the charge of universal profligacy which has been brought against him.   Nevertheless, it is the opinion of Sismondi (chap. xxix.) that his elevation was not less ascribable to his intrigues and effrontery than to his talents; and the public acts of his pontificate require no comment.

pontificate, the most intemperate indulgence. Not contented with the usual methods of papal extortion, he displayed his ingenuity in the invention of others more effectual: he en-
The Apos-larged and extended the rule of the Apostolical Chancery*;
tolical he imposed the payment of *annates* on ecclesiastical benefices;
Chancery. he multiplied the profitable abuse of dispensations; he increased in France the number of bishoprics; and commonly took advantage of the vacancy of a rich see, in order to make five or six translations, promoting each prelate to a dignity, somewhat wealthier than that which he had before held: so that all were contented (says Giannone†) while all paid their fees. In a word, he considered kingdoms, cities, castles and territories to be the real patrimony of Christ, and held the true virtue of the Church to consist, not in contempt of the world and zeal for the faith and evangelical doctrine, but in oblations and tithes, and taxes, and collections, and purple, and gold and silver. Such is the language of the Italian historians, and if it be somewhat exaggerated by their general prejudices against the popes of Avignon, the immense‡ treasures which were unquestionably amassed by John, prepare us to believe much that is asserted respecting the methods by which he exacted them.

* He reduced the system of Apostolical taxation to a code of canon law. A deacon or sub-deacon might be absolved for murder for about twenty crowns; a bishop for about three hundred livres: every crime had its price. See Denina, 14, vi.

† We might be disposed to receive this with some little suspicion, even from Giannone—since he was not only an Italian, but a decided anti-Gallican also—were not the facts directly derived from Giov. Villani.

‡ Giov. Villani (lib. xi. cap. xx.) asserts (on the authority of his own brother, resident at Avignon, who received his information from the treasurers of the pope) that the treasure found on the death of John XXII. amounted to more than eighteen millions of florins in gold coin; while that in services of the table, crosses, crowns, mitres and other trinkets of gold and precious stones, rose to about seven millions more—total, twenty-five millions of golden florins. The greater part of this was amassed by John, and chiefly by his reservations of all the benefices of all the collegiate Churches of Christendom. His ordinary pretext was the liberation of the Holy Land.

The "Storia or Nuova Cronìca," of Giovanni Villani, a citizen of Florence, begins at the earliest age and continues to the year of his death, 1348. It chiefly relates to the affairs of Florence, and is most instructive during the last century. His brother Matteo continued the History (with an addition by his own son Philip) as far as the year 1364.

But the circumstance, by which this pontificate was most distinguished, and which for a moment raises us from the sordid details of fraud and extortion to the recollection of the loftier vices of the Gregories and the Innocents, was a contest which the pope perseveringly maintained with the Emperor, Louis of Bavaria. Having entered at greater length, perhaps, than was necessary into the description of the two former conflicts between the empire and the holy see, and of that also between Philip and Boniface, we shall not pursue the particulars of this last and feeblest effort of declining papacy. The leading events are briefly these. The electors assembled at Frankfort in 1314 were divided; and while some chose Louis for successor to the throne, others supported Frederic, Archduke of Austria. John refused to confirm either of the pretenders. In a bull published in 1317, he maintained that all imperial vicars lost their authority at the death of the Emperor, and that it devolved on the Pope. " God himself," he continued, " has confided the empire of the earth, as well as that of heaven, to the sovereign pontiff. During the interregnum, all the rights of the empire devolve upon the Church; and he who, without the permission of the apostolic see, continues to exercise the functions entrusted to him by the Emperor in his lifetime, offends against religion, plunges into crime, and attacks the divine Majesty itself*. Nevertheless, the claimants continued to dispute the empire with the sword till the year 1323, when Frederic was defeated and taken prisoner. The Duke of Bavaria then took upon himself the imperial administration, without at all soliciting the sanction of the pope. Thereupon the latter pronounced sentence against him, and prepared to support Leopold, the brother of Frederic. Louis boldly appealed to a General Council, and to a future and legitimate Pope, and he received in return an ineffectual sentence of excommunication and deposition.

In the mean time, the war between the opposite parties had

marginal notes: The Pope's contest with Louis of Bavaria.

Appeal of Louis to a general Council.

---

* See Sismondi, Rep. It., ch. xxix. This claim was pressed more than once by the Avignon Popes—the more eagerly because the legitimacy of " the King of the Romans" was involved in that of the Emperor; and the Pope, who pretended to the prerogatives of the one, had a nearer interest in usurping the functions of the other.

been maintained with great fury in Italy, and upon the whole to the advantage of the Guelphs, through the powerful aid of the King of Naples, still faithful to the Roman see. Consequently Louis was pressed to cross the Alps. He assembled a parliament at Milan, and assumed with great solemnity the iron crown. From Milan he advanced to Rome: the celerity of his march anticipated all opposition, and the ceremony of his coronation was there performed, with abundant pomp and acclamation, in January, 1328. Vigorous measures of hostility were at the same time adopted—a sentence of degradation against John XXII., and the appointment of a new and imperial Pope, who assumed the name of Nicholas V. But though an emperor might at this time be sufficiently powerful to repel with impunity the pontifical censures, his aggressive attempts were at least as futile as those of his adversary. Nicholas was rejected by the Catholic world; and after two years of vain pretension, surrendered his title and his person* to John. The Emperor had been previously compelled to retire from Rome. So that after a fruitless contest of about seven years, the relative situation of the combatants was little altered; and the sentences of degradation and deposition, mutually reiterated, had no other effect than to prove to the world (though not so to the individuals engaged) that there was something in the claims of both parties extravagant and unfounded ; and that the temporal authority on the one hand, and the spiritual on the other, though occasionally confounded by the abuse of both, were in fact, as they were in essence and origin, independent.

We observe that, in one respect at least, Louis deviated during this contest from the tactics of his two predecessors, and adopted those of the French King. The appeal from the authority of the pope to that of a general Council was the

---

* According to the account of Giovanni Villani (lib. x. cap. clxiv.), he was delivered up by the Pisans, and sent to Avignon. He threw himself at the feet of the Pope, and prayed for mercy : " E con bel sermone eautorità se confessò peccatore *eretico* col Bavero insieme, che fatto l' havea." It should be added, that John treated him extremely well, and that he died a natural death at Avignon three years afterwards.

severest wound which could be inflicted on papal arrogance.
It was more than that,—since it led almost necessarily to the
limitation of papal power.   In an age of darkness, such an
appeal might have been treated as a wanton though bitter insult.   But reason was at length awakened, and men were beginning to consider what ought to be, as well as what had been.
The promulgation of a new and grand ecclesiastical principle,
on the authority of a king and an emperor, would excite some
consideration even among the most bigoted ; and there would
be few who did not begin to entertain a question respecting the
spiritual omnipotence of the Pope.

Another measure was taken by the Emperor, also after the
example of Philip, which tended more directly to the same end.
In the assembly held at Milan, at which several prelates
attended, John XXII. was formally impeached on the charge
of heresy.   Sixteen articles were specified, in which he
erred against the constitutions of the General Council ; and he
was pronounced to have virtually forfeited the pontifical dignity.   It was a bold proceeding in Louis, on the judgment of
a provincial meeting of his own partizans, to convict the Vicar
of Christ of heretical depravity*.   It was indeed to repel
usurpation by usurpation, and to seize the spiritual sword in
his strife to recover the material.   The accusations were probably false, and certainly fruitless ; they acquired no general
credit at the time, nor have they adhered to the memory of the
accused.   Nevertheless, the mere assumption of papal fallibility in matters of faith by two powerful monarchs, and the
vigour of the measures taken on that assumption, naturally
confirmed the confidence of those whom reason had already
led to the same conclusion.

But it also happened very strangely, that the same extraordinary charge was again incurred by John XXII. towards the
end of his life, and with much greater appearance of reason.   In
some public discourses delivered in the course of the years 1331

side note: Charges of Heresy against John XXII.

---

* The Pope's disputes with the Spiritual Franciscans had raised a considerable
party, even in the Church, against him.   Besides, all the theologians and sectarians, who were discontented with papal government, declared in favour of Louis.
See the latter part of this chapter.

and 1332, he had rashly declared his opinion, that the souls
of the faithful, in their intermediate state, were indeed permitted to behold Christ as a man ; but that the face of God,
or the Divine Nature, was veiled from their sight until their
reunion with the body at the last day *.   The publication of
this new doctrine produced a deep sensation throughout Chris-
The Beati-
fic Vision. tendom.   The immediate admission to the Beatific Vision, a
received and popular tenet, had been openly impugned by the
highest spiritual authority : it became necessary either to resign
the tenet or to condemn the pope.   Robert, King of Sicily,
warmly exhorted John, whom he had attached by a long and
useful alliance, to retract the offensive declaration.   Philip VI.
of France united with equal ardour in the same solicitation.
The most learned Dominicans, together with all the doctors
and divines of Paris, humbly urged the same entreaty.   Laymen joined with churchmen, the friends of the pontiff with his
bitterest enemies, in rejecting and denouncing his error.   The
pope was so far moved by such general and powerful interference, that he assembled, at the close of 1333, his cardinals
in public consistory ; and after having caused to be read in their
presence all the passages of all writers who had treated the
subject, (the labour of five days,) he protested that he had not
designed to publish a decision contrary to Scripture or the
orthodox faith ; and that, if he had so erred, he expressly revoked his error.

This explanation may possibly have been considered somewhat equivocal ; at least it had not the effect of allaying the
irritation which prevailed, and a second consistory was appointed for the same purpose in the December following.   But
on the evening preceding its assembly, John was seized by a
mortal malady.   Nevertheless, he summoned his cardinals,

* Mosh., Cent. XIV., p. ii., ch. ii. " The recompense of the saints, before the
coming of Jesus Christ, was the bosom of Abraham ; after his coming, his passion, and ascension, their recompense, till the day of judgment, is to be under the
altar of God, that is, under the protection and consolation of the humanity of
Jesus Christ.   But after the judgment they shall be on the altar, that is, on the
humanity of Jesus Christ, because then they shall behold not only his humanity,
but also his divinity as it is in itself ; for they shall see the Father, the Son, and
the Holy Ghost." These are the expressions of John, as given by Fleury, liv.
xciv., sect. xxi.   Raynald. ann. 1331. s. 43, et seq. Baluz. 1. Vit.

twenty in number, around him, and one of the last acts of his Jan. 3, long life (he died at 90) was to read in their presence a 1334. bull, containing the following declaration:—" We confess and believe that souls purified and separated from their bodies are assembled in the kingdom of heaven in paradise, and behold God and the Divine Essence face to face clearly, in as far as is consistent with the condition of a separated soul. Anything which we may have preached, said, or written contrary to this opinion, we recall and cancel *." Still even the expiring confession of the pontiff was not considered sufficiently explicit to satisfy the measure of orthodoxy; and thus it came to pass that John XXII., after having ruled the apostolical church for above eighteen years, which he passed for the most part in amassing treasures †, in fomenting warlike tumults, and in chastising heretics, died himself under the general imputation of heresy. But the error of the pontifical delinquent was discreetly veiled by the Church which it scandalized; and when Benedict XII., his successor, hastened in the year following to restore the unanimity of the faithful respecting the Beatific Vision, he described it as a question which John was preparing to decide, when he was prevented by death ‡.

The reasons which gave such popularity to the orthodox opinion on this subject, and excited such very general opposition to the other, were chiefly these:—If the Virgin, the Saints, and Martyrs, were not yet admitted to the Divine presence; if they were only in distant and imperfect communication with the Deity, it was absurd to uphold their mediatorial office; it was vain to supplicate the intercession of beings who had no access to the judgment-seat of Christ. Moreover, the mere insult thus offered to the dignity of the saints, and the dispa-

---

* Bzov., Ann. 1334. i. Fleury, liv. xciv., sect. xxxviii. J. Villan. l. xi. c. 19, &c. Bain. 1334. s. 36, 37.

† In the histories of his life we find many edicts directed against alchemists and the adulterers of coin,—proving at least how much of his attention was turned in that direction. He issued money from the pontifical mint, and counterfeited, with some loss of reputation, the florins of Florence. Giov. Villani, lib. ix., cap. clxx.

‡ In the bull *Benedictus Deus*, of which the substance is given by Fleury, l. xciv., sect. xliv., from Raynaldus, 1336, s. 2, 3.

ragement of their long-acknowledged merits, were offences
very sensibly felt and resented throughout the Catholic world.
Another reason is likewise mentioned; and it may, in fact, have
been the most powerful motive of dissatisfaction—if the dangerous opinion were once established, that the souls of the just
when liberated from purgatory must still await the day of
judgment for their recompense, the indulgences granted by the
Church would be of no avail; " and this (as the King of
France very zealously proclaimed) would be effectually to
vitiate the Catholic faith * !"

Benedict
XII.

Benedict XII. was born at Saverdun, in the county of Foix,
and was the son of a baker. He possessed considerable theological learning, but such little talent for the management of
an intriguing court, that he suspected and proclaimed his own
incapacity † for the pontifical functions. But it proved otherwise; for he brought to that office a mind sensible of the corruption which surrounded him and of the abuses which disfigured his Church, and he employed his useful administration
in endeavours to remedy such of them as were placed within
his reach. In the first exercise of his power, he dismissed to
their benefices a vast number of courtly ecclesiastics, who pre-

* See the end of the Tenth Book of Giovanni Villani. In the course of the
controversy, excited solely by his own vanity, John professed the most impartial
desire for truth ; but it was observed that he showered his benefices most liberally
upon those who supported the new opinion. Philip of France came boldly forward as the champion of orthodoxy, and the inviolable unity of the Church—
" dicendo laicamente come fidel Christiano, che invano si pregherebbero i Santi,
ò harebbesi sperenza di salute per li loro meriti, se Nostra Donna Santa Maria, e
Santo Giovanni, e Santo Piero, e Santo Paolo e li altri Santi non potessero vedere
la Deitade al fino al dì del Giudizio, e havere perfetta beatitudine in vita eterna ;
e che per quella opinione ogni indulgenza e perdonanza data per antico per Santa
Chiesa, ò che si desse, era vana. Laqual cosa sarebbe grande errore e guastamento
della Fede Catholica."

† The cardinals, twenty-four in number, agreed with an unusual decision and
unanimity, ascribed by some to divine inspiration, by others to a ridiculous mistake. Jacques Fournier (such was his name) being also a cardinal, was present
at his own election, and when he heard the determination of his brethren, he
reproached them with having elected an ass. He was certainly the least eminent
member of the sacred college ; and to that circumstance, according to Giovanni
Villani (lib. xi., cap. xxi.), he was indebted for his elevation. The cardinals,
intending in the scrutiny to throw away their votes, fatally concurred in heaping
them upon him—" ch' era tenuto il più menomo de' Cardinali."

ferred the splendour, and perhaps the vices, of Avignon to the discharge of their pastoral duties. A large body of cavaliers had been maintained by the pomp of his predecessor, with whose services Benedict immediately dispensed. He was sparing in the promotion of his own relatives, lest the king should make them the means of exerting influence over himself. He undertook the serious reform of the monastic orders —not confining his view to the less powerful communities, but purifying, with indiscriminate severity, the poor and the opulent, the Mendicants, Benedictines*, and Augustinians; and the order of Citeaux, to which he had himself belonged, was the first object of his correction. He established numerous schools within the monasteries, and also compelled the young ecclesiastics to frequent the universities of Paris, Oxford†, Toulouse, and Montpellier. In the education of the clergy he saw the only reasonable assurance for the stability of the Church. Lastly, he even displayed a willingness to restore the papal residence to Italy if it should appear that his Italian subjects were desirous of his presence; but the Imperialists were at that moment so powerful, and party spirit so highly inflamed, that he received little encouragement in that design.

Clement VI., who succeeded Benedict in the year 1342, did not imitate his virtues; but while, in his public deportment, he more nearly followed the footsteps of John XXII., he appears even to have outstripped that pontiff in the license of his private life. He was scarcely installed in his dignity, when he was addressed by a solemn deputation from the Roman

Clement VI.

* Vit. Benedict XII. ap. Baluzium. Benedict has been celebrated by the pen of Petrarch—

Te cui Telluris pariter Pelagique supremum
Contulit imperium virtus meritumque pudorque.

Yet we observe (in Bzovius, ann. 1339, s. l.) that on one occasion this virtuous pontiff *reserved* the appointment to all the prelacies of all the churches for the space of two years. Did he overlook in his reforming zeal the abuses by which he profited?

† About twenty years later, an archbishop of Armagh complained that when he was resident at Oxford, the University contained 30,000 students; whereas, at the time when he wrote (in 1358) it contained only 6000. The reason given for the decrease was, that the Mendicants, who occupied several of the chairs, had seduced so many of the young students into their order, that parents were no longer willing to expose their children to that risk.

Embassy
from
Rome.
people. It consisted of eighteen members *, one of whom was Petrarch; and it was charged with three petitions. The first was, that Clement would accept, personally and for his life only, the offices of senator and captain, together with the municipal charges; the second, that he would return to the possession of his proper and peculiar see; the third, that he would anticipate the secular Jubilee ordained by Boniface VIII., and appoint its celebration in the *fiftieth* year. The pope accepted for himself the proffered dignities, but without prejudice to the rights of the see; to the second, which was an important and wise request, he returned a friendly but decided refusal; but the third, which only tended to swell the profitable abuses of religion, he accorded without hesitation. The following is the substance of the bull which he issued (in 1343) for this purpose—" That the love of God has acquired for us an infinite treasure of merits, to which those of the Virgin and all the saints are joined;—that he has left the dispensation of that treasure to St. Peter and his successors;—and consequently, that pope Boniface VIII. had rightfully ordained, that all those who in the year 1300, and every following centurial year, should worship for a specified number of days in the churches of St. Peter and St. Paul, at Rome, should obtain full indulgence for all their sins. But we have considered (he continues) that in the Mosaic law, which Christ came spiritually to accomplish, the fiftieth year was the jubilee and remission of debts; and having also regard to the short duration of human life, we accord the same indulgence to all henceforward who shall visit the said churches and that of St. John Lateran on the fiftieth year. If Romans, they must attend for at least thirty following days; if foreigners, for at least fifteen."

Celebration of the
Jubilee, in
the year
1350.
This proclamation was diligently published in every part of Christendom, and excited an incredible ardour for the pilgrimage. During a winter of unusual inclemency, the roads were thronged with devout travellers, many of whom were compelled to pass the night without shelter or nourishment, in the fear of robbery and the certainty of extortion. The streets of Rome

---

* The orator on this occasion was Colas di Rienzo, afterwards the tribune of the republic.

presented for some months the spectacle of a vast moving multitude continually flowing through them, and inexhaustibly renovated. The three appointed churches* were thronged with successive crowds, eager to throw off the burden of their sins, and also prepared to deposit some pious offering at every visit.

It is affirmed, that from Christmas till Easter not fewer than a million, or even twelve hundred thousand strangers were added to the population of the pontifical city; for as many as returned home after the completion of the prescribed ceremonies were replaced by fresh bands of credulous sinners; and those again by others, in such perennial abundance, that, even during the late and unwholesome season of the year, the number was never reduced below two hundred thousand. Every house was converted into an inn; and the object of every Roman was to extort the utmost possible profit from the occasion; neither shame nor fear restrained the eagerness of their avarice. While the neighbouring districts abounded with provisions, the citizens refused to admit a greater supply than was scarcely sufficient to satisfy, at the highest expense, the simplest demands of the pilgrims; and thus those deluded devotees, after surmounting all other difficulties on their errand of superstition, were at length delivered up to be starved, as well as plundered, by the inhabitants of the holy city. Such was the moral effect produced upon the Roman people by a festival which was established for their pecuniary profit, and which disturbed the social system through every rank and profession, from one end of Christendom to the other †.

Conduct of the Romans.

---

* In visiting the three churches (says Matt. Villani), including the distance from his lodging and the return to it, each pilgrim performed about eleven miles. The streets were perpetually full, so that every one was obliged, whether on foot or on horseback, to follow the crowd ; and this made the progress very slow and disagreeable. The holy napkin of Christ was shown at St. Peter's every Sunday and solemn festival for the consolation of the pilgrims (*Romei*). The press then was great and indiscreet; so it happened that sometimes two, sometimes four, or six, or even twelve, were found there crushed or trampled to death."

† This account is abbreviated from Matteo Villani, lib. i., cap. lvi. It is to be observed, that the pope received a share of the oblations left by the pilgrims in the different churches. Clement VI. employed the fruits in an unsuccessful attempt to recover the property of his Church from the nobles, who had usurped it.

Clement's transactions in the foreign States.

Clement renewed with Louis of Bavaria those vexatious disputes which had been begun by John XXII., and conducted with so little advantage or honour to either party. Neither had the present difference, after many haughty words, any lasting result; though it seems probable that the pope might have succeeded in exciting a civil war in the dominions of his adversary, had not the latter escaped that calamity by death. The same pontiff defended his temporal prerogatives in a correspondence with Edward III. of England. At another time, publicly and in full consistory, he presented to Alphonso of Spain the sceptre of the Fortunate Islands. Nor was this right contested: the less so, perhaps, since St. Peter had claimed, in much earlier ages, the peculiar disposal of all insular* domains. Clement also made an important acquisition to the patrimony of the apostle by the purchase of the city of Avignon. The jurisdiction over that territory belonged to the queen of Naples, as Countess of Provence; and for 80,000 golden florins she consented, in a moment of poverty, to part with the valuable possession. A splendid palace, which Benedict XII. had begun, was now completed and amplified by Clement; and the luxury of the cardinals followed, at no very humble distance, the example of the popes. These circumstances seemed to remove still farther the prospect of the pope's restoration to his legitimate residence, and thus heightened the alarm which some were beginning to entertain for the stability of the papal power.

Clement VI. died five years afterwards, in 1352—celebrated for the splendour of his establishment, for the sumptuousness of his table, and for his magnificent display of horses, squires, and pages; for the scandalous abuse of his patronage; for manners little becoming the sacred profession, and for the most unrestrained and unmuffled profligacy †.

---

* Urban II., in his bull of 1091, presented the island of Corsica to the bishop of Pisa; and we all recollect that our Henry II. received from Adrian IV. the donation of Ireland. " En quoi (says Fleury) ce qui me paroit le plus remarquable n'est pas la prétention des Papes, mais la crédulité des Princes." But credulity, like many other weaknesses, is very commonly the offspring of interest.

† See Matt. Villani, lib. iii., cap. 43. He delighted to aggrandize his relatives by conferring on them baronies in France, and raising them, however young and

During the vacancy of the see, the cardinals, while in con- Oath or Capitulation taken in conclave.
clave, passed certain resolutions for the limitation of the pon-
tifical power and the extension of their own wealth and privileges; and the whole body bound themselves by oath to observe them. One of their number was then elected, Etienne
Aubert, bishop of Ostia, who took the name of Innocent VI.;
and almost his earliest act was to annul, as pope, what he had
subscribed as cardinal. We must detest his private perjury;
yet, as the sacred college had no power of legislation, unless
under the presidency of the pope, and as their office while in
conclave was expressly restricted to the election of a pope,
their constitutions could not legally be binding either on the
Church or on the future pontiff. The attempt of the cardinals
is chiefly important as it shows the power and the arrogance
into which they had risen during the disorders of the Church;
and the conduct of the pope is remarkable as having furnished
an example and a plea to several of his successors, who violated similar engagements in after times with the same perfidy.
In every instance the future pope was a voluntary party to the
compact deliberately made in conclave; in most cases he confirmed it after his election; he finally broke or evaded it in all.

Yet Innocent VI. was a man of simple manners and un- Innocent VI.
blemished moral reputation; and having found the Church
nearly in the same condition in which John XXII. bequeathed
it to Benedict, he imitated the latter in his judicious efforts to
reform it. But though he held the see for more than nine
years, it seems doubtful whether his mild and perhaps feebly-
executed measures were effectual in removing any important

---

abandoned, to the highest dignities. " At that time there was no regard to
learning or virtue: it sufficed to satiate cupidity with the Red Hat—Huomo fù
di convenevole scienzia, molto cavallaresco, poco religioso. Delle femine essendo
Archivescovo non si guardò, ma trapassò il modo de' secolari giovani Baroni: e
nel Papato non sene seppe contenere ne occultare ; ma alle sue camere andavano
le grandi dame, come i prelati, e fra l' altre una Contessa di Torenna fù tanto in
suo piacere, che per lei faceva gran parte delle grazie sue. Quando era infermo
le Dame il servivano, e governavano come congiunte parenti gli altri secolari. Il
tesoro della Chiesa stribuì con larga mano. Delle Italiane discordie poco si
curò, &c." We observe that some of the cardinals so appointed incurred the
severe reproach of Innocent VI. by their undisguised debaucheries. Matt.Villan.,
lib. iv., cap. lxxvii.

abuse. At least in the year 1358 we perceive him engaged in
a dispute with his German clergy, not respecting the relaxation
of their discipline, but upon a subject which was usually much
dearer to the popes of Avignon. Innocent demanded an extraordinary subsidy of the tenth of all ecclesiastical revenues,
for the use of the apostolical chamber. The clergy of the
three provinces of Treves, Mayence, and Cologne boldly refused
payment; the spirit of interested opposition spread rapidly;
and all orders of ecclesiastics throughout the whole empire
united to resist the demand. The pope yielded without struggle
or remonstrance; but he immediately sought his consolation
in the exercise of one of the grossest usurpations of his see.
He sent his messengers into every part of Germany, with
orders to collect half the revenues of all vacant benefices, and
to *reserve** them for the use of the holy see. The emperor
(Charles IV.) approved the resistance of his bishops†; but

Reserva-
tions.

* Even the see of Avignon was left without a bishop during this and the preceding pontificate; it was reserved, and its revenues usurped by these popes at
their own pleasure. Thus it would seem that the reforms of Innocent VI. were
not more disinterested than those of Benedict. See Vita Urbani V. ap. Baluz.
and Baluzius's Notes.

† In an assembly of the princes of the empire held on this subject in 1359,
Conrad d'Alzeia, Count Palatine, who was charged with the defence of the clergy,
addressed the meeting to this effect:—" The Romans have always considered
Germany as a mine of gold, and have invented various methods to exhaust it.
And what does the pope give in return but epistles and speeches? Let him be
master of all the benefices as to their collation, but let him leave the revenues to
those who own them. We send abundance of money into Italy for divers manu-
factures, and to Avignon for our children who study there, and who there solicit,
and let us not say purchase, benefices. No one is ignorant what sums are every
year carried from Germany to the court of Rome for the confirmation of prelates,
the obtaining of benefices, the carrying on of suits and appeals before the holy
see—for dispensations, absolutions, indulgences, privileges, and other favours.
In all former days the archbishops used to confirm the elections of the bishops
their suffragans; but in our time John XXII. violently usurped that right. And
now another pope demands from his clergy a new and unheard-of subsidy,
threatening his censures on all who shall refuse or oppose. Resist the beginning
of this evil, and permit not the establishment of this degrading servitude."—
(Fleury, l. xcvi., s. xxxviii.) It was in the same year that the emperor addressed
to the archbishop of Mayence the following complaints respecting the secular
habits of his clergy:—" De Christi Patrimonio ludos, hastiludia et torneamenta
exercent; habitum militarem cum prætextis aureis et argenteis gestant, et calceos
militares; comam et barbam nutriunt, et nihil, quod ad vitam et ordinem ecclesiasticum spectat, ostendunt. Militaribus se duntaxat et secularibus actibus, vita

on the one hand he denounced, in the strongest language, their pride, their avarice, and luxurious indulgences; while, on the other, he warmly demanded of the nuncio from Avignon wherefore the pontiff was so forward in taxing the property of the clergy, so remiss and languid in the restoration of their discipline? We should add, however, that Innocent, on his side, did not disregard that appeal, but turned himself to restrain the vices of the German prelates, while the emperor exerted his authority to protect them from the spoliations to which they were perpetually liable from powerful laymen.

He was succeeded, in 1362, by Urban V., whose reign was Urban V. distinguished by the first serious attempt to restore the pontifical court to Rome. On the solicitation of his Italian subjects, urged by the eloquence of Petrarch*, and on an understanding of perfect friendship and mutual co-operation with the emperor, he abandoned the splendid security of Avignon, and departed, with his reluctant court, for Rome. On his way, a popular tumult at Viterbo dismayed and even endangered some of the cardinals; but no other impediment was offered; and in October, 1367, the pope once more occupied the half-dismantled palace of his predecessors. He divided a peaceful residence of about three years between Rome† and Visits Montefiascone, where he passed the summer months; and his Rome. alliance with Charles IV. of Germany, whatever may have been the dispositions of his subjects, guaranteed him against any political outrage. Nevertheless, in 1370, probably on the persuasion of the French cardinals‡, he returned to Avignon, where he died immediately afterwards.

et moribus, in suæ salutis dispendium et *generale populi scandalum*, immiscent." —The passage is cited by Robertson, Hist. Charles V., b. ii.

* " Cogita tecum" (says Petrarch) " in die ultimi judicii an resurgere amas inter Avinionicos peccatores famosissimos nunc omnium qui sub cœlo sunt, an inter Petrum et Paulum, Stephanum et Laurentium, &c. &c." The same argument, which is the concluding one, may probably have been adopted a few years afterwards by Catharine of Sienna. Petrarch became a very ardent eulogist of this pope.

† The pope had the honour, during this period, of entertaining *both* the emperors as his guests. Charles IV. visited him at Montefiascone in 1368; John Palæologus in the year following at Rome.

‡ Spondanus, Ann. 1370, s. iv. St. Brigida, who was at that time in Italy, is related to have assured the pope, on the authority of an express revelation from

Gregory
XI.

Again was a Frenchman, Gregory XI., elected to the chair, and he professed his inclination to repeat the experiment which had been made by his predecessor; but his resolution was weakened and retarded by the intrigues of his countrymen. He listened, indeed, with attention to the prayer of a solemn deputation from the Roman people, in 1374; but he took no immediate steps to grant it. Two years afterwards he was still at Avignon, when he was again importuned on the same subject by a very different instrument of solicitation. There

Catharine
of Sienna.

was one Catharine, the daughter of a citizen at Sienna, who had embraced the monastic life, and acquired extraordinary reputation for sanctity. In the rigour of her fastings and watchings, in the duties of seriousness and silence, in the fervency and continuance of her prayers, she far surpassed the merit of her holy sisters; and the austerities which she practised prepared people to believe the fables which she related*: for she professed to have derived her spiritual knowledge from no human instructor—from no humbler source than the direct and personal communication of Christ himself. On one occasion especially she had been blessed by a vision, in which the Saviour appeared to her, accompanied by the holy Mother and a numerous host of saints, and in their presence he solemnly espoused her, placing on her finger a golden ring, adorned with four pearls and a diamond. After the vision had vanished, the ring still remained, sensible and palpable to herself, though invisible to every other eye. Nor was this the only favour which she boasted to have received from the Lord Jesus: she had sucked the blood from the wound in His side; she had received His heart in exchange for her own; she bore on her body the marks of His wounds—though these too were imperceptible by any sight except her own †.

the holy Virgin, that his return to Avignon would be immediately followed by his death—abiit nihilo-minus. Peter of Arragon likewise prophesied the Grand Schism from the same event.

* Fleury thinks that she believed them herself, and he may be right:—Une imagination vive, échauffée par les jeûnes et les veilles, pouvoit y avoir grande part: d' autant plus, qu' aucune occupation extérieure ne détournoit ces pensées. —Liv. xcvii., s. xl.

† On the body of St. Francis the wounds were *visible*—a distinction conferred, as his disciples assert, on him alone. See Spondanus, ann. 1376, s. iv.

We do not relate such disgusting impiety either because it was uncommon in those days, or because it was crowned by the solemn approbation of the Roman Church; for the wretched fanatic was canonized, and occupies no despicable station in the holy calendar: but it is a more extraordinary circumstance, awakening a deeper astonishment, that Catharine of Sienna was invited from her cell by the messengers of the Florentine people, and officially charged, by the compatriots of Dante and the contemporaries of Petrarch, with an important commission at the court of Rome; the office of mitigating the papal displeasure and reconciling the Church with the republic was confided to her enthusiasm. She was admitted to an early *Her embassy to Avignon.* audience. Her arguments, which she delivered in the vulgar Tuscan, were explained by the interpreter who attended her; and in conclusion, the pope (assured, no doubt, of her devoted attachment to the Church) expressed his willingness to leave the differences entirely to her decision*. But the embassy of Catharine was not confined to that object only; for, whether in obedience to the wish of the Florentines or to the suggestions of her own spirit, she urged at the same time the duties which the pontiff owed to his Italian subjects, to the tombs of the apostles, to the chair of his mighty predecessors; and her reasons are said to have influenced a mind already predisposed to listen to them.

Respecting the motives which created that disposition, it must be mentioned that the residence at Avignon was no longer recommended by that careless security which at first distinguished it from Rome. The open country had been invaded and the city menaced by one of those *companies* of associated brigands who were the terror of the fourteenth century. During the pontificate of Innocent VI. the inhabitants and the court had been compelled to seek for safety sometimes in their arms†, sometimes in their riches; and though the danger might not be very pressing, yet being near at hand and

---

* Spondanus, ann. 1376, s. ii. It does not appear, by the way, that the Florentines were ready to extend the same deference to her judgment. See Sismondi, chap. xlix.

† Matt. Villan., lib. vii., cap. xcvi.

fresh in recollection, it perhaps influenced beyond its importance the councils of Avignon. The pope's resolution, however, still wavered, and was at length decided by a second embassy from Rome, which arrived about two months after the
visit of St. Catharine. The envoys expressly assured him that,
unless he returned to his see, the Romans would provide a
pope for themselves, who would reside among them; his cardinal legate at the city gave him the same assurance; and it
afterwards appeared that overtures had already been made to
the abbot of Monte Cassino to that effect. This was no mo-

The Pope ment for delay. Gregory immediately departed for his capital,
returns to
Rome and and thence, whatever may have been his private intentions, he
dies there. was not destined to return.

The place of the death of the pope was at that time of more
lasting impression to the Church than his living residence, because the election of a successor could scarcely fail to be affected by the local circumstances under which he might be
chosen. There could be no security for the continuance of
the papal residence at Rome, until the crown should be again
placed upon the head of an Italian. At Avignon the French
cardinals, who were more numerous, were certain to elect a
French pope; but the accident which should oblige the conclave to assemble in an Italian city might probably lead,
through the operation of external influences, to the choice of
an Italian. That accident at length occurred, and its consequences will be pursued in the following chapter.

Section II.

General *History of the Church during this period.*

In the meantime, the account which has been given of the
pontiffs of Avignon is sufficient to throw some light on their
individual merits, and, what is of much more consequence, on
the general character and principles of their government. But
a deeper consideration of this important period suggests some
reflections which it is proper to express, while there are some
facts less closely connected with papal biography, but not less

strictly appertaining to the history of the Church, which have not been noticed, but which cannot wholly be overlooked. Accordingly, we shall first observe the decline which took place, during these seventy years, in the pontifical power, and point out some of its most efficient causes. We shall then inquire whether any attempts were made to obviate that decay by measures of reform or renovation. The heresies which divided the Church and the efforts which aimed to extinguish them, will be the last, and not the least instructive, subject of our examination.

I. The various and desultory warfare, alike savage in its circumstances and fruitless in its results, which was waged in Italy by the legates and mercenaries of the pope *, in defence of the patrimony of St. Peter, is described by the civil historians of those times; nor shall we descend to recount the intrigues which were employed in the same contest, or the bulls which were so repeatedly and vainly launched from Avignon. But the evil, which these measures were intended to repress, was deeply felt at the time, and was fatally pernicious in its consequences. We have observed that, even during his residence at Rome and in the fullness of his power, the pope was seldom in undisputed possession of the apostolical domains. But, in the season of his emigration, he could place little reliance on the friends whom he had deserted, while the licence of his enemies and depredators increased without restraint. Cities and populous districts were thus separated from the ecclesiastical states, and several among the Roman barons, who were his feudatories, usurped in perpetuity the lands of the Church. The deficiency thus occasioned in the pontifical treasury must needs be supplied from some new source; since the change in nation and residence had abated nothing of the pomp and prodigality of the Vicars of Christ.

Decline of the papal power.

---

* It is truly remarked by Sismondi, that the Avignon popes prosecuted these wars with greater ardour than they would have done had they been resident in Italy, or than they could had they drawn their resources only from Italy. They suffered no personal dangers, they saw nothing of the evils which they inflicted, and they derived their supplies from the contributions of the whole Church. The complaints which the Florentines had against the papal *Gubernatores* are enumerated with great warmth by Leonardus Aretinus. Hist. Florent., lib. viii., 181, 2.

Funds of the Church. The funds to which they had chiefly recourse for this purpose were twofold. By the more general and easy sale of indulgences they levied a productive tax upon the superstition of the people; at the same time they made a dangerous experiment on the submission of the clergy by various imposts on all ecclesiastical property*. The right of presentation to all vacant sees appears to have been first usurped by the Popes of Avignon. It was abused as soon as usurped ; and the system of reservation deprived the diocese of its pastor, while it carried away its revenues into the apostolical chancery. At the same time the frequent contribution of tenths and first-fruits, raised under crusading or other pretences, gave deeper offence to the sacred order, as it touched their interests more directly and personally. It was vain to imagine, that the monstrous system of papacy could long subsist, unless supported by the attachment and almost unanimity of the ecclesiastical body; nor could such concord easily take place, unless the pope could contrive to identify his interests with those of the clergy, or at least to persuade the clergy of such identity. But from the hour that his exigencies could only be supplied at their expense,—that his dignity, his luxuries, his very vices, tended to impoverish and no longer to enrich them; from that hour a very powerful, though very sordid instrument of connexion began to give way, and the discontent, which might originate in pure selfishness, found abundant fuel, as well as ample justification, in the manifold abuses which disgraced the papal court.

---

* The following are mentioned as the sources of the papal exactions from England during the fourteenth century :—(1.) Peter's Pence ; for the supposed support of the English pilgrims at Rome ; it scarcely exceeded 200*l.* a year. (2.) King John's census, of 1000 marks. This was tolerably well paid, till the time of Urban V., in 1366, when king, clergy, lords, and commons, proclaimed the payment illegal, and it ceased. (3.) The payment of first-fruits. The origin **First-fruits.** of this is referred to the presents which, in very early ages, a bishop at his consecration, or a priest at his ordination, paid to the officiating prelate. It was abolished by Gregory the Great, but soon grew up again, and insensibly came to be rated at a year's income. Presently, when prelates obtained their sees by provisions, those first-fruits flowed into the apostolical treasury. Those of smaller benefices were at first granted, seemingly in the thirteenth century, to bishops and archbishops. At length, Clement V. reserved for his own use all first-fruits, and John XXII. imitated his example. See Lingard's History.

Still there had been less danger from this disaffection had Rapacity of the Popes, and profligacy of the court. the popes pressed their impolitic exactions with any show of moderation; had they been contented to satisfy their necessities, or even to maintain with judicious liberality the ceremony and pomp of office. But so far were they removed from any such discretion, that it rather seemed their object so to reign as to unite prodigality with avarice—to spend profusely and hoard insatiably. It was this spirit of rapacity which presided over the councils of Avignon. The lofty pretensions, which animated and even dignified the pontiffs of former days, were degraded into mere lifeless instruments to the lowest worldly purposes. We seek not now for the deep religious enthusiasm of the earliest popes, for that had long been extinguished; but the exalted and magnanimous audacity of the Gregories and even the Innocents,—the settled *ecclesiastical* fanaticism (if we may use the expression), which so long dazzled the reason of man,—these too had at length given place to baser principles and passions. The cloud of mystery, which had so long hung over the chair of St. Peter, filling the nations with awe for the invisible power and majesty residing there, was at length dispersed and broken away, and in its place was discovered the nakedness of human turpitude. The charm of opinion began gradually to dissolve; and whatsoever prejudices many still retained in favour of the papal government, they were weakened by the sordid motives which now directed it; and an unpopular vice became still more detested, when it was found engrafted upon the ecclesiastical character.

Another cause, which materially assisted, during this period, in hastening the decline of papacy, was the shameless profligacy of the court of Avignon. There is no dispute as to this fact; and even moderate writers have strained their language, in order to present a just picture of that deformity. We refer not to the partial philippics of Petrarch; nor to the unholy name of Babylon, which may first have been affixed to the city of the popes, from a similarity in crime. But when Denina assures us, that the licentiousness of the clergy became excessive and universal, from the time that the scandals of Avignon

had removed all restraint and shame; and when Sismondi *
declares, that that people and that court made themselves
manners out of the vices of all other nations, those historians
do not exceed the testimony of contemporary authorities. The
causes and sources of this pestilence are disputed: it is ascribed
by the French writers to the importation of transalpine fashions
and morals into their less corrupt climate; while the Italians
retort the charge of greater impurity, and enlarge, perhaps
with more justice, on the temptations which may ensnare a
bishop who resides at a distance from his diocese, who is surrounded by a court of prelates also non-resident, without any
spiritual cure or any restraint from the observation of the
people. Howbeit, this argument would have had more weight
had the court of Rome been less polluted: but whatever may
have been the comparative delinquencies of Rome and Avignon,
it is at least certain, that the latter were more indecent and
more notorious; that offences, which (if they were really practised) had been heretofore veiled or only partially known, were
now exposed and stigmatized universally; and that the only
alternative thenceforward remaining to the pontifical government was to correct those flagrant abuses, or by their means to
fall †.

Decline of the papal power.
The publication of the celebrated bull called *Unam Sanctam*,
in which Boniface VIII. asserted the extreme pretensions of
his see to both descriptions of supremacy, may be viewed,
perhaps, as the great crisis in papal history. As far as that
moment, nothing had been ceded in the pontifical claims, and
nothing abated in the arrogance with which they were pressed.
It may be that their foundations had been silently crumbling
beneath them, but their actual instability was still concealed

* Denina, Delle Rivoluz. d'Italia, lib. xv., cap. vi. Sismondi, Rep. Ital., chap.
xlviii. See Baluz., Pref. in Vitas Pontif. Avenionensium.

† During the pontificate of John XXII., complaints against the clergy began
to break out very commonly in France, occasioned by the excess to which they
carried their jurisdiction, as well as other offences. But Philip the Regent protected them,—"Jura ecclesiarum auxerim potius quam imminuta velim." It is
remarkable, that it was to this declaration that the kings of France are indebted
for the title of *Catholic*,—so, at least, says Bzovius, Ann. 1329, s. xxiii.

by outward show and magnificent pretension. But from this point the descent was perceptible, and it soon became very rapid; and Philip, having penetrated the secret of the real weakness of the see, effectually brought about its humiliation. His attack on the personal safety of Boniface, though in a great measure defeated by the undaunted constancy of that pontiff, disclosed to the whole world the domestic insecurity of the Bishop of Rome.

Still it must be acknowledged that a Pope, as long as the seat of his government was his own capital, could not ever be the mere dependent of any sovereign; and this is the argument by which Roman Catholic writers most plausibly defend the temporal power of the chief of their Church. But no sooner had he crossed the Alps and transferred his court to France, than he descended to the condition of a subordinate prince. It was in vain that the formalities of respect, and even the show of equality, were observed: the influence of the king of France predominated in the councils of Avignon; and the sense and the notoriety of temporal dependence discouraged the ghostly pretensions of the pope, and blunted the edge of his weapons. For this, among other reasons, we are not surprised to observe, that the ecclesiastical censures lost much of their efficacy during this age; that they were received in various countries with various degrees of indifference, but that this indifference was everywhere increasing. Italy herself was the most conspicuous for the general neglect with which she treated them; and Italy, in her spiritual rebellion, did no more than imitate the pre-eminent obduracy of Rome. For Rome was irritated by the absence of her prelate; and her habitual contumacy and lawlessness found great pretence and some justification, when she was deprived even of the ordinary advantages of an episcopal residence.

Another severe, and even incurable, wound was inflicted on papal despotism by the threat of appeal to a General Council, which was first urged by Philip, and eagerly repeated by Louis of Bavaria. That there was a power superior to the pope within the Church itself was a principle which was sure to find many advocates even in the ecclesiastical body. Once broached,

Appeal to a General Council.

and on such high authority, it was commonly discussed, and by discussion gained ground; and though the progress of reason against established prejudice is usually very slow, the minds of many were prepared for this innovation during the first half of the fourteenth century; but it was not carried into full effect till somewhat later.

Of the dissensions which divided the Church during this period, and which we shall presently notice, none probably occasioned so great scandal at the time, as the disputes carried on by the more rigid Franciscans against the pope himself. Between the higher ranks of the secular clergy and their acknowledged head, we have observed differences not uncommon respecting their authority, their revenues, or the removal of their corruptions. But the regular orders had hitherto observed the strictest allegiance to a President, whose interests were inseparably connected with their own; and this was the first occasion on which the pontifical court was disturbed by the sound of monastic insubordination. There was danger in an example, which might be followed by any discontented branch of the priesthood; but the consequence, which really and immediately followed it, was to open the eyes of the laity to the deformities of the system, and to rouse them against those abuses, which ecclesiastics themselves no longer conspired to defend.

But another, and a still more certain instrument for the subversion of papacy had been now for some time in operation, and it acquired additional power during the fourteenth century; an instrument, independent of the accidents of papal " captivity " or ecclesiastical discord, and one which, however aided by such circumstances, would surely have accomplished its task without them. Human reason had at length been awakened from its long lethargy; and though its first flights were wild and irregular, it was beginning to extend its influence and to know its authority. The means of education were multiplied, its character was varied and exalted ; and what was most important to all purposes of general improvement, its advantages were no longer confined to a privileged body, but were diffused through every condition of society. The subjects, indeed, which still engrossed the greater portion of the learning of those days, were generally connected with theology, or with the constitution and discipline of the Church. Still it was not to churchmen alone that such discussions were confined. Those who profited by the ecclesiastical system were no longer the only persons qualified to argue respecting it. No sooner were the gates opened, than the laity rushed into that province with great eagerness; and the seeds of the Reformation were already scattered, though it was uncertain when they would break forth, or what fruits they would bear in their maturity.

II. The abuses which gave most offence at the commencement of this period, so as to excite the indignation of the better portion of the clergy, and even to claim the attention of the hierarchy, have been enumerated in a former page, as they were presented to the Council of Vienne. They were not corrected on that occasion, and they increased in consequence.

Attempts at reformation.

We must not, however, suppose, that no regulations were enacted under the Avignon popes for the amendment of the ecclesiastical system: they were very numerous*; but the misfortune was, that they were generally misdirected. They descended to insignificant particulars, or were fabricated by one portion of the clergy against another, or by the orthodox against the heretics; or they related to the imposts of the pope and the means of evading them : they never reached those grand deformities which endangered the Church, through the just offence which they gave to the laity. It is true that some papal constitutions were published both against the non-residence of the clergy and the holding of pluralities. But the first could not be consistently enforced by a prelate who had never visited his own see ; and the popes, though they held decisive

---

* A number of the Councils assembled for this purpose, and the principal canons enacted by them are mentioned by Semler, sec. xiv., cap. ii. The following are specimens :—Concil. *Coloniense*, ann. 1313. " Ne clericis publica pœnitentia imponatur, cum alii in albis procedunt, alii in nigris cappis, in facie laicorum. Ne fiant imprecationes contra aliquas personas." Concil. *Trevirense, ej. ann.* " Contra gerentes cucuteras, seu cucusas, mitras, virgatas, scacatas vestes. Contra convivia in exequiis... Ut ante vel post vel super altare sit imago, sculptura, pictura, in cujus Sancti meritum constructum sit... Si infans caput ex utero emiserit a muliere baptizetur; si solum caput vel pars corporis major appareat nec discerni potest sexus : dicat, *Creatura* Dei, ego, &c. &c., et erit baptizatus."

language*, were manifestly insincere in the second. Or, if we are to admit that one or two among them were really earnest in their wishes and endeavours, they were at least prevented from taking measures to effectuate them by the fear of offending the most powerful, though perhaps the least deserving, part of the sacred body.

Divisions and heresies.

III. When Francis of Umbria first established his rigid Order, his rule was celebrated by the applause of successive popes. The impious fables which he propagated, respecting the miraculous impression of the Saviour's wounds on his body, and other such matters, were countenanced and dignified by the authority of the Church; he was adopted with eagerness into the family of the Saints †; and the extreme austerity of the institution seemed in some fashion to be sanctified by the superstitious reverence thus studiously thrown around the name of the Founder. We are not, then, to be astonished when we observe, that several among his followers adhered to the very letter of his instructions with unprecedented pertinacity, and scorned the vulgar temptations to soften their severity. The example of relaxation set to them by almost every other

---

* John XXII., in 1317, put forth a constitution against all ambitious and avaricious clergymen, complaining of their non-residence, neglect of hospitality, the ruin of their churches, &c. And we observe, at the same time, that he deposed a bishop; not, however, on any of these grave charges, but for the offence of contumacy. (Bzov., ann. 1317, s. xiii.) The same pontiff also published an edict against pluralities, beginning " *Execrabilis quorundam*," &c., and continued in a strain of emphatic abuse. (See Vit. (3tia) Joh. XXII. ap. Baluzium.) Similar laws were launched, with the same inefficiency, by Benedict XII., and afterwards by Innocent VI. A curious story is told to prove the zeal of this last. Innocent, before his elevation, had a favourite chaplain, on whom had been conferred seven benefices. As soon as he became pope, the chaplain again presented himself, bringing with him a little godson, for whom he wished also to procure a benefice. But the pope, like a just man, answered him, " You have seven good benefices; resign the best of them to that boy." On which, when Innocent saw that the petitioner was discontented, he again said, " You have still six benefices, and fewer would suffice for your necessities: choose, then, for yourself the three best of them, and resign the others, that I may bestow them, for the honour of God, on three poor clergymen." The pope was highly applauded for that act, as having therein followed the path of spiritual, rather than carnal, affection. See Vita (4ta) Innocent VI., apud Baluzium.

† Both Francis and Dominic were canonized by the same pope, Gregory IX. (about 1235); so likewise was Anthony of Padua, and other less considerable personages.

Order, the desertion of the more numerous part even of their own brethren, the moderate indulgence enjoined by the Pope himself, were insufficient to seduce those honest fanatics from strict obedience to their law, or to abate the vivid faith which they placed in their master. For indeed it was to faith that their feelings amounted, when they maintained that St. Francis was a second Christ—nothing inferior or dissimilar to the first; and that the institution which he left behind him was the true gospel of salvation.

Entire and absolute poverty, the complete renunciation of all property, whether common or personal, was the fundamental principle of the society, the only principle of Christian obedience—the only rule of evangelical perfection. In defence of that position, it became them at the same time to profess and argue, that the practice of Christ and his Apostles had been rigidly formed upon the same rule; and this became accordingly the question in dispute with their theological adversaries. Those adversaries, as we may well suppose, were neither few nor of humble rank. A courtly and luxurious hierarchy were scandalized by that unqualified assertion of the necessity of poverty; and Christ's imperious vicegerent upon earth was shocked by so homely a picture of the humility of his heavenly Lord.

Some unsuccessful endeavours were made in the preceding century to bring the Fratricelli, or Minorites (so they were denominated) to a more reasonable view of the gospel institution, and of the *spirit* of their own rule: but it does not appear certain that any personal outrage was offered them until the year 1306; and even then it proceeded, as was naturally to be expected, from the more worldly members of their own fraternity. From Italy, many then fled into Provence, and were scattered over the south of France; and at this time they are represented to have united with the Spirituals, and the Beghards and Beguines. The name Spiritual is said to have been first assumed by the followers of a schismatic of that age, named Pierre d'Olive; the others were the Tertiarii, or third order of Franciscans. All were equally opposed to the existing system of papal government. As their principles were

henceforward identified, so also was their history ; and the
term *Spiritual* is that by which the observers of the rule of absolute poverty were commonly distinguished from their less
austere *Brethren of the Community.*

Disputes between the Pope and the Franciscans.

Clement V. interposed his mediation between these contentious mendicants ; and at the Council of Vienna he issued the
Bull *Exivi de Paradiso,* with the design of bringing them to
concord by mutual concession. He permitted to the Spirituals
the enjoyment of the most abject poverty; while at the same
time, to such Franciscans as resided in barren countries, where
the resources of mendicity were precarious, he allowed the use
of granaries and storehouses, as places of deposit for their
common alms. Nevertheless, though all acts of violence were
for the moment suspended, the division of the Order continued
as before, and the mutual animosity was in no degree abated;
and a distinction in dress at this time introduced by the Minorites, who adopted a meaner and coarser habit, contributed
no little to inflame the controversy.

Bull of John XXII.

Matters stood thus when John XXII. was raised to the
pontificate ; and since the moderation of his predecessors had
not availed to heal the schism, he entered without any delay
into the opposite system. We observe that the Fratricelli are
enumerated among the *heretics* condemned in an edict which
he published in 1317 ; and in the year following he made them
the object of a memorable bull :—" The glorious Church which
has neither stain nor wrinkle, which Christ loved, and for which
he delivered himself to death, that he might sanctify it by
washing it with water in the Word of Life—this Church the
Prophet knew by the revelation of the Spirit to be placed before all nations ; and admiring the splendour of so much dignity, he exhibited it under the similitude of royalty, saying—
A queen stood on thy right hand, in gilded garments, &c.*"

* " *Gloriosam Ecclesiam,* non habentem maculam aut rugam, quam Christus
dilexit, pro qua semet ipsum tradidit, &c. Nimirum ipsa Christi Sponsa Virgo
Mater Ecclesia, quia inclyto Capiti suo Domino Jesu Christo inviolabilis fidei
glutino copulatur, et ejus imperio prona obedientia substernitur, cum Illo unum
effecta, tam incomparabilis unionis merito rebus omnibus, more regio, principatur.
Quæ dum pia et devota religione terrena despicit, cælestia petit, omne sinistrum
premens, à dextris Sponsi gloriosa consistit. Et quia geminæ charitatis splendore

After describing the nature of the union between Christ and his spouse the Church, and especially eulogizing the charity of the latter, the pope proceeded to expose the errors of the Minorites.   He classed them under five heads, and showed how they combined the various enormities of the Donatists, of the Waldenses, and the Manicheans, while they also followed the " foul traces" of Montanus and Priscilla.   The burden of their offence was contempt of the " bonds of the Church," and disrespect for its ministers; howbeit, being convicted by the edict of John of certain condemned and stigmatized heresies, they were consigned by the same act to inquisitorial authority.   The agents of oppression executed their part with no delay; and the very same year four of the Fratricelli were seized at Marseilles, and burnt to death.

From this moment the contest assumed a much more serious character.   The devotion of the Spirituals was now sealed, and their resistance sanctified, by the blood of their martyrs; their zeal, their activity, their numbers everywhere increased; and the more violent were the proceedings of the inquisitors, the more advocates did the persecuted acquire, the more generally they rose into respect and consideration.   Their great principle respecting the poverty of Christ was now made the subject of solemn deliberation; and the most celebrated divines of the age, especially those of Paris, were officially consulted on the question, and finally the pope himself descended into the field of controversy—and happier had been his fortunes, and his memory more honoured, had he confined his hostility to that bloodless warfare.   At the end of 1322 he published a Constitution, in which he confuted the arguments of the Franciscans, and asserted for the monastic orders the right of property, instead of the simple *use* of their immediate necessaries.   The

---

omni ex parte rutilat, in vestitu aureo etiam angelicis spiritibus admiranda coruscat.   Cujus inæstimabilis decor, quia vario vivendi genere in una tamen charitate perficitur, quasi de vestis pulcherrima varietate lætatur. . . ."   Such were the senseless and even impious rhapsodies, with which a very bad pope celebrated the corrupt church, which he still further corrupted by his acts and his eulogies; —not that he was really blind to its deformities, but because he was too timid or too wicked to correct them, and because he believed that the system, with all its vices upon its head, would still last and be profitable *for his own time.*

Spirituals rejected the right with the same obstinacy with
which it was dictated by the pope ; and it was at least a singular contest, and worthy of a more religious age and more reasonable motives, where the one party indignantly repudiated
the worldly possessions which the other imperiously obtruded
—where a body of beggars preferred the endurance of a deadly
persecution to the sacrifice of the duty of poverty.

In this manner the dispute proceeded, until the rupture between John and Louis of Bavaria became open and decided.
Then the Emperor, as if to turn against the Church the old
ecclesiastical policy, hastened to profit by the divisions of his
adversary, and to foment the spiritual rebellion. The provinces of the empire were thrown open to all the denominations
of schism and heresy; and the multiform enemies of papacy
found refuge in the dominions of Louis, and honour at his
court. Marsilius of Padua, Cæsenas, Bonagratia, and William
Occam, were the most illustrious among those exiles. They
directed their eloquence, their learning, and their satire, both
personally against John, and generally against the system of
the Church; and their writings, which were eagerly read even
by that generation, were transmitted with still greater profit to
a less prejudiced posterity.

On the other hand, the Pope* was ardently supported by his
Dominican emissaries. Their thirst for heretical blood was
heated by a particular jealousy of the Franciscan Order.
Wherever an avenue was open they penetrated. They pursued
the fugitives even into the remote plains of Poland and Hungary, and introduced into those ignorant regions the machinery of the Inquisition. But France and Italy† were the scene

* The history of John XXII. abounds with edicts against the various denominations of heresy. We are also bound to mention that he published (in 1326)
one Constitution to repress the *too great zeal* of certain inquisitors in Sicily ; but
when we examine the nature of that zeal, we find that it had ventured to attack
"nostros et apostolicæ sedis officiales vel nuntios, &c." John, as well as several
other popes, extended more protection to the Jews than they enjoyed elsewhere.

† Vit. John XXII. ap. Baluz. Mosheim calculates, from various records pub
lished and unpublished, that the names of about two thousand persons, of both
sexes, may be enumerated, who suffered martyrdom in France and Italy for their
inflexible attachment to the poverty of St. Francis. Cent. xiv. p. 2. ch. ii.

of their most successful exertions; and these were not confined to the pontificate of John. Even the virtuous Benedict began his reign by an anathema against the Fratricelli; and it is remarkable, that, in the Constitution which he published on this occasion *, the articles of their heresy are swelled to fifty-five. Their denial of *the power of the pope to permit them to have property* is among the most curious, and not the least grave, of their offences;—some very gross absurdities were also imputed to them, which may have been calumniously, as indeed they may have been truly, alleged. But there is one observation here necessary, which will tend to account for the great multiplicity and vagueness of the charges advanced. A furious war was at that time raging in Italy between the imperial and papal factions; and it was a part of the crooked policy of the churchmen of Rome to confound political enmity with spiritual perversity, and to brand the adversaries of the visible church with the crime of heretical depravity. Among the adversaries of the church they usually classed its reformers—those who were indeed its only real friends; and thus it happened, that the term heresy came now to comprehend every opinion unfavourable to the ecclesiastical government of the day, and the gates of the Inquisition received without distinction a various and indiscriminate multitude. *Church principles.*

Still, as long as the reign of Louis continued, a secure asylum was offered to all descriptions of Dissenters; and these, being already connected by one common principle and one common wrong, may have adopted from each other the absurd opinions which some of them certainly held. But the spirit which united them was deep animosity against the pope, whom they accused in their turn of impiety and usurpation. In the year 1345†, Louis was succeeded by Charles IV.; and as that *Protection of the Franciscans and others by Louis of Bavaria.* *His death.*

---

* Bzov. ad ann. 1335. s. ii.

† About the same time died William Occham, "pestilentissimus Hæresiarcha." —Bzovius (ann. 1347, s. xxxvi.), though he designates this Englishman to have been " omnium incentor malorum, auctor scelerum, cultor tenebrarum, &c. &c.," still does not attribute his death to divine interposition;—which is the more surprising, because he had not hesitated to pronounce somewhat earlier (ann. 1321, s. xxi.) that Dante died through the peculiar vengeance of heaven, which visited his calumnies against the popes.

prince was chiefly obliged for his elevation to pontifical influence, so his policy followed the interests of the court of Avignon. If the principles of the Bavarian had continued to govern his dominions for another generation, it is not improbable that the empire would have wholly freed itself from papal supremacy, and raised the banners of reformation in the fourteenth century with no inconsiderable advantage to religion. But such anticipation of the more perfect triumph of a more enlightened age was cut short by the perfidy * of the imperial counsels. The numerous insurgents against the despotism of Rome, whom Louis had encouraged and protected and created, were betrayed by his successor into the hands of the avenger. The peaceful provinces of the empire, hitherto sacred from the inroads of persecution, were now thrown open to the Dominicans. Their irruption was supported by secular edicts and arms; and the extirpation of the " Voluntary beggars"—the enemies of the Church and the " *Roman empire*,"—was pressed with equal ardour by the Pope and the Emperor. The houses of the offenders were given to the tribunal of the Inquisition to be converted into prisons for heretics†; and their effects were publicly sold, for the equal profit of the inquisitors who ordered, of the magistrates who enforced, and of the poor who witnessed, their execution. The survivors fled towards the banks of the Rhine, to Switzerland, Brabant, and Pomerania; but they were followed by a tempest of mandates and bulls, and hunted by the keen Dominicans even into their most distant retreats; till at length it is admitted that the greater part of Germany was restored, after this sanguinary purification, to the peaceful embrace of the Church.

* This is no ground perhaps for imputing to Charles *personally*, that his intolerance was aggravated by treachery. The individual stands convicted of persecution only. But the circumstance of this change adds one to the many instances in which the steady, consistent perseverance of the Vatican has carried its point through the fluctuations of the imperial policy.

† See Mosheim, Cent. xiv., p. ii., ch. ii. Their crime is mentioned in the edict (published at Lucca in 1369) which condemns them. " They are a pernicious sect, who pretend to a *sacrilegious* and heretical *poverty*, and who are under a vow that they neither ought to have, nor will have, any property, whether special or common, in the goods they use—which they extend even to their wretched habits."

But neither edicts, nor bulls, nor inquisitors, could suppress the spirit of the schism, though they might extinguish its name; and those who preserved their obedience to the more rigid rule were still found to be so numerous, and the love of that discipline was still in some provinces so prevalent, that the popes at length thought proper to sanction the institution. Accordingly, the Franciscan order was by authority divided into two bodies, which subsist to this day—the more indulgent were called the Conventual Brethren, the more austere the Brethren of Observance. The disputes which afterwards disturbed this arrangement were partial and insignificant; and the historian may express his astonishment, mixed with sorrow, that so simple a method of reconciliation could only be reached through the paths of intolerance and oppression. *[marginal note: Authorized division of the Franciscan order.]*

The term Beghard was in this age commonly applied to the Tertiaries of St. Francis; and though in its origin probably innocent of such principles, it was now involved in the guilt and fate of the anti-papal heresies. The " Brethren of the free spirit," the harmless mystics of the last century*, had been some time known by that appellation; and sometimes they are designated as *Lollards* in the records of the following age. The reason of their confusion is, that both names were indiscriminately used by the Church to stigmatize those who dissented from it, without any new inquiry as to the grounds and points of their dissent. Mosheim, who has investigated this subject with great diligence, considers the Lollards † to have been a society of pious laymen, formed in the first instance at Antwerp for the purpose of visiting the sick and burying the dead during a season of pestilence; for the clergy are affirmed to have deserted their official duties as soon as they became attended with peril. The humane motives and religious practice of the new society caused it to spread throughout Flanders and many parts of Germany, and it was encouraged by the respect of the magistrates and the love of *[marginal note: Beghards and Lollards.]*

---

* See Mosheim, Cent. xiii., p. ii., ch. v.

† Mosheim, Cent. xiv., p. ii., ch. ii. The word Lolhard means a *singer*—as Beghard means one who *prays*. The former were also called the " Cellite brethren and sisters—the Alexian brethren"—from the cells in which they lived, and the saint who was their patron. See Semler, Secul. xiv., cap. i.

the inhabitants. Its success excited the jealousy, as indeed it reflected on the reputation, of all the clergy; but the Mendicants had perhaps a deeper motive for animosity against it when they found that their own profits suffered through its gratuitous charity. Accordingly, they raised the customary clamours of impiety and heresy: under the mask of extraordinary holiness, the Lollards concealed forsooth the blackest errors and the most enormous vices; they were denounced at the pontifical throne, and their name has passed into the language of the Church to designate a misbelieving and sanctified hypocrite.

Their im-
puted
tenets. They *may* have held some foolish opinions—among those generally attributed to them the following are the most peculiar: that the mind ought to be called away from the external and sensible parts of religion, and fixed on inward and spiritual worship; that the soul which is wholly absorbed in the love of God is free from the restraint of every law, and may gratify its natural appetites without sin; that perfect virtue and perfect beatitude may be obtained in this world; and that persons so circumstanced are removed above every worldly consideration; so that the moral virtues, as well as the religious ceremonies, might be neglected without offence. Moreover, they pretended that there were two Churches, the carnal Church, which was that of Rome; the spiritual, which was confined to their own society* . . . Such were the crimes imputed to them by the churchmen; and this last may really have been the

* Other charges are instanced by Bzovius (ann. 1307, s. ix.) They held that the mass, baptism, and extreme unction were useless ceremonies; that Lucifer was an injured being, and that the angels, as well as all the enemies of their own sect, would be finally condemned; that Mary did not continue a virgin after the nativity; that the body of the Lord in the Eucharist was not real; that marriage was only sanctified whoredom; that God neither punished nor regarded human sins. Besides this, they lay together promiscuously under the pretence of charity; they ate flesh when they would; they observed no festivals, and derided the merits and intercession of the saints; and finally, they were so obstinate under persecution, that whatever might be their sex or age, they unanimously preferred death to conversion. . . . In this strange and calumnious catalogue we may observe the malignity with which some tenets, merely rejecting the innovations of Rome, are mixed up with the most horrible crimes and blasphemies. Yet this was one of the most vulgar among the artifices of the churchmen of those days.

secret of their offence. Yet, though we should believe them
to have held almost every tenet with which they are charged,
(for the contempt of moral duties was clearly not a tenet, but
a consequence calumniously drawn by their enemies,) may we
not discern that the principle from which they departed was
excellent and holy? It led them into some extravagances;
but were those so gross, or nearly so detestable, as the deliberate absurdities which were committed by the Church itself
during the same period?—the insertion into the Liturgy of
" the words in which the angel Gabriel saluted the Virgin
Mary"—the institution of festivals in honour of the lance, the
nails, the crown of Christ *—the appointment of a holy day
for the solemn celebration of the wounds of Christ, miracu-
lously impressed upon the body of St. Francis! If we should
believe all the calumnies that churchmen have ever fabricated
in vilification of the mystics, we shall find among them nothing
so irrational, nothing nearly so impious, as those authorized
ecclesiastical mummeries.

The Lollards suffered some oppression in Austria and other
countries; but a war of extermination does not appear to have
been formally proclaimed against them. No doubt they were
confounded by the Inquisitors, sometimes erroneously and
sometimes wilfully, with the more avowed enemies of the papal
government; and thus they shared that vengeance which was
chiefly intended for the Spirituals and Beghards. But whether
through their greater obscurity or more manifest harmlessness,
they escaped in comparative safety without any direct attack;
and to this tolerance it may perhaps be attributed, that the
sect of the Lollards † (properly so called) never rose into great
power and never became dangerous to the Catholic Church.

During the reign of Clement V., a preacher named Dulcinus, Dulcinus.
attended by a woman called Margaret, his wife or his mistress,

---

* Others might be added. For instance, John XXII. re-established with fresh
indulgences the festival of " the body of Christ"—granting to all Christians a
general pardon of forty days for every reverence made, on the name of Jesus
Christ being pronounced by the priest. Giovanni Villani, lib. ii., cap. lxxix.

† The name Lollard, as is well known, was afterwards generally applied to
various adversaries of the popish establishment; but the real origin both of the
name and sect was probably such as has been here described.

presented himself in Lombardy, and erected in the neighbouring
mountains the standard of heresy. He was charged with contempt of the Catholic hierarchy, and with censuring the abuses
of their immoderate wealth; also with asserting a succession
of three theocracies—that those under the Father and the Son
were already passed; that the third, under the Holy Spirit,
was then in operation *. Lastly, to consummate his odium,
his followers, who were not very numerous, were assailed with
the primitive and accustomed calumny of promiscuous prostitution. A *crusade* was preached by the Church against these
miserable enthusiasts, and its armies were led to the assault
by a zealous bishop. Surrounded and pressed among the
Alpine passes, many had already perished from cold and want
before the sword was drawn to complete their destruction. It
did so most effectually; and Roman Catholic writers record
without emotion, that the heretic was torn in pieces limb from
limb, after his " spiritual sister" had suffered before his eyes
by the same torture. As the massacre is recorded without
emotion, so its consequence is told without understanding or
reflection—that the disciples of the martyr were multiplied by
the deed, and increased beyond number †.

The life and heresies ‡ of Wiclif also belong to this period;
but we shall at present leave them unnoticed, as more closely
connected with the history of the Council of Constance. And
if we pass from the name of that great patriarch of the Refor-

*His perse-
cution and
death.*

---

* His followers called themselves " The Spiritual Congregation and the Order
of the Apostles." " We alone (they said) are in the perfection in which the
apostles were, and in the liberty which proceeds immediately from Jesus Christ.
Wherefore we acknowledge obedience neither to the pope nor any other human
being: nor has he any power to excommunicate us ...The pope can give no absolution from sins unless he be as holy as St. Peter, living in entire poverty and
humility .. so that all the popes and prelates since St. Sylvester, having deviated
from that original holiness, are prevaricators and seducers, with the single exception of pope Celestine, Pietro di Morone, &c." See Fleury, liv. xci., sec. xxiii.

† Supra numerum. See Vita (4ta) Clementis V. apud Baluzium. Bzovius,
ad ann. 1310, sec. xiii.

‡ Wiclif's sixty-one heresies are carefully enumerated by Bzovius, (ann. 1352,
s. xv.) and that author expresses very sincere regret at his escape from the bishops
whom the pope had stirred against him. Indeed, notwithstanding his great protectors, the Reformer seems not to have been secure till the grand schism frittered
away the power of papacy.

mation to the mention of a transient sect of mere fanatics, we shall most faithfully exhibit the character of an age in which the long reign of ignorance and error was first disturbed by the irregular struggles of reviving reason. The beginnings of those great revolutions which renovate the whole frame of society, are invariably marked by some transient excesses, occasioned by the first fermentation of new and active principles in a body not yet qualified to give them full efficacy. And so it befell in the present instance—an age in which the true principles of Christianity were beginning once more to glimmer through the ecclesiastical system which had so long obscured them, was troubled by some of the wildest absurdities of superstition. The sect of the Flagellants first betrayed its existence about the middle of the thirteenth century; but it was discouraged by the authorities both spiritual and secular, and seemingly repressed: nevertheless, about the year 1340, it broke out again with additional violence. Its first re-appearance was in Italy, in the neighbourhood of Cremona*: suddenly a multitude, amounting to 10,000 persons, issued from the surrounding cities and villages, and paraded the country, flogging themselves and (in the first instance) begging. The contagion spread with a rapidity which will afflict, but cannot surprise, the observer of religious absurdities; and in the course of ten years scarcely a country in Europe was exempt from its visitation. As the Flagellants increased in numbers, they adopted some sort of system and method in their fanaticism; which, though it may have varied under different circumstances, possessed the same general character. Naked from the loins upwards, and marked on their front and back with red crosses, they spread themselves in numerous bands over the face of Europe. Twice every day, in the most public places, they performed their discipline, until blood flowed from the wounds; and they completed their duties by one nocturnal and private flagellation. No one among them begged. No one was admitted into the society who was entirely destitute; no one, unless he had made a full confession of his sins, unless he had received the consent of his wife, un-

The Flagellants.

---

* Bzov., ann. 1340, s. xxiv.

less he had forgiven his enemies every injury*. Their appearance and character chiefly moved the enthusiasm of the Germans, who opened their doors and entertained them at their
tables. But it is affirmed that they could never be persuaded
to partake twice of the same hospitality, nor to prolong their
visit beyond a single day: they then departed on their destina-
tion. Women were confounded with men in their irregular
ranks; and as they advanced in indiscriminate procession, each
bearing in his hand a wooden cross, they chanted in their
native language a hymn on the passion of Christ, and frequently interrupted their song by prostration and prayer.
Their eyes were ever downcast, and the aspect which they
wore was solemn and sorrowful.

The innocence of their demeanour, the severity of their discipline, the very singularity of their enthusiasm attracted a
multitude of proselytes; but as their numbers increased, their
conduct no longer escaped reproach, and the offences of individuals threw suspicion and obloquy on the whole body. Moreover, as they presently began to preach to the people, and as
their society was not authorized by the pope, many Lollards
and schismatics eagerly mingled in their companies, and carried
into them the name of heresy, and subjected them to that fatal
charge. Accordingly, we read in the Roman Catholic records
that the Flagellants were a sect who slighted the priesthood
and *the Gospel*—who had no reverence for the holy ceremonies,
or even for the body of the Lord: such was the confidence
(says Spondanus) which they placed in their own madness.
By thirty-three consecutive days of flagellation, they held
themselves absolved from the most heinous sins, to the disregard of the salutary penance and indulgences of the Church.
And lastly, they maintained that stripes were more honourable
than martyrdom; that the baptism by water had passed away,
and given place to the baptism by blood; and that through

---

* See Bzov., ann. 1349, s. ii. It is the testimony of an enemy. Spondanus,
(ann. 1349, sect. ii.) who confirms these particulars, also mentions that the Flagellants professed the authority of a letter, or writing, sent down to them from
heaven.

this last alone was there any road to salvation*. These charges were partly fabricated, and no doubt partly true; and even the limits of the truth and the falsehood are not difficult to discern; but the agents of persecution, who were presently in motion, were not retarded by any such considerations. They marched onwards in the path of destruction; and the Emperor Charles IV. encouraged and directed their zeal. It appears that, in the year 1351, a number of those pitiable enthusiasts were collected in Lithuania, in the exercise of their absurd practices. Pope Clement VI. proclaimed a holy war †; the Master of the Teutonic Order marched in person against them; and after a solemn fast and public prayer, that God would aid him in the extirpation of His enemies, for the glory of his Holy Name, he assaulted them, and massacred eight thousand: the remainder, about two thousand more, were carried away captive into Prussia, that they might be restored, by a second baptism, to the bosom of the Church. *Many of them massacred.*

When we examine the various denominations of heresy which appeared in the thirteenth and fourteenth centuries, and in the fourteenth most especially, we observe that almost all were directed, wholly or in part, openly or covertly, in tenet or in practice, against the sacerdotal government and the system of the Roman Church. It was not so with those of earlier ages. Among the numerous sects which divided the ante-Nicene Christians, it has been already remarked, that not one originated in any disaffection for the ministers of religion, or the ecclesiastical polity. In the times which followed, the Arian and Incarnation controversies, with their numerous names and progeny, were confined to matters of faith. During the prolonged disputes which succeeded about the worship of images, no clamour was raised against the corruptions or undue aggrandizement of the hierarchy. The dissensions of the ninth century regarded the nature of the Eucharist and the doctrine of *General character of these heresies.*

---

* See Mosheim, Cent. XIII., p. ii., ch. iii., and Cent. XIV., p. ii., ch. v.

† Bzov., ann. 1351, s. viii. The pretext alleged for this expedition was, that when two Mendicants, on some occasion, interrupted the devotion of the Flagellants, these had stoned one of them to death. It does not appear that they were armed.

Fatalism, and the former of those subjects was revived in the eleventh; but no sect had hitherto risen in revolt against the abuses and tyranny of the Church. The standard was first erected in the twelfth age; and from that moment there was never wanting a succession of bold and righteous spirits who rallied round it. The depravity of the Church system was indeed, in some respects, more scandalous in the fourteenth than in any preceding century : yet was there no lack, even in much earlier ages, of such enormities as might well have offended the reason and provoked the indignation of an evangelical Christian. But the fact was, that the civil institutions were at the same time so defective, and the dearth of knowledge so general, that the sins of the Church were overshadowed or kept in countenance by the secular depravity that surrounded them. Presently, as the social condition improved, the ecclesiastical abuses excited remonstrance and clamour; the foundations were shaken, and the edifice itself assailed; but the clamour was still the clamour of the few—the voice of enlightened individuals or of scattered sects : it did not yet endanger the established hierarchy, because it was not yet supported by the general prevalence of rational principles. The political system of the age still abounded with vices, and the learning in fashion was still perplexed with prejudice and fallacy. It is always with reference to such considerations as these that we are to estimate the danger of ecclesiastical abuses and the *necessity* of reformation. It is not sufficient to compare existing defects with those which have been tolerated in the same church, or in a different church, in a different age. Such a comparison would only tend to blind and mislead us. They must be examined in relation to the measure of civilization actually abroad—to the prevalence of knowledge, to the authority of reason, to the general principles of human conduct. Thus it will happen, that a much slighter defect, in days of improvement and inquiry, may prove more perilous to the system in which it is suffered to remain, than a much grosser deformity in a darker age :—it is the access of light which renders the stain conspicuous and offensive. And therefore it has ever been among the foremost duties of churchmen, and their surest wisdom, to detect the blemishes in their institution, and having detected, to remove them : since it avails them little to be free from the vices of preceding generations, unless they share the spirit, and adopt, to a great extent, the character and principles of their own.

NOTE ON THE FRANCISCANS AND OTHER MENDICANTS.

(I.) As something has been said in this chapter respecting the intestine divisions of the Franciscans, it is proper here to mention the sect of the *Fratricelli,* or Ultra-Spirituals, who made some figure in the dissensions of the fourteenth age. They arose, in that which preceded, from the stock of St. Francis ; and as they disclaimed any right even to the *use** of property, in which they surpassed the self-denial of the Spirituals, they may have deserved the praise which they arrogated, of being the *genuine* disciples of their Master. They professed great personal respect for Celestine V., who had been in some measure the founder of their order ; but they hesitated to acknowledge the legitimacy of his successors : they proclaimed the deep corruption of the Church, and they looked with ardent and almost pious enthusiasm for its immediate reformation.

This notion—that a thorough regeneration of the Church was near at hand, and that the reign of the true gospel was to be restored by the followers of St. Francis—was not the creation of the Fratricelli, nor was it indeed of very recent origin. As early as the beginning of the thirteenth century, a work was circulated, abounding with such like prophecies, under the name of the Eternal Gospel. It was founded on the text †— "I saw another angel fly in the midst of heaven, having the Everlasting Gospel to preach unto them that dwell on the earth ; " and it was such as Mosheim has designated it, the

The Eternal Gospel.

---

* In 1279, Nicholas III. published a celebrated Constitution, known as the Bull *Exiit,* in which he so interpreted the Franciscan Rule, as to prohibit to its observers every possession ; but to permit them the temporary use of houses, books, &c., of which the property, in conformity with the edict of Innocent IV., was to reside in the Church of Rome.

† Revelations xiv. 6.

senseless production of an obscure, silly, and visionary writer. The perfect scheme of revelation which it propounded was this —as there were three persons in the Godhead, so was it necessary that there should be three dispensations. The first was that of the Father, which ended at the coming of Christ—the second was that of the Son, which was now on the point of concluding, to give place to the third, and last. This rhapsody was ascribed, but not with sufficient foundation, to Joachim, abbot of Flora in Calabria, who flourished about the year 1200, who had declaimed against the abuses of the Church, and predicted their extirpation. But in spite of the respectable name, under which it had sought protection, the Eternal Gospel would not perhaps have attracted any general notice, had it not been adopted by the Franciscans, who eagerly appropriated the prophecies. Accordingly, about the year 1250, it was again published, with an elaborate Introduction, in which the assertion was advanced, that St. Francis was the angel mentioned in the Revelations; that the gospel of Christ was immediately to give place to this new and everlasting scripture; and that the ministers of this great Reformation were to be humble and barefooted friars, destitute of all earthly possessions *.

The Gospel might have passed unnoticed and despised; but the introduction contained a doctrine too daring, if not dangerous, to escape ecclesiastical reprehension; and in the very year following its publication at Paris, the book was suppressed by Alexander IV. Yet such was the tenderness of a pope for the reputation of the Mendicants, that the censures were lenient, and the edict was issued with reluctance.

The introduction has been commonly ascribed to no less distinguished an ecclesiastic than John of Parma, general of the Franciscans, though the opinion is more probable that it was composed by one Gerard, his friend. It is true, indeed, that writers of that order have entirely disclaimed the work, and imputed it to their rivals, the Dominicans, but without any plausible reason. And as the introduction was manifestly a Franciscan fabrication, so is it extremely probable that the Eternal Gospel also proceeded from the same forge.

* This account is chiefly taken from Mosheim (Cent. xiii., p. ii., ch. ii.), who has investigated the subject with great diligence.

We should also mention one Pierre Jean d'Olive, a native of Serignan, in Languedoc, who acquired some reputation towards the end of the same century, by a similar description of merit. He, likewise, was a leader of the Spirituals, a disciple of the Abbot Joachim, and a reformer of ecclesiastical iniquities. He published a work called *Postilla*, a commentary on the Revelations, in which he boldly denounced the Roman Church as the " Mystery, Babylon the Great, the Mistress of Harlots, and abominations of the Earth*." But he mixed so much wild and senseless superstition with his reforming zeal, that his labours were neither profitable to the Church, nor dangerous to the despotism of the pope. *Pierre d'Olive.*

(II.) We read from time to time of disputes, which arose in various countries between the Mendicants and the secular clergy, respecting the administration of several Church ceremonies, but most especially of the rite of Confession. It may, therefore, be useful to trace very concisely the history of that contest. A canon of the Fourth Lateran Council (commonly known as *Omnis utriusque Sexûs*) gave the entire power of receiving confessions to the priest; but Gregory IX., by a bull of Sept. 26, 1227, opened that privilege also to the preachers. The curés resisted; and in 1250 the Faculty of Paris loudly declared in their favour: so that Innocent IV., who in 1244 had shown every disposition to favour the Mendicants, prohibited them, in 1254, from hearing confessions without the permission of the priest. But Alexander IV. immediately revoked this bull, and presently afterwards issued others, to the interest of the Mendicants. Great heats were thus excited, and in the hope to allay them, Martin IV. published, in 1282, a sort of edict of compromise, by which the Mendicants were permitted to receive confessions, yet so that the same persons were still obliged to confess once a year to their own priest, according to the canon of the Lateran. *Contests between the Mendicants and Secular Clergy about Confession.*

Thereon arose a fresh question—whether the people were obliged again to confess to their priests the same sins which they had before confided to the Mendicants, and for which they had received absolution; and various appeals were made to the

* Revelations xvii. 5.

E 2

popes on this point. Nicholas IV. delivered no express response; but Boniface VIII. published a decretal called *Supra Cathedram*, in which he engaged to grant the privilege to the Mendicants by his own plenitude, in case they had previously asked the favour of the bishops, and it had been refused. Benedict XI. was still more decided; for he gave the Mendicants direct permission to hear confessions, and also decided that the people were not obliged to re-confess the same sins. This decretal, again, was revoked in the Council of Vienne, and replaced by the Clementine *Dudum*, which revived the Constitution of Boniface.

The above account, which is a bare outline of a tedious and angry controversy, is nevertheless sufficient to exhibit, not only the obstinacy with which the contending parties advanced or defended their privileges—not only the value which both of them affixed to the possession of that particular privilege, which contained indeed the grand secret of ecclesiastical influence, but also the vacillating policy of the Vatican, and the little consistency with each other or with themselves, which directed, in their councils, the chiefs of an infallible Church.

CHAPTER XXIII.

The Grand Schism of the Roman Catholic Church.

Remonstrance of the Romans to the College—its reply—The Conclave—Probable extent of popular intimidation—Constitution of the Conclave—various designs of the parties—violence of the people—Election of the Archbishop of Bari, Urban VI.—his character, and general reception—his first acts of harshness, and their effect—The Cardinals retire to Anagni, and annul the election of Urban—they choose Robert, Cardinal of Geneva, Clement VII.—his character—real merits of the question—Retreat of Clement to Avignon—Division of Europe—St. Catharine and other enthusiasts—Conduct of Urban to six Cardinals accused of conspiracy—Death of Urban, and election of Boniface IX.—The Jubilee—its extension—Sale of indulgences—Privileges granted to some German towns—Exertions of the University of Paris for the extinction of the Schism—Address to the King—three methods proposed in it—favourable circumstances—Death of Clement VII.—Election of Pietro di Luna, Benedict XIII.—Grand embassy of the King to Benedict—its failure—Continued exertions of the King and the University—attempts to influence Boniface—his assurance to the Roman deputies—The French withdraw their obedience from Benedict—Blockade of the palace at Avignon—Benedict restored to liberty and office—simoniacal rapacity of Boniface—The Jubilee of 1400—Boniface succeeded by Innocent VII.—Death of Innocent—Solemn engagement of the Conclave—Election of Angelo Corrario, Gregory XII.—Attempt at a conference—Perjury of Gregory—Retirement of Benedict to Perpignan—Convocation of the Council of Pisa—proceedings of that council—deposition of the two competitors—and election of Alexander V.—his birth and character—Conduct of the Antipopes—Intercourse of Alexander with the Roman people—his death—Election of Baltazar Cossa, John XXIII.—Sigismond emperor—Convocation of the Council of Constance—choice of the place—its advantages—number of members—its objects—Proposition of John XXII.—Two opinions respecting the course to be followed—Arrival of Sigismond—Question as to the power of the Council over the Pope—division of the Council—it decides on the method of cession—cession of the Pope—suspicions of the Council—Escape of John from Constance—question *de auferibilitate Papæ*—the Pope betrayed to Sigismond—his deposition, and the charges against him—his sentence—conduct and imprisonment—opinions of the justice of the sentence—Sigismond goes to Perpignan—Conference there—Union of all parties—Obstinacy of Benedict—he retires to Peniscola—is deposed by the Council of Constance—his conduct—the Council proceeds to the election of a new pope—Otho Colonna, Martin V. chosen—Observations—Death of Angelo Corrario—Pertinacity, death, and character of Pietro di Luna—Fate of John XXIII.—his liberation—return to Italy—counsels of his friends—he goes to Florence, and makes his submission to Martin—his treatment, conduct, and character—*Note;* on the White Penitents and other Enthusiasts.

THE number of Cardinals at the death of Gregory XI. was twenty-three, of whom six were absent at Avignon, and one was

legate in Tuscany. The remaining sixteen, after celebrating
the funeral ceremonies of the deceased, and appointing certain
officers to secure their deliberations from violence, prepared to
enter into conclave. But the rites of sepulture were scarcely
performed, when the leading magistrates of Rome presented to
Remon-   them a remonstrance to this effect :—In behalf of the Roman
strance of   senate and people, they ventured to represent, that the Roman
the Romans.
Church had suffered for seventy years a deplorable captivity
by the translation of the Holy See to Avignon; that during
that period the capital of the Christian world had suffered
more, both in its spiritual and temporal interests, than when it
was subject to the cruel domination of the barbarians; that
tumults, seditions, revolts, and sanguinary wars had desolated,
without interruption, the ecclesiastical states; that its cities and
its provinces were in part usurped by domestic tyrants, and
occupied in part by the neighbouring republics, or by the Lombard princes; that fire and sword were carried even to the
gates of Rome, which had neither power nor authority to repress such fury;—so that the aspect of the Holy City, the head
of religion, formerly venerable throughout the whole earth, was
no longer to be recognised through its strange and foul dis-
figurements. That the sacred edifices, those august monuments
of ancient piety, were left without honour, or ornament, or
reparation, nodding to their ruin ; that even the *Titles* of the
cardinals, abandoned by those who derived their dignities from
them, were left without roof, or gates, or walls, the abode of
beasts, which cropped the grass on their very altars. That the
Faithful were no longer attracted to Rome, either by devotion,
which the profanation of the churches precluded, or by interest;
since the pope, the source of patronage, had scandalously deserted his church—so that there was danger lest that unfortunate city should be reduced to a vast and frightful solitude,
and become an outcast from the world, of which it was still the
spiritual empress, as it once had been the temporal. Lastly,
that, as the only remedy for these evils, it was absolutely necessary to elect a Roman, or at least an Italian Pope—especially
as there was every appearance that the people, if disappointed
in their just expectation, would have recourse to compul-

sion. . . The cardinals replied, that as soon as they should be in conclave they would give to those subjects their solemn deliberation, and direct their choice according to the inspiration of the Holy Spirit. They repelled the notion, that they could be influenced by any popular menace; and pronounced (according to one account) an express warning, that if they should be compelled to elect under such circumstances, the elected would not be a pope, but an intruder*. They then immediately entered into conclave.

In the meantime the populace, who had already exhibited proofs of impatience, and whom the answer of the cardinals was not well calculated to satisfy, assembled in great crowds about the place of assembly. It may be true (though the circumstances rest for the most part on French and partial authority), that the civil magistrates had previously possessed themselves of the keys of the gates, which were usually confided to ecclesiastical officers, in order to preclude the escape of the cardinals to a more secure place of deliberation ; that in the room of the ordinary police they introduced a number of *Montanarii*, the wild and lawless inhabitants of the adjacent mountains, who paraded the streets in arms by day and by night; that a quantity of dry reeds and other combustibles was heaped together under the windows of the conclave, with threats of conflagration; that, at the moment when the college was proceeding to election, the bells of the Capitol and St. Peter's were sounded *to arms* † :—these, and other circumstances of direct constraint and intimidation, are asserted by some writers, and, though probably exaggerated, have undoubtedly some foundation in fact. But it is without any dispute that a vast crowd of people continued in tumultuous assemblage during the whole deliberation of the conclave ‡, and that the debates of the Sacred College were incessantly interrupted by one loud and unanimous shout—" Romano lo volemo lo Papa—Romano

The Conclave at Rome.

---

* " Quam si facerent, eos ex nunc avisaverunt, quod si ex ejus occasione aliquem eligerent ille non esset papa sed intrusus."—Aut. Vit. Greg. XI. ap. Bosquet. Maimb., Hist. du Grand Schisme, liv. i.

† *Ad sturnum*, according to the Roman expression of that time.

‡ Spondanus, ann. 1378, s. viii. et seq.

lo volemo—o almanco almanco Italiano!"—" We will have a
Roman for Pope—a Roman, or at least, at the very least, an
Italian !"

Let us now inquire, whether the College was then so constituted as to make it likely that its free choice would have
fallen upon a Roman, or even an Italian. Of the sixteen cardinals in conclave, eleven were French, one, Pietro di Luna, a
Spaniard, and four Italians. The unanimity of the French
would, of course, at once have decided the question; but it
happened that they were divided into two parties. Seven
amongst them were Limousins, natives of the same province;
and having succeeded, during the last twenty-nine years, in
electing four successive popes from their own country, they
were naturally eager to keep possession of so profitable a distinction. But the other four, unwilling to appropriate the pontificate to a single district, even though that district was French,
designed that the choice should fall on one of themselves. The
Limousins found in their superior numbers their hope of success and their excuse for perseverance ; and at length the
others, being more keenly excited by provincial than by national jealousy, began to turn their thoughts to a coalition with
the Italians. These last were equally bent on the election of
one of their own party ; and as their only chance of success
arose from the division of the French, they very readily joined
their forces against the exclusive ambition of the Limousins.
Such were the intrigues which commenced immediately after
the death of Gregory, and ripened during the eleven * days
which followed ; and such was probably † the state of parties
when the cardinals entered the conclave. There were materials
in abundance for long and angry dissension ; and though the
indignation of the Limousins against their compatriots might

---

* Gregory XI. died on the 27th of March, and the cardinals entered into conclave on the 7th of April.

† Fleury (liv. xcvii. s. xlviii.) seems persuaded that there was some secret understanding in favour of the Archbishop of Bari (who was afterwards elected)
even before the cardinals entered into conclave. But the view of Maimbourg is
more probable, that so wide a division, with so many opposite interests and passions, was not so easily reconciled,

finally have forced their consent to the election of an Italian, rather than a native of any other French province, still it was not without a struggle that they were likely to forego the courtly magnificence of Avignon, to which a French pontiff would surely have restored them, for a remote and tumultuous residence among the citizens of Rome.

But the internal disputes of the College were speedily silenced by the tempest from without. Even after the sacred body had been shut up in deliberation, the Bannerets, or heads of the twelve regions of the city, forced themselves, together with their disorderly followers, in contempt of custom and decency, into the recesses of the conclave. Here they repeated their demands with redoubled insolence, and direct menaces. The cardinals are recorded to have returned their former reply, with the additional declaration, that in case any violence were used, he, whom they should so elect, and whom the people would take for a real pope, would in fact be no pope at all*. The people received this answer with indignant clamours †; the disorder round the chapel augmented; the most frightful threats were uttered in case of hesitation or disobedience; and the same shout, which was indeed the burden of the uproar, continued to penetrate the conclave—" A Roman for our pope! a Roman—or at least, at the very least, an Italian!"

Popular tumults.

These were not circumstances for delay or deliberation. If any inclination towards the choice of an Italian had previously existed in the college, it was now confirmed into necessity; and on the very day following their retirement the cardinals were agreed in their election. Howbeit, they studiously passed over

Election of Urban VI.

---

* " Ista verba manifestè sonant minas; et ideo expressè nos dicimus, quod, si per vos aut ipsos aliqua contra nos attententur, et contingat nos talium occasione et timore aliquem eligere, credetis habere papam, et non habebitis, quia non erit." —Vita Greg. XI. ap. Baluzium.

† One of the cardinals addressed them from the window:—" 'State a pace— perchè i Signori Cardinali dicono cosi, che domani faranno dire una messa dello Spirito Santo, e poi faranno che voi sarete contenti.' Qui vero Romani maledicti tunc responderunt sic—' No—mò lo volemo, mò.' Et eterim ridebant inter se, et unus faciebat alteri signum, ut plus clamarent ut supra. In circuitu item Conclavi erat maxima multitudo cum caboris et flautis, et eodem modo clamabant fortiter juxta posse."—Vita (secunda) Greg. XI. apud Baluzium. We should observe, however, that this is not the description of a sanguinary mob.

the four Italian members of their own body, and casting their eyes beyond the conclave, selected a Neopolitan named Bartolomeo Prignano, the Archbishop of Bari. The announcement was not immediately published, probably through the fear of popular dissatisfaction, because a Roman had not been created; and presently, when the impatience of the people still further increased, the Bishop of Marseilles went to the window, and said to them, "Go to St. Peter's, and you shall learn the decision." Whereupon some who heard him, understanding that the Cardinal of St. Peter's, a Roman, had been indeed chosen, rushed to the palace of that prelate, and plundered it—for such was the custom then invariably observed on the election of a pope. Others thronged in great multitudes to offer him their salutations; and then they bore him away to St. Peter's, and placed him, according to ancient usage, upon the altar. It was in vain that the good cardinal, enfeebled by extreme old age and painful disease, disclaimed the title, and trembled at the honours that were forced on him. " I am not pope," said he : " and I will not be antipope. The Archbishop of Bari, who is really chosen, is worthier than I." They ascribed his resistance to modesty or decent dissimulation, and continued through the whole day to overwhelm him with the most painful proofs of their joy. In the meantime the other cardinals escaped from the conclave in great disorder and trepidation, without dignity or attendants, or even their ordinary habiliments* of office, and sought safety, some in their respective palaces, and others in the Castle of St. Angelo, or even beyond the walls of the city. On the following day, the people were undeceived ; and as they showed no strong disinclination for the master who had been really chosen for them, the Archbishop of Bari was solemnly enthroned, and the scattered cardinals reappeared, and rallied round him in confidence and security.

His character.

The archbishop's exalted reputation justified the choice of the college, and secured the obedience of the people. Through a long life, devoted to the service of the Church, he had recon-

* " Recesserunt pedes, unus sine Capa, alter cum Capa, alter sine Capucio, soli, sine sociis scutiferis."—Vit. Greg. XI. ap. Baluz.

ciled the most ardent disposition with the most devout humility, and improved by assiduous study a powerful comprehension. He submitted to the utmost severity of ecclesiastical
discipline; yet his deep and dangerous enthusiasm did not
close his mind against the liberal pursuit of learning, and the
patronage of learned men. His zeal for the Church was not
stained by the suspicion of bigotry, nor inconsistent with a
stern opposition to its abuses ; and among many other virtues,
he was perhaps chiefly famed for the rigorous exercise of justice. Such was the character to which Rome looked with
sanguine hope for the repair of her declining fortunes ; nor
was it, indeed, without the general approbation of Christendom
that Urban VI. ascended the apostolical chair. The cardinals
sent the customary communications to the courts of Europe of
the free and canonical election which they had made*, and
peaceably assumed their official stations about the person of
the pontiff.

The ceremony of coronation was duly performed, and several His injudi-
bishops were assembled on the very following day at vespers cious seve-
in the pontifical chapel, when the pope unexpectedly addressed rity.
them in the bitterest language of reprobation. He accused
them of having deserted and betrayed the flocks which God
had confided to them, in order to revel in luxury at the court
of Rome; and he applied to their offence the harsh reproach
of perjury. One of them (the bishop of Pampeluna) repelled
the charge, as far as himself was concerned, by reference to
the duties which he performed at Rome; the others suppressed
in silence their anger and confusion. A few days afterwards,
at a public consistory, Urban repeated his complaints and
denunciations, and urged them still more generally in the presence of his whole court. In a long and intemperate harangue,
he arraigned the vices of the prelates—their simony, their injustice, their exactions, their scandalous luxury, with a number
of other offences—in unmeasured† and uncompromising ex-

---

* A similar announcement was made to the six cardinals remaining at Avignon, who immediately recognized the new pope.

† " Nullo reprehensionibus modo imposito."—Ciacconius.

pressions ; and while he spared no menace to give weight to his censure, he directed the sharpest of his shafts against the cardinals themselves. There is not any dispute that his violence proceeded from an honest zeal for the reformation of the Church ; but the end was marred by the passionate indis- cretion with which he pursued it. The consistory broke up ; and the members carried away with them no sense of the iniquities imputed, no disposition to correct their habits or their principles, but only indignation, mixed with some degree of fear, against a severe and discourteous censor *.

Secession of the Cardinals. The cardinals continued, notwithstanding, their attendance at the Vatican for a few weeks longer, and then, as was usual on the approach of the summer heats, they withdrew from the city, with the pope's permission, and retired to Anagni. The four Italians alone remained at Rome. The others were no sooner removed from the immediate inspection of Urban, than they commenced, or at least more boldly pursued, their measures to overthrow him. On the one hand, they opened a direct correspondence with the court of France and university of Paris † ; on the other, they took into their service a body of mercenaries, commanded by one Bernard de la Sale, a Gascon; and then they no longer hesitated to treat the election of Urban as null, through the violence which had attended it‡.

* " Hunc et posteris diebus, cessante jam metu, venerari ut pontificem perse- verârunt. Sed fuit in illo homine natura inquieta et dura ; et tunc præter spem ad tantæ dignitatis fastigium sublevatus intolerabilis videbatur. Nulla patribus gratia, quod se potissimùm delegissent, nulla humanitas, nulla conciliatio ani- morum. Contumax, et minabundus, et asper malebat videri, et metui potius quam diligi. Ea perversitas Patres coegit metu et indignatione aliorsum respicere• Itaque clam inter se de electione conquesti," &c.—Leonardus Aretinus, Histor. Florent., lib. viii. ad finem.   Leonardus was himself personally attached to the popes of that succession.   By some the character of Urban is compared to that of Boniface VIII. Baluzius, the organ of the French opinion, represents him as a very monster—"Cujus electio facta arte diabolica."

† This learned and now influential body was courted with equal assiduity by Urban.   In a letter addressed to it on this same occasion, that pontiff compared it to a constellation irradiating every other academy ; to a fountain whence the purest doctrine perennially flowed ; to a tree bearing excellent fruit. See Spon- danus, Ann. 1378, s. xviii.

‡ There exists a letter written during that crisis by Marsilius d'Inghen, ancient rector of the university of Paris, who happened to be residing with Urban at that

To give consequence to this decision, they assembled with great solemnity in the principal church, and promulgated, on the 9th of August, a public declaration, in the presence of many prelates and other ecclesiastics, by which the archbishop of Bari was denounced an intruder into the pontificate, and his election formally cancelled.   In this doeument, the cardinals, after describing the tumults of the Romans, declared, that they elected the archbishop of Bari in the persuasion that, seeing the circumstances under which he was chosen, he would in conscience have refused the pontificate; that, on the contrary, forgetful of his salvation, and burning with ambition, he consented to the choice; that under the effect of the same intimidation he was enthroned and crowned, and assumed the name of pope, though he rather merited that of apostate and Antichrist.   They then anathematized him as an usurper, and invoked against him all aids and succours, divine and human. They immediately retired, for greater security, to Fondi, in the kingdom of Naples.   Still they did not venture to proceed to a new election in the absence, and it might be against the consent, of their Italian brethren.   A negotiation was accordingly opened; and these last immediately fell into the snare which treachery had prepared for ambition.   To each of them separately a secret promise was made in writing, by the whole of their colleagues, that himself should be the object of their choice.   Each of them believed what he wished; and concealing from each other their private expectations, they * pressed to Fondi with joy and confidence.   The college immediately entered into conclave; and as the French had, in the meantime, reconciled their provincial jealousies, Robert, the cardinal of Geneva, was chosen by their unanimous vote.   This event took place on the 20th of September (1378); the new pope assumed the name of Clement VII., and was installed with the customary ceremonies.

Robert of Geneva was of noble birth, and even allied to several of the sovereigns of Europe.   He possessed talents

Clement VII. elected at Fondi.

time. His description of affairs is such as we have given. See Fleury. l. xcvii., sec. lii.
    * They were now reduced to three, by the death of the Cardinal of St. Peter's.

and eloquence, a courage which was never daunted, and a resolution which was never diverted or wearied. Little scrupulous
as to means, in his habits sumptuous and prodigal, he seemed
the man most likely to establish his claims to a disputed crown,
and to unite the courts of Christendom in his favour. His age,
besides, which did not exceed thirty-six, gave promise of a
vigorous and decisive policy.

Question of   Nevertheless, his first endeavours had very little success. It
legitimacy. was in vain that the sacred college sent forth its addresses to
princes and their subjects, detailing all that had occurred at
Rome, Anagni, and Fondi, and protesting against the violence
which occasioned the illegal election of Urban. It was argued,
on the other hand, that the cardinals had assisted at the subsequent ceremonies of enthronement and coronation ; that they
had announced their choice in the usual language to all the
courts of Europe ; that they had continued their personal
attendance on the pope for some weeks afterwards, and had
even allowed four months to elapse, before they withdrew their
obedience. Besides which, many, no doubt, were well pleased
to see the chief of their church restored to his legitimate residence ; they disliked the irregular influence of the French, and
were glad to shake off their spiritual usurpation. In truth, the
reasons, which were advanced with such ardour and obstinacy
on both sides, were not perfectly conclusive for either ; and
though it is certain that the election was conducted under
some degree of intimidation *, the subsequent acquiescence of

* Sismondi (Repub. Ital., ch. l.) does not consider the choice of the cardinals
to have been decided by the tumult of the people, because after all they did not
elect a Roman, and therefore incurred some danger even by that compromise with
their independence. However, the real object of the populace was effected, if they
obtained a pope who would probably *reside* at Rome: *this*, and not the place of
his nativity, was the point which touched their interests,—and the election of a
Neapolitan secured it almost as certainly as that of a Roman.   Upon the whole,
it seems most probable (and the result of the second election confirms this) that,
had no external influence been exercised, the cardinals would have chosen an
Ultramontane, or, at any rate, not the Archbishop of Bari.   Sismondi's eloquent
description of this affair is chiefly drawn from the contemporary account of Thomas
d'Acerno, bishop of Lucera, who was present.   On the other hand, Baldus, a
celebrated lawyer and adherent of Urban, does not dispute the influence of the
popular uproar, but rests the 'legitimacy of that pope on the subsequent confirmation and obedience of the sacred college.

the cardinals makes it highly probable that the legitimacy of Urban would never have been questioned, had he followed the usual course of pontifical misgovernment, or even published his schemes of reformation with less earnestness, or more discretion. The severity of his rebukes rankled in the conscience of those who deserved them; and his menaces persuaded the court that, to preserve its beloved impurities, it must depose the master who presumed to arraign them. A pope so dangerous to the vices * of a powerful clergy could not hope to maintain without dispute an ambiguous right.

Such was the origin of the schism which divided the Roman Church for about forty years, and accelerated more than any other event the decline of papal authority †. We have related the particulars with some minuteness, not only in justice to the importance of the subject, but also to show that the great difficulties which were soon afterwards found, even by impartial judges, in determining the rights of the competitors, were not without foundation; but that both parties had a plausible plea for their respective obedience, though the true policy and interests of the Church clearly recommended an undivided adherence to the cause of Urban.

The hopes of Clement were fixed on the court of France; *France declares for Clement;* he knew that prejudices in his favour naturally existed in that kingdom, and he knew, too, that the first steps towards his

---

* He strictly forbade the cardinals, on pain of excommunication, to accept any presents. He endeavoured to restrain the luxury of all his prelates, and even to reduce their tables to a single dish,—a laudable moderation, of which he set the example himself. Again, he threatened the French, that he would create so many cardinals as to place them in a minority in the college. " Item Cardinali de Ursinis dixit quod erat unus Sotus." (Thomas d'Acerno, p. 725.) His harsh and offensive manner increased the unpopularity of his proposed reforms.

† The entire number of the schisms, which have disturbed the Roman Catholic Church, is variously estimated by its historians. Johannes Marius, a Belgian, historian of Louis XII., (a Latin translation of whose work is published, together with that of Theodoric of Niem,) makes the *fated* number to be twenty-four,— the last of which, the Schism of Antichrist, the most deadly of all, had not yet in his time befallen. The first in his catalogue is that of the Novatians; the sixteenth was that occasioned by Gregory VII.; the twentieth by Frederick Barbarossa; the twenty-second was that which we are now describing. His Book is divided into three parts, of which the second, "De Conciliis Ecclesiæ Gallicanæ," contains some useful information.

general acknowledgment must be taken there. Charles V., affecting great impartiality, and admitting the deliberation due to so grave a question, convoked at Vincennes a grand assembly of his clergy, nobles, and council. This august body, after individually abjuring the influence of all personal considerations, expressed an unanimous* conviction of the legitimacy of Clement. The king was guided by their voice, and declared on the 13th of November in his favour. The queen of Naples, the city of Avignon, and the six cardinals who resided there, had already come to the same determination. In the meantime, a passionate warfare of bulls and anathemas commenced on both sides; but happily the thunders must on this occasion have fallen harmless, even in the judgment of a moderate Catholic, since it was impossible certainly to decide which were the genuine bolts; and the ambiguous election of the rivals placed them both in the situation of Antipopes, rather than of Popes.

who retires to Avignon. But they were not contented with those innocuous conflicts; the rights which were ineffectually asserted by ecclesiastical censures, appealed for protection to the sword: a succession of combats desolated the south of Italy, and ended in the discomfiture of Clement. His first refuge was Naples; but at length, finding it impossible to maintain himself in Italy against an Italian rival, he retired to the residence most suited to his fortunes and his prospects, Avignon. From a city which was already consecrated by the tombs of so many popes, supported by the court and nourished by the clergy of France, he bade defiance to his transalpine adversary; and since he could not command, he was contented to divide, the spiritual obedience of Europe.

It does not enter into the plan of this History to pursue the affairs of the Church into all their connexions with political matters; to attend the march of papal armies, hateful alike in

---

* In a council previously held (on Sept. 8), to examine the rights of the dispute between Urban and the French cardinals, before the election of Robert of Geneva, the majority declared for the cardinals, though they advised the king still to suspend his decision. Gibbon remarks, that it was the vanity, rather than the interest of the nation, which determined the court and clergy of France.

their reverses and their triumphs; or to trace the flimsy threads of intrigue, by which the momentary interests of popes and kings have been suspended. It is enough to say, that, notwithstanding an intemperate ambition and some acts of singular imprudence, Urban continued to retain the greater part of his adherents. The kings of Scotland and Cyprus, the counts of Savoy and Geneva, the duke of Austria, and some other German princes, and even the kings of Castille and Arragon, were finally united with France in allegiance to Clement. But the other states of Europe remained faithful to the vows, which they had earliest taken; and it was no unreasonable reply to the antipope, Robert of Avignon, that he should be the last to reject that pontiff, whom the cardinal, Robert of Geneva, had officially recommended to universal obedience. The doctors and learned men of the age were similarly divided, and their division produced the most voluminous controversies. And lastly, as is observed by some Roman Catholic writers, many pious and gifted persons, who are now numbered among the saints of the Church, were to be found indifferently in either obedience ; which sufficiently proved (they assert) that the eternal salvation of the faithful was not in this case endangered by their error. In this holy society, Catharine of Sienna was again conspicuous, as the advocate and adviser of the *Roman* pope. She declared herself (says Maimbourg) loudly for Urban, and employed whatever talents, and eloquence, and force she possessed, in writing and exhorting all the world to acknowledge him. At the same time, in six epistles, which she addressed to himself, she discreetly recommended him to relax somewhat from that extreme austerity, which had made him so many enemies. To what extent Urban profited by that counsel we are scarcely able to decide, though some assert that he held his holy monitress in much veneration. But we are credibly informed that his predecessor, who had certainly been influenced by her persuasions, when at length, on his death-bed, his stronger reason prevailed, called around him his friends and assistants, and solemnly cautioned them against all pretenders of either sex, who should propound their private revelations as rules of conduct and policy. "Since I (he said),

Division of Europe.

having been seduced by such as these, and having rejected the
rational counsel of my friends, have dragged myself and the
Church into the perils of a schism, which is now near at hand,
unless Jesus, her Spouse, shall interpose in his mercy to avert
it *."

Such persons, notwithstanding, were found in abundance on
both sides ; and their wild visions were interpreted by the devotees of the day, and recorded by the grave historians of after
times ; and it was this, among other circumstances, which has
seduced Roman Catholic writers to the very consoling conclusion, that, though a schism did unquestionably exist, yet there
were none who could properly be termed schismatics; that the
adherents of Urban and of Clement were equally the children
of the Church; and that, while the faithful differed as to the
name of the bishop, they were united in unshaken allegiance
and attachment to the See †.

Cruelty of
Urban.

Certainly the character of Urban was not permanently
softened by the admonitions of his inspired instructress ; and
to many reported acts of harshness and rigour he presently
added one of positive barbarity. The following story rests on
satisfactory evidence. A plot for his deposition had been set
on foot, originating, as it would seem, with the King of Naples ;
and a paper, which had been circulated with that object, was
placed in the hands of some of his cardinals—for Urban had
immediately supplied the defection of his original court by a
large and, for the most part, respectable creation. How far they
countenanced the propositions contained in it does not certainly appear ‡ ; but as by one of those the provisional govern-

* " Ille positus in extremis, habens in manibus sacrum Christi Corpus, protes-
tatus est coram omnibus, ut caverent ab hominibus, sive viris sive mulieribus sub
specie religionis loquentibus visiones sui capitis ; quia per tales ipse seductus,
dimisso suorum rationabili consilio, se traxerat et ecclesiam in discrimen schis-
matis imminentis, nisi misericors provideret sponsus Jesus." See Gerson, De
Examinatione Doctrinarum, Pars. ii.. consid. iii.

† Never, says Maimbourg, was the unity of the See better preserved, than
during this schism.

‡ Respecting some of the particulars of this affair we have the directly opposite evidence of two contemporaries, who had both excellent means of information.
Gobellinus was attached to the house of Urban, and he relates, as the report
which had reached him, that the cardinals not only assented to the plan proposed
to them, but actually suborned false witnesses to convict the pope of heresy, and

ment of the church was vested in the hands of the sacred college, it is not improbable that some may have assented to them.
Urban discovered the conspiracy; he immediately seized six,
the most suspected of the body, and after subjecting them to
the utmost severity of torture, cast them into a narrow and
noisome dungeon. This affair took place at Nocera, in the
kingdom of Naples; but some reverses presently obliged the
pope to take refuge at Genoa. He carried his prisoners along
with him in chains, and afflicted with severe hardships; and,
during a year of sojourn in that civilized city, he could never
be moved by the counsels of his friends, or the prayers of the
republic which protected him, to release his captives. At length,
when on the point of departure, as he feared the inconvenience
or the scandal of dragging them after him through a second
journey, and as he could not exalt his resolution to the performance of an act of clemency, if, indeed, it were not justice,
he consigned five of them to sudden and secret * execution.
The other, an Englishman named Adam Eston, Bishop of
London, owed his preservation only to the frequent and pressing remonstrances of the English King. This affair took place
in the December of 1386.

In the October of 1389, Urban died at Rome; and as soon Election
as the glad intelligence reached Avignon and Paris, great and charac-
wishes were expressed and some hopes entertained in both face.
places, that the schism would thus terminate; that the Cardinals of Rome, wearied by the labours, the vicissitudes, and the
dangers of the conflict, would voluntarily unite themselves with

intended to burn him on the day of his condamnation,—and that this appeared
from their own confessions. Theodoric of Niem, who was on the spot, and one
of the judges appointed by the pope to try the cardinals, attests that all of them
constantly asserted their innocence, excepting one only, who confessed, in the
agony of the torture, anything that was asked him. Though neither author is
free from the charge of partiality, we must here give our credence to the latter
account, recollecting, that even that does not necessarily acquit the accused.
Fleury (l. xcviii., s. xx., xxi. &c.), who relates the particulars of the torture from
Theod. de Niem with painful minuteness, certainly believes the conspiracy.

  * Most assert that he threw them into the sea in sacks; others affirm that
they were strangled in prison, and their bodies consumed by quick-lime. It is
certain that they disappeared.

the college at Avignon, and acknowledge Clement for Pope, on the condition of his residence at Rome. In the University especially the public lectures were suspended, and no subject was discussed, except the probable determination of the Roman Cardinals. In the mean time, that body, on whose resolution at that moment so much depended, appear not to have been embarrassed by any hesitation as to the course before them. The members immediately assembled, to the number of fourteen; they entered into conclave, and elected, within a fortnight from Urban's decease, another Neapolitan for his successor. Pietro or Perrino Tomacelli, Cardinal of Naples, assumed, on the second of November, the name of Boniface IX., and was placed on the throne for which his ignorance * alone was sufficient to disqualify him. But the scandal of his ignorance was enhanced by his avarice. On the year following his accession, a Jubilee † was held at Rome, and the devout were exhorted to present themselves from every quarter. Unmoved by distance and expense, and even by the personal dangers which awaited them from the partizans of Clement or the *neutral* bandits of the mountains, great multitudes undertook, and many accomplished, the pilgrimage. The altars of the Roman churches were again enriched by the contributions of superstition; and if some part of the offerings was expended in the repair of the sacred edifices, by far the larger proportion flowed directly into the coffers of the pope. But Boniface was not contented with that partial stream, which had found its way to his capital; and being desirous, no doubt, that even those of his children, who had not listened to his call, should still participate in the spiritual consolation, he sent his emissaries

The Jubilee.

---

* Theodoric of Niem, lib. ii., cap. vi., " scribendi atque canendi imperitus. . . Nemo prosperatur in illo quod ignorat; unde inscitia ferè venalis facta fuit in ipsa Curia, tempore suo. Fuit tamen satis edoctus grammaticæ ac disertus, sed non habuit in aliqua scientia præeminentiam sive gradum."

† The indication of this Jubilee was the act of his predecessor. Urban VI., moved by the gradual abbreviation of human life, determined to reduce the interval (already reduced from 100 to 50) from 50 to 33 years,—this last space being the probable duration of Christ's sojourn on earth. See Spondanus, ann. 1389, s. ii. and iii. The new institution was to begin afresh from the year 1390; but it was not intended, as we shall presently observe, to supersede the secular celebration.

among all the nations by whom he was acknowledged, with commissions to sell the plenary indulgence to all indiscriminately, for the same sum which the journey to Rome would have cost them. This absolution extended to every sort of offence, and appears not to have been preceded even by the ordinary formalities of confession or penance,—it was purely and undisguisedly venal. The necessary consequences of this measure were sufficiently demoralizing ; but the evil was multiplied by the impostures of certain mendicants and others, who traversed the country with forged indulgences, which they bartered for their private profit.

Still dissatisfied, and determined to carry this lucrative mummery of the Jubilee to its utmost depth, and, as it were, to fathom the superstition of his age, Boniface communicated the privileges of the holy city to two towns of Germany, Cologne, and Magdebourg ; and permitted them also to hold their year of Jubilee, after the fashion and example of Rome. By this rash act he disparaged the supereminent sanctity of the see of St. Peter, of the tombs of the apostles, and the relics of so many martyrs! He called in question the exclusiveness of that glory, which was thought to encircle the throne of the Vicars of Christ ! He sacrificed—that which he least intended to sacrifice—even the temporal interests, even the pecuniary profits, which were ever closely connected with the *peculiar* holiness of the apostolical city. But his immediate greediness was gratified ; his collectors were present in both places to share the offerings of the faithful; and when he perceived that their fatuity was not yet exhausted, he extended the licence still farther, and accorded it to several insignificant places. At length, says Fleury, that pope became so prodigal of his indulgences, that he refused them to no one, provided he was paid for them; the effect of which was, that they grew into contempt *.

---

* The indulgence-mongers of Boniface IX., when they arrived in any city, suspended at their windows a flag, with the arms of the pope and the keys of the church. Then they prepared tables in the cathedral church, by the side of the altar, covered with rich cloths, like bankers', to receive the purchase-money. They then informed the people of the absolute power with which the pope had invested them, to deliver souls from purgatory, and give complete remission to

In the mean time the necessity of restoring the union of the church became more evident, and the expressions of that opinion more loud and general. Boniface himself professed an ardent though, as it proved, an insincere desire for the same consummation, and even addressed a letter to Charles of France (in April, 1393), in which he exhorted him seriously to under-take the sacred office of conciliation *. The king consented ; the University of Paris eagerly caught at any hope of removing the scandal and the daily growing evils which attended it, and applied itself to discover the most efficient means. After mature deliberation, a public harangue was delivered before that body (in the June of 1394), by Nicholas de Clemangis, a doctor appointed to the office, and after receiving their approbation, was presented to the king. It contained in substance, that there were three methods of healing the schism, any one of which might be adopted with reasonable hope of success :— the method of cession,—the method of compromise,—the method of a General Council. By the first the voluntary resignation of both competitors was recommended, in the presence of both Colleges ; these were then to proceed in conjunction to another election. By the second, the opposite claims might be referred to certain arbitrators appointed by both parties, with the power of final decision. As to the third, it was suggested, in case of its adoption, that the assembly should no longer consist of prelates only, many of whom were ignorant or passionately partial, but also of several Doctors in theology and law, members of the most celebrated Universities. Of the above methods, the University pronounced its own decided opinion in favour of the first,—as being the most prompt and expedient, the most proper to prevent expense and other difficulties, the most agreeable to the consciences of the faithful in both obediences, the most respectful to the honour of the princes, who had declared

Projects of the University of Paris.

all who bought their wares. If the German clergy exclaimed against this base traffic of spiritual favours, they were excommunicated. See Sismondi, Repub. Ital. ch. lxii.

* It appeared, on subsequent explanation, that Boniface saw only one solution of the difficulty,—the expulsion of his rival, and the universal acknowledgment of himself.

for the opposite parties.   Yet was there an objection to this
method, which, to many, as human nature is constituted, might
have seemed at once conclusive against it :—was it probable,
that, for the attainment of a public good, two men, in the enjoyment of very great power, dignity, and wealth, could both be
persuaded to make a voluntary cession of those personal advantages, and to withdraw to a private, and perhaps insecure
retirement, from the loftiest eminence of ambition ?   Yet this
difficulty does not appear to have been much considered, in the
outset, though it became manifest, even to the most sanguine,
long before the termination of the contest.

In the same Exposition, in which the remedies were thus
pointed out, some of the monstrous evils which then afflicted
the Church were exhibited with little exaggeration ; while all
were naturally ascribed to the prevalent disease of the moment
—the Schism.   It was forgotten that the greater number were
rooted in the system itself, and only flourished somewhat more
rankly on account of its accidental derangement.   The Church, Abuses of
it was declared, had fallen into servitude, poverty, and con- the Church.
tempt.   Unworthy and corrupt men, without the sense of justice or honesty, the servants of their intemperate passions, were
commonly exalted to the prelacy ; these plundered indifferently
churches and monasteries, whatever was profane and whatever
was sacred ; and oppressed the inferior ministers of religion
with intolerable exactions.   The dominion of simony was universal ; benefices and cures were conferred only on those who
had means to buy them ; while the poor and learned candidate
was hated the more for that very learning which made him
dangerous to corruption.   And not only were the dignities of
the Church publicly bartered ; not only were relics and crosses
and the sacred vessels commonly exposed to sale ; but the
very sacraments themselves, those especially of ordination and
penance, had their price in gold.

A political circumstance occurred at this moment which was
favourable to the hopes of union.   A truce for four years was
signed between the kings of England and France—the most
zealous supporters of the opposite parties.   At the same time,
the University of Cologne, though it acknowledged Boniface,

and had probably profited by his patronage, entered into correspondence with that of Paris for the extinction of the schism;—and lastly, as if to place the result within the immediate reach of the pacificators, Clement VII. was so violently* affected by the proceedings at Paris, that he was struck with apoplexy, and died.

Death of Clement VII.

As soon as this intelligence reached Paris, the deputation from the University instantly petitioned the king, that he would cause the cardinals to suspend the election, until some general measure should be taken to ensure the union; also, that he would assemble his prelates and nobles, and order processions and public prayers to the same end throughout his kingdom. Accordingly, a royal messenger was dispatched to Avignon, to prevent the meeting of the College, and prepare it for a special embassy; and on the success of this mission hung the hopes of Christendom. The envoy arrived at Avignon only ten days after the decease of Clement; but he found the cardinals already in conclave! Still, as the election was not yet made, he transmitted to them the letter of the king; but the College, suspecting its contents, and determined at any risk to have a pope of their own creation, deferred the opening of the letter till their actual business should be completed. They then hastened to a decision; and Peter of Luna, Cardinal of Arragon, was raised by their unanimous voice to the divided throne.

Election of Peter of Luna, Benedict XIII.

Howbeit, they previously took a precaution, which was certainly necessary for their own credit, though there were few, probably, who expected any real advantage from it. Before the election, they drew up an act, by which they solemnly engaged to labour for the extinction of the schism, and to give every aid to the future pope for that purpose. It was moreover specified, that if any one among themselves should be raised to the pontificate, this act should be equally binding

* When the earnest and reasonable exhortations of the University were pressed upon him—when he was assured that the evil had gone so far, that some began almost to advocate a *plurality* of popes, and the appointment of one to every kingdom—the infatuated bigot only started from his seat in anger, and declared that " the letters were poisoned, and tended to bring the Holy See into discredit."

upon him; and that he should even be prepared to cede his dignity if his cardinals should judge it expedient for the concord of the Church. They then took oaths on the altar to observe this engagement.

Peter of Luna had long been distinguished for ability and address; he had discharged with vigour the offices intrusted to him; but there was also an opinion respecting him, which seems more than any other to have procured his elevation, and even at first to have reconciled all parties to it—this was, that he ardently desired the union of the Church. This zeal he had been forward, while cardinal, to proclaim upon all occasions—even so far as to censure Clement for the want of it; and many hoped that it would burn with equal fervour under the pontifical robes. The University addressed to him congratulations, which were seemingly sincere, and Benedict XIII. (the name assumed by him) repaid them with the strongest protestations of good intention.

A grand Council was then held at Paris, in which the method of cession again received the approbation of the great majority; and it was agreed that an embassy should be sent to Avignon to treat with the pope. The king added his authority, to give weight to this measure; and the more certainly to secure its success, he sent his brother and both his uncles (the Dukes of Burgundy and Berri) to conduct the negotiation. Benedict received them with respect and deference; but when they opened the subject of their mission, and pressed the necessity of the cession, as the only road to concord, he found many reasons to urge against that particular method, as indeed against the other two, which had also occurred to the University. In the place of them, he proposed a conference with his rival, at which he affected to believe that matters might be accommodated. The ambassadors persevered in their proposal; and even the cardinals, on their strong solicitation, declared, with one exception*, for the method of cession. Nevertheless, Benedict, during several weeks of repeated conferences and debates, inflexibly persisted in his refusal. At length the illustrious

Grand embassy from Paris to Avignon.

* The cardinal bishop of Pampeluna, a Spaniard, and compatriot of the pope.

mission returned to Paris without any other result than the discovery of Benedict's insincerity.

Notwithstanding this failure, the king addressed himself very warmly, to unite the different courts and learned bodies of Europe in favour of the method which still seemed to promise the greatest hopes. Messengers traversed the country in all directions, and every state and every city in Europe was agitated by the same momentous question. The speculations of the learned and the projects of the powerful were equally engrossed by it; and it seemed as if the fate of all governments and the welfare of all subjects depended on its solution. At this time the University of Paris, which took the foremost part in these discussions, and possessed much more influence than any other learned body, openly expressed dissatisfaction with Benedict, and even threw out some menaces of a General Council, in case of his further contumacy.

Benedict watched these proceedings with anxiety; but the variety and discordance of the materials which it was necessary to combine for his destruction gave him the confidence to persist;—upon which the doctors of Paris advanced one degree towards more efficient measures. And as Luna had unreservedly sworn to adopt the method of cession in case his cardinals should hereafter recommend it, and as his cardinals had strongly recommended it, and as he had then unequivocally rejected it, little sympathy could be expected from any quarter with a prelate whose selfish opposition to the interests of religion was made more detestable by an act of deliberate perjury. The measure was, to draw up a strong exposition of Benedict's general delinquency and of the particular grievances of the complainants, and to appeal from his censures, whether past or future, to the future pope*: a step which very temperately opened the path for more vigorous proceedings.

Conduct of Boniface. In the meantime, the courts which acknowledged the rival pope made great exertions to bring him to the arrangement— which to them seemed so reasonable, and to him so unjust and extravagant. From Sicily to the extremities of Germany,

---

* On this occasion numbers of polemical tracts and pamphlets were published on both sides, containing, as Fleury has observed, many words but few reasons.

assemblies were held and resolutions adopted; and the vows and talents and energies of all men were directed to the same object: consequently, deputations and embassies were sent to Rome from all quarters. Boniface at first was contented to reply, that he was the true and only pope, and that universal obedience was due to him. But presently, in the year 1398, when the emperor at length interfered more directly, and pressed the method of cession, he found it expedient to dissemble; and by the advice of his cardinals, he promised submission, provided (a very safe proviso) that the antipope of Avignon should also resign his claims*. Yet even so guarded a concession alarmed the avaricious fears of the citizens of Rome. They trembled lest their bishop and his prodigal court, and the train of his dependents and expectants, and sycophants, should again be seduced to some foreign residence. That event, too, at that moment, would have been peculiarly afflicting, since in two years (in 1400) the second grand and general Jubilee was to take place; and the inhabitants had already begun to make provision for the season of spoliation. Accordingly, a body of the notables of the city waited upon the pope, and professed towards him the most sincere and unprecedented † affection: they declared that they would never desert him, but sustain, with their very lives and property, his just and holy cause. " My children," replied Boniface, " take courage; rest assured that I will continue to be pope; and whatever I may say, or however I may play off the king of France and the emperor against each other, I will never submit to their will."

While such was the disposition of the Roman competitor, Subtraction of obedi-ence. during the July of the same year the court and university of Paris at length perceiving that a mere contest of acts and declarations would never weary the pontiff of Avignon, proceeded to a measure of greater efficacy—one which no Catholic nation had hitherto, on any occasion, dared to adopt against any

---

* Spondanus, ann. 1398, s. ii.

† Fleury, liv. xcix., s. 18. Boniface artfully availed himself of this unusual display of loyalty on the part of his subjects to secure an extent of temporal authority over them, such as no former pope is said to have possessed. See Ægidius Card. Viterb. apud Pagi, Vit. Bonif. IX., s. xliii.

pope:—" By the aid and advice of the princes and other
nobles, and of the Church of our kingdom, as well clergy as
people, we entirely withdraw our obedience from pope Benedict XIII., as well as from his adversary, whom, indeed, we
have never acknowledged.   And we ordain, that no one henceforward make any payment to pope Benedict, his collectors, or
agents, from the ecclesiastical revenues or emoluments. We
also strictly prohibit all our subjects from offering to him any
manner of obedience."   Such was the substance of the royal
proclamation; and arrangements were at the same time made
to deprive the pope of the presentation to all benefices for as
long a time as it should remain in force.   This edict was received with such general respect and submission, that the very
domestics and chaplains of Benedict retired from their offices;
and what was still more important, the cardinals themselves
withdrew in a body from his court.   But he, nothing moved
by that unanimity, was the more forward on repeated occasions
to assert that he was the true and genuine pope; that he would
remain so in despite of king, duke, or count—and that he was
prepared to renounce his life rather than his dignity.

Blockade of the palace. Recourse was then had to the only method which gave any
just hope of success.   A military force was sent against
Avignon; and as the inhabitants of that city also declared
their adhesion to the king and the cardinals, nothing now remained in opposition to the royal will and the force of the
nation, except the pontifical palace.   But Benedict had secured
some faithful mercenaries for its defence; and an effective
blockade was thought sufficient for the objects of his enemies.
Thus for the space of four years he continued a close prisoner
in his own residence, without any strength to resist the means
employed against him, or any disposition to yield to them.
But at length the vigour of that powerful confederacy was dis-
sipated by the persevering intrigues of one feeble individual,
and the variety of interests and principles in the mass opposed
to Benedict led by slow degrees to a disunion which preserved
him.   The first who betrayed his party was a Norman officer,
Robinet de Braquemont, who, through the confidence reposed
in him, and his constant access to the palace, found easy means

of liberating the pope.   It was on March 12, 1403, that the Escape of Benedict. successor of St. Peter concealed his apostolical sanctity under the disguise of a menial; and having thus eluded the penetration of his guards, took refuge in a small town near Avignon. As a pope was never wont to travel, unless preceded by the holy sacrament, Benedict carried out with him a little box containing the consecrated element; and even for the literal observance of that custom, he placed the box upon his breast.

As soon as he found himself in safety, he caused his beard, which he had nourished during the persecution of his captivity, to be shaved off; and recovering with his freedom the consciousness of his dignity, he resumed the habits and authority of a pope.   No sooner was the circumstance of his liberation made known, than several noble individuals rendered to him the accustomed homage.   Immediately the college of cardinals passed over to him and sought a reconciliation.   The citizens of Avignon eagerly tendered their offers of service.   Benedict forgave the truancy and accepted the repentance of all.   At the same time, the party in France, which for some time had been opposed to the *subtraction** of obedience, and which had lately gained strength, now boldly declared its adhesion.   The king was privately induced to join it; and notwithstanding the resistance of the more consistent promoters of ecclesiastical concord, it prevailed.   By an edict of May 30, an entire and unequivocal restitution of obedience was enjoined: thus, after a partial interruption of about five years, the tide of papacy resumed for a season, even in France itself, its prescribed and customary † course.

The reason which was advanced by the king to justify so Rapacious government of Boniface. complete a change in his policy was, that the example of France had not been followed by other nations‡; and that,

---

* It is the word used by ecclesiastical writers—Subtractio, soustraction.

† The first proof of moderation and gratitude which Benedict gave after the Act of Restitution was, to appoint afresh to certain benefices, which had been filled up during the subtraction.   The king then sent an embassy to *pray* him to confirm such provisions as had been then made.   *He returned a direct refusal.* On this Charles published his commands, that those who had been so appointed should, at any rate and without any fees to the pope, remain in possession.   This was conclusive.

‡ In 1399, king Richard expressly consulted the University of Oxford on the

while the pontiff of Avignon was confined to his palace walls, the intruder at Rome was acquiring new strength and confidence. We shall, therefore, now recur very briefly to the system of government which Boniface had adopted. It appears to have been directed by one principle only—to extract the largest possible sums from the superstition of the people and the ambition of the clergy, and the folly and credulity of both. During the first seven years of his pontificate, his proceedings were veiled by some show of decency, through a reluctant respect which he paid to the virtues of some of the ancient cardinals. But as these successively died, and were replaced by others of his own creation and character, he broke out into the undisguised practice of simony*. This was the most copious and constant source of his gains; but when the simple and honest sale of benefices proved insufficient for his demands, he had recourse, besides, to direct acts of fraud and robbery. In the distribution of Graces and Expectatives, the poorest candidates were invariably placed at the bottom of the list; but this was not sufficient—even the promises that had been made them were frequently cancelled in favour of some wealthier competitor, to whose more recent patent an earlier date was affixed, with a clause of preference. The fluctuating health and approaching decease of an opulent incumbent were watched with impatient anxiety, and appointed couriers hurried to Rome with the welcome intelligence. Immediately the bene-

grand question of the age. The answer of that body was very decided against any refusal of obedience to Boniface, *because he was indeed the true pope*. On the same ground, they objected to the method of cession, and insisted in preference on that of a General Council—to be convoked, of course, by their own genuine pope. Thus they assumed at once the point at issue—if Boniface had power to convoke a council of universal authority, Boniface was truly pope—and the schism was at an end.

* See Theodoric of Niem, De Schismat., lib. ii., cap. vii., viii., ix., x., xi., xii., &c. This author, a native of Westphalia, was attached as secretary to the Roman court during the whole of the schism; and besides the history of this event, in four books, (the last of which is entitled *Nemus Unionis,*) he composed the Life of John XXIII. He exposed pontifical depravity with freedom, it may be with rancour. Spondanus (ann. 1404, s. xvi.) especially ascribes his account of the simony of Boniface to an *ulcerosus stomachus*, and of course other Roman Catholic writers are scandalized by his little reserve. But we doubt not that his narrative is essentially true. Spondanus excuses the rapacity of Boniface by his necessities, and brings some authority for the assertion *that he died poor.*

fice was in the market; and it not uncommonly happened that the same was sold as vacant to several rivals, even under the same date. The ravages of a frightful pestilence only contributed to fill the pontifical coffers; and a benefice was sometimes sold in the course of a few weeks to several successive candidates, of whom none survived to take possession. At length, in the year 1401, the pontiff proceeded so far as to cancel by a single act nearly all the graces, dispensations, and expectatives which he had previously granted, and to declare them wholly void—that he might enter afresh and without any restraints upon the task which seemed almost to be terminated, and reap from the same exhausted soil a second harvest of shame and iniquity. By such methods * Boniface enriched himself and impoverished his clergy; and however we may abominate his rapacity, we have little cause to feel any compassion for the sufferers, who were possibly influenced by the same passion, and who were certainly involved in the same simoniacal scandal with himself.

The superstition of the laity was also taxed to the utmost The Jubilee point of endurance; the excessive abuse of the Jubilee has been of A.D. 1400. mentioned as the favourite resource of Boniface, and the circumstances of the time combined to sharpen his appetite for that feast. The year 1400 was that destined, according to the original institution of Boniface VIII., for the celebration of the *secular* solemnity; and it appears that, though the innovations of later popes had met with general reverence, there were still several rigid devotees who, holding them in inferior estimation, looked forward with pious impatience to the approach of the legitimate festival. Neither was this impression confined to the nations in the obedience of the Roman competitor; the

---

* The system of Annates, or the payment of a year's first fruits to the apo- Annates. stolical chamber, was brought to perfection by Boniface IX. It did not, however, originate with him; Clement V. having learnt that some bishops in England exacted such claims from their diocesan clergy, felt justified in transferring the right to the see of Rome. This took place in 1306; thirteen years afterwards, John XXII., when he reserved *for three years* the first fruits of all vacant benefices, excepted the bishoprics and abbeys. Boniface IX. extended the usurpation to the prelacies, and *made it perpetual*. Fleury, l. xcix, s. xxvii. Spondanus, ann. 1339, s. ii.

followers of Benedict acknowledged by their respect for the
apostolical city the authority of the see, though they rejected
the usurper who occupied it; and the French especially pressed
in great multitudes to obtain the plenary indulgence at Rome.
Charles published an ordonnance to restrain the emigration of
his subjects; he saw with sorrow, not perhaps their slavish
superstition, but the exportation of their wealth to a foreign and
even hostile treasury.   Still in many, the religious zeal overpowered the sense of civil duty, and these proceeded on their
pilgrimage.   But several were intercepted and pillaged on
their road by partizans at enmity with the pope; and those
who escaped this danger were exposed, on the termination of
their journey, to the pestilence which was laying waste the
holy city.   Some perished miserably; and others, whose resources were exhausted through their devotion and their sufferings, when they applied for aid to the apostolical coffers, were
dismissed with a cold and contemptuous refusal.

Innocent
VII. suc-
ceeds
Boniface.
Four years afterwards Boniface died; his cardinals immediately entered into conclave, and elected a successor, nearly
under the same conditions which had been accepted and
violated by Benedict. He assumed the name of Innocent VII.;
but the two years of his imbecile government produced no other
change, than the secession of Genoa and Pisa to the obedience
of his rival.   Both parties expressed equal desire for the extinction of the schism; both were equally insincere; and the
attention of the courts of Christendom and the feelings of the
pious friends of the Church were insulted by the verbose correspondence and recriminations of two aged hypocrites.   Innocent died in 1406; and the Roman cardinals then seriously
deliberated on the expediency of deferring the new election,
until some measures could be taken in concert with the college
at Avignon.

But their fears of an interested populace contended with
their wisdom and their virtue; they likewise dreaded the risks
which the temporal sovereignty of the see must incur during
the interregnum—their indecision terminated in a half-measure.
They bound themselves by oath, that whichsoever of them
should be chosen, should hold himself in perpetual readiness

to resign, in case the concord of the Church and the union of
the two colleges should require it; and that he should immediately make public that such was the condition of his election.
This act having been assented to with great solemnity, they
threw their eyes upon a prelate, whose advanced age, whose
holy reputation *, whose habitual integrity, whose ardent love
of the Church and regard for its best interests, placed him beyond all suspicion, almost beyond the possibility, of perfidy.
Angelo Corrario, a Venetian, the titular patriarch of Constan- Election of
tinople, was the character which they sought.   Seventy years Angelo
Corrario, or
of immaculate piety, by which he was endeared to the whole Gregory
Church, were a pledge for the extinction of any selfish passions XII.
which at any time might have lurked in his bosom; and the
austerity of his devotion, which emulated the holiness of the
ancient pontiffs, guaranteed the strict observance of his engagement.   Accordingly, on the instant of his election, he eagerly
ratified his covenant †, and proclaimed his intention to restore

* They sought not (says Aretinus) for a man of business or address, but for
one of honour and integrity; and at length they unanimously fixed their choice
upon Angelo Corrario, " virum prisca severitate et sanctimonia reverendum."

† The short account of Leonardus Aretinus, the attendant and faithful adherent of Angelo, should be cited. " Is conclavi egressus promissionem, votum,
et juramentum, quæ privatus fecerat, tunc in potestate constitutus iterato novavit.
Atque ita loquebatur de Unione primo illo tempore, ut, si cætera deessent, pedibus
et baculo se iturum ad eam conficiendam asseveraret. Statimque adversario scripsit benigne illum ad pacem invitans et abdicationem mutuam offerans. Adver-
sarius autem tantisdem ferme syllabis ad eum rescripsit; eadem invitatio fuit,
eademque cohortatio... Locus deinde necessarius visus est in quo et Pontifices
ipsi et collegia convenirent. Ad hoc Savona pari consensu recepta est... Pros-
perè huc usque et plane ex sententia. Deinde paulatim res labascere cœpit et
cuncta indies deteriora fieri. Voluntas autem illa Pontificis recta nequaquam
satis habere firmitatis reperta est ad pontificatum deponendum; cujus rei culpam
multi in propinquos ejus referebant, &c... Erat in altero Pontifice non melior
sane mens, sed occulebat callidius malam voluntatem, et quia noster fugiebat,
ipse obviam ire videbatur... Sed cum de congressu eorum per internuntios agere-
tur, noster tanquam terrestre animal ad littus accedere, ille tanquam aquaticam
a mari discedere recusabat... Cum per hunc modum desideria Christianorum qui
pacem unitatemque optabant in longum ducerentur, non tulerunt Cardinales
nostri sed deserto Pontifice Pisas abiere," &c. Leonard. Aretin. in Rer. Italicar.
Historia. " Ego (the historian presently continues) Pontificem secutus sum potius
familaritatis gratia, quam quod ejus causam probarem. Quanquam fuit in Gre-
goria permagna vitæ morumque honestas et prisca quædam, ut ita dixerim, bonitas,
scripturarum quoque scientia et indagatio subtilis et recta... Denique in cunctis
fermè rebus mihi satisfaciebat, 'præterquam in Unionis negotio."... Id. loc. cit.
Gibbon has referred to this passage in his 70th Chapter.

union to the Church by any risk or sacrifice. Should it be necessary to perform the journey on foot with his staff in his hand, or to encounter the sea in the most wretched bark, he vowed that he would still present himself at the place of conference. His declarations were received with joy and confidence, and it was thought that the flock of Christ had at length obtained a faithful shepherd.

After his restoration to liberty, the policy of Benedict had entirely changed—all his original desire for the extinction of the schism appeared to be revived; he had made overtures to that effect both to Boniface and Innocent ; and when the new pope (Gregory XII.) addressed him on the subject, he renewed his usual protestations. But they were no longer able to deceive either the court or the doctors of Paris ; it was found that, however profuse in general professions, he invariably evaded the cession, whenever it was strongly recommended to him; and he was not the better loved for the frequent exactions of tenths and annates, to which his necessities even more than his avarice obliged him.

Projected Conference at Savona.   At length it was arranged, at a meeting of certain deputies of both parties, that the long-promised conference should be brought about ; and the place selected for the purpose was Savona. Some hopes were entertained from this project, and it was pressed with earnestness both at Rome and Avignon. The time was fixed for the Michaelmas of 1407 ; and when it arrived, Benedict was found at the appointed city, full of his customary declarations. But where was Angelo Corrario, the sworn advocate of concord, the model of ancient holiness ? Every solicitation, to observe the direct obligation of his oath, had been urged upon him in vain. To the most overpowering arguments he opposed the most contemptible pretexts. He was secretly determined to evade the conference; and he did finally absent himself. Then followed another interchange of accusations and protestations, which had no other effect than to persuade men, that an understanding secretly subsisted between the two pretenders, and that they had conspired to cajole the world and retain their offices by their common perjury*.

* Spondanus, ann. 1408, s. v.

We shall not pursue the tedious details of their elaborate
duplicity; nor is it important to notice the multifarious correspondence which perplexed the dispute, nor even closely to
trace the circumstances which led to its conclusion *. It is
enough to mention the leading facts. In the first place, in
contempt of one important clause † of the oath taken in conclave, Gregory created four new cardinals; on which the others,
in just indignation, deserted his court and retired to Pisa,
where they fixed their residence. Presently afterwards (in
1408) the king of France took measures to seize the person of
Benedict; but that accomplished politician, having constantly
retained a small fleet in his service on the plea of personal
security, set sail on the rumour of this danger, and, after a
short cruise on the coast of Italy, found a safer refuge at Perpignan in Spain,—for the Spaniards continued to adhere to Flight of
their countryman, through all his vicissitudes, and through all Benedict
his perfidy. At Perpignan he assembled his bishops, and held to Spain.
his councils, and awaited the termination of the tempest.

But his cardinals remained in France; and now perceiving The Cardi-
that they were abandoned by their master, they turned their nals con-
attention more zealously than before to the extinction of the Council of
schism. To that end, they negotiated in perfect sincerity with Pisa, A.D.
the rival college at Pisa; and the consequence was an imme- 1409 ;
diate coalition. By this event, the first substantial ground
towards the closing of the schism was gained. It was now
clearly ascertained, that the voluntary cession of the pretenders,
under any conceivable circumstances, was hopeless. The latest
proof of that truth was the strongest; since Angelo di Corrario,
the most unblemished of mankind, had chosen to stain his grey
hairs with deliberate perjury, rather than resign the possession
—the very short possession—of a disturbed and disputed dignity. No resource henceforward remained, except compulsion;

* The celebrated embassy sent from France both to Rome and Avignon, just
before the Council of Pisa, is described by Gibbon, chap. lxx.

† "That both parties shall promise to make no new cardinals during the treaty
of union." Gregory probably considered this part of the obligation as conditional.
And, as it is not likely that Benedict should have made any such promise, he
might feel that the engagement was not binding upon himself. Had he been
more scrupulous, when the obligation was direct and unequivocal, we might have
given him the benefit of this supposition.

and the union of the colleges afforded the only prospect of that result. Some difficulties were still to be overcome, but the convocation of a general council promised to remove them. Accordingly the council was summoned to assemble at Pisa in the March of 1409.

The Council of Pisa met under circumstances wholly different from any other similar assembly. In the division of churchmen it represented the unity of the Church. Disregarding the opposite pretensions to individual legitimacy, it asserted the undivided authority of the see; and thus, since there might be many antipopes, but not possibly more than one pope, the object to which its proceedings necessarily tended, was to reject the two actual claimants, and substitute one true and catholic pontiff. It was summoned by the cardinals, twenty-four of whom were present, and it was attended by a great number of prelates *, as well as by the generals of the Mendicant orders, and the deputies of several universities. Ambassadors from the courts of Germany, France, England, and others, were likewise present; though the object of the first was rather to question the legitimacy than to sanction the deliberations of the council. The scruples of these envoys gave rise to an important discussion, which was occasionally renewed afterwards; and which, as far as the principles of the disputants were concerned, divided the high papist party from the moderate catholics. It was argued on the one side, from the language of the canons and the unvarying practice of the Church, that a general council could not legally assemble, unless by the authority and express summons of the pope, whereas the meeting at Pisa had received the sanction of no pontiff. On the other hand, it was maintained, that no pope did then in fact exist; that both pretenders, by their long-continued perfidy and contumacy, had involved themselves in the guilt of schism and heresy † ; and that, under such circumstances, if

---

* Besides the three patriarchs, 180 archbishops and bishops, and about 300 abbots, were present in person or by representatives, and 282 doctors in theology. —Spondanus, ann. 1409, s. ii.

† This last assertion does not appear, at first sight, so obvious—but the word heresy was now used in a much more comprehensive sense than in the early Church:—perseverance in schism was at this time sufficient to constitute heresy.

the necessities of the Church demanded it, the cardinals had full power to call a council*. Recollecting, as we do, the false foundation on which the claims of the pope really rested, we can scarcely pretend to doubt on which side the reason lay. But among the controversialists of that time, the spuriousness of the decretals was still unknown, and almost unsuspected; and pretensions directly derived from them were acknowledged with respectful acquiescence.

The council then proceeded to fulfil its object. The first step was to summon the pretenders to appear in person or by deputy, and on their non-appearance to pronounce them contumacious. The next, to trace the proofs of their insincerity and collusion, and to expose their perjury. The next, to command the Christian world to withdraw its obedience from the one and from the other. Then followed the sentence of condemnation;—and here we may pause to remark, that the prelate who pronounced it was the titular patriarch of Alexandria, supported on either hand by those of Antioch and Jerusalem. The two schismatics, after a long enumeration of their crimes, were cut off from the Church; and the holy see was declared vacant. Then the cardinals, after binding themselves by oath to continue the council after the election, for the general purposes of Church reform, entered into conclave. They remained six days in deliberation, and their choice fell upon the cardinal and elect of Milan, Peter of Candia, who took the name of Alexander V. Peter of Candia,

Peter, native of Candia, a Venetian subject, had risen from Alexander so low an origin, that he professed to retain no recollection of V. his parentage—a circumstance (he boasted) which gave him a great advantage over his predecessors, since it exempted him from all temptation to nepotism†. One day, as he was begging alms, while yet extremely young, an Italian monk took compassion on him, and introduced him into his convent. From Candia, as he gave great promise of intellectual attainment, he was carried into Italy; and thence, for the gradual completion

---

* That there were cases, in which they possessed that right, does not appear to have been disputed—that, for instance, of the insanity of a pope.

† It was the boast of his friends, that, from being a rich archbishop, he had become a poor cardinal, and that the popedom had reduced him to beggary.

of his studies, to the universities, first of Oxford, and afterwards of Paris. There he acquired great theological reputation, and retained along with it a mild, liberal, and convivial disposition. He was already advanced in age when raised to the pontificate. After a few more sessions, in which a commission was appointed for the investigation of ecclesiastical abuses, and some unimportant regulations enacted, the council was adjourned for an interval of three years, till the April of 1412.

The authority of the council of Pisa was recognized by all the national churches of Europe, excepting Arragon, Castille, Bavaria, and Scotland; and Rome itself, by placing Alexander in the list of its genuine bishops, has offered it the same acknowledgment. Its proceedings were conducted without any reproach of irregularity or dissension, and it dispersed under the auspices of a legitimate pope. It remains to inquire what was the effect produced upon the antipopes by decisions so Conduct of solemnly delivered. On the determination of an assembly, the anti- which expressed the power and united the vows of almost popes. every nation of Europe, what course did the repudiated schismatics adopt? Did they endeavour to conciliate the party which they were too weak to resist, and too infamous longer to cajole? Did they resign those claims by which they might still indeed disturb the peace of Christendom, but which could scarcely promise any substantial dignity to themselves? No; they clung to the fragments of their fortunes with the same attachment which had bound them to prosperity; and the more generally it was admitted that *both* were pretenders and antipopes, the more violently each proclaimed himself to be the genuine pope. Benedict could still boast of the obedience of Spain; but this was a narrow field to content the ambition of the successor of the Gregories and the Innocents. But the reverses of his rival were even more remarkable. He only escaped captivity by traversing the ambush of his enemies in the disguise of a merchant, while his chamberlain, who resembled him in person, and had assumed his robes, was taken in his place, and subjected to some severity of treatment. Having in such guise escaped to two galleys which awaited him, and which conveyed him to Gaieta, he then reclaimed his dignity, and imitated, with his scanty train of courtiers, the pomp of the imperial city. He was protected, indeed, by Ladislaus, and neither Germany nor Hungary had yet nominally withdrawn from his obedience. But he was poor, and as he had no patronage, he had no resources; and his few followers continued to adhere to him through fear of the king of Naples, rather than from any attachment either to his person or his cause.

Alexander V., the feebleness of whose character made him liable to the influence of any more vigorous spirit, fell almost entirely under the guidance of a Neapolitan, named Baltazar Cossa, legate at Bologna. This extraordinary person, by birth *Baltazar Cossa.* a nobleman, by habit and inclination a soldier, by profession a churchman, and in rank a cardinal, was one of the boldest champions of the council of Pisa. And when it appeared that the possession of Rome could only be recovered from Ladislaus by military measures, Baltazar undertook to conduct an expedition for that purpose. The Roman people acknowledged the authority of Alexander, and sent to him a deputation with the keys of the city. The pope was then at Bologna. He received the envoys with magnificence; he expressed his pleasure at their emancipation from the seductions of Angelo Corrario; and in respect to the desire which they testified to have their pope among them, and to revive the Jubilee*, (for these vows were united in their petition,) he appointed the year 1413 for that solemnity. This circumstance is worthy of thus much attention, as it shows how unblushingly the Romans at that time avowed the real motive of their attachment to the vicar of Christ; and also how basely a pope, who could not plead either weakness or poverty, pandered to their cupidity. But Alexander V. was not destined to witness the execution of his decree, nor even to receive the venal applauses of his people. He died at Bologna the year after his election (May 3d, 1410) *Elevation of John XXIII. to the see,* and the cardinals, after a very short deliberation, appointed Baltazar Cossa in his place.

The world was surprised at this election; for though he possessed good natural talents and a rapid decision in matters

* Fleury, l. c., sec. xliii.

of business and other temporal concerns, Baltazar was of a violent temper, and remarkable for the licentiousness of his morals; his demeanour and manners corresponded with his reputation; and the military air, which so little became the habit of the cardinal, seemed wholly to disqualify him for the chair of St. Peter. On the other hand, his fearless character gave promise of that vigour which was now required for the restoration of the Church; and it was hoped that if he did not awaken to the spiritual duties of his station, he would at least consent to observe its decencies.

John XXIII. (Baltazar assumed that name) did not at first deceive either of those expectations: his manners were softened on his elevation, and his morals ostensibly amended; and he framed his political arrangements so well, that the king of Naples declared in his favour. Then Gregory, for the second time an exile, embarked his person and his suite in two trading vessels, and sought almost the only spot in Europe which continued to obey him. Charles Malatesta opened to him the gates of Rimini; and there, together with three cardinals who still followed him, he had space to deplore the passion or the weakness through which he had exchanged a holy reputation and dignified independence for banishment, insecurity, and infamy.

and of Sigismond to the empire.

The death of the emperor at this moment opened an occasion to the pope to recommend Sigismond as successor; and as Sigismond was actually chosen, a friendly intercourse was immediately established between the two parties. The still disturbed condition of the Church, and the abuses which universally prevailed, demanded indeed their cordial and honest co-operation; and in this at least they agreed, that a General Council was the only remaining remedy, and that no time should be lost in convoking it. On the dissolution of that of Pisa, it had been arranged that another should be called after three years. Accordingly, John had summoned the prelates to Rome at the appointed time; but so few presented themselves, that it was not judged expedient to proceed to any important enactments.

The place which was now selected for a more efficient meeting was the city of Constance, in Switzerland. Much depended on that selection. Much depended on the local influence which might probably be exercised, and which would certainly affect the deliberations of the body. Constance was under the direct control of Sigismond; and it is well known* that the pope foresaw some of the consequences of that arrangement, and consented to it with extreme reluctance. It is known, too, that he felt a much stronger inclination to march in arms for the recovery of his capital, which the death of Ladislaus had again opened to him, than to conduct the peaceful procession of his cardinals towards the appointed city. Nevertheless, his outward conduct betrayed no disposition to recede, whatever may have been his private wishes or his secret intrigues; and having fixed the 1st of November, 1414, for the opening of the council, he was present for the performance of his duties on that day.

Convocation of the Council of Constance, A. D. 1414.

The situation of Constance in many particulars justified the preference which the emperor had obtained for it. Its pleasant and healthful situation on the shores of an extensive lake; its central position with respect to France, Germany, and Italy; and not least, the circumstance that it was at that time the

* Leonardus Aretinus relates a curious anecdote on this subject, which throws light on the still disputed character of John. " The pontiff privately communicated to me his design. ' The whole matter (said he) depends on the place of the council, and I will not have it where the emperor is the stronger. I shall therefore give to the legates whom I send to decide this matter, credentials of full power and discretion for public appearance's sake, but I shall privately restrict them to certain specified places'—and then he mentioned those places. Afterwards, when the legates came to take leave, having dismissed all excepting myself, he secretly addressed them and showed of what weight the matter was on which they were sent. Then, speaking kindly to them, he praised their prudence and fidelity, and said that they knew what ought to be done better than himself. While he was thus talking and repeating those civil things to them, he was himself overpowered by a feeling of kindness, and in an instant changed the design so long determined by him. ' I had meant (he said) to give you a list of certain places, from which list you should on no account depart; but at this very instant I change my mind, and commit everything to your prudence. It is for you to think what may be safe and what dangerous for me.' And thus he tore in pieces the paper on which he had written the names of the places. The legates therefore going to Sigismond chose Constance—a transalpine city, and subject to the emperor. When John heard this, he was incredibly afflicted, and lamented his evil stars, that he had so lightly deviated from his former mind and counsel." Leonard. Aretin., In Rerum Italic. Historia.

grand depôt of all commercial intercourse between the two last countries, made it favourable for the access and accommodation of a numerous and opulent assembly. As the council lasted for nearly four years, the number of its members and their attendants must have greatly fluctuated ; but if it be true that at certain times not less than 30,000 horses * were maintained for its use, we may conceive the splendour as well as the multitude of the assemblage. It was divided into four sections, following the grand national division of Europe; and all the members were arranged under the banners of Italy, of France, of Germany, or of England. Most of the leading ecclesiastics† of Europe were present ; but the greater proportion of eminent laymen who thronged to Constance distinguished that council, more than any other circumstance, from all that had preceded it.

Its professed objects. Its professed objects were the extinction of the schism and the reformation of the Church. The persecutions of John Huss and Jerome of Prague, which formed a part of its labours, will be described and traced to their true motives in a following chapter. Even the subject of the Reformation must for the moment be deferred, since we must confine our present attention to the thread which we have pursued through so many windings, and trace the history of the schism to its conclusion. And to some indeed it might appear, and not without specious reason, that the schism was virtually extinct already; and that the feeble antipopes of Perpignan and of Rimini might have been safely left to waste their complaints and anathemas unnoticed. And so it might possibly have proved. But, on the other hand, the politics of Europe were at that time so fluctuating and faithless, that the slightest circumstance of national interest, or even of personal caprice or jealousy, might at any moment have transferred the obedience of a kingdom, and restored to Gregory or to Benedict the ad-

---

* Apprehensions being entertained about the means of providing for so many animals, it was ordered that the pope should be limited to twenty horses, the cardinals and princes to ten each, the bishops to five, and the abbots to four only. Raynald., ann. 1414, s. xiii.

† Nine-and-twenty cardinals and three hundred bishops and archbishops were present at the second session, on March 2, when the pope made his abdication.

hesion of a powerful party. So that there seemed no positive security for the concord of the Church until the two schismatics should be deprived of the faintest shadow of authority. Hence it was that all parties were chiefly anxious to attend to this subject, and to complete the work which had been so far advanced at Pisa*.

But here, at the very outset, a difference arose of the most essential importance, as to the manner of attaining that end. It will be observed, that the present assembly approached that question under circumstances dissimilar from those which guided the former. At Pisa, the impossibility of deciding between the two claimants having been admitted, neither of them was recognised by the council. The fathers were indeed personally divided in their obedience ; but as a single legislative body they acknowledged neither Peter of Luna nor Angelo Carrario. Thus their course was obvious—to declare the See vacant, and to proceed to a canonical election. But the council of Constance, being held in continuation of that of Pisa, being bound by its decisions and resting on its validity, admitted of necessity the rights of John XXIII. And thus, whatsoever course its deliberations might take, it had to deal with a pope of undisputed legitimacy. For though some feeble murmurs would be raised at Rimini and Perpignan, Constance at least was not the place where they could find an echo.

Under these circumstances the council met together and soon afterwards John caused his own proposition to be laid before it. It was simply this—that the fathers should first of all things confirm all the acts of the council of Pisa; that they should next deliberate on the best means of carrying them into effect ; and lastly enter upon their labours for the reformation of the Church. In this paper the pope merely called upon the

Proposition of the Pope.

---

* The bare circumstance that there were three competitors for the chair after the council of Pisa, and only two before it, has led many historians to consider that assembly as having increased the schism. But to us it seems otherwise. It reduced the antipopes to an insignificance from which they never recovered, and it united the great body of Christendom in the same views, and with a common principle. If it was not immediately successful, neither was the council of Constance perfectly so. But the proceedings of Pisa were the foundation of the re-union, and it was by building on them that the work was finally completed.

fathers publicly to declare, what they never for a moment disputed, the legality of that council from which he derived his
authority; and if that declaration were once made, he felt
assured that there could be no other method of proceeding
against two denounced anti-popes, than by arming the real
pope with additional authority to crush them. It was very
natural that John should take this view of the subject: indeed,
as far as the strict justice of the question was concerned, it was
the correct view; and assuredly the distinction between a pope
and a schismatic was sufficiently broad, to be made ground for
decided action with an assembly of Roman Catholic ecclesiastics.

Objections
of the
Council.

Nevertheless there were many, and some of the most celebrated doctors of the age were among them, who considered
the subject in a widely different light. These loudly maintained, that, as the council of Constance was a continuation of
that of Pisa, it was bound steadily to pursue the same object;
that this object had been the extinction of the schism, and that
it was still so; and that a solemn obligation rested on all the
prelates present, even on the pope himself, to adopt whatsoever
means should appear most efficacious for that purpose. It was
immediately obvious to what end this opinion tended—that the
method of cession, which had been attempted with such imperfect success at Pisa, would be again brought forward as the
only healing measure; and that the true and recognized pope
would be called upon for the same humiliation, and probably
subjected to the same compulsion, with two anathematized
pretenders.

The subject was warmly debated, but without any approach
to a decision, because the emperor was not yet arrived; and as
much certainly depended on his views, so the attention and
even the hopes of both parties were earnestly fixed upon him.
Sigismond possessed considerable talents and accomplishments;
he spoke several languages with fluency and even eloquence,
and was the patron of learning, in an age when it still needed
powerful protection. The dignity of his personal appearance
has attracted the commendations of history*; and if his moral

* Leonardus Aretinus (Rer, Italicar. Historia) speaks of him thus:—" Fuit

character was not free from stain, and if his military enterprises generally ended in disgrace, he has been abundantly honoured for his zeal in the service of the Church, and his exertions against heresy and schism.

His previous intercourse with John, and the obligations which he certainly owed to him, led many to believe that he would throw his weight into the pontifical scale—nor was reason wanting to incline him to that side.   But it proved otherwise. He probably reflected, that, should he determine unequivocally to support and enforce the rights of John, no other method re- mained to reduce the antipopes, except violence—the princes of Arragon and Rimini would not otherwise renounce their obedience.   The disposition of Sigismond was known ; but mat- ters had not yet proceeded to any determination, when legates presented themselves both from Gregory and Benedict.   The latter, indeed, merely insulted the council by the usual vague and faithless offers of conference and compromise.   But the former declared their authority to make a formal cession on behalf of their master, in case that *both* his rivals should abdi- cate also.   From that moment the exertions of the great ma- jority of the fathers were directed to one object—to accomplish by some means or other the abdication of John.

Now, as they never affected on any occasion to throw the slightest doubts on his legitimacy, it became them to take their measures with deference and caution ; and when they pressed upon him the general obligations of his office, and argued, that he was bound, as chief of the Church of Christ, willingly to lay down, not his dignity only, but life itself, if the interests of that Church required it, we shall not wonder that the pope was unmoved by so indeterminate an appeal.   But the council felt its strength ; and the above appeal was accompanied by the new and bold proposition, that a general council possessed the power, in a peculiar exigency, to *compel* the pope to abdica- tion.   This assertion gave rise to long and warm discussions ;

Questions as to the relative power of the Council and the Pope.

procul dubio vir inclytus, præclara facie, corpore tum specioso, tum robusto ; mag- nitudine animi sive pace sive bello eximia ; liberalitate vero tanta, ut hoc unum illi vitio daretur, quod largiendo et erogando sibi ipsi facultates detraheret ad negotia bellaque obeunda.''

the Italian prelates maintained the papal cause, but with less vigour and ability than the circumstances required, and even than the merits of the question admitted. The superiority of learning and genius was on the side of the French; and the powerful harangues of Pierre d'Ailly and the celebrated Gerson, Chancellor of the University, added weight to a doubtful cause. It seemed clear that the party of John must yield.

In the meantime, the Archbishop of Mayence, the Primate of the German Church and Elector of the empire, arrived with great pomp at Constance, and immediately declared his adherence to the cause of the pope. Frederic of Austria and the Duke of Burgundy were likewise enlisted on the same side. But Sigismond had now decidedly espoused the opposite principles; and thus the French and Italian, which first divided the council, now really became the imperial and papal parties. This was the crisis of the contest; and the great majority of three of the nations was manifestly on the side of the emperor. Still, before they proceeded to the question, it was feared that, as the Italian prelates were the most numerous and under the most direct influence, and would, probably, be unanimous for the pope, they might be able to outvote the majorities of the other nations. It was, therefore, advanced as a fair proposal, and finally arranged, that each nation should separately ascertain its own sense, and that then, on the general meeting, the majority of nations, not the numerical majority of votes, should

The Council declares for the cession,

prevail. On the day appointed, they met together, and it then appeared that the decision in favour of the method of cession was unanimous—to the astonishment of the whole council, the greater portion even of the Italians themselves had adopted that opinion.

During the progress of these deliberations, there were some who judged, from the customary tenacity of other popes, that still further measures might afterwards be called for. And in that apprehension, a long list of personal charges against John XXIII,, some of which involved the most abominable offences, was handed about among the fathers; and a copy came under the inspection of the pope himself. John then saw the real nature of the tempest that was hanging over him, and immediately determined to avert it by timely submission. He expressed that intention amidst the acclamations of the whole assembly; and after some unimportant disputes respecting the formula of cession, he publicly pronounced (on the 2nd of March) his solemn and voluntary abdication*. and the Pope abdicates.

The cession of John was, of course, conditional on that of the antipopes; and as no difficulties were any longer offered by Gregory, the accomplishment of the union rested wholly with Peter of Luna. To this end a conference was proposed at Nice, between Sigismond and the King of Arragon; and as it seemed that Benedict was to be one of the parties, John claimed his right to be also present on the occasion. This demand excited some suspicions of his sincerity; and these were confirmed by a proposal, which he soon afterwards made, to transfer the council from Constance to Nice. It was difficult, after the instances of pontifical duplicity which had disgraced the last forty years, to put trust in the honesty of any pope; and the character of John was not such as to command any peculiar confidence. Consequently, the council required of him a formal deed or procuration of cession; and he, without hesitation, refused it. Guards were then placed about the gates of the city, but, on the urgent remonstrance of the pope, removed. Howbeit, whether he had previously meditated an escape from the power of the council, as soon as it proved too great for him, or whether he was driven to that resolution (as may also have been) by the distrust and even harshness with which he was treated, it is certain that, on the morning of March 21, the Emperor and the Fathers learnt with dismay and astonishment, that the pope was no longer at Constance. Flight of John XXIII.

---

* The formula finally agreed on was to the following effect :—" We, John XXIII., for the repose of the people of Christ, profess, promise, vow, and swear, before God, the Church, and this sacred Council, freely and with our entire good will, to give peace to the Church by the method of a simple and pure cession to be made by us of the Sovereign Pontificate, and to accomplish it effectually through the wisdom of the present Council,—whensoever Peter of Luna and Angelo Corrario shall similarly renounce, in person or by their delegates, the Popedom to which they pretend. And we also promise to do the same thing, howsoever that may occur, whether by cession or by death, or by any other way, so that it shall become possible to unite the Church of God through our cession, and thus to extirpate the present schism."

He had quitted the city, in the night, in a military disguise; and, having instantly embarked, had descended the Rhine as far as Schaffhausen, a city of his protector, Frederic.

The consternation of the council was somewhat abated by a communication received from John on the following day, in which he renewed his assurances of sincerity, and justified his retreat from Constance by the argument, that his personal security was necessary to give obligation to the promise of cession; and hereupon he was joined by several cardinals and other prelates. But the great majority remained behind, in close co-operation with the emperor; and both they and he immediately engaged in the most vigorous measures. For, on the one hand, Sigismond put in motion the temporal forces of the assembly, and directed a powerful army against the States of Frederic; and on the other, the Fathers of the Council and the doctors of Paris, with Gerson at their head, advanced in mighty spiritual array against the pontifical deserter. And while the imperial soldiers approached the walls of Schaffhausen, the bulwarks of popery were assaulted from the pulpits of Constance.

Further contest between the Council and the Pope.

The momentous question was now publicly argued, whether a Council General of the Church did not possess an authority superior to the pope. The rights of the council were advocated by the eloquence of Gerson*, and asserted by the general consent of the Fathers of Constance. The opposite opinion was maintained by the seceders at Schaffhausen; and these even ventured to assert, that the council itself was virtually dissolved by the absence of the pope. It has generally been the error of high churchmen to advance the loftiest pretensions at the most unseasonable moments; and instead of receding at a crisis of violence and danger, to rush with a sort of effeminate rashness into perils, which would not otherwise have reached them. A decided breach now took place between the two parties; but after some vain replications and negotiations, it became perfectly clear on which side the real strength lay. The Court of Schaffhausen daily diminished, and the Council proceeded by

* De Auferibilitate Papæ ab ecclesia.

vigorous acts to give efficacy to the principle of its own superiority. Nevertheless, the pope would not acknowledge his
defeat, but rather determined to risk the experiment by a
second flight; intending, as it would seem, to throw himself on
the protection of the Duke of Burgundy, and establish his residence at Avignon. He halted at Brisac, and a deputation
from the council found him there; he fixed the following morning to give them audience, but on the following morning John
XXIII. was no longer at Brisac. We shall not trace the fruitless negotiations which followed: it is sufficient to add, that
during their progress the Duke of Austria prevailed upon the
pope to take refuge at Fribourg, under his own sacred protection—for the Duke, being severely pressed in his contest with
the Emperor, and foreseeing his entire discomfiture, was desirous to possess the means of reconciliation. Having suc- John is be-
ceeded in this desire, he hastened to violate his vows, and to trayed.
sacrifice his virtue and reputation, by surrendering the person
of his guest. And thus, says Maimbourg, the unfortunate
pope, who, disorderly and licentious as he was, failed not to
be an object of great compassion through the treachery practised against him by his protector, was betrayed, and found
himself a prisoner in the Castle of Fribourg, the very place
where he had thought to find an asylum.

The council then turned to the affair of his deposition, observing in this matter the same forms which had been followed
at Pisa in the process against Gregory and Benedict. The list
of accusations presented against John XXIII. consisted of fifty
articles; but the whole weight of his offences might be comprised under five or six heads. He was charged with all the Accused,
various modifications of simony; with squandering and alien-
ating the property of the Church; and with oppressing the
people by unjust acts and exorbitant imposts. His escape
from Constance, and his subsequent endeavours to elude the
demands of the council, were urged against him with the
greater minuteness, as they were the most recent and the least
pardonable of his offences. Another class of charges related
to his official, another to his private delinquencies. It was
asserted that, as pope, he had disregarded the divine offices,

neglected to repeat his breviary, and rarely assisted at the celebration of mass; and that, even when he did so, he recited the service rapidly and carelessly, like a sportsman or a soldier*. It was added, that he had wholly disregarded the fasts and abstinences of the Church. As to the scandals of his private life, they were traced with minute diligence, even from his childhood to his flight from Constance. In his earliest youth the intemperance of his disposition betrayed itself: his most innocent years were charged with falsehood, impudence, disobedience to his parents, a tendency to every vice. His progress in life was a progress in iniquity. Murder by violence and by poison, adultery, incest, the most abominable impurities were imputed to him, as unquestioned and notorious. Such is the substance of the allegations recorded by Roman Catholic writers against their spiritual Father; but it must not be forgotten, that, in the list formally presented to the council and to the pope, these last charges were suppressed. This might be with a view to spare the Catholic Church so monstrous a scandal; or through consideration to the conscience and character of the Cardinals, who had so lately elected such a pope; but it might also be because they rested on slight foundations, and proceeded from that popular licence, which so eagerly calumniates the fallen fortunes of the great.

It is not disputed that the paper, which received the approbation of the council, contained many heinous charges, expressed in very unequivocal language, and confirmed by numerous testimonies. But the pope, when it was presented to him for inspection and refutation, calmly replied, with the most submissive respect for the council, that he had little curiosity to read either the charges or the depositions; but that of this the fathers might rest assured, that he should receive their decision, whatever it might be, with perfect deference: in the meantime, that his best defence was in their justice. This was politic, for from the moment in which the council determined upon the method of cession, John very clearly perceived that the pontificate had passed from his hands. For a time,

---

* "Et si aliquoties celebravit, hoc fuit currenter, more venatorum et armigerorum." Act. Concil. Const.

indeed, he probably hoped, through the support of the dukes of Austria and Burgundy, to retain a partial obedience and wear a divided mitre; but no sooner did he become the prisoner of the council, than even that hope abandoned him; and his only remaining object was to secure, in a private station, his personal freedom and security. Accordingly, he addressed a respectful and even pathetic letter to Sigismond, in which he reminded him of services formerly conferred, and supplicated in return his friendship, or at least his clemency. This appeal was written in a tone of deep humiliation, and with an affectation of attachment, which could scarcely be sincere. But neither emperor nor council was softened by this tardy display of obsequiousness. At a full session, held on the 29th of May, John XXIII. was solemnly deposed from the pontificate. By *and deposed.* the same sentence he was condemned to imprisonment during the pleasure of the council, which reserved to itself the power of imposing such other penalties as should, in due season, be declared.

This sentence was communicated to John in his confinement *His conduct* at Cell; he perused it without any emotion, and requested a short interval of solitude. After two hours, he ordered the deputies again into his presence; and then, first reading all the articles in succession, with a firm voice and unruffled manner, he declared to them that there was no particular which did not receive his complete approbation; and that, as far as in him lay, he cordially confirmed and ratified the sentence. To this assurance he added a voluntary vow, that he would never at any time protest against that sentence, nor make any attempt to recover the pontificate—that, on the contrary, he renounced purely and simply, and from the bottom of his heart, any right which he ever had, or might still have, to that dignity; that, in proof of this, he had already removed from his chamber the pontifical cross, and would throw off the pontifical garments as willingly, if he had any others to put on in their place; that he wished with all his soul that he had never been pope at all, since he had not enjoyed one single happy day since his exaltation; and so far was he from wishing to be restored to that dignity, that should any desire his re-election, he would never at any time consent to it. He then threw himself, with his former humility, on the mercy of the council and the emperor—not, however, without reminding them, that he possessed legitimate means of defence, of which he had not yet availed himself, but to which he should certainly appeal, should they drive him, by more rigorous measures, to further extremities.

and imprisoned. This conduct, which was not only politic, but generous, succeeded not in obtaining for him any mitigation of his sentence. He was led away in close confinement, first to Heidelberg, and afterwards to Mannheim, where he was imprisoned for three years. Neither did it avail him anything to have once possessed the friendship of Sigismond. Nay, so far was the severity of the sentence enforced, that he was deprived of the services of his Italian attendants, and surrounded by Germans, with whom his ignorance of the language permitted no other intercourse than by signs *. Such rigour, exercised against a fallen pope, awakened sympathy and swelled the ranks of his advocates ; and there were many who maintained, both then and afterwards, that his deposition was illegal and compulsory, since the charge of heresy, on which alone a pope could be canonically deposed, was not that which occasioned the degradation of John XXIII. The court of France openly professed this opinion ; and the offence, which Charles VI. on that occasion took at the exceeding zeal of the University, repressed the ardour and diminished the credit of that illustrious body.

In the meantime, the Council advanced onwards in the course which it had chosen. It had now assumed the despotic † con-

---

* Platina and Nauclerus assert the severity with which John was treated. Theodoric of Niem gives a different account, on the authority, as he says, of well-informed persons. There are differences, too, in some other particulars, which we have not thought it necessary to specify. The historians who have been principally consulted for the contents of this chapter (besides the original authorities) are Maimbourg, the Continuator of Fleury, Lenfant (Hist. du Conc. de Constance), Pagi (Breviar. Gest. Pontif. Roman.), and Spondanus.

† Hence it proceeded, *papaliter*, to interfere with the state also. Previously to Sigismond's departure for Perpignan, through France, it published an edict— " Quicunque, cujuscunque status aut conditionis existat, *etiamsi regaiis*... euntes aut redeuntes impediverit, perturbaverit—sententia excommunicationis percellitur —et ulterius omni honore et dignitate ipso facto est privatus." Act. Concil. Constan., Sess. xvii. This sudden assumption of the power of deposition astonished all sovereigns, but especially insulted the king of France.

trol of the Church ; and in its first exercise of that power, it published a declaration that the cardinals could not proceed to a new election without its consent. By its next decision the formalities attending the session of Gregory were duly completed, and the old man was permitted to *resign* that which no one acknowledged that he possessed. The attention of the council and the whole Catholic world was then turned entirely towards the determination of Peter of Luna.

His determination was simply this,—to cling to the ruins of his fortunes—to clasp the name and shadow of the pontificate —to persevere in his pretensions and his perjury to the end of his life. Nevertheless, it was necessary to treat him with temper and deference, as long as he was supported even by a single prince. The method of conference was that which he still proposed, and the council now assented to it ; and as the king of Arragon was prevented by sickness from travelling to Nice, Sigismond professed his willingness to undertake in person the journey to Perpignan. It was in vain that Benedict exhausted the resources of his ingenuity to retard, at least, if he could not impede, the advance of the emperor : his artifices were foiled by the firmness of a candid mind resolutely bent on a noble object ; and on the 18th of September Sigismond arrived, with a small number of attendants, at the place of conference. *Conduct of Benedict.*

An extraordinary scene was then enacted. Ferdinand of Arragon sincerely desired the extinction of the schism; ambassadors from the courts of Castille and Navarre, and others who were present, united their powers for the same object. The emperor pressed it with all his talents and all his power— Benedict alone opposed himself to the unanimity of Christendom. Whatever was most convincing in argument or persuasive in rhetoric was repeatedly urged upon him by the princes and their deputies. If any pretext for his resistance had hitherto been furnished by the pertinacity of his competitors, this, they maintained, was now removed by the cession and deposition of Gregory and John. The condition, on which he had sworn to abdicate, was at length accomplished beyond dispute ; and his honour, his conscience, his promises, his oaths, unequivocally *Conference at Perpignan.*

obliged him to fulfil his part. Henceforward the concord of Christendom depended wholly upon him. After eight-and-thirty years of schism, disorder, and desolation, Benedict was the only remaining obstacle to the union, repose, and welfare of the Christian world. The Church herself, if she was indeed intrusted by the Almighty to his care and guidance, now stretched forth her arms to him, from the abyss of misery in which she was sunk, and sadly supplicated that he would raise her from her degradation; that he would voluntarily sacrifice that dignity, which he could not possibly retain much longer; and that he would invest his few remaining years with the gratitude and blessings of mankind, rather than adhere, amid universal detestation, to a mere name, which an early death, followed by eternal infamy, was now at hand to tear away from him.

These arguments, urged by the highest secular powers, were confirmed by other authority, which may have given them additional value in the eyes of a churchman and a pope. There were two holy brothers named Vincent and Boniface Ferrier*, who had hitherto faithfully adhered to the cause of Benedict, and whose acknowledged piety and supposed inspiration seemed to lend it some sort of sanctity. These venerable persons now joined their friendly eloquence to turn the heart of Benedict; and they fortified their appeal by declaring, that, as the reproach of schism must henceforward rest on his party, they should be compelled, in case of his further opposition, to desert him †.

Pertinacity of Benedict. Benedict was not moved by any of these considerations. Whether it was that, in the conscientious belief that he was

* This same Vincent Ferrier is addressed by Gerson from Constance, as a patron of the sect of the Flagellants, whom the chancellor earnestly exhorts him to abandon. Nevertheless he is designated as "Theologus et Orator toto orbe inclytus." The documents are given by Von der Hart, tom. iii., pars vii.

† Theodoric of Niem mentions that Vincent Ferrier did then, in fact, take so decided a part against his former master, as to declare it a merit to persecute or kill him. "Quod sit vir pravus et fallax et fictus, decipiendo populum Dei, quodque justè persequendus sit usque ad mortem ab omnibus Christianis," &c.... Vit. Johann. XXIII. p. 63. This holy zealot had as little charity in his enmity, as discretion in his friendship.

the true Pope, he considered it a religious, or (what might be equally sacred in his mind) an ecclesiastical duty, to preserve his office to the end of his life; or whether (as is more probable) the love of power grew with the progress of his years, and the decay of his vigour, so as finally to close his heart against any representations of reason or decency,—he maintained his constant resolution inflexibly. As he had always been the legitimate, so was he now, forsooth, the only pontiff: the deposition of both his adversaries confirmed him, without competition, in the possession of the see. So that, if the schism were still permitted to subsist (he continued), the scandal must rest with the Council of Constance, not with him. For his own part, he was determined never to abandon the bark of St. Peter, of which the helm had been confided to him by God; and the older he became, and the nearer he approached to death and the judgment, the stronger was his obligation to resist the tempest, and avert the anger of heaven by persevering in the course assigned to him. In conclusion, he enforced the necessity of at once uniting all the faithful in universal obedience to himself. Benedict was now in his seventy-eighth year; nevertheless, he argued his own cause before a public assembly for seven entire hours, with such courage, fervour, and impetuosity, as to leave it uncertain whether his extraordinary energy was derived from ambition, or from fanaticism, or from a strange combination of both.

The result of this singular contest was not yet perfectly manifest. On the one side was the secular and spiritual power of Europe, the authority of kings, the prayers of the people, the consent of the Catholic Church—reason, and justice, and every wise and every good principle, arrayed against the infatuated obstinacy of one crafty, faithless old man. Yet the thoughtful were still in some suspense, and many had greater fears from the inveterate subtilty of Benedict, than hopes from the union of so many princes. But it proved otherwise; the parties engaged in the conference had no personal interest in favour of that pretender; and his perversity was so remote from reason, that it served rather to cement the confederacy against him. It was resolved, however, to make one final attempt at persuasion. But

here Benedict, perceiving the firmness of his adversaries, and
fearing their ultimate design, withdrew his person from their
power, and quitted Perpignan. He retired, after some hesitation, to a place called Paniscola,—a fortress situated near
Tortosa and the mouth of the Ebro, an ancient possession of
the house of Luna. Four cardinals, and a small body of
soldiers followed him.

Any hopes which he may have derived from this proceeding, beyond that of mere personal security, were disappointed.
The Assembly at Perpignan, being now relieved from the constraint which his presence still occasioned to those who yet
acknowledged him, immediately, and by a formal act, renounced
its obedience. Not long afterwards, Scotland, which had taken
no part in these measures, but continued to adhere without
scruple to its first decision, being now persuaded that Benedict
was the only remaining obstacle to the general concord, followed the example of the Conference. And then, at length*,
the Council of Constance felt itself empowered to inflict the
final blow. The sentence of deposition was pronounced against
Peter of Luna, according to the prescribed forms; and the bolt,
which had fallen almost harmless from the Assembly of Pisa,
descended on this occasion with greater efficacy, because its
object was already virtually deposed, through the secession of
his royal adherents.

*His depo-
sition, 1417
A. D.*

In the mean time, the aged ecclesiastic, against whom the
storm which himself had raised was now in justice directed,
was not moved to any act of concession, or any show of humiliation. Twice deposed by two General Councils—twice anathematized by the great and almost unanimous consent of the
Catholic Church—deserted by the secular powers, who had so
long countenanced his perfidy and protected his adversity—
abandoned by the most venerable, even among his spiritual
followers—and confined to a narrow and solitary residence—
the Pope of Paniscola still preserved the mockery of a court,
and presided in his empty council-hall. And thence, in the
magnanimity of disappointment and despair, he launched his

* On July 26th, 1417.

daily anathema against Ferdinand of Arragon, and retorted, with ludicrous earnestness, the excommunications of the Christian world.

The Council of Constance, having thus at length, through the perseverance of its imperial director, removed the three competitors whose disputes had rent the Church, proceeded to provide for its future integrity; and, that no pretext might possibly be left for subsequent dissension, it was determined, for this occasion only, to make an addition to the Elective Assembly. The entire college of the united Cardinals consisted, at that time, of thirty members; and to this body a second, consisting of six ecclesiastics from each of the *five** Nations, was associated. It was further regulated, that the consent of two-thirds both of the sacred college and of the deputies of each nation should be required for the validity of the election,—so many were the interests which it was necessary to reconcile, so severe were the precautions required, to secure for the future pontiff the undivided obedience of Europe. Accordingly, on the 8th of November, 1417, the electors entered into conclave, and after a deliberation of three days, they agreed in the choice of Otho Colonna (Martin V.), a noble and virtuous Roman.

Election of Martin V. by the Council, and termination of the schism.

The character of Martin pointed him out as the man destined to repair the ruins of the Church. The announcement was received with enthusiastic expressions of delight; the Emperor was the first to prostrate himself at the holy prelate's feet, in a transport of rapture, which was shared, or affected, by the vast assembly present. And it was not without reasonable ground of confidence—it was not without many motives for self-satisfaction, and many just claims on the gratitude of that age and that Church, that Sigismond and the Council at length approached the termination of their labours. To us, indeed, looking back from our brighter elevation upon the means of the disputants and the subject of the strife, it will, perhaps, appear, that so powerful a combination of temporal and spiritual

Observations.

* As soon as the fate of Benedict was decided, the Spanish nation was added to the four, which had hitherto constituted the Assembly.

authority might have accomplished in a much shorter space
the destruction of a profligate pope and two denounced pretenders—that the force employed was disproportionate to the
end—that the methods were indirect and dilatory, marked by
too much ceremony and too little vigour. But we should thus
determine inconsiderately, and without due regard to the
maxims and prejudices of those days. When we reflect, that a
century had scarcely yet elapsed since Boniface VIII. was exulting in the plenitude of spiritual despotism; that, even to the
end of the Avignon succession, the lofty attributes of papacy
remained, as heretofore, unviolated and almost unquestioned;
when we recollect, too, how slow and difficult are the triumphs
of reason over prescriptive absurdities, we shall rather admire
the firmness exhibited at Constance, and the courage with
which some papal principles were overthrown, than censure that
Assembly for not having more hastily accomplished what it
did at length accomplish effectually.

Fate of the
Pretenders.
The Council continued its sessions* for a few months after
the election of Martin, and was then dismissed, or rather adjourned, for the space of five years. Pavia was the place appointed for the next meeting; and the pope proceeded towards
Rome, to occupy and refit his shattered vessel. Nevertheless,
with whatever security he may have approached his See, he
must sometimes have reflected, that there still lived three men,
who had enjoyed in their turns the dignity which he now held,
and who had clung to it with extreme pertinacity. It was fair
to presume that their ambition would not depart from them,
except with life; and that any casual circumstance, which
might offer to any one of them the means of recovering any portion of his power, would find him eager to embrace it. So long
as they breathed, the concord of the Church could scarcely be
deemed secure; let us then follow their history to its termination. Gregory did not long survive the act of his cession; he
lived long enough to emerge from the condition of dishonour
and guilt, into which his weakness had thrown him, and little

* These were forty-five in number; lasting, at various intervals, from November 16th, 1414, to August 9th, 1418.

longer; and if his last act had been less obviously the effect of compulsion, we might have admitted it as some atonement for his previous delinquency.

Peter of Luna continued for about six years to proclaim his legitimacy, and exult in his martyrdom. Every day the walls of Paniscola were astonished by the repetition of his anathemas; yet the bolts were innocuous : but for the temporary departure of Alfonso of Arragon from the principles of his predecessor, they would scarcely have been heard beyond the fortress gates; nor did they disturb, in any degree, the repose of Christendom. He died suddenly, in the year 1424*, in extreme old age; but his vigour, which was still fresh and unabated, gave some colour to the suspicion of poison, which attends his death. It is at least certain, that, as soon as he perceived his final hour approaching, he commanded the attendance of his *two* Cardinals, the faithful remnant of his court, and addressed them with his wonted intrepidity. And then, even at this last crisis, when ambition and interest could not possibly sway him longer, he asserted with his parting breath, that he was the true and only pope, and that it was absolutely essential for the purity of the Church to continue the succession. On this he adjured his two hearers, on pain of his pontifical malediction, to elect a successor. Having secured their obedience, he died; and it is related in ecclesiastical records, that six years afterwards his body was found entire, and without symptom of decay; and that, being then transported to Igluera, a town of Arragon, the property of his family, it long continued, and perchance may still continue, to resist the visitation of corruption.

His character has not escaped equally inviolate; and the censures by which it is perpetually assailed cannot in justice be suppressed or softened. His talents were unquestionably vivid and active; but they were of a mean description,—the mere machines of intrigue and subtilty,—the energies of a con- Character of Benedict.

* The year is disputed. We follow Spondanus, ann. 1424, s. iii. The circumstance that he held, at least, the name of Pope for thirty years--a space longer than any predecessor—has been seriously urged as an argument *against* his legitimacy. " Non videbis dies Petri,' the prophetic address to the successors of the apostle, had not been accomplished in the case of Luna ; therefore he could not be a genuine successor.

temptible and contracted soul.   He was eminent in sanctity, and the integrity of private life.   Still, what manner of integrity or sanctity is that, which is found consistent with ambition, and selfishness, and perjury; which can wrap itself in duplicity at any call of interest, and pursue a seeming expediency through fraud, and faithlessness, and falsehood?   But at least (it is said) Benedict was sincere in believing that he was the true Pope, and that through his perseverance alone the succession could be preserved uninterrupted.   Was he so sincere?   When he advocated so warmly the necessity of mutual concession, during the reign of his predecessor, then, at least, he was not persuaded that the purity of the Catholic Church was identical with obedience to the pretenders of Avignon.   Had he been so persuaded, he could not himself have accepted the pontificate as a conditional boon; nor bound himself by oath to cede, on specific terms, that trust, which afterwards he proclaimed it his religious duty to maintain, under every circumstance.   Assuredly, if his sincerity in this respect must be admitted, we must, at the same time, acknowledge, that he was not impressed with it till *after* his elevation; and that it was then so closely connected with his ambition, as to make it impossible for the historian, as it might be difficult even for himself, to distinguish between them.

The two cardinals obeyed the parting injunction of their master, and chose for his successor one Gilles Mugnos, who called himself Clement VIII.   But, not long afterwards, Alphonso finally withdrew his protection from his creature; Mugnos retired, without a struggle, to his former obscurity; and the succession of pretenders, which had been imposed upon the Church by the Conclave at Anagni, was at length at an end.

End of
John
XXIII.   One other object of our curiosity still remains, Baltazar Cossa, the President, the adversary, and the victim of the Council of Constance.   Very soon after the dissolution of that Assembly, the Republic of Florence, which had been unceasingly attached to the cause, or at least to the person and sufferings, of the captive, earnestly solicited his liberation from Martin V.; and it appears that, presently afterwards, whether

through the imprudence *, the policy, or the generosity of that pope, Baltazar was restored to liberty. He returned to Italy, and presented himself as a simple ecclesiastic among his former associates and dependents. His popular qualities had secured him many adherents, and their affection was not shaken by his adversity. In some places he was welcomed with cordial salutations, but Parma was the principal scene of his triumph and temptation; for there he found a powerful party prepared to revive and support his abrogated claims to the chair. These warmly pressed him to resume his dignity, and their solicitations were seconded by several individuals who had tasted his former bounty, or had hopes from his future gratitude; all joined in protesting against the violence which he had suffered at Constance, and conjured him once more to array himself in the pontifical vestments, which were rightfully his own. This was not all: even in the calculations of success there seemed some ground for hope. The independent states of Italy would probably declare in his favour, and the numerous petty tyrants, who had usurped the patrimony of the Church, would assuredly unite against the acknowledged pope. These circumstances were represented to Baltazar, and he fully comprehended their

* The account of Leonardus Aretinus (in Rerum Italic. Historia), who had the means of knowing the truth, is not so favourable to the motives of either party, as that which we would more willingly adopt. " John, after his captivity and abdication, was imprisoned in Bavaria. But many had a scruple, whether his deposition and abdication, being forcible, was legitimate. And if that was doubtful, the legitimacy of Martin also came into dispute. With this apprehension, and, at the same time, lest the Princes of Germany, possessing this image (idolum) of a Pope, should some day take some advantage of it, Martin engaged in measures for his redemption and restoration to Italy. Therefore, when on his liberation he arrived in France, and then learnt the counsel of Martin (which was *to confine him for life at Mantua*), before he arrived at Mantua, he turned off towards Genoa ; and there being free, and his own master, whether induced by conscience, or by despair of success in any hostile enterprize, he voluntarily came to Florence, and throwing himself at the feet of Martin, recognized him as the true and only pontiff. In adventu ejus tota civitas obviam profusa multis lacrimis et incredibili commisseratione respexit hominem de tantæ dignitatis fastigio in tantas calamitates prolapsum. Ipse quoque miserabili prope habitu incedebat, &c." . . . The Florentines, on the other hand, were not very fond of Pope Martin ; and he is related, by the same historian, to have been almost childishly affected by a song then popular among the rabble, of which the burden was—
Papa Martino non val un quattrino.

importance. Some wrongs, too, some unnecessary hardships, he had unquestionably endured at the hands of the emperor and council. Baltazar patiently listened to the seductions of his friends; and then without returning them any answer, he suddenly took his resolution. He departed from the city hastily, and without any attendants; and proceeded to Florence, where the pope then resided, in the garb of a fugitive and a suppliant. Immediately, without requiring any formal security for his person, he sought for Martin, and in the presence of a full assembly cast himself humbly at his feet; and while he recognized him with due reverence as the legitimate Vicar of Christ, he repeated his solemn ratification of the acts of the Council, and of his own deposition.

Most of those, who witnessed this spectacle, were affected to tears; for they beheld the man, in whose presence all had once been prostrate, now voluntarily humbling himself before the throne which he had so lately occupied, and before an individual who had honoured him, for nearly five years, as his lord and pontiff. Martin V. shared the general emotion; and the reciprocal conduct of these two prelates furnishes an instance of magnanimous generosity, which too rarely illustrates the annals of the Church. The pope resolved to exalt his predecessor as near to his former dignity as was consistent with his own supremacy. Baltazar Cossa was appointed cardinal and dean of the Sacred College; in all public ceremonies, whether of chapels, consistories, or other assemblies, Baltazar was placed by the side of the pontiff, on a loftier seat than any other ecclesiastic; he was honoured by the confidence of his master, and he repaid it by undeviating fidelity.

His conduct and his character. That fidelity may, indeed, have cost him no struggle; and if we should believe his former declaration, that from the moment of his elevation to the chair he had never enjoyed one day of happiness, the most enviable portion of his life may really have been that in which he was followed by general commiseration. But whether he passed his remaining days in successful conflict with a bad and powerful passion, or whether (as seems to us more probable) he surveyed with philosophical disdain the dignity of which he had felt the cares, and had not valued the vanities—in either case he exhibited a vigour and expanse of mind which is rarely found in man. It is true that the usual portraits of John XXIII. would not prepare us to expect such virtue in him. But that pope has been, in truth, too hardly treated by historians. His enemies, in all ages, have been the powerful party; and the monstrous imputations which originated at Constance, have been too eagerly repeated both by Protestant and other writers. Baltazar Cossa was a mere soldier*—deeply stained, no doubt, with the loose immorality which then commonly attached to that profession, but not destitute of candid and manly resolution, nor of those worldly principles which make men honourable. It is entirely unquestionable that he was never actuated, even in appearance, by any sense of religion; that he was wholly disqualified even for the lowest ministry in God's Church: but he lived in an age in which the ecclesiastical and military characters were still deemed consistent, and in a Church which had long permitted the most dissolute demeanour to its directors. As Grand Master of a military order, Baltazar Cossa might have descended to posterity with untarnished celebrity; and even the Apostolical chair, had he possessed it some fifty years later, would have pardoned, under the protection of his warlike enterprise, the pollution and scandal of his vices.

NOTE ON THE WHITE PENITENTS AND OTHER ENTHUSIASTS.

(I.) Giovanni Villani (lib. xi., cap. xxiii.) relates, that in 1334 one Venturius of Bergamo, a Mendicant preacher, a man

---

* He is said to have exercised in his youth the trade of a pirate. " Dum simplex Clericus ac in adolescentia constitutus existeret, cum quibusdam fratribus suis piraticam in mari Neapolitano, *ut fertur*, exercuit, &c." To the habits thus acquired is attributed a peculiarity which followed him even to the popedom, of devoting the night to business and the day to sleep. Theod. of Niem, Vit. Johann. XXIII. His character is fairly discussed by Sismondi (Rep. Ital., chap. lxii.), who truly remarks, that had he been as abandoned as he is sometimes described, he would scarcely have been *twice* raised to the pontificate (for he was really chosen when Alexander V. was made pope), nor retained so many valuable friends to the end of his life. Leonardus Aretinus describes him to have been " Vir in temporalibus quidem magnus; in spiritualibus vero nullus omnino et ineptus." Rer. Italic. Historia.

of no eminence or family distinction, created a strong, though temporary, sensation in Lombardy and Tuscany. The object of his preaching was to *bring sinners to repentance;* and so great was the success, and so visible were the fruits of his eloquence, that more than 10,000 Lombards, of whom many were of the higher ranks, set out to pass the season of Lent at Rome. They were clad in the habit of St. Dominic; they travelled in troops of twenty-five or thirty, preceded by a cross; and their incessant cry was " Peace and mercy." During fifteen successive days, the time of their passage through Florence, they were entertained by that enlightened people with respect and charity; and so great became the renown and influence of the preacher, that they came to the knowledge of the court of Avignon, and awakened the jealousy of Pope Benedict. Venturius was arrested, and summoned before the Inquisition on the charge of heresy; and though acquitted by that tribunal, he was still retained in confinement by papal authority. " Such," says Villani, " are the rewards which holy persons receive from the prelates of the Church—unless, indeed, the above was inflicted as a just chastisement upon the overbearing ambition of that friar, though doubtless his intentions were excellent."

(II.) We read in Spondanus, that in the year 1374 there arose in Belgium a sect of Dancers, who paraded the streets, entered houses and churches half naked, crowned with garlands, dancing and singing, uttering unknown names, falling senseless on the ground, and exhibiting other marks of demoniacal agitation. Many were found to imitate them; and thus much (says the historian) appears certain, that this effect was produced through the visitation of an evil spirit; for they were healed by the charms of the exorcists, and by the reading of St. John's gospel, or of the expressions by which Christ is recorded to have cast out devils, as also of the Apostles' Creed. The same writer proceeds more reasonably to attribute their disease to the want of religious instruction. But it was needless to seek particular causes for the appearance of one of those distempers which have disfigured the best ages of the Church at a time when the disorders of the ecclesiastical

government were so generally felt and confessed; when the
people were beginning to exercise in so many quarters a freedom of opinion, yet feebly moderated by reason or knowledge;
and when religion was the subject to which the greater portion
of this irregular independence was directed.

(III.) We shall, therefore, content ourselves with mentioning
one other eruption of enthusiasm, which was more violent, indeed, and more celebrated than the last, but apparently even
more transient. In the year 1399, when the Christian world
was astounded by the triumphs of the Turks and the Tartars
from without, and shocked by the schism and by the vices
which it exposed and occasioned within, a body of devotees
descended the Alps into Italy, and began to preach peace and
repentance. They were entirely clothed in white, and carried
crosses or crucifixes, whence blood appeared to exude like
sweat. They were headed by a priest, a foreigner, whom some
affirm to have been a Spaniard, others a Provençal, others a
Scotsman, and who affirmed himself to be Elias the prophet,
recently returned from Paradise. The awful announcement
which he was commissioned to make was the immediate destruction of the world by an earthquake; and his tale and his
prophecy were eagerly received by a generation educated in
habits of religious credulity. Lombardy was the scene of his
first exhortations; he traversed its cities and villages, followed
by multitudes, who assumed at his bidding the cross, the rai-
ment and at least the show, of repentance. From Lombardy
he proceeded to the Ligurian Alps, and entered Genoa at the
head of 5,000 enthusiasts, natives of an adjacent town. They
sang various new hymns in the form of litanies, and among
them the celebrated *Stabat Mater dolorosa*, the reputed composition of St. Gregory: they passed several days in that city
preaching peace, and then returned to their homes. The
Genoese caught the contagion, and transmitted it onwards to
Lucca and Pisa. Those of Lucca immediately proceeded,
4000 in number, to Florence, and, after being entertained by
the public hospitality, departed. Then the Florentines adopted
that new religion (as ecclesiastical writers designate it) with
equal fervour; and thus was it propagated from one end of

Italy to the other, till its course was at length arrested by the sea.

This pious frenzy was not confined to the lower classes, nor to the laity, nor even to the inferior orders of the clergy. Prelates and even cardinals are recorded to have followed, if they did not guide the current; and the numerous procession from Florence was conducted by the archbishop. And if, indeed, we are to believe the wonderful effects which are ascribed to the preaching of these fanatics, we shall scarcely censure the compliance which countenanced, or at least which tolerated them. All who joined in those pilgrimages made confession and testified sincere repentance. Every one pardoned his neighbour, and dismissed the recollection of past offences; so that the work of charity was multiplied with zeal and emulation, and enmities which no ordinary means could have reconciled were put asleep. It was a festivity of general reconciliation. Ambuscades, assassinations, and all other crimes were for the season suspended; nor was any violence committed nor any treason meditated, so long as the "religion" of the White Penitents continued in honour. But this was not long; the imposture of the prophet was presently discovered and exposed, and within a very few months from the time of its appearance, the order fell into disregard, and wholly disappeared*.

CHAPTER XXIV.

Attempts of the Church at Self-reformation.

General clamour for Reformation—with different objects—first appearance of a Reform party in the Church—exposure of Church abuses by individual ecclesiastics—Pierre d'Ailli—Nicholas Clemangis—John Gerson—German and English Reformers—Zabarella—the real views and objects of those ecclesiastics—how limited—position, exertions, and disappointment of the *Council of Pisa*—good really effected by it—*Council of Constance*—language of Gerson—the Committee of Reform—its labours—the question as to the priority of the Reformation or of the election of the new Pope—division of the Council—argu-

---

* The authors who have mentioned these enthusiasts are Theodoric of Niem, an eye-witness, Poggio, in his History of Florence, Sigonius, Platina, Muratori.

ments on both sides—calumnies against the Germans—death of the Bishop of
Salisbury—Address to the Emperor—defection of two Cardinals and of the
English—final effort of the Germans—triumph of the Papal party—and elec-
tion of Martin V.—necessary result of this—the principles and motives of the
Italian clergy—the Fortieth Session—object of the Reformers—the Eighteen
Articles—remarks—other projects of the Committee—respecting the Court of
Rome—their general character—respecting the secular Clergy—ecclesiastical
jurisdiction—the monastic establishments—the real difference in principle
between the two parties—first proceedings of Martin V.—fresh remonstrances
of the nations—Sigismond's reply to the French—the Pope negotiates with
the nations separately—publishes in the 43rd Session his Articles of Reformation—and soon afterwards dissolves the Council—the Concordats—character
of the Pope's Articles—Annates—exertions of the French—the principle of
the superiority of a General Council to the Pope established at Constance—
decree for the periodical convocation of General Councils—assemblies of Pavia
and Sienna—meeting of the *Council of Basle*—death of Martin V.—crisis of
the Church—Accession of Eugenius IV.—his character—determines on opposition to the Council of Basle—the objects of that assembly—Cardinal Julian
Cesarini—Contest between the Council and the Pope—two epistles of cardinal
Julian to the Pope—citations from them on the corruption of the German
clergy, on the popular discontent, on the transfer or prorogation of the Council, on the danger to the temporalities of the Church, on Eugenius's efforts to
destroy the Council—political circumstances interrupt the dispute—the Pope
sanctions the Council, and they proceed to the reformation of the Church—
Substance of the chief enactments on that subject—against concubinage, fees
paid at Rome—on papal election, &c.—some subsequent canons—Industry of
the Pope's party in the Council—his successful negotiations at Constantinople
—the quarrel renewed—the Pope assembles the Council of Ferrara—secession
of Cardinal Julian—his example not imitated—differences about the legitimacy
of the Council of Basle—the cardinal of Arles—the eight propositions against
Eugenius—strong opposition in favour of the Pope—he is deposed—Amadeus,
Duke of Savoy, (Felix V.) appointed successor—dissolution of the Council—
Nicholas V. succeeds Eugenius, and Felix abdicates—Diet of Mayence—The
Council of Bourges—Pragmatic Sanction—its two fundamental principles—
character of its leading provisions—its real permanence—the intended periodical
meeting of General Councils—its probable effects on the condition of the
Church—Ecclesiastical principles of the Councils of Constance and Basle—
treatment of Huss and Jerome of Prague—Spiritual legislation of the Council
of Basle—intolerance of those assemblies—Discovery of the art of printing.

THOUGH churchmen are usually slow to perceive the corruptions of their own system, and unwisely dilatory and apprehensive in correcting them, still the abuses of the Roman Catholic
Church were now become so flagrant—they had so commonly
thrown off decency and shame—they were so wholly indefensible by reason or even by sophistry—and at the same time so
oppressive and so unpopular, that a cry for Reformation began
to be raised by the acknowledged friends, the ministers, and

even the dignitaries of the communion. We intend no reference at this moment to the murmurs of those discontented
spirits who saw deeper into the iniquities of the system, and
aimed their yet ineffectual resistance at its root—those faithful
messengers of the Gospel who prepared the way for Luther
and Cranmer, but whose warnings were lost upon a selfish and
short-sighted hierarchy. The exertions of Wickliffe and Huss,
the real reformers of the Church, will be noticed hereafter : at
present we shall confine our attention to the endeavours by
which the wiser and more virtuous among her obedient children strove, through a considerable period, to remove her most
repulsive deformities, and restore at least the semblance of
health and dignity. We shall observe with curiosity and advantage the particular evils to which the zeal of those reformers
was directed, and the perverse and narrow and fatal policy
which thwarted it. It is not that any effectual remedies could
have been applied by those hands—nor any perfect renovation
of their Communion accomplished by men who were ignorant
of the actual seat and character of the disease. The restoration of an evangelical Church was not the object, nor could it
have been the result, of their efforts; but the permanence of
their own system was the matter really at stake—for it is very
clear that the dominion of Rome would have been greatly
strengthened by seasonable self-correction, and that an authority so deeply fixed in the firmest prejudices of mankind might
have been preserved somewhat longer had it been exercised
with more discretion, and modified according to the changing
principles of the times.

In our progress through the earlier annals of the Church,
the shadow of reformation is continually before our eyes, and
its name presents itself in every page—not only in the records
of the monastic establishments, which could not otherwise have
been perpetuated than by an unceasing process of regeneration,
but also in the general regulations of popes and of councils.
The necessity of new enactments, the pressure of existing abuses,
the excellence of the ancient discipline were admitted in all
ages, and the admission was sometimes followed by salutary
legislation. Indeed, it is unquestionable that those among

the chiefs of the Church, who have best secured the gratitude
of their own communion, as well as the commemoration of
history, have deserved that distinction not by a timid acquiescence in the defects of the existing institutions, but by a generous endeavour to correct them: so that the word at least was
familiar and respectable in the eyes of prelates and of popes,
and the principle might be avowed, under certain restrictions,
without any suspicion, or even insinuation, of heresy.

The first occasion, however, on which the advocates of
reform can be said to have appeared as a party in the Church,
was the first assembly for the extinction of the schism. Among
the Fathers of Pisa a powerful spirit of independence prevailed,
and the circumstances of the preceding century had given it a
direction and an object. There are, indeed, many earlier instances of the boldness of ecclesiastics in individually denouncing the imperfections of the Church, and in synodically legis-
lating for their removal: but it was not till the secession to
Avignon had lowered the majesty of Rome and impaired the
resources of her pontiffs; it was not till the division which followed had filled the world with proofs of their weakness and
baseness, of their necessities, their vices, and their extortions—
that a principle very hostile to papal despotism established
itself, not only among princes and enlightened laymen, but
even among the prelates of the Catholic Church. Indeed, General
when we observe the language in which certain eminent eccle- complaints
siastical writers, during the conclusion of the 14th and the against the
abuses of
beginning of the following century, have exposed and stigma- the Church.
tized ecclesiastical disorders, our wonder will rather be, that
the system, which they so boldly denounced, did not sink
beneath the burden of its own sinfulness, than that persons,
who were interested in its preservation, should have combined
to amend and restore it. Among these were men of the noblest
character and most extended learning; men of all nations, and,
during the schism, of all obediences; at the same time, they
were persons attached to popery and patronized by popes.

Among the *French*, Pierre d'Ailli, cardinal of Cambrai, was Pierre
a moderate, but earnest, advocate for reform; in his treatise * d'Ailli.

* " De difficultate Reformationis in Concilio Universali." It was addressed to

on that subject, written about 1410, he censured with great
severity the luxurious insolence of his own order ; and it was
he who has retailed a proverb current in those days, "that the
Church had arrived at such a condition, as to deserve to be
Clemangis. governed only by the reprobate*." Nicholas of Clemangis, a
native of Champagne, who had been secretary to Benedict XIII.,
in an address to the council of Constance, ascribed the schism
and desolation of the Church to the frightful ungodliness of its
pastors. "The earliest ministers of the Gospel were devout,
humble, charitable, liberal, disinterested, and they despised
the good things of this world. But as riches increased, piety
diminished ; luxury, ambition, and insolence took the place of
religion, humility, and charity : poverty became a disgrace,
and economy a vice ; avarice came to the aid and support of
ambition ; and the property of ecclesiastics being no longer
sufficient for their desires, it grew into practice to seize that of
others, to pillage, assault, and oppress the inferiors, and to
plunder every one under every pretext." Such being the substance of his general † censures, he did not hesitate more par-

Gerson, in reply to the Treatise of the latter on the same subject. His more
celebrated work was that " De Ecclesiastica Potestate," in which he gave his
views of the origin of ecclesiastical, as well as of papal power, and of their relation
to each other. It may be found in the 6th volume of Von der Hardt. He was
born in Picardy in 1350, and both Gerson and Clemangis were his pupils. Bayle,
Vie de Pierre d'Ailly.

* " Adeo ut jam horrendum quorundam proverbium sit, ad hunc statum
venisse Ecclesiam, ut non sit digna regi nisi per reprobos." The passage is cited
by Lenfant, Hist. Conc. Const., l. vii. s. l.

† Not that his censures were confined to the avarice and rapacity of the clergy ;
a considerable share of them is directed to their incontinence — for instance,
" Quid illud, obsecro, quale est ? quod *plerisque* in Diocesibus rectores parochi-
arum ex *certo* et conducto *cum suis Prælatis pretio* passim et publicè Concubinas
tenent ? Quod subditorum excessus et vitia, omniaque officia, quæ judiciis præesse
sunt solita, publicè venundant ? Sed adhuc levia hæc sunt." Nor was he more
merciful to the canons and monks ; he was even particularly severe on the insolence and vanity of the latter, whom he considers as the Pharisees of their age.
Respecting the abominations committed in the nunneries, his expressions are
strong and exaggerated. " Nam quid, obsecro, aliud sunt hoc tempore puellarum
monasteria, nisi quædam, non dico Dei sanctuaria, sed Veneris execranda prostibula, sed lascivorum et impudicorum Juvenum ad libidines explendas receptacula,
Ut idem hodie sit puellam velare, quod ad publicè scortandum exponere." (Nicol de
Clemangiis, de Ruina Ecclesiæ, cap. xxxvi. Apud Von der Hardt, tom. i., Conc.
Constan.) Gerson, also, in his sermon at Rheims, used these words : " Et utinam

ticularly to ascribe the first rank in vice and scandal to the popes. " When they saw that the revenues of Rome and the patrimony of St. Peter were inadequate to their designs of aggrandizement, it became necessary to discover new resources for the support of that project of universal monarchy. And nothing could be conceived more lucrative than to deprive metropolitans, bishops, and other ordinaries, of the right of election to benefices, and to reserve the nomination and collation to themselves: and these they never conferred, except for large sums of money, which they often obtained in advance, by granting expectative graces to all sorts of persons indiscriminately, or at least without any distinction in regard to capacity or morals." Such was, in truth, the origin of the *Apostolic Chamber;* and the mysteries of that fiscal inquisition had, no doubt, been intimately revealed to the secretary of Benedict XIII. The last whom we shall mention, and the greatest among the reformers of France, was the chancellor of the university of Paris, John Gerson. In a sermon delivered before John the council of Rheims in 1408, that eloquent doctor exposed Gerson. the vices of the clergy, with the same freedom which he afterwards* employed at Constance in defining the legitimate limits of papal authority. From the exposure of the evil he proceeded to investigate its origin; and as the general degeneracy of every rank in the priesthood was commonly traced by the writers of that age to the licentiousness of the Roman court, so any effort to purify the descending stream was reasonably directed to its supposed source.

If the most distinguished among the reforming party were natives of France, the *Germans* engaged in greater numbers, and with greater consistency, in the same project. They appear, moreover, to have been the earliest in the field; for we observe that Henry de Langenstein, of Hesse, a German, pub-

nulla sint Monasteria mulierum, quæ facta sunt prostibula meretricum, et prohibeat adhuc deteriora Deus." Ser. factus in Concil. Remensi. Op. Gers., vol. ii., p. 625. Edit. Paris. See Lenfant, Conc. Const., l. vii., c. 13.

* In 1410 he addressed to Pierre d'Ailly his treatise " De Modis Uniendi et Reformandi Ecclesiam in Concilio Universali." His more celebrated work, " De Simonia abolenda Constantiensis Concilii Ope," was written during the council. Both may be found in Von der Hardt, tom. i.

lished, in 1381, a vigorous treatise on "the Union and Reformation of the Church*." The five last chapters of his work
were employed in depicting the universal profligacy of the
clergy. After denouncing the simonies and other iniquities of
the popes, the cardinals, and prelates, he descended to expose
the concubinage of the priests and the debaucheries of the
monks; he represented the cathedrals as no better than dens
of robbers, and the monasteries as taverns and brothels. He
seems at the same time to have looked somewhat more deeply
into the question of Reformation: for he beheld with dissatisfaction the great multitude of images, which he held to be so
many incentives to idolatry; and expressed his offence at the
multiplication of festivals, and the frivolous nature of the controversies which divided the Church.

From *England* the voice of remonstrance proceeded with
not less energy. "The Golden Mirror of the Pope, his Court,
the Prelates, and the rest of the Clergy†," was composed
during the pontificate of Boniface IX., the most triumphant
era of schism and simony; and the Treatise of Richard Uller-
ston, an Oxford doctor, is said to have guided the views of the
bishop of Salisbury, who effectually served the cause by his
personal zeal, both at Pisa and Constance. The *Italians*, as
they were the only people who profited by pontifical corruption,
so were they more commonly found to defend and uphold it.
But even among them were a few splendid exceptions; Pileus‡,
archbishop of Genoa, and Zabarella §, cardinal of Florence,
acknowledged and deplored the general unworthiness of the
order to which they belonged. Lastly, even the *Spaniards*
themselves, the perverse adherents of Benedict XIII., vented

---

* " Consilium Pacis de Unione ac Reformatione Ecclesiæ in Concilio Universali
quærenda." It occupies sixty columns in the beginning of Von der Hardt's
second volume.

† "Aureum Speculum Papæ, ejus Curiæ, Prælatorum, aliorumque Spiritualium."
The work gained great celebrity on the Continent.

‡ See his *Ingenua Parænesis* ad Sigismund. Imper. *De Reformatione Ecele-
siæ in Conc. Const. prosequenda*, apud Von der Hardt, tom. i., part 15.

§ There still exists a long and elaborate Treatise, published by Zabarella, " De
Schismate Innocentii et Benedicti Pontificis," either before the meeting of the
Council of Pisa, or during its earliest deliberations.

at Constance, in some satirical compositions, the indignation which it was not yet politic to express openly.

We have thus seen how generally * it was admitted at that period, even by the friends and ministers of the Church, that great abuses existed therein, that they demanded immediate and effectual correction, and that such could only be administered by removing the cause of the evil. Let us examine then, for one moment, the view which they took of their own imperfections. We may observe that the lamentations and censures, so abundantly poured forth by those writers, were confined almost wholly to one subject—the degeneracy and corruption *of the clergy.* This, indeed, was acknowledged to extend to the lowest rank from the very highest—this was admitted to comprise every form of sin and degradation—but this, according to their notions, was the limit of the evil. Under this one head was comprehended (or very nearly so) the sum and substance of the ecclesiastical derangement. The purity of the *system* was seldom or never questioned; the perfect integrity and infallible wisdom of the Church, and the divine obligation to believe and obey, without thought or question, all that it had

Limited objects of those complaints.

---

* In the "History of the Council of Constance," by Theodric Vrie, written at the time and dedicated to Sigismond, the Church herself is made to speak the following lines, more remarkable for the bold truths which they contain, than for delicacy of expression, or metrical correctness. (Lib. i. Metrum Secundum.)

> Heu Simon regnat; per munera quæque reguntur,
>   Judiciumque pium gaza nefanda vetat.
> Curia Papalis fovet omnia scandala mundi,
>   Delubra sacra facit perfiditate forum.
> Ordo sacer, baptisma sacrum cum Chrismate Sancto
>   Venduntur, turpi conditione foro.
> Dives honoratur, pauper contemnitur, atque
>   Qui dare plura valet munera gratus erat.
> Aurea quæ quondam fuit, hinc argentea Papæ
>   Curia procedit deteriore modo.
> Ferrea dehinc facta, dura cervice quievit
>   Tempore non modico; sed modo facta lutum.
> Postque lutum quid deterius solet esse? Recordor—
>   Stercus. Et in tali Curia tota sedet.

Semler, in cap. ii., secul xv., "De Publico Ecclesiæ Statu," enumerates a great multitude of compositions produced by the discontented spirits of the 14th and 15th centuries. Several are given at length by Herman Von der Hardt, Hist. Concil. Constant.

enjoined or should enjoin, in practice, or precept, or ceremony, or discipline, was as strongly inculcated by the most eminent reformers, as by the most perverse upholders of the avowed abuses; only, it was maintained by the former, that the men, who administered this heaven-descended system, were sunk in a depravity from which it was necessary to raise them, and that no measures could effect this benefit, which did not first provide for the re-organization of the highest ranks. After all, it was but the surface of the subject which they surveyed; and thus the remedies proposed could not be other than in-effectual.

At the same time it must be admitted that those remedies were properly adapted to the end which they were intended to attain. The demoralization of the inferior clergy was un-doubtedly occasioned, in a very great measure, by the non-residence, the avarice, and the venality of their more elevated brethren; and these views were communicated almost neces-sarily by the contagion of the court of Rome. And since it was become the practice of that court to attract all aspiring ecclesiastics by the undisguised sale of the most honourable dignities, its malignant influence spread like a pestilence through the Church. Those, therefore, who maintained that no reform could have any effect unless it commenced at the head, and whose first endeavours were turned to extirpate the scandals of the Vatican, pursued their own views with boldness and sagacity, and aimed well to uproot the evil which they saw—only, their views were too narrow, and the evil lay deeper than they were able to discover, or than they dared to avow.

Designs of the Council of Pisa; One professed object of the council of Pisa was "to reform the Church in its head and its members;" and many of the fathers there assembled were earnest in that intention. We have seen, indeed, to what insufficient limits their project was confined: still was it no inconsiderable design in that age, nor unworthy of a bold and generous character, especially in ministers and prelates of the Roman Church, to repress the licentiousness, and to moderate the power, of the successor of St. Peter. The boldness of the enterprise may be measured by its difficulty; for, if it was little that the reformers attempted, it was much more than they had the means of accomplishing. The moment, however, was exceedingly favourable; and when after the deposition of the two pretenders, the see was vacant, and the election about to be made under the very eyes of the council, an oath was imposed upon the cardinals, that he among them who should be raised to the pontificate, should not dissolve the council, until after the reformation of the Church had been completed. The choice of the college, directed by the counsels of Baltazar Cossa, fell upon Alexander V. Gerson presently preached before him, and did not omit to press the paramount duty of correcting many abuses. A great number of the fathers held the same expectation. But eluded by Alexander, who was a Greek and a pope, had no design to diminish his own profitable privileges, nor any scruple in evading his solemn obligation. In the 22nd and 23rd sessions he published certain declarations, that, out of regard for the necessities of the Churches, he remitted all arrears due to the apostolical chamber; that he resigned henceforward his claim on the property of deceased prelates, and the revenues of vacant bishoprics; that he would make no more transfers of benefices, without previously hearing the parties concerned; and that provincial councils should be more frequently assembled for the salutary regulation of the Church. The consideration of any extensive plan of reform he thought expedient to defer until the next general council; but this was to be assembled in three years.

With these unsubstantial concessions—and even from these there was one dissentient cardinal,—the prelates of Pisa were dismissed; and if they returned to their several sees with the consciousness that they had not fully accomplished any one of the objects for which they were convoked, yet were they not without consolation, nor were their labours without fruit. They had not, indeed, healed the divisions of the Church; they had not restrained the abuses of papal power; they had not checked the profligacy of the cardinals; they had not imposed any limit on the spreading domination of simony. Nevertheless, they had fulfilled an important destiny in the declining history of their Church; they had proclaimed the supremacy of a general council, and deposed the two disputants who divided the papacy : they had freely censured the vices of the Apostolical See, and had demanded its reformation ; they had secured the early convocation of another council for the remedy of their grievances ; and lastly, and most especially, they had opposed to pontifical despotism that independent constitutional spirit, which was the safeguard of the ancient Church, and which spreading from Pisa to Constance, from Constance to Basle, and striking deeply, though latently, during the times of iniquity which succeeded, at length achieved, under happier auspices and in a bolder spirit, its great and effectual triumph.

Proceed-
ings of the
Council of
Constance.
A much more numerous congregation of prelates and eccle-siastics of every rank, of ambassadors, of doctors of law, and other distinguished laymen, constituted the august assembly of Constance.   The place was favourable to the hopes of reform ; for the German soil was more auspicious to that cause than the irreligious and interested cities of Italy.   Ac-cordingly, we observe that its necessity was more loudly pro-claimed, and its principles defined with greater boldness and exactitude.   Gerson once more led the assault against papal delinquency.   He attacked the Decretals, the Clementines, and most of the Constitutions of the Popes ; he overthrew many of the pretensions thence derived, and he exposed, in a strain now familiar to his audience, their simony, their avarice, and anti-Christian usurpations *.   " All the bulls of John begin with a falsehood ; for, if he was truly the *servant of the servants of God*, he would employ himself in rendering service to the faith-ful, and assisting the poor, who are the members of Christ Jesus. But so far is he from calling the poor about him, or persons distinguished for their learning or their virtue, that he sur-

---

* " Non Christi, sed mores gerunt Antichristi ; " and again, " Non legimus Christum illi contulisse potestatem beneficia, dignitates, episcopatus, villas, terras dispensandi aut distribuendi, sed nec unquam legimus Petrum hæc fecisse.   Sed solùm hanc potestatem ei tribuit specialem, scriptam *Matt. xvi.*, quam etiam minimo mundi episcopo concessit."   Such expressions might be flattering to the dignity of the surrounding prelates.   But he was an injudicious friend to the Roman Catholic Church who appealed to the Bible as the test of its purity. John Huss, had he been present, at this discourse, might have pressed that argu-ment somewhat farther.

rounds himself with lords, and tyrants, and soldiers. Let him, then, rather assume the title of Lord of Lords; since he dares to boast that he possesses the same power which Christ possessed in his divine and human nature *. It was well, indeed, for Gregory the Great to call himself the Servant of the Servants of God. He nourished the poor, and was poor himself; he conferred benefices only on men of virtue and capacity; he preached the Gospel himself to his clergy and his people; he composed works to confirm believers in their faith; he held a rein over the luxury of the Roman people, and rescued them by his prayer to God from a pernicious pestilence." Accustomed to the bitterness of such taunts, the pope and his luxurious court may have been insensible to their shamefulness, or even questioned their justice; but among the mitred multitudes who were present, some were doubtless awakened by the eloquence of Gerson to a better sense of their faith, their duties, and their obedience.

The Council had not been many months in existence before

---

* "Quia præsumit dicere esse tantam suam potestatem, quantam Christus habuit, secundum quod Deus et secundum quod homo." Opera Gersoni, apud Lenfant, Hist. Conc. Const., l. vii., s. xiv. The same doctor, in his sermon, "De Signis Ruinæ Ecclesiæ," mentions eight such indications: (1.) Rebellio et inobedientia; (2.) Inverecundia; (3.) Immoderata inæqualitas, qua alius et sæpe dignior esurit; alius et frequenter indignior præ multitudine et magnitudine beneficiorum ebrius est; (4.) Fastus et superbia prælatorum et aliorum ecclesiasticorum—tantus fastus in Dei Ecclesia, præcipuè in temporibus istis, non tam multos movet ad reverentiam quam multos ad indignationem; et plures invitat ad prædam, qui se reputarent fortasse Deo sacrificium offerre, si possent quosdam divites ecclesiasticos spoliare; (5.) Signum sumitur ex tyrannide præsidentium—tales sunt pastores qui non pascunt gregem Domini sed semetipsos; (6.) Conturbatio principum et commotio populorum; (7.) Recusatio correctionis in principibus ecclesiæ; (8.) Novitas opinionum. Moderno quidem tempore unusquisque interpretari et trahere non veretur sacram scripturam jura, sanctorumque patrum instituta ad libitum suæ voluntatis, prout amor, odium, invidia, spes promotionis, aut vindicta eum inclinat .... Præter hæc sunt alia signa, videlicet recessus justitiæ, distinctio studiorum, prælatio puerorum, et ignorantium et pravorum, et *hæc erit destructio Latinorum.* Plura alia sunt descripta in Prophetis de dejectione sacerdotalis honoris, ex quibus et prædictis, sapiens potest concludere ruinam temporalium de propinquo imminere. A multis annis non fuerunt tot malevoli, tanti corde rebelles et animo accensi contra ecclesiam sicut his diebus. Quos in longum compescere nequaquam valebimus, nisi signis virtutum manifestis ad benevolentiam eos inclinaverimus." Gersoni Opera, vol. i., p. 199, Ed. Paris, 1606. This sermon was preached before the Council of Constance.

it entered seriously into this department of its duties; and a Committee of Reform (Collège Reformatoire) was appointed to examine into particular abuses, and prepare a general project for the approbation of the whole assembly. This College, named on the 15th of June, 1415, was composed of nineteen persons, viz., four deputies from each of the four nations, and *three Cardinals.* The deputies were chosen indifferently from bishops, doctors in theology, and doctors in law. There had been some previous contest, whether or not the cardinals should be at all admitted as members of this body; since it was now well understood by all parties, that the question of a general reform practically resolved itself into a reform of the court of Rome: not only because any other measures would have been wholly useless, unless attended by that, but also because the whole opposition to the removal of abuses proceeded from that quarter. Of the three interested parties who were at length admitted into the committee, Pierre d'Ailli, the cardinal of Cambrai, was one.

The College appears to have held its first deliberations on the 20th of August; and the subject to which they were directed was the translation of bishops. Other important matters were discussed by it during the autumn following; but whether it was paralyzed by the pontifical intrigues, or whether some of its members were deficient in zeal, its exertions did not keep pace with the eagerness of the reformers without. The German "Nation" published, about the end of the year, a remonstrance against the tediousness of its proceedings; the pulpits of Constance resounded with expressions of exhortation and reproof; and elegies, and squibs, and satires were circulated to the same effect in the social, and even in the public, meetings of the fathers.

Division on
the expedi-
ency of de-
ferring the
Pope's elec-
tion. The labours of the committee were continued through the whole of 1416 till late in the succeeding year; and by that time, as we shall see presently, they had produced many wise and salutary resolutions. But in the course of 1417 a new subject of controversy arose, which deeply affected the success of those measures. As soon as the See, through the cession or deposition of its three claimants, was declared vacant, a very

important question was moved—whether it were not wise to defer the new election until after the work of reformation should have been accomplished. Whatever was honest, and intelligent, and dispassionate in the party of the reformers maintained the necessity of that expedient. They knew the ambitious and selfish spirit of papacy; they knew how the elevation to the apostolical chair could blight the best principles, and contract the noblest heart ; they knew that disinterested integrity in *that* situation was beyond the magnanimity of man. They determined not to create with their own hands a destroyer of their own works. The nations, which took this side in the dispute, were the Germans and the English, and they were supported with the utmost sincerity and firmness by the emperor. The Cardinals conducted the opposite party with equal constancy and greater craft : they were warmly supported by the Italians ; the Spaniards, who on the deposition of Luna had been admitted to the deliberations, were on the same side; and even the French, hitherto the most enlightened advocates of reform*, for the most part, threw themselves into the ranks of its opponents. The contest continued during the whole summer, — numerous harangues were delivered, and much violence and much sophistry was wasted on both sides. On the one hand, the universal deformity and prostitution of the Church were exhibited and exaggerated in the most furious invectives: on the other, it was argued that the Church without the Pope was a headless trunk, which was indeed the most frightful of all deformities ; and that it became, in consequence, the first duty of every reformer to supply that deficiency (such was the nonsense seriously propounded by the friends of corruption), and thus restore the spiritual body to its integrity.

This was indeed the last ground of hope which remained to the Cardinals ; and it was really firm and tenable, because the majority of the nations had declared in their favour. They contested it with every weapon, and with the uncompromising, unscrupulous activity of men whose personal interests were

---

* This sudden change is ascribed to their national jealousy of the English, the victors of Agincourt.

concerned in the result. On one occasion they presented a
memorial to Sigismond, in which they urged, on the plea of
their majority, their right to proceed to immediate election : at
the same time they affected to repel, with some loftiness, the
imperial interference in matters strictly ecclesiastical. On
another, they published an offensive libel upon the Germans,
in which they accused that nation of a disposition to favour
the opinions of the Hussites—to defer the election of a pope,
in order to reform, without his co-operation, his office and his
court, savoured strongly (so the cardinals argued) of the anti-
papal perversion of those heretics ! The stigma of heresy—a
weapon which the defenders of ecclesiastical abuses have
managed with great address in every age of the Church—
exasperated those honest and orthodox Christians, and they
repelled it with great, and (as they thought) virtuous indignation. About the same time Robert Hallam, bishop of Salisbury, died. He was among the stoutest of the Reformers of
Constance, and had exercised very considerable influence, not
only over the councils of his compatriots, but over the mind of
the emperor himself *.

Conduct of
Sigismond
and the
Germans.
On the 9th of September, five days after his decease, an
assembly was held on the same subject ; and the result was a
remonstrance, in the name of the cardinals, to Sigismond, on
the extreme danger impending over the Church from any delay
in the election of a Pope. It is remarkable, that the language
of this document expressed a sense of the necessity of reform,
and great readiness to undertake it ; but it was urged, that the
question ought to be deferred, until a head had been given to
the Church. But the emperor rose ere the address was
finished, and indignantly quitted the assembly. Howbeit, the
cardinals persisted, without any fear or compromise ; two days
afterwards, a second † memorial, more explicit and decided
than the former, was presented and read ; and so firm was the
attitude of that party, that the only two members of the Sacred
College, who had hitherto supported the opposite opinions, now

* Von der Hardt calls him Cæsar's *fidus Achates.*
† They may both be found in the first volume of Von der Hardt's Hist. Conc.
Constat., Præfat. in part, xx., p. 916 et seq.

joined their colleagues. A still more important defection immediately followed this; the English also passed over to the papal party.

From the moment that the decision of the majority of the council was contravened by Sigismond, it was very easy to persuade even the most honest reformers, that the dignity and authority of the whole assembly was at stake, and that it was the duty of all parties to combine, in order to repel the presumptuous interference of the Emperor—and many were probably influenced in their change by that motive. But the Germans still maintained their former resolution; and though many of them also may have been guided by considerations (of nationality or loyalty) foreign to the original question of reform, a fresh memorial, which they immediately presented to the Council, pressed very forcibly the real argument on which the contest now turned. In this paper they maintained, with great boldness and reason, " that the General Council stood in the place of the Church and completely represented it; that the schism had arisen from the general corruption of that body, and that such corruption could only be remedied during the vacancy of the see; that if a pope were once elected—however virtuous and upright the individual exalted might be, however proved and old in integrity and piety—he would speedily be stained by the vices which infected the chair, and debased the ecclesiastics surrounding it; that he would grope in the darkness and solitude of his own honesty, till his private excellence would give way before the overwhelming depravities of a system, which no man could possibly administer and be virtuous,—while, on the other hand, a substantial reform, previously effected, would shelter him from the pressure of unjust and wicked solicitations." The wisdom and truth contained in these positions inflamed still further the perversity of the cardinals; and what they could not hope to effect by reason, or even by menace, they prepared to accomplish by more certain means. Among the German prelates there were two who Triumph of possessed, more completely than their brethren, the confidence the papal both of the Emperor and the "Nation"—the Archbishop of Riga party. and the Bishop of Coire. Each of these respectable persons had private reasons (which were not concealed from the cardinals) for being discontented with his own see. A negotiation was opened. To the former they promised the bishopric of Liege, which he coveted; to the latter, the archbishopric of Riga—both were converted. Their compatriots followed them; and the tumults, which had shaken the council for so many months, were appeased by the translation of two venal prelates*.

The Emperor, thus deserted by the entire Church, still offered an ineffectual show of resistance; and at length, to throw at least some dignity over his defeat, he stipulated as the conditions of his consent, that the Pope should enter, without any delay, even before his coronation, upon the work of reform; that he should conduct it in concert with the Council; and that he should not depart from Constance until his task was accomplished. The cardinals, with their coadjutors†, soon afterwards assembled in conclave; and on the 11th of November following, Martin V., an Italian and a Roman, was raised to the pontifical throne.

The historian cannot fail to perceive, what was indeed obvious at the time to the most intelligent men of both parties, that the battle of reform had in fact been fought on other ground, and that the field for which so many efforts had been made, and were still to be made, was already lost. Some nominal improvements might yet, perhaps, be extorted from the reluctant pontiff—some trifling abuses he might be brought to sacrifice in order to save and perpetuate the rest—with some unmeaning shadow he might consent to amuse and delude the world—but the hope of any substantial measure of renovation was gone. Notwithstanding the strong sense of the Church's degradation and danger with which so many of the fathers were deeply penetrated—notwithstanding the security and even applause with which their complaints and invectives were uttered and heard—notwithstanding the learning, the virtue, and the powerful talents which were united in the same cause—it was no difficult matter for a small body of very crafty ecclesiastical

and election of Martin V. Observations.

* Von der Hardt, tom. iv., p. 1426.
† See the preceding chapter, p. 105.

politicians, closely bound together by common and personal interests, and wholly unscrupulous as to means, to neutralize the exertions of a much more numerous party, which, though earnestly bent on one general purpose, might be divided as to a thousand particulars. For a space of nearly three years, numberless causes of discord, personal, professional, national, might spring up, while the watchful cardinals were ever at hand to encourage and mature them. Every change of circumstance presented a new field of action; and in so harassing and protracted a contest, superior discipline and a keener sense of interest might finally supplant or wear away the adverse majority.

Moreover, the College could always count, with perfect confidence, on the zeal and fidelity of its Italian allies. The whole multitude of the Transalpine clergy conspired, with scarcely an individual exception, in opposition to reform. Yet this combination did not probably arise either because they were very rich or very powerful, or very generally demoralized. *In riches*, the bishops and abbots of Italy could bear no comparison with the lordly hierarchy of Germany or England; partly because their disproportionate numbers diminished the share of each in the common fund, and partly because the private devotion of ancient days had there been less munificent than among the younger and ruder proselytes of the North. *In power* and popular influence they were precluded from any extravagant progress by the wider diffusion of intelligence, and the free and daring spirit of the prevalent Republicanism. In truth, among the Italian *people*, the last sparks of religious fervour were at this time nearly extinct; and whatever attachment they still retained for their Church was without enthusiasm, and not uncommonly without faith. The venerable family of Saints, once so fruitful in every province, was now rarely and languidly propagated. The din of polemical controversy, the surest indication of theological zeal, was seldom heard; and even *heresy* itself, which was building its indestructible temples in the North and West of Europe, gave little occupation or solicitude to the churchmen of Italy. Many of the causes which tend generally to swell sacerdotal authority (we are not

Conduct and character of the Italian clergy.

K 2

now speaking of the peculiar dominion of the pope) had ceased to operate in that country. *In morality*, the Italian clergy were upon the whole less dissolute than those to the North of the Alps; and for that reason they were less deeply impressed with the necessity of reform. To this praise the court of Rome did indeed present an infamous exception. But the pontifical palace may seem to have attracted to its own precincts most of the noxious vapours which else would have spread more general infection; and the prelates of Italy found their profit in the very vices of Rome. Besides, they had been so long habituated to consider the authority of that see as national property, and shared with such selfish exultation the glory of its foreign triumphs and the sense of its imposing majesty, that they rallied round it with ardour, on the first rumour of hostility. They saw that some of its dearest prerogatives were threatened—they saw that some of its most profitable usurpations were assailed: but they did not see the FRIENDLINESS of the design—they did not perceive that an increase of vigour and stability would assuredly follow the immediate sacrifice:— they snatched at the short-sighted policy of the moment, and, by defending the abuses of their Church, insured its downfall.

On the 30th of October, in the interval between the triumph of the cardinals and the election of the Pope, the fortieth, one of the most important sessions of the Council, took place. Then was made a very seasonable effort, on the part of the reformers, to impose some specific obligation upon the future pope; and

Project of Reformation.

on this occasion the scheme which the Committee of Reform had been so long engaged in preparing was formally approved, and recommended to the immediate adoption of the pontiff and council—for the majority were still sincere in their intentions, though they had blindly cast away the means of effecting them. To do justice to this subject, we must shortly mention the heads of this project, since it may be considered as embracing the utmost extent of change which it was thought expedient, or found possible, under any circumstances to introduce. The articles to which the future reformation was to be directed were eighteen:—(1) The number, the quality, and the nation of the cardinals; (2) The reservations of the holy

see; (3) Annates; (4) Collations of benefices and expectative
graces; (5) What causes ought to be treated in the court of
Rome; (6) Appeals to the same court; (7) The offices of the
Chancery and Penitentiary; (8) Exemptions granted and unions
made during the schism; (9) Commendams; (10) The confirmation of elections; (11) Intermediates, i. e., revenues during
vacancy; (12) Alienation of the property of the Roman and
other Churches; (13) In what cases a Pope may be corrected
and deposed, and by what means; (14) The extirpation of
Simony; (15) Dispensations; (16) Provision for the Pope and
the Cardinals; (17) Indulgences; (18) Tenths. To these it
should be added, that, in the session preceding, a decree had
passed to regulate and secure, as far as possible, the periodical
meeting of General Councils.

In the resolutions which the committee published respecting
the above articles, a sort of principle is discernible, of throwing
aside the new Canon law, and reviving in its place the more discreet and venerable institutions of more ancient days. Thus
they resolved that the popes should judge no important cause
without the counsel of his cardinals—and even, in some instances, without the approbation of a General Council. And
again, that there were certain cases in which a pope might be
judged and deposed—decisions wholly at variance with the
Canons of the Vatican, which committed to the pope alone all
judgment of major causes, and gave authority to bulls originating with himself; and which also laid it down that a pope
could not be judged or deposed on any other charge than that
of heresy.

The Committee of Reform also prohibited the popes from
reserving * the *spoils* of the bishops, the revenues of vacant
benefices, and the *procurations*, or provisions made for bishops
during their visitations. It imposed some restraint on pluralities and dispensations. The pope was forbidden to permit

Regarding the pope.

---

* On the subject of reservations, Lenfant remarks, that *mental* reservations of
benefices were not yet introduced. These differed from others in that they were
not published. If a benefice was vacant, and either the Ordinary had conferred
it, or any one went to Rome to obtain it, the datary would answer, that the pope
had made a mental reservation to present it to whom he thought proper.

the same person to hold more than one bishopric or abbey at
the same time, unless with the consent of the sacred college,
and for important reasons—though even this restriction appears
to have been liable to exceptions, in countries especially where
the benefices were poor*. Another resolution enforced the
residence of the higher clergy, on pain of deprivation in case
of six months of absence, unless with special permission from
the pope. Another forbade the pope to impose tenths on his
clergy without the consent of a general council. Another revoked, with some trifling exceptions, all the exemptions which
had been granted during the schism. The abuse of exemptions had, indeed, proceeded so far as to awaken the conscience
even of the pope himself, who subsequently ratified this article.

The popes had usurped the power of translating from see to
see without consulting the inclination of the prelates affected
by the change. These *forcible* translations were prohibited by
the committee; but it does not appear that Martin V. consented
even to so slight an encroachment upon his despotism. It had
also been a custom, probably established by Innocent III., for
the popes to reserve to the holy see the power of giving absolution for certain offences (called reserved cases), which were
thought to be placed above episcopal cognizance. The pretext
for this innovation was, to invest those crimes with additional
terrors, and to repel men from their commission by the difficulty of obtaining absolution. The common effect was this:
that many, unable or indisposed to undertake so long a pilgrimage, disregarded entirely both confession and penance;
while others, whose easier circumstances permitted the journey,
poured forth their penitential gold with great profusion into
the apostolical coffers. This subject was for some time debated

* In Apulia, for example, and in some parts of Spain, the Reformers allowed
the pope to give dispensation for four benefices. In England, on the other hand,
they would not permit it, on any account, to be granted for more than two. Clemangis asserts (De Corrupto Ecclesiæ Statu, cap. xi.) " that there were at that
time ecclesiastics who held as many as 500 ample benefices." And the same
writer further affirms " that the monks of his day were at the same time monks,
canons regular, secular; that under the same habit they possessed the rights,
offices, and benefices of all orders and of all professions,'' Lenf. Hist. Conc.
Const., l. vii., s. xxxii.

in the committee; but it was at length unanimously decided
that the established usage should remain.

As those here mentioned composed the most important restrictions which it was designed to impose upon the pope's authority, so the meditated reform of his cardinals and his court *The court
would have introduced changes still less considerable. Four *of Rome.*
resolutions were passed respecting the number of the Sacred
College, and the qualifications necessary for admission; as also
that every new nomination should receive the approbation of
the majority of the college. Others were enacted for the better
administration of the apostolical chancery and chamber, respecting prothonotaries and participants; the auditors, or judges
della Rota (the parliament of the pope); scriptors of the penitentiary; abbreviators of bulls; clerks of the chamber; correc-
tors of the apostolical letters; *auditores contradictariorum,* and
auditors of the chamber; acoluthes, subdeacons, chaplains,
referendaries, penitentiaries, and registrars—not for the abolition of any of those offices *, or of others which might have
been added to the list, but only for their more judicious regulation. Thus we observe that it did not then enter into the views
of any party to diminish the state and dignity of the see, or to
curtail any of the consequence which it might derive from those
circumstances; but that the Reformers of those days would
have been well satisfied in that matter, had the pope consented
to part with the most obvious and superficial abuses.

The resolutions of the committee respecting the secular *The secular
clergy, while they proclaimed the general corruption, were *clergy.*
more especially levelled against two crimes, the same which,
from the days of Gregory VII., had been the constant mark
for the shafts of Reform—simony and concubinage. The
enactments which were made, particularly against the former
of these offences, were reasonable and salutary. But there
could be little prospect of their execution so long as the court
of Rome was left in possession of so much pomp and splendour, without any fixed and sufficient funds for its support.

* The only office, as far as we can observe, which the Reformers abolished
was the "Auditorship of the Chamber of Avignon," which, since the return of
the pope to Rome, had become an obvious sinecure.

Even had it been possible, by a single act of the council, at
once to extirpate simony from the Church, Rome was the hot-
bed where it would of necessity have sprung up again, and
thence spread its pestiferous branches over the whole surface
of Christendom.   Other ecclesiastical abuses were likewise assailed.   It had frequently happened*, to the great scandal of
the people, that bishops held sees, and incumbents parishes,
without having taken priest's orders.   The college of Reform
had already regulated that the pope should grant no dispensation to bishops on this point for longer than one year: it extended the same limit to the inferior clergy.   Another and very
important task it also undertook—to draw the limits which
were hereafter to divide civil from ecclesiastical jurisdiction,
and to specify the causes which appertained to either.   The
want of some definite arrangement on this subject had, for
some time, disturbed the course of justice, and led to perpetual
broils between the clergy and the laity.   Nevertheless, as it was
through that very indistinctness that the former had been enabled to push their claims so far, it might be uncertain whether
its removal, though finally advantageous to both parties, would
be very popular among them.   Several useful regulations were
likewise devised for the purification of the various religious
bodies, and especially of the Mendicants.   It seems, indeed,
to have been generally admitted by the leading reformers, that
in the universal degeneracy of the Church, the most conspicuous instances of profligacy and profaneness were exhibited
by the monastic establishments.

Points at
issue be-
tween the
parties.

Such are the outlines of the Project† by which the reformers
of Constance proposed to restrain the abuses of papacy, and to
restore, correct, and consolidate the Catholic Church.   And
here we should again remark, that the authors of that project
were themselves zealous, and even bigoted churchmen.   Re-

---

* Lenfant, Hist. Conc. Const., liv. vii., s. 46.

† The above account is founded on four authentic documents published by M.
Von der Hardt, from the MSS. of the library of Vienna, and recognised by Len-
fant as " containing all the resolutions of the committee of reform."—Hist. Conc.
Constan., liv. vii., s. xxvii.   See Von der Hardt, tom. i., partes x. xi. xii.   *Collegii
Reformatorum Constant. statuta,* sive *Geminum* Reformatorii Constant. *Protocol-
lum,* &c. &c.

specting the divine authority, the power, the infallibility * of
the Church, they professed opinions as lofty as the loftiest
notions of their adversaries.   Still the space which divided the
two parties was broad and clear, and it was included in one
question—In what does this infallible Church consist? In what
is it fully and faithfully represented?   Does a council-general,
without the pope, possess the mighty attributes in question?
Or a council-general with the pope? or the pope without a
council-general? The last opinion, the extreme of high papacy,
had not perhaps very many advocates; at least the second was
that on which the Italians took their stand, as being the more
tenable: the first was the rallying principle of the reformers,
who may be designated the low papists. It cannot be too carefully impressed, that the mighty struggles at Constance respected, in as far as *principles* were concerned, not the character of the Church, on which all were agreed, but the extent to
which the Pope possessed the attributes of the Church.   And
this distinction being rightly understood, we shall find no difficulty in accounting—when we shall arrive at that subject—
for the seeming inconsistency, with which the council of Constance deposed a legitimate pope with one hand, while it consigned the heretics, Huss and Jerome, to barbarous execution
with the other.

We have observed, that at the Fortieth Session eighteen
articles, which were the heads of the resolutions of the committee, were submitted, by the approbation of the council, to
the future pope, and that Martin V. was elected a few days
afterwards. Again, on the very day following his coronation,
the nations assembled and pressed the observance of his obligation. The pope appears to have promised with great facility; but at the same time he appointed six cardinals to co-operate with the deputies of the nations in revising their former
labours. Divisions presently arose: the cardinals were indefatigable in creating difficulties; so that the patience of the
Germans being once more wearied, they addressed (about the

*The Re-
formation
eluded by
Martin V.*

* It is only necessary to refer to the writings of the leading reformers, Gerson,
Pierre d'Ailli, &c., and the acts of the councils both of Constance and Basle.

end of 1417) a fresh memorial to the new committee. The
subjects urged on this occasion principally regarded reservations, appointment to benefices, expectative graces, and other
papal usurpations, and abuses of the Church patronage. Very
soon afterwards, the French remonstrated with equal warmth
against the procrastinations of the committee, and even presented a petition to Sigismond, in which they exhorted him to
employ his powerful influence with the pope. But Sigismond
had not forgotten their late opposition, nor was he unmindful
of the fatal wound which they had inflicted on the cause. He
dismissed their deputies without honour; and while he bade
them reflect, how steadily they had thwarted his wish to
accomplish the reformation *before* the pope should be elected,
he recommended them, now that they had obtained their pope,
to apply to *him* for their reform. At the same time, the Spaniards raised a clamour against simony and other abuses, and
went so far as to throw out some menaces against the Pontiff
himself; indeed some of them were suspected of still harbouring a secret attachment for their perverse compatriot, the Pope
of Paniscola. Martin was somewhat moved by this show of
unanimity; and thinking to gain better terms by dividing his
adversaries, he contrived to open a separate negotiation with
each nation, on the plea that he could thus more intimately
consult their several interests. The scheme succeeded; and as
all parties were wearied alike with dispute and delay, matters
were now hurried to a conclusion. On the 21st of March,
1418, the Pope, no longer disguising his eagerness to dissolve
the council, held the Forty-third Session, and published his own
articles of reformation; and they should be recorded for their
very insignificance. The first revoked (with a large field for
exceptions) such exemptions as had been granted *during the
schism;* the second commanded a fresh examination of such
unions of benefices as had taken place during the same period.
The third prohibited the appropriation of the revenues of vacant
benefices to the apostolical chamber. The fourth was a general
edict against simony. The fifth respected papal dispensations
to hold benefices without being in orders. The sixth forbade
the imposition of tenths and other taxes on ecclesiastics, unless

for some great advantage to the Church, and with the consent
of the cardinals and local prelates. The seventh regulated the
dress of the ecclesiastics, according to the modesty of the ancient
laws; and the last, and the most shameless of all, declared
that, by the above articles, and by the concordats granted to
the nations, the Pope had satisfied the demands of the committee of reform, as expressed in the Fortieth Session of the
Council, and discharged his own obligations.

The Concordats were as delusive as the articles*; and Martin, conscious of this, had not yet made them public, but continued to press the immediate dissolution of the council. It
was in vain objected, that many matters of great importance
still remained unsettled: it was replied, that the patrimony of
the Holy See was in the hands of depredators; that Rome
itself was exposed to the scourges of famine and pestilence, of
foreign and intestine war; that it was the paramount duty of
him, whom the whole world now acknowledged as the successor of St. Peter, to place himself on the throne of the apostle.
Accordingly, on the 22d of April, the council assembled for the
forty-fifth and last session: and the Bull, which released the
fathers from their unsuccessful labours, showered upon them
and their domestics a profusion of indulgences, as if to complete, by an additional mockery, the insult with which their
hopes had been destroyed†. On the 2d of May the Concor-

*Dissolu-
tion of the
Council.*

---

* That granted to the Germans contained twelve articles, which are enumerated by Semler, Secul. xv., cap. ii., p. 38. Since they did not go to the effectual
removal of any grand abuse, it is unnecessary to cite them here.

† As this memorable Bull happens to be short, it will be well to record it. " We
Martin, Bishop, servant of the servants of God, ad perpetuam rei memoriam, by
the requisition of the holy council, do hereby dismiss and declare it terminated,
giving to every one liberty to return home. Besides, by the authority of God the
omnipotent, and of his blessed apostles, St. Peter and St. Paul, *and by our own*,
we accord to all the members of the council plenary absolution from all their sins,
" semel in vita ;" so that each among them may obtain this absolution in form,
within two months after the gift shall be made known to him. We also give
them the same privilege *in articulo mortis;* and we extend it to servants as well
as their masters, on condition that, after the day of notification, both the one and
the other shall fast every Friday during one year, for the absolution for life, and
another year for the absolution in articulo mortis ; unless there be some legitimate
hinderance, in which case they shall perform other pious works. And after the
second year, they shall be held to fast every Friday during life, or to do other

dats were published; and that which was granted to the
French was immediately rejected by them, as contrary to the
liberties of the Gallican Church. But the object of Martin
was already accomplished; *the Council of Constance had
ceased to exist;* and in defiance of the urgent remonstrances of
the emperor, the pontiff turned his footsteps towards Italy. He
turned towards the soil, where papacy was national and indigenous, and where, amidst all the turbulence of contending
cities and factions, the spiritual despotism of the Vicar of
Christ had never yet been contested.

We should here observe, that, while very lofty language was
employed at Constance on both sides respecting the principle
on which the government of the Church rested; while some
maintained that it was a pure monarchy, others that it was a
monarchy tempered by a mixture of the aristocratical and even
republican character; other disputes were less publicly, though
not less passionately, agitated between those parties, respecting
much more vulgar considerations. The reader cannot fail to
have remarked, that of the concessions made by Martin, those
which were not absolutely nugatory regarded the temporalities
of the Church, and the power of the pope to levy contributions
upon the clergy. The reforming prelates had pressed these
from the beginning among other grievances; but it proved at
last, that the subject, on which those pecuniary discussions had
chiefly turned, was entirely unnoticed in the pope's decree.
The exaction of *Annates,* or the first year's income of vacant
benefices, seems to have been that, among all the resources of
the apostolical chancery, which was most profitable to the re-
ceivers, and most unpopular among all other ecclesiastics. The
claim was of a very modern date; it could not be traced higher
than Clement V.; and it scarcely assumed the shape of a right
till the pontificate of Boniface IX. The French " nation"

Disputes on Annates.

works of piety, on pain of incurring the indignation of the omnipotent God, and
of his blessed apostles St. Peter and St. Paul." Such were the consolations
which were offered to the most enlightened body which had ever yet assembled in
the name of the Church, in return for their disappointed expectations, by the
very man whom they had raised to power, and whose first use of it was to betray
them. They demanded a substantial reform, and he paid the debt in indulgences.

urged the abolition of this tax with especial zeal from the very opening of the council; and the ambassador of Charles VI. was instructed at all events to carry this measure. The fathers, in a general assembly, even passed a resolution to that effect: but the cardinals still exclaimed and remonstrated, and protested; and, as their last resource, they ventured to appeal from the council to the future pope. The French replied to this appeal with much spirit and reason*; and had the reformation preceded the election, there can be no doubt that the imposition would have been removed. But the cardinals finally prevailed, and the odious exaction, under some slight and indefinite restrictions, was re-established.

But though the reforming party, which really constituted the great majority of the council, was finally defrauded of all the substance of its project, and dismissed with a very thin veil to cover its defect, yet the recollection of one great triumph might supply substantial ground of consolation. The superiority of a general council to the pope was unequivocally decreed at Constance. The prelates of Pisa had done little more than overthrow two claimants to the See, neither of whom was universally acknowledged, or rightfully established. But the legitimacy of John XXIII. was never questioned even by his bitterest enemies; and Martin, whose succession to the dignity was only legal through the legality of the previous disposition and of the power exercised by the deposing council, was the least qualified of all men to discredit either the act or the authority; so that, whatsoever struggles and protestations may afterwards have been made by individual popes, the general principle was immutably established in the Church †.

The fathers of Constance also carried home with them ano-

* The substance of the paper is given by the Continuator of Fleury, l. civ., s. lxxiv. Some curious particulars of the dispute between the French and the cardinals on the subject of Annates may be found in Von der Hardt, tom. i. pars xiii.

* It is well known that Transalpine divines dispute the principle even to this moment; but they have no ground to stand upon. If they admit the legitimacy of the Council of Constance, they must receive that decision; if not, they impugn the succession of their popes ever since that council—for they all flow uninterruptedly from Martin V. No sophistry can liberate them from this dilemma.

ther source of comfort and hope. In the thirty-ninth session,
held on the 9th of October, 1417, it was enacted, as a perpetual
law of the Church, that general councils should be held on
every tenth year from the termination of the preceding, in such
places as the pope, with the consent of the council sitting,
should appoint. But in the first instance, as the actual exigencies of the Church did not seem to allow even that short
interval, another council was to be assembled in five years from
the dissolution of that of Constance, and a third in seven years
after the second. In obedience to this Constitution, Martin V.
twice attempted to collect an obsequious assembly in Italy ; but
his summons was disregarded by the foreign prelates, to whom
neither Pavia nor Sienna offered any prospect of independence.
The scanty synods were hastily dissolved, and the only act
which is recorded of the latter was to grant as ample indulgences to those who should contribute gold for the extinction
of the Bohemian heretics, as to those who should serve *the cru-*
sade in person. Basle, at length, was appointed for the meeting of the real representatives of the Church, and they crowded
thither in great multitudes during the spring and summer of
1431.

In the meantime, on the 19th of the preceding February,
Martin V. died. His long pontificate had been principally
devoted to two objects, the recovery of the states of the Church
and the amassing of wealth, and he had succeeded in both.
As to the former, he had restored the interests of the see nearly
to the condition in which they stood before the schism. As
to the latter, he destined the treasures which he collected
rather for the aggrandizement of his own family than for the benefit of the Catholic Church, or even of the pontifical government. At the same time, it is admitted that he possessed considerable talents, and a vigorous and consistent character; and
he has escaped the imputation of any great vice, excepting
avarice. At this crisis, the character of the successor to the
chair was of consequence almost incalculable to the Church.
The council of Basle was irrevocably summoned; and its
principles, its policy, and its power could easily be foreseen
from the experience of Constance. What policy, then, was

Marginal notes:

Decree for the decennial meeting of General Councils.

Council of Basle, 1431 A.D.

the new pope to pursue ?   Was he openly to oppose, or craftily to elude, or generously to co-operate in, the work of reformation? The durability of the Roman Catholic Church depended on the answer.

The cardinals were not, indeed, disturbed by such distant considerations; and the views with which most of them entered the Conclave extended not beyond their private intrigues or immediate interests.   Being unable at once to agree, they proceeded to the scrutiny; and their secret arrangements being not yet satisfactorily concluded, they continued to throw away their votes upon the names which held the lowest consideration, and were the last in the chance of success.   And thus it happened, that at the conclusion of one of these scrutinies, to the astonishment and dismay of the whole college, one Gabriel Condolmieri, the least and most insignificant member of the sacred body, was found in possession of two-thirds of the suffrages*.   There was no space to repent or retract; the election was already valid, and the bark of St. Peter was *thus* consigned, in the most anxious moment of its destiny, to the hand of Eugenius IV.

Election and character of Eugenius IV.

Had that pontiff been as deeply impressed with his own incapacity as the rest of the Christian world, he might occasionally have followed the counsel of wiser men; but on the contrary, he was the most presumptuous, as he was the most ignorant, of mankind †.   The rigorous habits of a monastic life had equally contracted his principles and blinded his judgment; so that he perpetually mistook precipitation for decision, and then thought to redeem his rashness by his obstinacy.   Without talents or any steady policy, through the very restlessness of his character he exercised an influence which was everywhere felt, and everywhere felt for evil‡.   And if it

---

* It is thus that Sismondi describes the elevation of Eugenius, without any question as to the credibility of his authorities. But we are bound to add, that several ecclesiastical historians, of various ages, whom we have consulted on this subject, are silent as to the circumstance mentioned in the text. Sismondi (chap. 66) cites Andreæ Billii Histor. Mediolan, l. ix., p. 143.

† He was remarkable for a downcast look. " Vultu alioqui decoro et venerabili, nunquam oculos in publico attollebat, ut a parente meo, qui eum sequebatur, accepi."—Volaterra, lib. xxii., p. 815, ap. Bayle.

‡ Contemporary Italian historians exert all the talents of partisanship in his

were just to select from the long list of pontifical delinquents
one name to which the downfall of the Church should more
particularly be ascribed, we should not greatly err in attaching that stigma to Eugenius.

The unexpected accident of his elevation inflated still further
an inconstant mind.   Some success which he gained in a
struggle with the Colonna family for the treasures of his predecessors filled him with unbounded confidence; and it was
in such a mood that he plunged into hostilities with the Council of Basle.   His first endeavours were directed to crush it,
ere it came into operation or even existence; but finding that
hopeless, and convinced that an assembly so solemnly convoked and so earnestly desired must meet, or seem to meet, he
determined to neutralize its character by changing its place.
Accordingly, he notified to the president, towards the end of
the year, that " by his own full power," he had *transferred* it
to Bologna, in Italy.   The president was the Cardinal Julian
Cesarini, a man whose eminent talents qualified him for that
office, in which he was placed by Martin, and confirmed by
Eugenius, and who may have deserved the reputation which
he has received from Bossuet, of being " the greatest character
of his age."   At any rate he was, on this occasion, more mind-
ful of his duties to the Church than of his obligations to his
master, and respectfully refused obedience to the pontifical
mandate.

Julian Cesarini, Cardinal of St. Angelo.

Objects of the council.
Three purposes were specified, for which the Council of Basle
was convoked*; (1.) The reunion of the Latin and Greek
Churches; (2.) The reform of the Church in its head and

favour. But Sismondi, who has estimated with less prejudice his political, as
well as his ecclesiastical character, speaks of him very differently. " Dans les
révolutions violentes où on le voit sans cesse engagé, en guerre avec son clergé,
avec ses sujets, avec ses bienfaiteurs, il manque presque toujours en même temps
et de la bonne foi, et de la politique. Il y a peu de tyrans à qui on peut reprocher
plus d'actes de perfidie et de cruauté; il y a peu de monarques imbécilles, qui
aient donné plus de preuves d'incapacité et d'inconséquence." Republ. Ital.,
cap. lxx.

* " Concilium hoc congregatum est propter extirpandas hæreses, faciendum
pacem, reformandum mores." Epist. (2) Juliani Card. ad Eugen. IV. Julian
places first that which seems to have been in his mind the most important object:
the third, the reformation, he regarded rather as the means of restoring the unity
of the Church.

members ; (3.) The reconciliation of the Hussites. We shall confine our account, for the present, to the second of these, and resume the thread which was broken at Constance : in so doing, it will be our misfortune again to observe the one party furiously contending against its own lasting interests, and repelling the friendly hand which would have purified and saved a foul and falling system ; and the other party, thwarted by perpetual impediments, insults, artifices, so as to confine its exertions to unworthy objects, and not effectually to accomplish even those. The former, consisting for the most part of Italians, were the myrmidons of absolute papacy ; while the latter comprehended almost all that was enlightened and generous and virtuous among the clergy of the rest of Europe.

Though many of the prelates had been long assembled, the first public session * was not held until the 14th of December, 1431 ; and from that time forwards, for the space of two entire years, the energies and patience of the fathers were wearied, and their passions excited, and their attention wholly diverted from the great object of their meeting by uninterrupted contentions with Eugenius. They had come together from all parts of Europe, and their numbers were swelled by the addition of many of the inferior clergy ; they arrived, deploring the debasement, and eager for the regeneration of their Church ; they were confident, too, in their power, and it was to this power that they chiefly trusted to repress the excesses of papacy ; yet when they would have advanced with ardour to realize these hopes, they found themselves engaged in a tedious and irritating contest for their own independence. In the course of this contest they published and republished those decrees of Constance which proclaimed the superior prerogatives of the council. They reiterated the authorized assertions, that a council general represents the Church, and is the Church ; that, as such, it derives its attributes *immediately* from Jesus Christ ; that, as such, it is impeccable ; that it is thus pos-

Contention between the council and the Pope.

---

* The method in which that very large body proceeded through its deliberations was both generally judicious, and particularly calculated to neutralize the majority of Italian deputies. It is given at length by the Contin. of Fleury, liv. cvi., s. 6.

sessed of infallibility—a boon which had been denied not only
to popes who had erred in matters of faith, but to the angels *
themselves, for they had sinned; that on these accounts the
pope was subject to the council in all things regarding (1)
faith, (2) the extirpation of schism, and (3) the reformation
of the Church: that he was only the *ministerial* † head of the
Church, inferior in eminence to that mystical body ‡; and consequently (for this was the point to which the whole tended)
that he possessed no power over the council, either to dissolve
or transfer it. But all these, and all similar assertions, fell
without any effect upon the mind of a pontiff, who was in real
monastic sincerity persuaded that there existed in the Church
no other legitimate authority whatsoever except his own. It
was in vain to appeal to ancient canons against modern usurpations, where ignorance had conspired with interest to overthrow reason and justice. It was in vain that all the learning
and genius and eloquence of the Church were arrayed on the
same side—their weapons were unfelt or unheeded by a stupid
and selfish bigotry.

Warnings of Cardinal Julian. During this controversy (if such it may be called) Cardinal
Julian boldly maintained the principles of the Council and
the cause of the Catholic Church. His mind was naturally
capacious: deep and assiduous study, which so commonly con-
tracts a feeble understanding, had enlarged and enlightened
his; and a mission which he had personally undertaken for
the conciliation of the Bohemians had brought before his eyes

* The "synodal response of the council" may be found in substance in the Continuator of Fleury, lib. cvi., s. 14. The original is in Labbe's Hist. Concil.

† This is urged by Æneas Sylvius, Comment. de Gestis Basil. Concil., lib. i.,
v. 16. The same writer also argues that the pope is more properly the *Vicar of
the Church* than the Vicar of Christ.

‡ This last position, together with some of the others, was proved by arguments
derived (1) from reason, (2) from experience, (3) from authority, in the synodal
response addressed to Eugenius at the second session. The argument from authority chiefly rested on the text from the 18th chapter of St. Matthew—"If thy
brother shall trespass against thee, and will not hear thee, and shall neglect to
hear the witnesses, tell it unto the Church; but if he neglect to hear the Church,
let him be unto thee as a heathen man and a publican. Verily I say unto you,
whatsoever ye shall bind on earth shall be bound in heaven, and whatsoever ye
shall loose on earth shall be loosed in heaven." Still the question remained, what
constituted the Church?

the causes, the obstinacy, and the contagiousness of spiritual rebellion. He was one of the few Italians who had penetrated the truth, so long manifest to the northern prelates, that a thorough reformation in *discipline* was necessary for the pre- servation of the Church. We cannot so well illustrate the condition of affairs at that period, as by citing some passages from the two celebrated epistles which he addressed from Basle to Eugenius*. " One great motive with me to join this coun- cil was the deformity and dissoluteness of the German clergy, on account of which the laity are immoderately irritated against the ecclesiastical state; so much so, as to make it matter of serious apprehension whether, if they be not reformed, the people will not rush, after the example of the Hussites, upon the whole clergy, as they publicly menace to do. Moreover, this deformity gives great audacity to the Bohemians, and great colouring to the errors of those who are loudest in their invec- tives against the baseness of the clergy: on which account, had a general council not been convoked at this place, it had been necessary to collect a provincial synod for the reform of the German clergy; since, in truth, if that clergy be not cor- rected, even though the heresy of Bohemia should be extin- guished, others would rise up in its place." . . . " If

---

* The first epistle begins in these words—"Multa me cogunt libere et intrepide loqui ad sanctitatem vestram; periculum videlicet eversionis fidei ac status eccle- siastici, et subtractionis obedientiæ a Sede Apostolica in iis partibus; denigratio quoque famæ ejusdem sanctitatis. Cogit et me charitas qua erga V. S. afficior et qua mihi affici scio. Ita enim opus est ut, intellecto discrimine, cautius rebus agendis postea consulatur." The following sentiment is worthy of the best ages of Christianity: " Et si dicat S. V. Habuimus guerram (bellum); ego respon- debo, quod etiam si guerræ adhuc durarent, etiam si essetis certi perdere Romam, et totum patrimonium ecclesiæ, potius subveniendum est fidei et animabus, pro quibus Dominus noster Jesus Christus mortuus est, quam arcibus et mœniis civi- tatum. *Carior est Christo una anima* quam non solum temporale ecclesiæ patri- monium, sed etiam cœlum et terra." . . Again, " Pro Deo, non permittat sibi V. S. talia persuaderi, *quia timeo dissidium in ecclesia Dei.* Vereor ne ad- venerit tempus, de quo dicit Apostolus, quod oportet primum ut fiat discessio." The fears of the cardinal were obviously directed, *not* to a second schism, a mere orthodox division of the Church, but to the absolute revolt of its children. But its destiny was not yet accomplished; one more century of turbulent, contested, and flagitious domination was yet required to fill the cup. But if the overflow did not take place at the time, it at least proceeded from the country, indicated by Julian.

you should dissolve this council, what will the whole world say when it shall learn the act? Will it not decide that the clergy is incorrigible, and desirous for ever to grovel in the filth of its own deformity? Many councils have been celebrated in our days, from which no reform has proceeded; the nations are expecting that some fruit should come from this. But if it is dissolved, all will exclaim that we laugh at God and man. As no hope of our correction will any longer be left, the laity will rush, like Hussites, upon us. This design is already publicly rumoured. The minds of men are pregnant; they are already beginning to vomit the poison intended for our destruction. They will suppose that they are offering a sacrifice to God when they shall murder or despoil the clergy. Sunk in general estimation into the depth of evil, these last will become odious to God and the world; and the very moderate respect which is now felt for them will entirely perish. This council is still some little restraint upon secular men; but as soon as they shall find their last hope fail them, they will let loose the reins of public persecution." . .
" Should the council be dissolved, the people of Germany, seeing themselves not only deserted but deluded by the Church, will join with the heretics, and hate us even more than they. Alas! how frightful will be the confusion! how certain the termination!" . . . "Already I behold the axe laid at the root. The tree is bending to its fall, and can resist no longer. And certainly, *though it could stand of itself, we ourselves should precipitate it to earth.*" . . . "Again, should a prorogation be proposed and a transfer of place, to the end that in the presence of your holiness greater blessings may be accomplished, no man living will believe it." . . "We have been deluded (they say) in the council of Sienna: so it is again in this: legates have been sent out, bulls have been issued; nevertheless, a change in the place is now sought, and a delay in the time. What better hope will there be then?" . . "Most blessed father, believe me, the scandals which I have mentioned will not be removed by this delay. Let us ask the heretics, whether they will delay for a year and a half the dissemination of their virulence? Let us ask those who are scandalized at the

deformity of the clergy, if they will for so long *delay* their indignation ?   Not a day passes in which some heresy does not
sprout forth ; not a day in which they do not seduce or oppress
some Catholics ; they do not lose the smallest moment of time.
There is not a day in which new scandals do not arise from
the depravity of the clergy ; yet all measures for their remedy
are procrastinated !   Let us do what can be done now.   Let
the rest be reserved for this *year and a half.*   For I have
great fears that, before the end of the year and a half, unless
means be taken to prevent it, the greater part of the clergy of
Germany will be in desolation.   It is certain that, if the word
should be once spread through Germany that the council is
dissolved, the whole body of the clergy would be consigned to
plunder." . . . " But I hear that some are apprehensive lest the
temporalities should be taken away from the Church by this
council.   A strange notion !   Though, if this council did not
consist of ecclesiastics, there might be some question on the
subject.   But where shall we find the ecclesiastic who would
consent to such a project ? not only from its injustice, but from
the loss the body would sustain from it.   And where the layman ? there are none, or next to none.   And if some princes
should haply send their ambassadors, they will send for the
most part ecclesiastics who would in no wise consent.   Even
the few laymen who will be present will not be admitted to
vote on matters strictly ecclesiastical ; and I scarcely think
that there will be, upon the whole, ten secular lords present,
and perhaps not half so many.   But if we dismiss the council,
the laity will then come and take our temporalities indeed.
When God wishes to inflict any misfortune upon any people,
he first so disposes that their dangers shall not be perceived
nor understood.   And such is now the condition of ecclesiastics ; they are not blind, but worse than blind ; they see the
flame before them, and rush headlong into it." . . " Within these
few last days I have received intelligence which should tend
still further to divert you from dissolving the council.   The
prelates of France have assembled at Bourges, and, after long
and scrupulous investigation, have decided that this council is
not only legitimate, but must also of necessity be celebrated

both in this place and at this time; and so the French clergy
is about to join it. The reasons which have moved them to
this were sent at the same time, and have been forwarded to
your holiness. Why then do you longer delay? You have
striven with all your power, by messages, letters, and various
other expedients, to keep the clergy away; you have struggled
with your whole force utterly to destroy this council. Nevertheless, as you see, it swells and increases day by day, and the
more severe the prohibition, the more ardent is the opposite
impulse. Tell me now—is not this to resist the will of God?
Why do you provoke the Church to indignation? Why do
you irritate the Christian people? Condescend, I implore you,
so to act, as to secure for yourself the love and good will, and
not the hatred, of mankind."

The eloquent expressions of reason and truth were wasted
upon the sordid soul of Eugenius. He persisted in measures
of opposition; they were met by a process of citation on the
part of the council; and this was retorted by a bull of dissolution; both were equally ineffectual. At length, on the 12th
of July, 1433, the fathers proceeded one step farther; they
suspended the pontiff from his dignity, and prohibited all
Christians from paying him obedience. Eugenius, in the plenitude of his own power, annulled their decree; and this noisy
but innocuous altercation might have continued for some time
longer, without any advantage or any honour to either party,
had not some accidental circumstances interrupted it. The
political enterprises of the pope had not been more happily
conducted than his ecclesiastical measures. During the winter
of 1433 he was threatened by a complication of disasters. The
Colonna attacked him at home; the duke of Milan assailed
him from abroad; his subjects were universally discontented,
and their menaces resounded in his capital; while Sigismond
had declared loudly in favour of the council, and had even
countenanced it by his presence. Under these circumstances,
Eugenius suddenly lowered his pretensions, and withdrew his
opposition. The offensive bulls were revoked; and under the
plea of co-operating with the council, and with the design of
embarrassing it, he sent two legates to Basle to represent his
authority.

This hollow reconciliation took place early in 1434 ; and as the difficulties of the pope increased during the following spring, so far as to oblige him to fly from his capital and take refuge at Florence, the fathers were at length enabled to turn with some reviving hopes to the subject of reformation.

Nineteen* sessions, during four invaluable years, had already been consumed without any benefit either to the pope, the council, or the Church.   In the twentieth, which did not meet until January 23, 1435, some edicts were at length published for the repression of ecclesiastical abuses ; and during the fourteen months which followed, other canons were enacted to the same end.   Their substance may be expressed in very few lines.   (1.) Severe penalties were proclaimed against concubinary clergy, including all who, having suspicious women in their service, had disregarded the command of the superior to dismiss them.   (2.) It was prohibited (in the name of the Holy Spirit) to pay any fees in the court of Rome, or elsewhere, for confirmation of elections, for admissions, postulations, or presentations ; for provision, collation, disposition, &c. &c., by laymen ; for institution, installation, or investiture, in cathedral or metropolitan churches or monasteries, in dignities, benefices, or other ecclesiastical offices ; for holy orders, for benedictions, or concessions of the pallium ; for bulls, for the seal, for common annates, *servitia minuta*, first-fruits, deports †, or on any other colour or pretext.   The exaction,

Articles of Reformation.

---

* We should, perhaps, mention that, in the nineteenth session, the council renewed the ancient decrees about the conversion and *excommunication* of Jews, and the necessary distinction in their dress and residence ; and also on the establishment of oriental professorships in the various universities—the last in confirmation of a lifeless canon of the council of Vienne.   Previously, too,—in the twelfth session—a general decree had been promulgated with a view to restore episcopal *elections* to their original form, and to deprive the pope of reservations ; but it was so general, that little practical effect could be expected from it.

† (1.) The *deport* was the year's income of vacant cures paid to the pope or bishop.   It was a tax instituted by the popes of Avignon, under the pretext of holy wars.   (2.) The *grace expectative* was the pope's assurance of presentation to a particular benefice when it should become vacant.   This right originated in simple recommendation ; afterwards it changed into command.   To the first letters, called monitory, letters preceptory were added ; and when it was necessary, letters executory were also addressed to some papal commissioners, whose duty it became to compel the Ordinary to present, on pain of excommunication.   This procedure

Deport.

Grace expectative.

payment, or promise, of such fees were forbidden under the
penalties of simony. "And even (it was enacted), which
may God prohibit, if the Roman pontiff himself, who is bound
more than any other to observe the holy canons, should throw
scandal on the Church by violating, in any way, this decree,
he shall be brought to trial before a general council." This
passed in the twenty-first session (June 9, 1435); and it is
curious to observe the desperate exertions with which the pope
and his legates and inferior myrmidons put every resource of
craft and intrigue into action, in order to prevent, to annul, or
to neutralize this measure. But they were defeated by the
firmness of the majority of the council in a good cause; and if
many more such triumphs had been obtained by the same
party—if many more such restrictions on the worst excesses of
Rome had been imposed and enforced, her supremacy over the
Catholic Church had not so speedily passed away from her.

(3.) The twenty-third session (March 25, 1436) regulated
the election of the pope, and confirmed the decree of the thirty-
ninth session of Constance, which had prescribed a formula of
faith, to be approved on oath, on the day of election. The
oath was to be renewed every year on the anniversary of the
election. It proceeded to moderate the nepotism of the pontiffs,—so far, at least, as to confine their *secular* favours—the
dukedoms, marquisates, captaincies, governorships, and other
offices which were at their disposal as temporal monarchs—to
the second degree of relationship. New laws were also published for the better constitution of the Sacred College, which

Reserva-
tion.

gradually gained ground from the twelfth age. (3.) The *reservation* was a declaration, by which the pope pretended to appoint to a benefice, when it should
become vacant, with prohibition to the chapter to elect, or the ordinary to collate.
From special, the popes proceeded to *general* reservations; from general to universal; at least John XXII. reserved, by a single edict, all the cathedrals in
Christendom. This usurpation was attacked with success both at Pisa, Constance,
and Basle; and the rights which the French Church acquired in that matter at
Basle, passed into the Pragmatic Sanction, and thence, with some modification,
into the Concordat. The council of Trent abolished reservations entirely. The
practice is traced as high as Innocent III.... Both the second and third of these
were contrary to the canons of the third Lateran council, held by Alexander III.
in 1179, which published a general prohibition against all dispositions of benefices
previous to vacancy.—Fleury, Institut. au Droit Eccles., p. ii., ch. xv.

differed in very trifling, if in any, respects from the enactments of Constance on the same subject. The legislation of Basle also descended to some less important subjects : it consulted the delicacy of " timorous consciences " by specifying the degree of obedience due to *general* sentences of excommunication ; it restrained the punishment of interdicts to the offences of the city or its government: any sins of an individual citizen were held insufficient to provoke that indiscriminate chastisement. It prohibited appeals, while the causes were yet pending ; it condemned the spectacles which took place in the churches on particular festivals ; it promulgated decrees for the greater solemnity of the divine offices, and for the more decorous dress and deportment of the officiating ministers.

Such is the substance of the enactments of the council of Basle for the reform of the Church. It is true that, at a much later period of its continuance, it published, in the thirty-first session (January 24, 1438), two decrees,—the one for the limitation of *appeals* to Rome, the other to revoke and prohibit expectative graces, and subject the *provisions* of the pope to certain specified restrictions ; but these, even had they been very fundamental improvements, were passed at a period when the legitimacy of the council itself was much disputed, and probably they never acquired general authority. Those which we have above enumerated may be considered as comprising all that the assembled fathers really accomplished, during deliberations which continued, at least nominally, through the space of nearly twelve years.

The two legates, to whom the pontifical interests had been intrusted by Eugenius, followed with abundant zeal and capacity their private instructions. No device which seemed calculated to thwart the progress of reform had been neglected by them. Every objection had been magnified into a difficulty, every difficulty had been swelled into an insurmountable impediment. The meanest sophistry had been confronted with the boldest reason ; artifice, fraud, seduction had been arrayed against upright purposes and generous principles*; delays had

Conduct of the Pope's Legates.

---

* " Scitis vosmetipsi quoties hæ vobis *dilationes* nocuerint, quotiesque paucorum mora dierum longissimum traxit spatium ; qui jam octavum annum in dila-

been created, falsehoods propagated, subterfuges invented, and all that minute machinery set in motion, which is at all times employed in the defence of corrupt systems, by those who find their profit in the corruption *. To the honour of the re-formers of Basle be it recorded, that the intrigues which were eternally in operation to divide or to degrade them were ineffi-cient; the firmness of those respectable ecclesiastics †, their intelligence and their honesty reflected upon the Catholic Church a splendid gleam of glory in the moment of her danger and tribulation ; and their perseverance might still have wrought some great advantage, had not a new circumstance arisen to foil it.

Final breach be-tween the Pope and the Coun-cil.

The conciliation of the Greek Church was one of the avowed objects of the council ; and as the deputies were expected from the East to confer on that subject, their convenience and in-clinations as to the *place* of conference required some attention : both (it was justly said) would be best consulted by substi-tuting for Basle some city in Italy. It was in vain that the council then proposed Avignon or Savoy; the pope would listen to no such compromise, but pressed the superior advantages of an Italian city. At the same time both parties had opened

tionibus agitis, semper dilationes ex dilationibus vidistis emergere,"—*Cardinalis Arelatensis*, ap. Æn. Sylv. de Gest. Basil. Concil.

* "Quis est qui existimet Romanum pontificem ad sui emendationem con-cilium conjugare ? Nempe ut peccant homines, sic etiam impunè peccare volunt." Æneas Sylv. de Gest. Basil. Conc. l. i., p. 20.

† The expressions of Æneas Sylvius almost rise into eloquence. " Ubinam gentium talis patrum est chorus, ubi tantum scientiæ lumen, ubi prudentia, ubi bonitas est, quæ nomen patrum æquare virtutibus queat ? Oh integerrimam fra-ternitatem ! oh verum orbis terrarum Senatum ! Quam pulchra, quam suavis, quam devota res fuit, hìc celebrantes episcopos, illic orantes abbates, alibi vero doctores divinas legentes historias audire ! .... et unum ad lumen candelæ scri-bentem cernere, alium vero grande aliquid meditantem intueri.... Illic cum ex-euntem cella aut Christianum aut alium quempiam ex antiquioribus vidisses, non alium certe videre putasses, quam vel magnum Antonium, vel Paulum simplicem ; et illum sane Hilarioni, illum Paphnutio, illum Amoni æquiparasses. Plus autem hoc in loco quam in Antoniana solitudine reperisses, siquidem Hieronymo etiam et Augustino obviasses, quorum litteræ in conclavi fuerunt, in eremo non fuerunt.... Custodiebatur inter dominos magna charitas, inter famulos bona dilectio, inter utrosque optimum silentium," &c. &c. De Gestis Basil. Concil., lib. ii., p. 57. It should be mentioned that this description is not general, but relates only to the fathers who constituted the conclave for the election of the new pope—the élite of the council,

negotiations at Constantinople; and the contests which had been enacted at Basle were repeated, with a different result, before the patriarch and the emperor. In that refined court the superior tactics of the papal party prevailed; and in the intestine commotions of the hierarchy of the West, the Oriental autocrat listened more partially to the monarch than to the senate of the Church. Besides, while his emissaries were thus advancing his views abroad, the pope's domestic embarrassments had gradually diminished, and with them his fears and his prudence. Thus elated, he determined again to engage with the council in open warfare. Accordingly we observe that, about the twenty-third and twenty-fourth sessions, his legates assumed a higher tone than formerly: on the other hand, the council breathed nothing but indignation and defiance; and thus, after a short and feverish suspension, the former quarrels were renewed, and not even the semblance of concord was ever afterwards restored.

The second contest began nearly where the first had ended. The pope manœuvred to transfer the council to Italy. The council cited the pope to Basle (July 31, 1437), to answer for his vexatious opposition to the reform of the Church. And the pope, in that plenitude of power to which he had never formally abandoned his pretensions, declared the council transferred to Ferrara. In the 28th session (Oct. 1, 1437), Eugenius was convicted of contumacy; and on the 10th of the January following, he celebrated, in defiance of the sentence, the first session of the council of Ferrara. On that occasion he solemnly annulled every future act of the assembly at Basle, excepting only such as should have reference to the troubles of Bohemia.

On the eve of the opening of the Council of Ferrara, Cardinal Julian, whose fidelity to the body over which he presided, and earnestness in the discharge of that office, had never been questioned, suddenly departed from Basle, and passed over to the party of the pope. The defection of so considerable a person, at so dangerous a crisis, might naturally have shaken the firmness of the fathers; and we can also readily believe that, after Cesarini had taken his resolution, he exerted his great

Desertion of Cardinal Julian.

talents to induce as many as he could influence to follow him. It remains however as a memorable fact, that, among the numerous prelates assembled at Basle, four only were persuaded to imitate the example of their president; nor does it appear that, even after the arrival of the Greeks in Italy, any one bishop, or doctor, or dignified ecclesiastic deserted the cause in which he had first engaged. The sovereigns of Europe remained equally firm, and the king of France even prohibited his subjects from joining the assembly at Ferrara.

Questions on the legitimacy of the Council. It is almost needless to say, that the legitimacy of the Council of Basle has been a subject of dispute among Roman Catholic writers, and that they have differed, according to the diversity of their opinions on the extent and nature of papal supremacy. It has been commonly designated the *Acephalous* Council; and some have maintained that its authority expired as early as the tenth session; but even Bellarmine allows that its decrees were binding on the Church, until it commenced its deliberations respecting the *deposition* of the pope. This last is the more general opinion even among the Transalpine divines —of whom none have been found so rash and inconsistent as to dispute its canonical convocation and origin. If it be admitted then, thus generally, that during those few sessions which it devoted to the reform of the Church it was a true and infallible council, the controversy respecting the sessions which followed can have little importance in the eyes of the historian; since they were consumed in an obstinate contest with a perverse pontiff, without producing any lasting alteration either in the principles or administration of the government of the Church.

We shall not pursue that contest into any detail. The Cardinal Archbishop of Arles, who was born in France near the borders of Savoy, was elected, no unworthy successor to the chair of Cesarini *. Eugenius was presently " superseded

---

* " Vir omnium constantissimus et *ad gubernationem Generalium Conciliorum natus.*" Æn. Sylv. Comment. de Gestis Basil. Conc., lib. i. p. 25. This particular commendation is explained by subsequent expressions. We shall select two of a very different character. (1.) The Cardinal, on an important occasion, fearing to be left in a minority, out-manœuvred the opposition, and prorogued the

from all jurisdiction;" but it was not until the middle of April,
1439, that the council published its celebrated "Eight Propositions" against that pontiff, as a measure preparatory to his
deposition.   On this occasion great dissensions arose; the prelates of Spain combined almost unanimously with the Italian
party; and the opposition was powerfully conducted by the
Archbishop of Palermo (Panormus or Panormitanus*,) who
had recently made the sacrifice of his private principles to the
will of his sovereign.   His talents and his eloquence were ad-
mired by all; his sophistry influenced the weak or the waver-
ing; and when the Fathers next assembled for the resumption
of the debate, the benches of the prelates were almost deserted;
—of the multitudes collected at Basle, scarcely twenty mitred
heads could be numbered in that congregation †.   The cardi-

Council. His friends were delighted—"Alii quidem eum, alii vestimentorum
fimbrias, deosculabantur, secutique ipsum plurimi, prudentiam ejus magnopere
commendabant, qui, licet origine esset Gallicus, Italos tamen hac die summa
hominis astutia, superasset." Ibid. p. 37. (2.) A violent pestilence broke out at
Basle, and swept away some distinguished members of the council. Every one
supplicated the cardinal to retire into the country; all his domestics, all his
friends, joined with one voice in the same entreaty—"Quid agis, spectate Pater !
fuge hunc saltem lunæ defectum, salva tuum caput, quo salvo salvamur omnes;
quo etiam pereunte omnes perimus. Quod si te pestis opprimat, ad quem confu-
giemus? quis nos reget? quis ductor hujus fidelis exercitus erit ? Jam tuam
Cameram irrepsit virus, jam Secretarius tuus, jamque Cubicularius tuus mortem
obiit. Considera discrimen, salva teipsum et nos...." Sed neque illum preces
neque domesticorum funera flectere potuerunt, volentem potius cum vitæ periculo
salvare concilium, quam cum periculo concilii salvare vitam. *Sciebat enim, quoniam, se recedente, pauci remansissent, facileque committi fraus in ejus absentia po-
tuisset.* Ibid. lib. ii. p. 48. The man, who united more than Italian subtlety
with the courage and self-devotion here discovered, was undoubtedly born to rule
his fellow-creatures.

* His speech is reported in the Commentaries of the *then* admirable advocate
for the independence of the Church, Æneas Sylvius. His work is chiefly employed on those Acts of the Council, which more immediately preceded the election of Felix V. Panormitanus urged, among other things, that the pope's error
in dissolving the Council was not a heresy ; since, though the superiority of the
General Council was a truth, it was not an article of faith—so that the council
had not sufficient ground for deposing Eugenius. This seemed unpardonable
sophistry to Æneas Sylvius—to Pope Pius II. it probably appeared a very feeble
defence of papal rights.

† The Council of Basle was composed, besides numerous prelates and abbots,
of a great multitude of inferior clergy, who appear to have formed the majority;
and we observe, from the narrative of Æneas Sylvius, that, during the violent
debates which preceded the deposition of Eugenius, the prelates were for the most

nal of Arles was prepared for this defection; and he had devised a remedy, suited no less to the character of the declining days of Papacy, than of its most prosperous. He commanded the relics of all the saints in the city to be brought from their sanctuaries, to be carried by the priests to the place of assembly, and deposited by their hands in the vacant seats of the bishops. At this spectacle (says Æneas Sylvius), and on the invocation of the Holy Spirit, the multitudes present were moved by an extraordinary impulse of devotion, which overflowed in tears. And throughout the whole Church there was a soft and affectionate bewailing of pious men, who implored in sorrow the divine assistance, and deeply supplicated the Omnipotent God to give aid to the Church whose children they were. The session (the thirty-third) was then peacefully dissolved ; but in that which followed (June 25th, 1439) the contested measure was carried; and, after eight years of open, or disguised hostility, Eugenius IV. was at length deposed.

Election of Felix V. and dissolution of the Council.

On the 5th of November following, Amadeus, Duke of Savoy, was elected to the See thus vacated, and assumed the name of Felix V. But as Eugenius retained, without any defection, the obedience of Italy and some other countries, the success of the anti-papal party had no other effect than to create a second schism. Among the sovereigns of Europe, the most powerful, though ill affected to Eugenius were far from approving the violent proceedings of the council; and the German, as well as the French court became more distant and guarded in its intercourse with the fathers of Basle; while

part on the side of Panormitanus, that is, of the pope, and the inferior orders on the other. In the session (the thirty-third) described in the text, " Nullus Arragonensium prælatorum interfuit, nullusque omnino ex tota Hispania. Ex Italia soli Grossitanus Episcopus et Abbas de Dona. Doctores autem et cæteri inferiores magno in numero Arragonenses fuerunt, et omnes fere, qui aderant, ex Italia Hispaniaque (*nec enim inferiores, sicut Prælati, principem timuerunt*). *Maximaque* tunc Arragonensium et Cathelanorum *virtus in inferioribus emicuit,* qui sese minime necessitati ecclesiæ denegarunt." " Si enim episcopi haud multi erant, plena tamen omnia fuerunt subsellia procuratoribus episcoporum, archidiaconis, præpositis, prioribus, presbyteris et divini et *humani juris doctoribus,* quos aut quadringentos aut certe plures esse dijudicavi, &c." This republican constitution of the council must, indeed, have rendered it peculiarly obnoxious to the prejudices of a monastic pope.—Comment. Æn. Sylvii, l. ii. p. 43.

the inferior princes appear to have recognized or rejected the one pope or the other, as suited the seeming policy of the moment. And this confusion continued with little interruption until May, 1443, when the council celebrated its forty-fifth and last session, It then dissolved itself—or rather transferred its (nominal) sittings to Lyons or Lausanne; while the rival assembly, which was still lingering at Florence, withdrew, by a simultaneous secession, to Rome.

Felix V. maintained his scanty court, and the faint show of pontifical majesty, at Lausanne; and though the sovereigns both of France and Germany made some exertions to remove the schism, it continued until the death of Eugenius in 1447. Nicholas V. succeeded; and the more general recognition which he received from the courts of Europe, as well as his more popular reputation, induced Felix, whose ambition was destitute of selfishness, as his character was moderate and virtuous, to negotiate respecting the cession of his dignity. Certain conditions were accordingly proposed and accepted, and in the year 1449, the creature of the Council of Basle for ever resigned his claims on the chair of St. Peter. The happy escape from this second peril, which menaced the unity of the Church, filled the people with universal joy; the errors of the Hussites and the scandals of the clergy were for the moment forgotten; and everywhere, after the fashion of the times, a commemorative verse was chanted,— *Nicholas V.*

Cession of Felix.

Fulsit lux mundo; cessit Felix Nicolao.

Though the general measures of reformation, published by the Council of Basle, were very inadequate to the necessities of the Church, even in the eyes of an orthodox reformer, yet by concurrence with some national assemblies held in Germany, and especially in France, they became instrumental in improving the ecclesiastical government and discipline in both those countries. In Germany, a project, which had been prepared at Nuremburg, in 1438, having failed to obtain the approbation either of the Council or the Pope, a Diet was opened at Mayence in the March of the year following. The deputies from Basle, and some emissaries of Eugenius were present; and the Assembly, after some deliberation, received all the general *Diet of Mayence.*

decrees of the Council *. We do not learn, however, that any means were taken to give them efficacy, or to establish them as the permanent and living code of the German Church. At any rate, its independence was soon afterwards betrayed by Frederic III. ; and in the negotiations between the empire and the Holy See, which were conducted by his secretary, Æneas Sylvius, that accomplished politician was less faithful to the interests which he thus represented, than to those over which he was destined hereafter to preside. The concordats, arranged at Aschaffenburg in 1448, resigned most of the advantages which the Germans had derived from the proceedings at Basle, and left the papal rights nearly in the situation in which they had been placed by Martin V. †

Council of Bourges, 1438 A.D. The French were at the same time conducting their national exertions with greater method and decision, and with a much better prospect of permanent effect. The first meeting of their prelates at Bourges was contemporary with that of the Council of Basle. Some useful resolutions were then passed. But the Grand Assembly, which fixed the liberties of the Gallican Church, was held in the same city in the year 1438. It was convoked by Charles VII., who presided in person ; it was thronged by his most illustrious subjects, secular as well as ecclesiastic ; and it was attended by the authorized legates both of Eugenius and the council. The result of their deliberations was the celebrated Pragmatic Sanction ‡, the great bulwark of the national Church against the usurpations of Rome—that to which the French divines afterwards clung with so much resolution and tenacity, even after it had been betrayed to the enemy by an interested monarch.

---

* The Diet of Mayence withheld its sanction from those decrees which were directly levelled against Eugenius.

† The Annates, the great bone of contention, were retained in substance by the pope. Instead of the arbitrary reservation of benefices, he obtained the positive right of collation during six alternate months of every year. Episcopal elections were restored to the chapters—the pope only nominating in case of translation, or of a person, canonically disqualified, being presented for confirmation.— See Hallam, Middle Ages, chap. vii.

‡ Pragmatic sanction was a general term for all important ordinances of Church or State—those, perhaps, more properly which were enacted in public assemblies, with the counsel of eminent jurisconsults, or *Pragmatici*.

The Gallican Liberties, while they embraced a number of *Gallican Liberties.* particular provisions, were founded on two grand principles :— (1.) That the pope has no authority in the kingdom of France over anything concerning temporals. (2.) That, though the pope is acknowledged as sovereign lord in spirituals, his power even in these is restricted and controlled by the canons and regulations of the ancient councils of the Church *, received in this kingdom.

The articles constituting the Pragmatic Sanction were chiefly *The Pragmatic Sanction.* founded on the decrees of the twentieth, twenty-first, and twenty-third sessions of the Council of Basle. Some of these were, indeed, modified, with a view to accommodate them to the peculiar circumstances of the country, not (as was expressly declared) from any disrespect to the authority of that assembly; but the greater part were at once adopted into the Church of France, and ardently embraced by the clergy and the nation. Yet can it scarcely be necessary to remind the reader that most of the abuses thus removed concerned no more vital question than the *patronage* of the Church—that the object of most of those vaunted resolutions was only to relieve the clergy (and, to a certain extent, the people of France) from the *contributions* which, under a thousand names and pretexts, were exacted by the apostolical chancery; that the avarice of the Holy See was the most unpopular among its vices; and that mere pecuniary motives were at the bottom of more than half the grievances which alienated its children from it †.

---

* "La première est, Que les Papes ne peuvent rien commander ni ordonner, soit en général soit en particulier, de ce qui concerne les choses temporelles és pays et terres de l'obeyssance et souveraineté du Roy Tres-Chrestien : et s'ils y commandent ou statuent quelque chose, les sujets du Roy, encores qu'ils fussent clercs, ne sont tenus pour obeyr pour ce regard.

"La seconde, Qu'encores que le Pape soit reconnu pour suzerain és choses spirituelles ; toutefois en France la puissance absolue et infinie n'a point de lieu, mais est retenue et bornée par les canons et règles des anciens conciles de l'Eglise réceus en ce royaume. Et in hoc maximè consistit Libertas Ecclesiæ Gallicanæ." See Commentaire sur le Traité des Lib. de l'Eglise Gall. de Pierre Pithov. Paris, 1652.

† The Pragmatic Sanction consisted of twenty-three articles, several of which regarded the police of cathedral churches, the celebration of the divine offices, and other matters not connected with papal prerogatives. There are also some

We shall not here relate the exertions which were made by Pius II. to subvert the principles, of which, as Æneas Sylvius, he had been the warmest advocate, and to overthrow the liberties which his own hand had planted. The nominal repeal of the Pragmatic Sanction by Louis XI. was never ratified by his subjects, nor effected in defiance of their dissent; and the articles which were enacted at Bourges continued for the most part in force until the reign of Francis I. The consequence was, that the French people, being in a great degree sheltered from the extortions of Rome, were less disposed to question her general rights, and to rebel against her spiritual prerogatives. The most sordid and disgusting particulars of her system were not so commonly presented to their view. A smaller contribution, indeed, flowed into her treasuries, and her emissaries were more sparingly scattered in that country; but her name was less odious, as her vices were less obtrusive. And while in Germany the re-establishment of the papal despotism, with all its train of annates, reservations, and indulgences, produced, by an inevitable necessity, the violent revolt and final independence of the oppressed, so the Catholics of France submitted with less reluctance to her mitigated sway.

Periodical Meeting of General Councils.   The most important decree promulgated at Constance was, perhaps, that which fixed the periodical meeting of General Councils; for it was in vain to have established the supremacy of those assemblies, unless continual opportunities were afforded them for its exercise. The spirit of Rome was invariable, and in perpetual action; it could not be counteracted and restrained, unless by frequent collision with the restraining body. The wisest resolutions, unless enforced by the constant protection of the power which created them, would be neutralized or crushed in the pontifical grasp. The justice of this apprehension was proved by the fate of the very decree of which we are now

few which are so connected, which have yet no reference to patronage—they respect the periodical assembly, and the superior authority, of General Councils, and the number of the Sacred College. But elections, reservations, collections, expectative graces, and annates formed, after all, the burden of the grievances; and to those we may fairly add appeals to the court of Rome, which were now become only an additional method of raising money.—See Histoire de l'Orig. de la Pragm. Sanct., &c., par Pierre Pithov.

speaking. It was perseveringly eluded by the popes who followed, and with so much success, that no other General Council
was convoked before the end of the century. After the separation of the fathers of Basle, the repose and prerogatives of
the pontiffs were never seriously disturbed until the destined
season at length arrived, in which they were invaded by a
harsher voice and a far ruder hand.

It has been made a question among ecclesiastical writers,
whether the decennial meetings of those bodies, as decreed at
Constance, would have conferred benefit or the contrary on the
Roman Catholic Church. It is argued on the one hand, that
they presented the only check upon the excesses of the Roman
court, which were hurrying the Church to its destruction ; that
in the progressive light and information of the age, an absolute
spiritual despotism could not possibly endure much longer,
and that the monarchy of the Church could only hope for stability through an infusion of the popular principle : since even
the clergy themselves were no longer well affected towards an
unlimited government : that many abuses in morals and discipline, which were continually growing up, were most effectually
corrected by the authority of Councils.

On the other hand, it is disputed whether the benefits derived
from the three assemblies which had taken place were, in fact,
so very substantial ? Whether they were at all proportionate
to the weighty machinery which was moved to produce them ?
Whether the non-residence of so many prelates and other
clergy, during such long periods, was not a new evil of immense importance ? Whether those divisions and passionate
contests among spiritual ministers, which seemed the necessary
fruit of general councils, did not cast as many scandals on the
Church as those which were removed ? Whether the immediate danger of a positive schism, which had actually been
occasioned by the proceedings at Basle, did not at least counterbalance those remote perils, which timely remedies might
(or might not perhaps) have averted ?

To a Protestant, impartially comparing these considerations, Observa-
it is, in the first place, obvious, that a cordial co-operation tions.
between an enlightened pope and a body of intelligent eccle-

siastics, for the single purpose of correcting abuses in government and discipline, and otherwise modifying the system by
seasonable alterations, would have afforded the best human
probability of preserving the papal supremacy undisputed, and
deferring the hour of a more perfect reformation.   But on the
other hand, it is equally manifest that, as the court of Rome
was at that time constituted, so generous a co-operation, so
provident a sacrifice of instant profit for future security, could
not possibly have formed the policy of the Vatican.   Those
who have long been in possession of usurped prerogatives have
seldom the courage, when the moment of retribution ap-
proaches, to concede a part, though they should thereby save
the rest ; they cling pertinaciously to their meanest acquisitions
until the hand of the reformer is at length provoked to resume
the whole.   It was thus with the bishops of Rome : educated
in a profligate court, and in the narrowest principles, they
commonly obtained their elevation by intrigue or bribery.   The
pontifical dignity was itself beset by seductions sufficient to
corrupt the most generous mind.   So that it was in vain to
look to Rome for any other policy than the most contracted
and the most selfish.

   If these conclusions be true, the periodical meetings of General
Councils would have only introduced periodical convulsions and
schisms.   And, although some partial benefits would no doubt
have proceeded from their deliberations, they would scarcely
have prolonged the duration of a system of which unity was a
necessary characteristic.   The *manner* of its destruction might,
indeed, have been different ; it might have been torn in pieces
by intestine discord, instead of sinking before the impulse from
without.   But its doom was irrevocably sealed ; and the seeds
of dissolution were too amply sown in the very vitals of the
papal Church to admit of any effectual reformation.

General principles of the Councils of Constance and Basle.
   Again ; however justly we may applaud the reforming projects of the fathers of Constance and Basle, as indicating some
consciousness of shame or of danger, some foresight, at least,
if not some virtue, yet it is certain that their general principles
were in no respect more moderate than those of the Vatican.
We have already observed how the former of those councils,

after investing itself with all the spiritual attributes and authority of the Church, immediately overstepped the boundary *,
and drew, like the popes whom it superseded, the temporal
sword.   But we have still to describe the most arbitrary and
iniquitous act of the same assembly.   The Holy Fathers, be it
recollected, had met for the reformation of their Church.   The
word was perpetually on their lips, and they denounced, with
unsparing vehemence, some of the corruptions of their own
system.   In the midst of them were two men of learning,
genius, integrity, piety, who had intrusted their personal safety
to the faith of the council, John Huss and Jerome of Prague;
and these, too, were reformers.   But it happened that *they* had
taken a different view of the condition and exigencies of the
Church; and while the boldest projects of the wisest among
the orthodox were confined to matters of patronage, discipline,
ceremony, the hand of the Bohemians had probed a deeper
wound; they disputed, if not the doctrinal purity †, at least
the spiritual omnipotence of the Church.   Those daring innovators had crossed the line which separated reformation from
heresy — and they had their recompense.   In the clamour
which was raised against them all parties joined as with one
voice: divided on all other questions, contending about all
other principles, the grand universal assembly was united, from
Gerson himself down to the meanest Italian papal minion, in
common detestation of the heresy, in implacable rage against
its authors.   Those venerable martyrs were imprisoned, arraigned, condemned; and then by the command, and in the
presence of the majestic *senate* of the Church, the deposer of
popes, the uprooter of corruption, the reformer of Christ's holy
Communion—they were deliberately consigned to the flames.
Is there any act recorded in the blood-stained annals of the
popes more foul and merciless than that?   More than this.
The guilt of the murder was enhanced by perfidy; and for the

---

* If the fathers of Constance offended the King of France by the orders which
they issued respecting the safe-conduct of Sigismond in his journey to Spain, so
did those of Basle irritate the princes of Germany by an assumption of temporal
authority; and this was their great mistake.

† See the following Chapter.

purpose of justifying this last offence (for the former, being
founded on the established Church principles, required no
apology) they added to those principles another, not less flagitious than any of those already recognized—"that neither
faith nor promise, by natural, divine, or human law, was to be
observed to the prejudice of the Catholic religion *." Let us
here recollect that this maxim did not proceed from the caprice
of an arbitrary individual, and a pope—for so it would scarcely
have claimed our serious notice—but from the considerate
resolution of a very numerous assembly, which embodied
almost all the learning, wisdom, and moderation of the Roman
Catholic Church.

Various edicts of the Council of Basle. General Councils, claiming to act under the immediate influence of the Holy Spirit, were consequently infallible, as well
as impeccable. We shall, therefore, mention one or two of the
subjects to which their unerring judgment was directed. In
the July of 1434, the council of Basle confirmed a bull, previously published by Eugenius IV., respecting the veneration
due to the sacrament of the Eucharist, and the indulgences
granted at the Feast of the Holy Sacrament; with an order for
its universal observance in the Church. The thirty-sixth
session (Sept. 17, 1439) of the same assembly was occupied in
drawing up a decree in favour of the Immaculate Conception
of the Holy Virgin †. This article of faith was solemnly enjoined to all good Catholics; and an universal festival was
instituted in its honour, " according to the custom of the

* ' Cum tamen dictus Johannes Huss, fidem orthodoxam pertiuaciter impug-
nans, se ab omni conductu et privilegio reddiderit alienum, nec aliqua sibi fides
aut promissio de jure naturali, divino vel humano, fuerit in prejudiciem Catholicæ
fidei observanda: idcirco dicta sancta synodus declarat, &c.' The words are
cited by Hallam (Middle Ages, chap. vii.), without suspicion. We find it asserted,
however, by Roman Catholics, that they exist in no MS. except that in the Imperial Library at Vienna; and that even there the formal signatures attached to
the other articles are not subscribed to this; hence they infer its spuriousness.
We should remark that Von der Hardt has published it (tom. iv., p. 521) without
any expression of doubt.

† That is, that the Holy Virgin was preserved in her conception from the stain
of original sin. We observe that bachelors in theology, and others in the university of Paris, were compelled to subscribe, on oath, to their belief in this doctrine. In Spain it is considered an essential part of the Catholic faith at this
moment.

Roman Church." Two years afterwards, at their forty-third meeting, the same fathers confirmed, after a very long delibe- ration, the feast of the *visitation* of the Holy Virgin. They enacted that it should be celebrated throughout the whole Church by all the faithful; and they accorded to those who should assist at matins, at the processions, at the sermon, at mass, at the first and at the second vespers, a hundred days of indulgences for each of those offices. At the same time, while they were thus extending the reign of superstition over their obedient children, they were contesting the double communion with the Bohemian rebels, and refusing every concession to reason and to scripture, excepting such * as was extorted from them by force. Some individuals must certainly have existed among them who had penetrated the *inward* depravity of their system and saw the tottering ground on which it stood; but they believed, no doubt, that things would continue to be as they had been: they were blind to the slow but irresistible progress of inquiry and knowledge.

From the days of St. Bernard to those of Bossuet the extir- pation of heresy formed a part or an object† of every scheme of Church reform proposed by churchmen. The principle of toleration was unknown in the ecclesiastical policy; it may have guided the private practice of many enlightened indivi- duals, but it was never inscribed in the code of the Church. Those very Councils from whose generous professions and

Limits of the good effects of General Councils.

---

* The concession of the council respecting the double communion amounted, at last, only to this, that whether the sacrament was administered in one kind or in both, it was still useful to communicants—" for there could be no doubt that Christ was entire in either element ; and that the custom of communicating the laity in one kind, introduced with reason by the Church and holy fathers, long observed and approved by theologians and canonists, should pass for a law, neither to be censured nor altered without the authority of the Church." This decree was published in 1437, in the thirtieth session.

† For instance, at Constance it formed a *part* of the scheme of the reformers. To " repress simony, and prosecute Jerome of Prague" were joint subjects of the same remonstrances. To restore the unity of the Church was to reform the Church. But at Basle the reformation in discipline was chiefly recommended as the *means* of extirpating heresy. (See the passages above cited from Cardinal Julian's two letters.) But it never occurred to either Council to consider whether the heretics might not possibly be right; or, being wrong, whether they might not safely be tolerated.

popular constitution a wiser legislation might have been expected, did but exclude it more fiercely, and banish it more hopelessly. But in return for their adherence to the favourite vice of the Church, did they amend any maxim of its government? Did they uproot any unscriptural tenet, any superstitious belief, any profitable imposture, any senseless- ceremony, or degrading practice? Did they wash away any spiritual stain from the sanctuary, now that the light from abroad was breaking in upon it? On the contrary, they not only persevered in maintaining every absurdity which had been transmitted to them, but showed a preposterous anxiety to increase the number. It is perfectly true that, in mere matters of discipline, they were fearless innovators, and that they assailed with ardour the more palpable iniquities of the Vatican. But this was the extent of their daring; this was the limit, as they thought, of safe and legitimate reform; all beyond it was inviolable ground. Thus it was, that to question the sanctity of their spiritual corruptions was deemed profane and heretical; and their eyes were wilfully closed against the unalterable truth, that the Church of Christ cannot permanently stand on any other foundation than the Gospel of Christ.

In the meantime, while the fathers of Basle, who saw some part of their danger, were ineffectually contending with an infatuated pontiff, who was blind to the whole, the art of printing was discovered; and the star of universal knowledge, the future arbiter of Churches and of empires, arose unheeded from the restless bosom of Germany.

CHAPTER XXV.

History of the Hussites.

(I.) General fidelity of England to the Roman see—the beginnings of Wiclif, and the hostility he encountered—to what extent his opposition to Rome was popular—his death at Lutterworth, and the exhumation of his remains in pursuance of a decree of the Council of Constance—his opinions on several important points—he was calumniated by the high churchmen—his translation of the Bible.—(II.) The writings of Wiclif introduced into Bohemia—Origin and qualities of John Huss—his sermons in the Chapel of Bethlehem—Division in the University of Prague—Secession of the Germans, in hostility against Huss —he incurs the displeasure of the archbishop of Prague—of John XXIII.—is summoned before the Council of Constance—his attachment to the character of Wiclif—Opinions ascribed to the Vaudois and Hussites by Æneas Sylvius— many of them disclaimed by Huss—Notion respecting tithes—the restoration of the cup to the laity—demanded not by Huss, but by Jacobellus of Misnia— the principle of persecution advocated by Gerson—Huss proceeds to Constance —the safe-conduct of the emperor—the motives of Huss—assurances of protection—nevertheless Huss is placed in confinement—and eight articles alleged against him—Condemnation of Wiclif—a public trial granted to Huss—the insults and calumnies to which he is exposed—three articles to which he adheres—Principles of the Council—Huss refuses to retract—Declaration of Sigismond—Various solicitations and trials to which Huss is subject during his imprisonment—Overture made to him by Sigismond—Interview between Huss and John of Chlum—the sentence passed on Huss—the process of his degradation—and execution—two principal causes of his destruction.—(III.) Jerome of Prague appears before the council—his retractation—subsequent avowal of his opinions—and execution—Observations.—(IV.) Movements occasioned in Bohemia by these executions—the name of Thaborite assumed by the insurgents—the triumphs of Zisca—massacre of the Adamites—the Bohemian deputies proceed to the Council of Basle—the four articles proposed by them—and the consequent ineffectual debate—the scene of negociation then removed to Prague—Various parties there—Defeat and massacre of the Thaborites—a compact concluded between Sigismond and the Separatists—real principles of Rome—the Pope refuses to confirm the compact, and the dissensions continue—under Pius II. and Paul II.—Many of the opinions of the Hussites perpetuated by the " Bohemian Brothers," who became celebrated in the next century.

I. The Roman see had been long accustomed to consider the English as the most obedient and exemplary among its subjects—an equivocal merit, which it rewarded by more oppressive extortions and more contemptuous insult. It is true that

our kings and statesmen had made at various times some
vigorous exertions to mitigate the papal dominion; but the
popes were enabled to thwart or elude their efforts by the
fidelity of the clergy and the people*.   Nor was it only the
praise of ecclesiastical obsequiousness that our Catholic ancestors deserved of the holy see; that of immaculate doctrinal
purity was ascribed to them with equal justice.   They received
with reverence every innovation in their belief, every demand
on their credulity, which proceeded from the unerring oracles
of the Church; but they faithfully discouraged any new opinions originating in any other quarter.   The continental heresies
of the twelfth and thirteenth centuries had not been allowed
to defile their sanctuary; still less had it been profaned by
any weeds of indigenous growth.   The land in which Wiclif
was already preparing his immortal weapons for the contest
was that on which the pontifical regards were fixed with the
deepest complacency and most unsuspecting confidence.

John Wic-
lif.
John of Wiclif† was born in Yorkshire about the year 1324.
He was educated at Oxford; and the great proficiency which
he made in the learning of the schools did not prevent him
from acquiring and deserving the title of the Evangelic, or
Gospel Doctor.   His earlier life was distinguished by a bold
attack on the corruptions of the clergy, and by great zeal in
the contest with the Mendicants, which, in 1360, disturbed the
university and the Church.   He was raised to the theological
chair in 1372; he had previously defended the cause of the
crown against the pope, respecting the payment of the tribute
imposed by Innocent III., and he was known to harbour many
anti-papal opinions: but he was not yet committed in direct
opposition to Rome.   Soon afterwards he formed part of an
embassy to Avignon, instructed to represent and remove the

---

    * The statutes of *provisors* and *præmunire*, enacted in 1350, anticipated most
of the articles of the Pragmatic Sanction of France, since the first restrained the
usurpation of Church patronage by the pope, and the second protected the temporal rights of the crown; but neither of them was observed, and the pope continued to fill the sees with foreign prelates.

    † We do not profess, in the present history, to treat in any detail the ecclesias-
tical affairs of England; and in the following short account of Wiclif there is
little which may not be found much more fully and eloquently expressed in Professor Le Bas' " Life of Wiclif,"

grievances of the Anglican Church.   It was not till his return His opposi-
from that mission, when his language was heated by long- tion to the court of
treasured indignation, or by the near spectacle of pontifical Rome.
impurity, that the reformer first incurred the displeasure of the
English hierarchy.   He was cited before a convocation held at
St. Paul's in 1377; and it seems probable that he owed his
preservation to the powerful protection of John Duke of Lancaster.   At the same time the Vatican thundered; and the
heresy of Wiclif was compared to that of Marsilius of Padua
and others, who had been sheltered against the oppression of
John XXII. by the imperial patronage.   But the papal bull
was so little regarded at Oxford*, that it was even made a
question whether it should not be ignominiously rejected; and
when the offender was subsequently summoned to Lambeth,
he was dismissed with a simple injunction to abstain from diffusing his opinions.   Howbeit, the pope and his myrmidons
continued eager and constant in the pursuit; and there are
many who believe that it was the timely circumstance of the
schism which alone defrauded persecution of its intended
victim.

On the other hand, the ardour of Wiclif† was still further
inflamed by the appearance of this new deformity—when he
saw " the head of Antichrist cloven in twain, and the two parts
made to fight against each other."   He even proceeded so far
as to exhort the princes of Europe to seize that signal opportunity of extinguishing the evil entirely.   But in their eyes it
did not perhaps appear to be an evil at all—at least it was
still so deeply rooted in the prejudices of the people, that its
extirpation, even had they thought it desirable, had not yet
been practicable.   It was the misfortune of Wiclif, as it was
his greatest glory, that he anticipated, by almost two centuries,

---

* " Diu in pendulo hærebant, utrum papalem Bullam deberent cum honore
suscipere, vel omnino cum dedecore refutare."—Walsingham.

† One of the latest labours of his life was another attack on the delinquencies
of the clergy, which he described under thirty-three heads in the tract " How
the Office of Curates is ordained of God."   The more profound sense of those delinquencies which he had derived from inveterate habits and principles of piety,
gave an ardour to the expressions of his advancing age which surpassed that of
his youthful enthusiasm.

the principles of a more enlightened generation, and scattered
his holy lessons on a soil not yet prepared to give them perfect
life and maturity.

As long as Wiclif confined, or nearly confined, his vehement
reprehensions to the delinquencies of the clergy, or the anti-
Christian spirit of the court of Rome, so long he obtained many
and powerful disciples, and could count on their attachment
and fidelity.   But no sooner did he rise from that manifest
and intelligible ground of dissent, and advance into the region
of doctrinal disputation, than the enthusiasm and number of
his followers declined, and even John of Lancaster strongly

His doc-
trinal con-
troversy.
enjoined him to desist.   In 1381-2 he opened his sacramentary
controversy; some considerable tumults followed; he was cited
in consequence before the convention at Oxford, and banished
from that city.   He retired to his rectory at Lutterworth; and
after two more years diligently employed in the offices of piety,
he died there in peaceful and honourable security—security
which was alike honourable to his own character, to the firmness of his illustrious protectors, and to the moderation of the
English prelacy.   His opinions were never extinguished; and
his name continued so formidable to the champions of the
Church, that after an interval of thirty years—after all personal
malice and jealousy had long passed away—the council of Reformers at Constance published that memorable edict, by which
" the body and bones of Wiclif were to be taken from the
ground, and thrown far away from the burial of any church."
The decree met with a tardy obedience: after the space of
thirteen years, the remains were disinterred and burnt, and
the ashes cast into the adjoining brook.   " The brook (says
Fuller, in words which should be engraven on every heart) did
convey his ashes into Avon; Avon into Severn; Severn into
the narrow seas; they into the main ocean.   And thus the
ashes of Wiclif are the emblem of his doctrine, which now is
dispersed all the world over."

His opi-
nions.
His doctrine was formed with an entire disregard of all spiritual authority, and on the foundation of scripture alone—for
" the Scripture alone (as he said) is truth."   Various innovations
of the Roman Church were opposed by him with various degrees

of confidence.   Respecting Images and the Invocation of the
Saints he wrote at no great length, but with reasonableness
and moderation.   He rejected Transubstantiation, according
to the sense of the Church; but he admitted a sort of *real*
presence, without affecting to determine the manner.   His
notion concerning Purgatory seems to have gone farther from
the belief in which he was educated as he gradually advanced
in knowledge; but he never entirely threw off his original impressions.   At last, indeed, he might appear to have considered it as a place of sleep; but his expressions are vague, and
betray the ignorance which he was not careful to conceal either
from others or from himself.   On other matters he expressed
much bolder opinions.   He rejected auricular Confession; he
held pardons and indulgences to be nothing but " a subtle
merchandise of anti-Christian clerks, whereby they magnified
their own fictitious power; and instead of causing men to
dread sin, encouraged them to wallow therein like hogs."
Excommunication and interdicts were repudiated with equal
disdain.   He reprobated the compulsory celibacy of the clergy
and the imposition of monastic vows, and visited with the austerity of a Puritan not only the vain and fantastic ceremonies
of the Church, but even the devout use of holy psalmody.   In
the granting of Absolution he treated the office of the priest as
strictly ministerial and declaratory; and he hastily pronounced
Confirmation to be a mere ecclesiastical invention, for the purpose of unduly elevating the episcopal dignity.   He appears
not to have disputed that the pope was the highest spiritual
authority in the Church; but he rejected with equal scorn his
ghostly infallibility and his secular supremacy; and his abhorrence of the court of anti-Christ was so strong as to be a continual incentive to the bitterest censure.   According to the
original institution, he considered bishops and priests as the
same order; and he ascribed (through a defect in historical
knowledge) the distinction which afterwards divided them to
the imperial supremacy.   He objected to the possession of any
fixed property by the clergy, and maintained that the ecclesiastical endowments were, in their origin, eleemosynary, and

that they remained at the disposal of the secular government*.

Such were, the opinions which Wiclif promulgated in the theological chair, and in the fourteenth century. His reputation and his dignity raised him far above contempt; but at the same time they embittered the malignity of his enemies. Yet, monstrous as many of his real tenets must have appeared in that age, recourse was had to the usual expedient of charging him with absurd inferences and notions† wholly at variance with any that he professed—as if the churchmen of those days had some secret consciousness of the weakness of their cause, and despaired to make the enemies of their system generally detestable, unless they could also stigmatize them as foes to the acknowledged principles of religion, of morality, and of reason. We are not surprised by such calumnies; neither is it strange that the dissemination of his actual doctrines (for they were diligently disseminated by emissaries‡ employed by him for that purpose) was followed by some tumults and disorders. The first open struggles of reason against prescription and prejudice—its first appeals to the sense and virtue of mankind against particular interests and established absurdities are seldom unattended by popular heats and commotions; and the wonder in this case rather is, that the prematurity of the Reformation did not occasion the martyrdom of the reformer.

For many of Wiclif's opinions were too advanced and ripe for the bleak season in which he lived. They were calculated, indeed, for the consideration of all virtuous and disinterested men; and they were sure to *create* in succeeding generations a

---

* It is observed that, with these opinions, Wiclif held the Divinity Professorship at Oxford, a prebendal stall, and the rectory of Lutterworth. He thought it excusable, no doubt, to conform to the system which he found established, and his enemies at the time thought it no crime in him that he did so; yet he would have stood higher with posterity had he disdained the plausible excuse, and placed the unequivocal seal of private disinterestedness and generosity upon his public principles.

† They are to be found in great numbers, chiefly among the articles of impeachment levelled against his name and memory, and published by popes and councils. One error ascribed to him is, "that he represented God as subject to the devil."

‡ Men whom he called his "poor priests." See chap. x. of Le Bas' Life of Wiclif.

disposition towards better principles of belief and practice; but they could look for no general reception among those to whom they were first addressed.   Therefore was it wisely determined by that admirable Christian, when he sent them forth into a prejudiced and ignorant world, to promulgate along with them the sacred volume on which they professed to stand.   His translation and circulation of the Bible was that among his labours which secured the efficacy, as it was itself the crown, of all the others.   This was the life of the system which he destined to be imperishable—this the treasure which he bequeathed to future* and to better ages, for their immortal inheritance.

II. The queen of Richard II. was a Bohemian princess; and on the death of her husband she returned, with a train of attendants, to her native land.   It is commonly believed that these persons introduced a precious, but a dearly preserved, possession among their countrymen—the works of Wiclif. Others suppose this present to have been made by an Englishman who had travelled to Prague; others by a Bohemian who had studied at Oxford.   All may possibly have contributed; but in respect to the more important fact there seems to be no dispute—that the writings of Wiclif kindled the first sparks of the Bohemian heresies.   During the latter days of that venerable teacher, a youth was growing up in an obscure village of Bohemia, who was destined to bear, in his turn, the torch of truth, and to transmit it with a martyr's hand to a long succession of disciples—and he was worthy of the heavenly office. John of Huss, or Hussinetz, was very early distinguished by the force and acuteness of his understanding, the modesty and gravity of his demeanour, the rude and irreproachable austerity of his life.   A thoughtful and attenuated countenance, a tall and somewhat emaciated form, an uncommon mildness and affability of manner added to the authority of his virtues and the persuasiveness of his eloquence.   The University of Prague,

John of Huss.

* The effect was felt even in the next generation, and the high churchmen began to tremble. By a decree published by the Convocation at St. Paul's in 1408, it was prohibited either to compose or consult any private translation of the Scriptures, on the penalties attached to heresy.

His aca-
demical

at that time extremely flourishing, presented a field for the expansion of his great qualities; in the year 1401 he was appointed president, or dean, of the philosophical faculty, and was elevated, eight years afterwards, to the rectorship of the University.

and theo-
logical dis-
tinction.

The Church divided with the academy his talents and his reputation. In the year 1400 he was made confessor to Sophia of Bavaria, the Queen of Bohemia; and in 1405 he had obtained general celebrity by many eloquent sermons delivered *in the vulgar tongue* in his chapel * at Prague. In those fervent addresses to the people who composed his audience, he frequently inveighed against the corruption of the court of Rome, her indulgences, her crusades, her extortions, and all the multitude of her iniquities; and his harangues were received with impassioned acclamation. Nevertheless, his name was not yet tainted by any charge of heresy; and as late as the July of 1408, Subinco (or Suinco), Archbishop of Prague, declared in a public synod, that the kingdom over which his spiritual guardianship extended was free from the stain of any religious error. But about this time the University of Prague was disturbed by a violent dissension. The German students, who formed the majority, and to whom a greater share in the government, the dignities, and emoluments of the institution had been allotted by the original statutes†, were vigorously assailed by the native Bohemians; who claimed, as a national right, that, according to the example of Paris, those enviable prerogatives should be transferred to themselves. Huss engaged with zeal in the cause of his countrymen. The king decided in favour of his own subjects, and he was considered to

* Called the Chapel of Bethlehem. An opulent citizen of Prague had built and endowed it for the maintenance of two preachers, " qui festis profestisque diebus verbum Dei Bohemico sermone plebibus insinuarent." Æn. Sylv., Hist. Bohem., cap. xxxv.

† The University, founded in 1347, by the Emperor Charles IV., was composed of four nations, Bohemia, Bavaria, Saxony, and Poland; and as the three last (even the last) were chiefly Germans, and had three votes in four, three-fourths of the professors, doctors, &c., were Germans. On the other hand, in the economy of the University of Paris (where the division was also quadripartite) the natives had three voices. The declaration of King Wenceslas in favour of his subjects was made on October 18, 1409.

have been chiefly influenced to that resolution by Huss. Many German doctors resigned their offices and retired from the kingdom ; and they carried with them, whithersoever they went, deep rancour against the author of their defeat and secession.

Again, about the same time, probably in the beginning of 1409, Huss was extremely zealous in bringing over his country from the cause of Gregory XII., in whose obedience it persisted, to that of the cardinals assembled at Pisa ; and this laudable forwardness appears to have been the first offence which awakened the displeasure of the Archbishop. At least it is manifest that this was the period at which the indignation of that prelate* first broke out ; and in the December of the same year, the pope himself (Alexander V.) issued some prohibitory decree against Huss and his followers.

The existence and circumstances of the great schism, and the obvious evils produced by it, had long been a popular theme of censure for the Bohemian reformer. And after its extinction, John XXIII. furnished him, in 1411, with fresh matter for reprehension. That pontiff sent forth his emissaries to preach a crusade against Ladislaus, King of Naples, and to accord the usual indulgences. The minds of many had been previously inflamed against this mockery of the cross of Christ by the preaching of Huss ; and so it proved, that, on three several occasions, the pontifical missionaries were interrupted by violent exclamations in the midst of their harangues. Three offenders were accordingly seized by the order of the senate, and privately executed ; but the blood which flowed from the prison into the street betrayed their fate. The people rose ; and having gained possession of their bodies, carried them in procession to the various churches, chanting holy anthems. They then buried them in the chapel of Bethlehem, with the aromatic offerings usually deposited on the tombs of martyrs. Other commotions followed ; the clergy* of Bohemia

---

* Subinco, Archbishop of Prague, is characterised by Maimbourg as " a man who feared nothing when the service of God and the interests of the church were at stake." Such a compliment, from the pen of Maimbourg, is at least suspicious.

† If we are to believe Æneas Sylvius (Historia Bohemica, cap. xxxv.), the clergy, in the first instance, were favourable to Huss ; and the reason which he

conspired very generally against the principles of the reformer;
Summoned and John XXIII. cited him, but without effect, before the tri-
before the Council of Constance. bunal of the Vatican. In fact, so great was the agitation
which these disputes had now excited, that when the Council
of Constance assembled presently afterwards, it issued an immediate summons for the appearance of Huss. With whatsoever disregard that ecclesiastic may have treated the mandate
of the pope, he proved, without hesitation, his allegiance to the
Council. He knew the hostility and the faithlessness of the
court of Rome; but in the august representation of the Church,
in the full congregation of holy prelates assembled for the reformation of abuses, and the redressing of wrongs, he might
find some foundation for confidence, and some hope of justice.

Opinions imputed to Huss.   It is proper now to examine what was the nature of those
spiritual offences which excited such attention throughout
Christendom, and such terror among the directors of the
Church. In the first place, the Bohemian innovator was accused of disseminating the mortal venom which he had imbibed
from England. His devotion to the faith and memory of
Wiclif, for it was for some years concealed, became at length too
deep and ardent for dissimulation ; and it is even related, that
in his discourses from the pulpit of Bethlehem, he was wont to
address his earnest vow to Heaven, that, whenever he should
be removed from this life, he might be admitted to the same
regions where the soul of Wiclif resided; since he doubted not
that he was a good and holy man, and worthy of a habitation
in Heaven *. It is certain, that on the first movement against

malignantly gives for that fact seems to prove at least his own conviction of its
truth. " Sequebantur Johannem clerici ferè omnes, ære alieno gravati, sceleribus
et seditionibus insignes, qui rerum novitate evadere pœnas arbitrabantur. His et
nonnulli doctrina celebres juncti erant; qui cum in ecclesia consequi dignitatem
non potuissent, iniquo animo ferebant sacerdotia majorum censuum his committi,
qui, quamvis nobilitate præirent, scientia tamen videbantur inferiores." The
probability seems to be, that Huss may have won, in the beginning of his
preaching, the partial support of the secular clergy by the bitterness with which
he inveighed against monastic abuses; but that they deserted him, as soon as
they saw his views more perfectly developed.

    * " Qui, cum se libenter audiri animadverteret, multa de libris Viclefi in me-
dium attulit, asserens in iis omnem veritatem contineri ; adjiciensque crebro inter
prædicandum, se, postquam ex luce migraret, ea loca proficisci cupere, ad quæ Vi-

Huss, the Archbishop collected all the books of Wiclif, to the number of two hundred volumes, embossed and decorated with precious ornaments *, and caused them to be publicly burnt. The same element which consumed the writings of Wiclif was destined to prey upon the body of his disciple; and it came like a signal that his vow had been registered above, and that his master awaited his coming at the gates of Paradise.

It was another general charge against Huss, that he was " infected with the leprosy" of the Vaudois; and that it may be seen how many gross offences were thought to be contained in this single accusation, we shall here follow the enumeration of Æneas Sylvius,—only premising that many opinions are there ascribed to Huss, which, in his examinations before the Council, he expressly disavowed. The most important among them were these: that the pope is on a level with other bishops; that all priests are equal except in regard to personal merit; that souls, on quitting their bodies, are immediately condemned to eternal punishment, or exalted to everlasting happiness; that the fire of purgatory has no existence; that prayers for the dead are a vain device, the invention of sacerdotal avarice; that the images of God and the saints should be destroyed; that the orders of the mendicants were invented by evil spirits; that the clergy ought to be poor, subsisting on eleemosynary contributions; that it is free to all men to preach the word of God; that any one guilty of mortal sin is thereby disqualified for any dignity secular or ecclesiastical; that confirmation and extreme unction are not among the holy rites of the Church; that auricular confession is unprofitable, since confession to God is sufficient for pardon; that the use of cemeteries is without reasonable foundation, and inculcated for the sake of profit; that the world itself is the temple of the omnipotent God; and that those only derogate from his majesty, who build churches, monasteries, or oratories; that the sacerdotal vestments, the

clefi anima pervenisset; quem virum fuisse bonum, sanctum, cœloque dignum non dubitaret." Æn. Sylv., Hist. Boh., l. xxxv.

* " Quorum major pars argenteis atque inauratis fibulis et pretiosis integumentis ornabatur." Harpsfield. ap. Contin. Fleury. Æneas Sylvius mentions the same fact nearly in the same words.

ornaments of the altars, the cups and other sacred utensils, are
of no more than vulgar estimation ; that the suffrages of the
saints who reign with Christ in Heaven are unprofitable, and
vainly invoked; that there is no holiday excepting Sunday;
that the festivals of the saints should by no means be observed ;
and that the fasts established by the Church are equally destitute of divine authority.

To these opinions, which he is accused of having habitually
propounded in his chapel of Bethlehem, and of which he disclaimed many of the most important, he appears in truth to
have subsequently added another, by no means calculated to
conciliate the clergy.   During a period of suspension from his
preachings at Prague, he retired to his native village, and addressed to large rustic congregations the popular doctrine, that
tithes are strictly eleemosynary, and that it is free for the
owner of the land to withhold or to pay them, according to the
measure of his charity.   But the subject, on which the greatest
heats were afterwards excited, and in which, indeed, the other
points of difference were for the most part forgotten, was the
distribution of the sacramental cup to the laity.   And this
innovation upon the modern practice of the Church is not, as it
singularly happens, ascribed to Huss, though it originated in
the same country, and at the same time. A celebrated preacher
of the day, named Jacobellus, whose learning and piety are
alike unquestioned*, first promulgated the tenet, that the communion in both kinds was necessary for salvation ; and as the
opinion was shown to rest not only on the authority of Scripture, but also on the practice of the ancient Church, " the
heretics embraced it with immoderate exultation, as evincing
either the ignorance, or the wickedness, of the Roman See."
Wenceslas, the King of Bohemia, regarded the rise of these
principles with a careless and, as some assert, a stupid indifference ; his queen protected the person, if she did not profess
the principles, of her confessor ; and thus the secular sword
slept peacefully throughout these disputes, though it was loudly

Distribu-
tion of the
Cup to the
Laity.

* " Per id tempus populum prædicando instruebat Jacobellus Misnensis, literarum doctrina et morum præstantia juxta clarus." Æn. Sylv., loc. cit.

evoked by the zeal of the Archbishop, and though Gerson*
himself raised his voice to awaken it.

It has been matter of surprise to many writers that Huss, The safe
with the consciousness that he had taught many of the above conduct of
tenets, and with the knowledge how detestable they were held Huss.
by the churchmen, should have advanced so readily from a
position of comparative security, and placed himself at once in
the power of his enemies. It was not that he was ignorant
of his danger. A letter which he addressed to a friend immediately before his departure for Constance contains passages
almost prophetic of his imminent fate. He had the precaution,

---

* Sufficient extracts from Gerson's Letter to the Archbishop are given by Cochlæus, Historiæ Hussitarum, lib. i., p. 21, (ed. Mogunt. 1549,) and as it is curious
to observe in what language the great Church Reformer of his day justified the
principle of persecution, we shall cite some passages from it, only premising that,
very nearly at the same moment, the pope, John XXIII., was inditing an epistle
to Wenceslas to the same purport. " Inveniuntur adhuc hæreses extirpatæ ab
agro ecclesiastico diversis viis, veluti falce multiplici. Inveniuntur quidem pri-
mitus extirpatæ falce vel acuto sarculo miraculorum, attestantium divinitùs Catholicæ veritati, et hoc tempore apostolorum. Inveniuntur extirpatæ postmodum
per falcem disputationis argumentativæ per doctores. Sunt extirpatæ deinde per
falcem sacrorum Conciliorum, faventibus imperatoribus, quum disputatio doctri-
nalis particularium doctorum inefficax videbatur. Tandem accessit, velut in de-
sperata peste, securis brachii secularis, excidens hæreses cum auctoribus suis et in
ignem mittens. *Providens hac tanta serveritate et misericordi, ut sic dicatur, cru-
delitate* ne sermo talium, veluti cancer, serpat in perniciem tam propriam quam
alienam. Et ante multo tempore non sinere peccatoribus ex sententia agere, sed
statim *ultiones adhibere magni beneficii est indicium.*" After showing that none
of the ancient methods of extirpation were applicable to the existing heresy, he
thus proceeds :—" Superest igitur, si de præmissorum nihil prosit, quod *ad radi-
cem* infructuosæ, immo MALEDICTÆ, *arboris ponatur securis brachii secularis.* Quale
vos brachium invocare viis omnibus convenit, et expedit ad salutem omnium vobis
creditorum." . . . The doctrines attributed to Huss were condemned by the University of Paris, and the act was published with the signature of Gerson, as
Chancellor: it contains the following passage : " For though there appears among
the opinions of these heretics some zeal against the vices of the prelates, which in
truth are very great and manifest, yet it is a zeal *not sufficiently enlightened.* A
discreet zeal tolerates and deplores the sins which it finds in the house of God,
when it cannot wholly remove them. It would be impossible to correct vice by
vice, and error by error; as the devil is not compelled by Beelzebub, but by the
spirit of God, whose will it is that the correction of abuses be undertaken with
great prudence and regard to circumstances of time and place." This,
too, is language which might very well have proceeded from the court of
John XXIII.

however, to obtain an act of safe-conduct * from the emperor,
which was understood to be a pledge for his personal protection during the whole period of his absence from Bohemia. But
that admirable Christian was unquestionably impelled by
motives too deep for the calculation of ordinary minds. He
felt an intense conviction of the truth of his doctrines, and he
was resolved, should need be, to lay down his life for them.
That conviction, attended by that resolution, gave a confidence
to his character, which, while it left him without fear, might
at the same time animate him with the highest hopes. He
was filled with that deliberate enthusiasm, which sometimes
raises the soul of man above that which we call wisdom; and
which, while it provokes the sneer of ordinary beings, has produced those lofty deeds of disinterestedness and self-devotion
which redeem human nature.

Doubtless Huss was so influenced when he published, both
before his departure from Bohemia and during his journey,

* The following are given as the words of this frequently controverted "safe-
conduct:"—"Honorabilem magistrum Johannem Huss, S. T. Baccalaureum,
etc., de regno Boemiæ, in Concilium Generale ... transeuntem ... vobis omnibus
et vestrum cuilibet pleno recommandamus affectu, desiderantes, quatenus ipsum,
cum ad vos pervenerit, gratè suscipere .... omnique prorsus impedimento remoto
transire, stare, morari et redire liberè permittatis, sibique et suis."—(Act. Public.
apud Bzovium, ann. 1414, sect. 17.) It is not at all obvious that the Council was
bound by this safe-conduct—the less so, as the professed object of Huss's journey
was to clear himself of heresy in the presence and judgment of the Council: but
the Emperor was certainly so bound; and that which he committed, and which
the Council persuaded him to commit, was direct, unqualified treachery. It was
manifestly the duty of Sigismond to receive Huss from the hands of the Council,
and restore him to his native country; then the affair might have been taken up
de novo, without any reflection on the faith of any party. The best illustrations
of the rights of this question are such facts as prove the light in which it was
viewed by succeeding generations. Thus we observe, that before the assembling
of the first Diet of Worms (1521), the Elector of Saxony privately required of the
Emperor Charles V. a formal renunciation of the Decree of Constance—"that no
faith be kept with heretics." On the same occasion we find that great pains were
again taken by the Catholics to induce the Emperor to violate his safe-conduct to
Luther; on which Louis, Elector Palatine, is recorded to have said—"That all
Germany would not stain itself with the shame of public perfidy to oblige a few
ecclesiastics;" and Charles himself to have uttered that celebrated apophthegm
—"That if good faith were banished from the rest of the world, it should find
refuge in the breast of kings."—See Beausobre's Hist. Reform., liv. iii.

repeated challenges to all his adversaries to appear at Constance and meet him in the presence of the pope and the council :—" If any shall there convict me of any error, of any doctrine contrary to the Christian faith, I refuse not (he proclaimed) to undergo the last penalties of heresy *." These expressions betoken confidence in his own principles and in the integrity of the council. He had yet to discover that his controversy was not with candid opponents, contesting his avowed opinions before an impartial tribunal; calumny and secret malice, and ecclesiastical bigotry, were more dangerous enemies ; and his fate was seemingly irrevocable from the moment in which he placed his life in the power of that Catholic assembly.

He was attended by some Bohemian noblemen, and he received the strongest assurances of protection from John XXIII. "Though John Huss (said that pope) should murder my own brother, I would use the whole of my power to preserve him from every injury during all the time of his residence at Constance†." Nevertheless, within a month from his arrival, after having professed before a meeting of the council his readiness to repel every charge, he was placed under a surveillance which was immediately changed to strict confinement. It should not be forgotten, that this first violation of the safe-conduct was peculiarly the act of the Council. Sigismond, who was not present, strongly remonstrated against it; and the pope (from whatever motive ‡) disclaimed all share in the proceedings.

He is put under confinement by the Council.

* " Significo toti Boemiæ et omnibus nationibus, me velle sisti primo quoque tempore coram Concilio Constantiensi, in celeberrimo loco, præsidente Papa, etc. . . . . Eo conferat pedem quisquis suspicionem de me habuerit, quod aliena a Christi fide docuerim vel defenderim. Item doceat ibi, adstante Papa, me ullo unquam tempore erroneam et falsam doctrinam tenuisse. Si me de errore aliquo convicerit, etc. . . . . non recusabo quascunque hæretici pœnas ferre."—Huss. Bohemic., apud Bzovium, ad ann. 1414.

† Lenfant. Hist. Conc. Constant., lib. i., § xxviii.

‡ The cardinals were the agents in this affair; and John does not appear to have been present at that congregation. But we should not forget that when Sigismond wrote to command the immediate liberation of Huss, on the strength of his own safe-conduct, the pope opposed the execution of the order. Lenfant. Conc. Constant., l. i., § 50.

Accused,   This advantage was instantly pursued by his enemies, of
whom the most ardent were found among his countrymen;
and accordingly eight* articles of accusation were prepared,
and presented to John XXIII. When a copy of them was
delivered to the accused, where he lay sick in prison, he requested that an advocate might be granted him to defend his
cause; but that was refused, on the plea of a general prohibition by the canon law to undertake the defence of any one
suspected of heresy. And then, instead of striving to obviate
the various intrigues which were employed for his destruction,
he devoted the tedious leisure of his imprisonment, and the
resources of a mind superior to ordinary agitations, to the
composition of various moral and religious treatises†.

The next step in the process against him was the condemnation of the doctrines and memory of Wiclif. It was in the
eighth session, held on the 4th of May, 1415, that a list of
forty-five articles was drawn up, which embodied all (and more
than all) the errors of that reformer; that it received the
solemn censure of the fathers; and that the vengeance of that
orthodox body pursued the spiritual offender even beyond the
grave.   It is a singular circumstance, and serves well to illustrate the position in which the Council then stood, as an
assembly of reformation, that in the very sermon which opened
that session, and which introduced the opinions of Wiclif to
universal abhorrence, the Pope and his court were treated with
equal severity, and rebuked in language ‡ which would have

---

* It seems almost unnecessary to enumerate these charges,—they were as follows:—(1.) That communion in both kinds is necessary for salvation;—(2.) that
the bread remains bread after the consecration;—(3.) that ministers in a state of
mortal sin cannot administer the sacraments; and that any one in a state of
grace can do so;—(4.) that the Church does not mean the pope nor the clergy;
that it cannot possess temporal goods, and that the secular powers can rightfully
take them away;—(5.) that Constantine and other princes erred when they endowed the Church;—(6.) that all priests are equal in authority; so that ordi-
nations and privileges reserved to the popes and bishops are the pure effect of
their ambition;—(7.) that the Church loses the power of the keys when the pope,
cardinals, and the rest of the clergy are in mortal sin; (8.) that excommunications may be disregarded with safety.

† On marriage—on the Decalogue—on the love and knowledge of God—on
penitence—on the three enemies of man—on the Lord's Supper—and others.

‡ The Bishop of Toulon preached the sermon—"ubi puram dixit veritatem de

been held blasphemous, had it proceeded from the lips of a heretic.

It was an object of great importance with the Council, bent, as it certainly was, on the destruction of Huss, and conscious, as it probably was, of the weakness of its own cause, to avoid the scandal of a public disputation. Accordingly, Huss was continually persecuted by private interrogatories, frequently accompanied by intimidation and insult; and depositions against his orthodoxy were collected with great diligence and great facility, since every kind of information was admitted against a suspected heretic. On the other hand, he vehemently remonstrated against this inquisitorial secrecy, and demanded for his defence an audience of the whole Council. His Bohemian friends pressed the same point with equal earnestness. But in vain would they have solicited from that body this most obvious act of justice, if the Emperor had not also been impressed with its propriety, and insisted, with great firmness, that the trial should be public.

Consequently the Fathers assembled very early in June for that purpose. The first charge was read. The defendant was called upon for his reply. But when he appealed in his justification to the authority of the Scriptures, and the venerable testimony of the fathers, his voice was drowned in a tumult of contempt and derision. He was silent; and it was interpreted as guilt. Again he spoke; again he was answered by disdainful jests and insults; and the assembly at length separated without any serious determination. The second audience was fixed for the 7th of June; and that greater decency might be preserved, the Emperor was requested to be present on that occasion. It is carefully recorded by historians, and not, perhaps, without some sense of superstitious awe, that the day on which the fate of that righteous man was in fact decided was signalized by a total eclipse of the sun—total, as was observed, at *Prague*, though not quite so at Constance. But the

and tried.

fathers were not moved by that phenomenon to any principle of justice, or any feeling of mercy. The various charges already prepared were pressed upon the culprit, less clamourously indeed, but not less eagerly than before. His accusers were numerous and voluble, and armed with the most minute subtleties of the schools. Many among them were English; and these urged their arguments as warmly as if they had thought to redeem the land of Wiclif by the persecution of Huss, and to wash away the stains, which one heretic had cast upon them, in the blood of another.

Numerous depositions were likewise produced and read, alleging errors which he had advanced in his writings or in his sermons, or even in his private conversations. Alone, and unsupported, save by two or three faithful Bohemians, and worn and enfeebled by confinement and disease, he presented a spirit which did not bend beneath this oppression. The opinions imputed to him related chiefly to the Eucharist, and the condemned propositions of Wiclif. There were some which he entirely disavowed; others which he admitted under certain modifications; others which he professed his readiness and his ability to maintain. Among the first was the charge respecting Transubstantiation, on which subject he repeatedly and unequivocally asserted his entire concurrence in the doctrine of the Church. Among the last, the positions (they were ascribed to Wiclif) to which he clung with the greatest pertinacity appear to have been three. (1.) That Pope Sylvester and the Emperor Constantine did evil to the Church when they enriched it. (2.) That, if any ecclesiastic, whether pope, prelate, or priest, be in a state of mortal sin, he is disqualified for the administration of the sacraments. (3.) That tithes are not dues, but merely eleemosynary. In defence of these, and perhaps some other opinions, the few arguments which he was permitted to advance were temperate, if not reasonable and scriptural: at least they proved his uprightness and the integrity of his heart; but they were received, as before, with reiterated shouts of derision. The question, indeed, was not whether the opinions of Huss were founded in truth, or otherwise: that consideration seems not to have influenced any one mind in the whole assembly, excepting his own; the question really to be decided, the only question with which the Council affected any concern, was, whether they were the doctrine of the Church. Whatsoever had once been pronounced by that infallible body was law, and the alternative was obedience or death.

On the following day Huss was admitted to the mockery of another and final audience; and on this occasion he was chiefly pressed on twenty-six articles, derived (fairly or unfairly) from his " Book of the Church." A scene similar to the preceding was terminated, on the part of the judges, by urgent solicit-ations to the accused to retract his errors. This act of submis-sion was advised by several of the fathers; it was strongly recommended by the Emperor; but Huss was unmoved. "As to the opinions imputed to me, which I have never held, those I cannot retract; as to those which I do indeed profess, I am ready to retract them when I shall be better *instructed* by the Council." The province of the Council was not to instruct, but to decide—to command obedience to its decision, or to enforce the penalty.

If Huss had hitherto nourished any reasonable hope of safety, it was placed in the moderation of the Emperor; but at this conjuncture even that prospect was removed. For, towards the conclusion of the session, Sigismond delivered his unqualified opinion, " that among the errors of Huss, which had been in part proved, and in part confessed, there was not one which did not deserve the penal flames;" to which was added, " that the temporal sword ought instantly to be drawn for the chastisement of his disciples, to the end that the branches of the tree might perish together with its root." *Con-demned.*

Huss was again conducted to his prison, and thither was still pursued by fresh solicitations on his constancy; and that which had stood firm before public menace and insult might have yielded to private importunity, to bodily infirmity, to friendship, to solitude. First of all, an official formula of re-tractation was sent to him by the Council; it was express as to his abjuration of all the errors which had been proved against him, and as to his unconditional submission to the Council; but it was free from any harsh or offensive expressions. Huss *Attempts to induce him to re-tract;*

calmly persisted in his resolution. " He was prepared to af-
ford an example in himself of that enduring patience which he
had so frequently preached to others, and which he relied upon
the grace of God to grant him." Many individuals, of various
characters, but alike anxious to save him from the last inflic-
tion, visited his prison, and pressed him with a variety of
motives and arguments; but they were all blunted by the rectitude of his conscience and the singleness of his purpose. One
of his bitterest enemies, named Paletz*, was among the number; but though his counsels had been successful in degrading
the person of the reformer, they failed when they would have
seduced him to infamy.

by the
Council;

Numerous deputations were sent by the Council, to which he
always replied with the same modesty and firmness, equally
removed from an obstinate perseverance in acknowledged
error, and a base retractation of that which he thought truth.
About the same time it was resolved to commit his books to
the flames, as if to warn him by that prelude of the approaching catastrophe. But in a letter which he wrote to some friend
on the occasion, he remarked that *that* was no ground for despondency, since the Books of Jeremiah had suffered the same
indignity; but the Jews had not thus evaded the calamities
with which the prophet had menaced them.

Notwithstanding his public and recent declaration, the Emperor appears even to the very conclusion of this iniquitous
affair to have entertained some lingering scruples respecting
his safe-conduct. These had been silenced, it is true, by the
sophistry of the doctors; and he had even been taught to believe that his protection could not lawfully be extended to a
man suspected of heresy; that monstrous charge superseded
the ordinary economy of government, and dispensed with the

* It was supposed that the spiritual influence of a confessor might possibly be
sufficient to lead him to retract; and Huss requested that the same Paletz might
be the person so commissioned—partly to prove that he could pardon his worst
enemy; partly to show how willing he was to confide the inmost secrets of his
heart even to one who might be disposed to proclaim them most loudly. The
Council did not think proper to accede to this generous request. It sent a monk
to him, who gave him the same counsel as the others, and absolved him without
any penitential imposition.—See Lenfant's Hist. Conc. Const., liv. iii., § xxxv.

imperious obligations of moral duty! Howbeit, notwithstanding the spiritual authority on which this principle was advanced, Sigismond would have greatly preferred some reasonable compromise to that violent termination which was now
near at hand. Accordingly, when he saw the fruitlessness of
every other attempt to bend the spirit of Huss, he resolved
himself to make one final effort for the same purpose. On the by the Em-
5th of July, on the eve of the day destined for his execution, peror.
the prisoner was visited by an imperial deputation, commissioned to inquire " whether he would abjure those articles of
which he acknowledged himself guilty?"—and in regard to
those which he disavowed, " whether he would swear that he
held thereon the doctrine of the Church?" One objection to
which Huss had throughout attached great importance was
removed by this proposal—the obligation to *retract* that which
he had never maintained. But the grand, the insurmountable
difficulty still remained—to abjure against conviction that which
he did actually profess. Upon the whole, he saw no reason
for any change, and returned to the Emperor the same sort of
answer with which he had met all preceding solicitations.

It remained for him still to encounter one other trial ; if, John of
indeed, we can so designate the upright counsel of a faithful Chlum.
and virtuous friend—for such was the circumstance which completed and crowned the history of his imprisonment—and it
should be everywhere recorded, for the honour of human
nature. A Bohemian nobleman, named John of Chlum, had
attended Huss, whose disciple he was, through all his perils
and persecutions, and had exerted, throughout the whole affair,
every method that he could learn or devise to save him. At
length, when every hope was lost, and he was about to separate from the martyr for the last time, he addressed him in
these terms : " My dear master, I am unlettered, and consequently unfit to counsel one so enlightened as you. Nevertheless, if you are secretly conscious of any one of those errors
which have been publicly imputed to you, I do entreat you not
to feel any shame in retracting it; but if, on the contrary, you
are convinced of your innocence, I am so far from advising
you to say anything against your conscience, that I exhort you

rather to endure every form of torture than to renounce anything which you hold to be true." John Huss replied with
tears, " that God was his witness how ready he had ever been,
and still was, to retract on oath, and with his whole heart, from
the moment he should be convicted of any error by *evidence
from Holy Scripture**." In the whole history of the sufferings
and the fortitude of Huss, there is not one discoverable touch
of pride or stubbornness; the records of his heroism are not
infected by a single stain of mere philosophy : he was firm, indeed, but he was humble also; he expected death, and he feared
it too; he neither sought the Martyr's crown, nor affected the
ambition of the Stoic : his principles of action were drawn from
the same source as the articles of his belief; he was a pure and
perfect Christian, and he thought it no merit to be so.

There was a long interval between his imprisonment and
his audience, and again a tedious month intervened between
his audience and execution. This period was passed in prepa-
ration to meet his fate, not in struggles to avoid it. " God, in
his wisdom, has reasons for thus prolonging my life. He
wishes to give me time to weep for my sins, and to console
myself in this protracted trial by the hope of their remission.
He has granted me this interval, that, through meditation on
the sufferings of Christ Jesus, I may become better qualified
to support my own †." The time of those sufferings at length
arrived. On the morning of July 6, 1415, he was conducted
before the Council, then holding its fifteenth session; and after
various articles of accusation had been read, a sentence was
passed to the following effect:—" That for several years John
Huss has seduced and scandalized the people by the dissemination of many doctrines manifestly heretical, and condemned
by the Church, especially those of John Wiclif. That he has

Huss is
sentenced,

* Huss, on the eve of his execution, wrote to the Senate of Prague to the following effect:—" Be well assured that I have not retracted or abjured one single
article. The Council urged me to declare the falsehood of every article drawn
from my books; but I refused, unless their falsehood could be demonstrated from
Scripture. So do I now declare, that I detest every meaning which may be
proved false in those articles, and I submit in that respect to the correction of
our Saviour Jesus Christ, who knows the sincerity of my heart." See Contin. of
Fleury, l. ciii., lxxviii.

* Opera Joh. Huss. epist. 14, apud Lenfant.

obstinately trampled upon the keys of the Church and the ecclesiastical censures. That he has appealed to Jesus Christ as
sovereign judge, to the contempt of the ordinary judges of the
Church; and that such an appeal was injurious, scandalous,
and made in derision of ecclesiastical authority*. That he
has persisted to the last in his errors, and even maintained
them in full council. It is therefore ordained that he be publicly deposed and degraded from holy orders, as an obstinate
and incorrigible heretic." The prelates appointed then proceeded to the office of degradation. He was stripped, one by
one, of his sacerdotal vestments; the holy cup, which had been
purposely placed in his hands, was taken from them; his hair
was cut in such a manner as to lose every mark of the priestly
character; and a crown of paper was placed on his head,
marked with hideous figures of demons, and that still more
frightful superscription, *Heresiarch.* The prelates then piously
devoted his soul to the infernal devils †; he was pronounced to
be cut off from the ecclesiastical body, and being released from
the grasp of the Church, he was consigned, as a layman, to
the vengeance of the secular arm. It was in the character of
" advocate and defender of the Church" that the Emperor
took charge of the culprit, and commanded his immediate execution.

The last, which was not perhaps the bitterest of his sufferings, was endured with equal constancy and in the same
blessed spirit. On his way to the stake he repeated pious
prayers and penitential psalms; and when the order was given and exe-
to kindle the flames, he only uttered these words—" Lord cuted.
Jesus, I endure with humility this cruel death for thy sake;
and I pray thee to pardon all my enemies." The ministers
executed their office; the martyr continued in uninterrupted

---

* Probably, in the long list of Huss's imputed heresies, there was no single
article which inflamed the Council against him nearly so violently as this appeal.
The point which, above all others, that assembly was interested to establish was
its own omnipotence and infallibility—its agency under the *immediate* operation
of the Holy Spirit—in fact, its divine power. Consequently, an appeal to any
superior, even though it were Christ himself, was derogatory to the heavenly
attributes with which the council had clothed itself.

† " Animam tuam devovemus infernis Diabolis."

devotion; and it was not long before a rising volume of fire
and smoke extinguished at the same time his voice and his
life. . . . . His ashes were carefully collected and cast into
the lake. But the miserable precaution was without any effect,
since his disciples tore up the earth from the spot of his martyrdom, and adored it with the same reverence and moistened
it with those same tears which would otherwise have sanctified
his sepulchre.

The points of difference strictly doctrinal between Huss and
his persecutors were, after all, neither numerous nor important,
since we are bound in this inquiry to give credit to the solemn
disavowals of the accused rather than to the malignant imputations of his accusers. Lenfant, in his accurate history* of
this affair, has investigated very minutely the real extent of
the offences of Huss, and reduced them under two heads.
(1.) He unquestionably refused to subscribe to any general condemnation of the articles of Wiclif. There were many particulars on which he dissented from that reformer, but in several
others he professed the same notions; and among these last
were disparagement of the pope and the Roman Church, and
opposition to tithes, indulgences, and ecclesiastical censures.
(2.) It was also made a dangerous charge against him, that
the spirit of ecclesiastical insubordination, which had already
appeared in Bohemia, was principally occasioned by his
preaching. Such was the burden of his offence. And though
all the leading authors and orators of the time were as unsparing as Huss himself in their denunciations of papal and
ecclesiastical enormities, even from the pulpits of Constance;
though it was even usual with them to ascribe to these abuses
the heresies of the day; still the independent exertions of a
Bohemian preacher in the same cause were stigmatized by
them as indiscreet and immoderate zeal—because the principles from which that zeal proceeded were not in accordance
with their own hierarchical pretensions—because the Bible,
and not the Church, was the source from which it flowed. And
as to the disaffection of the Bohemians, if the Council really
hoped to repress it by the perfidious execution of the most

* Hist. Conc. Const., lib. iii., § 52, 60.

pious and popular of their teachers, the events which presently followed were a lesson of bloody and indelible instruction both to those who indulged that error and to their latest posterity.

III. In less than a year from the execution of Huss, the same scene of injustice and barbarity was acted a second time, though with some variety of circumstances, in the same polluted theatre. Jerome, master in theology in the university of Prague, and a layman, was the disciple of John Huss. Huss (says Æneas Sylvius) was superior in age and authority; but Jerome was held more excellent in learning and eloquence. While the former presided in the chair, the latter delivered his lectures in the schools; and the same opinions were taught with equal zeal and effect by the one and by the other. In the troubles which had been excited through those opinions, Jerome had had, perhaps, the greater share; there was at least no favourable feature to distinguish his offence from that of his master. Accordingly, he was summoned to Constance soon after the meeting of the Council; and he appeared there on the 4th of April, 1415, not unprepared for the treatment which awaited him. It should be observed, that he also obtained a safe-conduct from the emperor; but that in his case the conditional clause, *salva semper justitia,* was inserted; whereas that of Huss contained no such provision.

At his first audience (on May 23rd) he exhibited great firmness; but at the second, which took place only thirteen days after the execution of Huss, it was expected that the impression made by that frightful example would render him more tractable. And so assuredly it proved; for on his third examination (on September 11th) he submitted, after suffering much insult and intimidation, to make a formal and solemn retractation. He " anathematized all heresies, and especially that of Wiclif and Huss, with which he had been previously infected (infamatus); he denounced the various articles which expressed it as blasphemous, erroneous, scandalous, offensive to pious ears, rash, and seditious; and professed his absolute adhesion to all the tenets of the Roman Church."

It was admitted that, in this mournful exhibition of human inconstancy, he had satisfied every demand which was made

Marginal notes: Jerome of Prague. / His retractation.

upon his weakness, both in substance and in form; nevertheless, he was still retained in confinement. After a short space, his enemies pressed forward with new charges against him. They found many eager listeners among the members of the Council; and Gerson* himself again took up the pen of bigotry, and again sought to dip it in blood. Matters continued thus until the 23rd of May, 1416, when a final and public audience was granted to his repeated entreaties. On this occasion he recalled, with sorrow and shame, his former retractation, and openly attributed the unworthy act to its real and only motive—the fear of a painful death. His bitterest foes desired no further proof against him; and only seven days were allowed to elapse before he was condemned, and executed on the same spot which had been hallowed by the sufferings of his master. The courage which had abandoned him in the anticipation of the flames returned with redoubled force as he approached them. The executioner would have kindled the faggots behind his back: " Place the fire before me," he exclaimed; " if I had dreaded it, I could have escaped it." " Such (says Poggio † the Florentine) " was the end of a man incredibly excellent. I was an eye-witness to that catastrophe, and beheld every act. I know not whether it was obstinacy or incredulity which moved him; but his death was like that of some one of the philosophers of antiquity. Mutius Scævola

and execution.

* He composed at this time (in October, 1415) his treatise " De Protestatione et Revocatione in Negotio Fidei, ad eluendam Hæreseos notam." He sought to cast suspicion on such retractations; and this was the first step towards the execution of Jerome. The composition may be found in Von der Hardt, tom iii., p. iv.

† In a letter addressed to Leonardus Aretinus, of which the whole is valuable, as describing the entire transaction, and painting the character of Jerome. It is cited by Beausobre, Histoire de la Réformation; lib. ii.; by Von der Hardt, tom. iii., pars iii.; and other writers. There was, indeed, a little more of philosophical parade, and a little less of the genuine Christian spirit in the death of Jerome than in that of his master. Æneas Sylvius, however, whose eye was not likely to perceive this distinction, or to value it when perceived, includes both in the same sentence of admiration. " Pertulerunt ambo constanti animo necem et quasi ad epulas invitati ad incendium properârunt, nullam emittentes vocem, quæ miseri animi posset facere indicium. Ubi ardere cœperunt, hymnum cecinerunt, quem vix flamma et fragor ignis intercipere potuit. Nemo philosophorum tam forti animo mortem pertulisse traditur, quam isti incendium." Hist. Bohem., cap. xxxvi.

placed his hand in the flame, and Socrates drank the poison
with less firmness and spontaneousness than Jerome presented
his body to the torture of the fire."

Whatsoever may have been the respective excellence, in their Reflexions
living or in their martyrdom, of those two venerable heralds of on the conduct of the
the Reformation, the conduct of the Council was not at all less Council.
iniquitous in respect to its second, than to its first victim. If
in the one instance the violation of the safe-conduct displayed
unblushing perfidy, the contempt of the retractation was at least
as shameless in the other. The first crime was followed by
no remorse; it seems rather to have led to the more calm and
deliberate perpetration of the second. The *principle* by which
the deeds were justified was never, for an instant, questioned in
either case. And we should, at the same time, bear in mind
(for it is a consideration deserving repeated notice), that this
was not a principle exclusively papal—no peculiar emanation
from the apostolical chair or the Court of Rome—it was a principle strictly ecclesiastical, animating the Council as the representative of the Church, and inflaming the individual bosom of
the churchmen who composed it. It was embraced by the
French and English, as warmly as by the Italians themselves;
nor was it pressed to any greater extremity by the champions
of ecclesiastical corruption, than by the men who called themselves its reformers.

IV. The condition of Bohemia is described to have been
singularly flourishing at that moment. There was no other
region * more abundant in useful productions, or in which the
people were blessed with greater comforts; none more distinguished for the splendour of its churches and monasteries, and
the wealth of its Clergy. Unhappily, that body had used with
little moderation the advantages enjoyed by it; and its excesses
had for many years excited the murmurs of the laity. This

---

* Cochlæus (lib. i. p. 314) cites some verses " Conradi Celtis primi apud Ger-
manos Poetæ Laureati," in praise of the city of Prague :—
       Visa non est Urbs meliore cœlo ;
       Explicat septem hæc spatiosa colles,
       Ambitu murorum imitata magnæ
         Mœnia Romæ.

disaffection had ever shown itself in occasional outrages; but
no systematic hostility had yet been arrayed either against
the persons or the property of the sacred order. Howbeit, no
sooner were the proceedings of the Council made known
throughout the country, than the people gave indications of a
ferocious spirit; the nobles * likewise addressed a bold remonstrance to the fathers; and as their rising opposition was
met by new edicts † of condemnation, which still farther inflamed it; and as Martin V. at length published a Bull ‡ of
Crusade against the contumacious heretics, every hope of reconciliation was removed, and the difference was fairly committed to the decision of the sword.

It was one of the earliest and most innocent acts of insubordination to spread three hundred tables in the open air, for
the public celebration of the communion in *both* kinds §.   And

> * They had previously addressed several remonstrances to the Emperor on the
> subject of Huss's imprisonment, representing that there was no person, great or
> small, who did not see the violation of his safe-conduct with indignation. Their
> letter to the Council immediately followed the execution of Huss, and was dated
> September 2. The Great considered the act as an affront to the kingdom of Bo-
> hemia; the populace exclaimed against the fathers, as persecutors and execu-
> tioners, and assembling in the chapel of Bethlehem, decreed to the victim the
> honours of martyrdom. It is related, that Jerome of Prague was prematurely
> associated with his master in this popular canonization; and it is remarkable that
> this crown was conferred upon him within a few days from that, on which he
> made his retractation.
>
> † Among the edicts published at Constance against the Hussites, there was
> one, in 1418, which prohibited the singing of songs in derision of the Catholic
> Church.
>
> ‡ The Bull, published by Martin in 1421, contained a prohibition to keep faith
> with heretics, as distinctly conveyed as words can express it,—" Quod si tu aliquo
> modo inductus defensionem eorum suscipere promisisti; scito *te dare fidem hære-
> ticis*, violatoribus Fidei Sanctæ, *non potuisse, et idcirco peccare mortaliter, si serva-
> bis;* quia fideli ad infidelem non potest esse ulla communio." It is addressed to
> Alexander, Duke of Lithuania, and published by Cochlæus, a prejudiced Catho-
> lic. Lib. v. p. 212.
>
> § After all, it appears nearly certain, that Huss was not the author of the re-
> storation of the cup. Lenfant follows the account of Æneas Sylvius, and argues
> that he was not. The retrenchment of the cup appears to that author to be a ne-
> cessary consequence of the doctrine of transubstantiation, which Huss seems to
> have professed to the last. The Catholics of Constance, and even Gerson himself,
> (for he published a very elaborate and artificial treatise on the subject,) appear
> to have been more perplexed in the defence of this, than of any other of their
> abuses. Antiquity, of course, is the great object of appeal; and yet the antiquity

Insurrec-
tion of the
Bohemians

as the sense of some one specific grievance is necessary for the union of a large multitude in revolt against any established power, so it was wise in the Bohemian insurgents to select one among their spiritual wrongs, as the principal motive of resistance, and to select that which would be most intelligible to the lowest classes. Again, the distinction of a name was useful in rousing enthusiasm, and preserving the show of concord. And as this *chosen people* stigmatised the surrounding nations as Idumæans or Moabites, as Amalekites or Philistines ; themselves were the well-beloved and elect of God; Thabor was the mount on which they pitched their tents, and Thaborite the appellation which they adopted. The first effects of their indignation were directed against the monks and clergy. These were plundered and even massacred without pity and without remorse. The sacred buildings were overthrown, the sanctuaries profaned, the altars stained with blood ; and all those abominations were unsparingly committed, which commonly attend a premature resistance to inveterate oppression.

Sigismond conducted the armies of the Church ; Zisca led the rebels against them ; and the name of Zisca is signalised by several triumphs over the imperial crusaders, which evinced not only his great military genius and resolution, but the deep religious enthusiasm and devotion of his followers. Atrocities were perpetrated by both parties, as if in emulation of each other, and of the heroes of former holy wars ; and so keen was the thirst for blood, that the Hussites indulged it in the massacre of a sect of brother heretics. A number of unfortunate enthusiasts, usually designated Adamites, were collected in an insular spot, in the neighbourhood of Zisca's encampment. They are accused by various writers of the habit of nudity, and of many scandalous crimes ; and in this matter it is probable that they have been much calumniated. It may be, as Mosheim is disposed to think, that they were infected with some of the absurdities of Mysticism; or, as Beausobre * learnedly argues,

Their triumphs, Zisca.

of this practice could scarcely reach two centuries (Lenfant, lib. iii., § xxxi.); and it certainly never acquired the force of a law till the contrary was declared to be heresy in the 10th Session of this Council (May 14, 1415).

* This very ingenious writer, in his dissertation on the " Adamites," addressed

that their difference from the Catholics was confined to the use of the cup. It is beyond dispute, that they did not maintain all the opinions of the Thaborites; and it would seem that some fatal quarrels had taken place between individuals of the two sects. Zisca surrounded and destroyed them without any discrimination or mercy; but lest we should on this account consider him as having surpassed the wickedness of his Catholic adversaries, we may remark, that by this very act he has incurred the deliberate praise of their historians *, and redeemed in their eyes some portion of the guilt of his apostasy.

Divisions.
Orebites
and Or-
phans.

Zisca died in 1424, and divisions immediately ensued among his followers. Two other factions, the Orebites and the Orphans, distracted the Bohemian reformers; but they united on occasions of common danger. In 1431 they repelled another formidable crusade, which was conducted by the celebrated Cardinal of St. Angelo; and in this affair the rout was so complete, that the Pope's Bull, as well as the hat, cross, and bell of the Cardinal, fell into the hands of the victors †. In the meantime, a more moderate party arose and acquired influence among the Hussites; its hopes were turned to a pacific accommodation with the Church; and with that view it was arranged, that the Bohemians should send deputies to treat with the Council of Basle. Accordingly some of the most renowned among their military and ecclesiastical directors appeared at that city on the day appointed. The fame of their fierce exploits made them objects of deep and fearful curiosity with that peaceful assembly; they were treated with respect, for they had earned it by their sword; and no violation of their safe conduct, or other breach of faith, was on this occasion meditated.

Embassy
to Basle.

They were introduced, on February 16, 1433, to a general meeting of the fathers, and immediately proposed the condi-

in two books to M. Lenfant, and published together with the " History of the Council of Constance" by the latter, certainly clears the Adamites from the worst of charges that have been brought against them, which he shows to have been Catholic calumnies. Still the question, why Zisca destroyed them, is scarcely answered satisfactorily.

* See Cochlæus, lib. v., p. 218.

† See Lenfant, Guerre des Hussites, l. xvi. s. v. &c.

tions of reconciliation, which were four in number*. (1.) The use of the cup in the administration of the sacrament. (2.) The free preaching of the word of God. (3.) The abolition of the endowments of the clergy. (4.) The punishment of heinous transgressions and moral sins. A separate debate was then opened upon each of these articles; and John of Rokysan, the most conspicuous among the Hussite divines, commenced by a defence of the double communion, which lasted for three entire mornings. He was answered by John of Ragusa, an ingenious Dominican, who so far surpassed the prolixity of his opponent, as to occupy eight mornings in the delivery of his arguments †; six others were then consumed by the reply of Rokysan. The other subjects were contested with scarcely less tediousness ; and when the debate had thus continued for nearly two months, and when it was found that, so far from any progress having been made towards accommodation, the obstinacy of both parties was only confirmed and inflamed, the Duke of Bavaria, the secular protector of the Council, sought for other expedients to bring them to terms. But in this attempt he failed likewise; and after the Catholics had advanced some counter-propositions, which were rejected by the Hussites, the conference terminated, and the deputies returned to recount to their compatriots the failure of their mission.

But the Catholics, being now better informed as to the variety and nature of the dissensions which divided their opponents, thought to profit by that circumstance, if they should carry the controversy into the hostile territories ; a solemn embassy was accordingly appointed to proceed to Prague. Negotiations were again opened; and again the Catholics essayed

---

* According to Cochlæus (lib. v., p. 205), these were first agreed upon in a general assembly " Baronum terræ Bohemiæ et Moraviæ, et dominorum inclytæ urbis Pragensis, militarium, clientum, civitatum et communitatum," A.D. 1421. This will account for the moderation of the demands contained in them.

† It is observed that John of Ragusa gave great offence to his opponents by the frequent use of the word heresy, as applied to their opinions. With them it was still a question whether it was not the Church which was in heresy; with the Dominican, the Church was infallible. With them it was error to differ from the Scripture; with John, to differ from the Church. Thus the term, taken in a different sense, was as obnoxious in their eyes as in those of the Dominican.

the arts of persuasion in vain. They then introduced such amendments into the four articles as effectually destroyed their force, or altered their meaning; but these were firmly rejected by the larger and more determined portion of the separatists.

The Calix-tines.
There existed, however, among these last, a more moderate and very influential party, which was strongly disposed to waive all other subjects of complaint, provided the double communion were fairly conceded by the Church. These were called Calixtines *—from the *chalice* † to which their demands were confined—and they were distinguished from the Thaborites, who constituted the more violent faction; and the sum of whose grievances was by no means comprehended in the four articles, though they might consent in their public deliberations to suppress the rest. Among the Calixtines were several of the substantial citizens and leading members of the aristocracy; and of such too the Catholic party was chiefly composed. As these, next after the clergy, were the principal sufferers by the continuance of anarchy and the devastations of war, they entered without much difficulty into the designs of the Council. And since it was now obvious, that no reconciliation was to be expected from discussion, it was determined to make another appeal to the sword.

Renewal of War.
Massacre of the Tha-borites.
A civil war was immediately kindled throughout the country (in 1434); the party of the council was directed with ability by a distinguished Bohemian, named Maynard: his schemes were at first advanced by dissensions which raged between the Thaborites and the Orphans; and he afterwards conducted matters with so much address, that he engaged them when united, and entirely overthrew them. On this occasion it so

---

* Cochlæus (lib. v., p. 192) mentions early differences between the Magistri Pragenses and the Thaborites. The former were the more moderate Dissenters; the Church Hussites and Jacobellus Misnensis, Rokysan, and other distinguished reformers, belonged to them. But the Thaborites, who were the Puritans, and also the soldiers of the party, had Zisca with them, and the two Procopiuses—both eminent warriors—so that they were for some time the stronger faction.

† Tot pingit calices Bohemorum Terra per urbes,
    Ut credas Bacchi numina sola coli—
is a contemporary distich. It should be observed, that every other picture was an object of aversion, at least to the more rigid reformers.

happened, that the most hardened and desperate among the insurgents fell alive into the power of the conquerors; and as they were numerous, and objects, even in their captivity, of fearful apprehension, Maynard resolved to use artifice for their destruction.   Among the prisoners there were also several who were innocent of any previous campaigns against the Church, and who were neither hateful as rebels, nor dangerous as soldiers.   These it was the design of the Catholics to spare; and the better to distinguish them from the veterans of Zisca, they caused it to be proclaimed, that the government intended to confer honours and pensions on the more experienced warriors, the heroes of so many fields.   These were accordingly invited to separate themselves from their less deserving companions, and to withdraw to some adjacent buildings, where more abundant entertainment and a worthier residence were prepared for them.   They believed these promises; and then it came to pass (says Æneas* Sylvius) " that many thousands of the Thaborites and Orphans entered the barns assigned to them; they were men blackened, and inured and indurated against sun and wind; hideous and horrible of aspect; who had lived in the smoke of camps; with eagle-eyes, locks uncombed, long beards, lofty stature, shaggy limbs, and skin so hardened and callous as to seem proof, like mail, against hostile weapons.   The gates were immediately closed upon them; fire was applied to the buildings; and by their combustion that ignominious band, the dregs and draff of the human race, at length made atonement in the flames, for the crimes which it had perpetrated, to the religion which it had insulted." . . . Among the crimes with which the Thaborites are reproached, was there any more foul than that by which they perished? or can any deeper insult be cast on the religion of Christ than to offer up human holocausts in his peaceful name?   In the balance of religious atrocities the mass of guilt must rest at last with those who established the practice of violence, and consecrated the principles of Antichrist.

* Hist. Bohem., cap. li., ad finem.

But the adversaries of Rome were not thus wholly extirpated : under the spiritual direction of Rokysan, they were still so considerable, that Sigismond did not disdain to negotiate with them. The result was, that a concordat or compact Compact of was concluded at Iglau in the year 1436, by which the Bohe-
Iglau. mians conceded almost all their claims ; but in return, the use of the cup was conceded to them, not as an essential practice, but only through the indulgence of the Church*. Some arrangement was likewise made respecting the ecclesiastical property which had been despoiled by the rebels. This affair was conducted with the countenance of the Council. The first result was favourable ; and the contest with Rome might then, perhaps, have ceased ; the Bohemians, fatigued with tumult and bloodshed, might have returned to the obedience of the Church, contented with one almost nominal concession, if the chiefs of the hierarchy could have endured any independence of thought or action, any shadow of emancipation from their immitigable despotism. For this was, in fact, the spirit which guided the Councils of Rome ; it was not the attachment to any particular tenet or ceremony which moved her to so much rancour; but it was her general hatred of intellectual freedom, and the just apprehensions with which she saw it directed to the affairs of the Church.

In September, 1436, Sigismond made his entry into Prague, amid congratulations almost universal ; and the calamities which had desolated the country for two-and-twenty years
The Pope appeared to be at an end †. But the Pope refused his assent
refuses his
ratification. to the concordat; he refused to confirm the appointment of

* The Council of Basle, in its thirtieth session, published its decree on the Eucharist, in which are these words :—" Sive autem sub una specie sive duplici quis communicet, secundum ordinationem seu observationem Ecclesiæ, proficit digne communicantibus ad salutem." Cochlæus, lib. viii., p. 308. Communicants might be saved according to either method, so long as that method was sanctioned by the Church.

† The appointment of a double administrator of the Sacrament in every Church, one for the Catholic, the other for the Separatist, was of somewhat later date. Lenfant places it in 1441, and mentions that great good proceeded from it.

Rokysan to the See of Prague, though the Emperor had promised it; and though all the factions of the people were united
in desiring it.   Wherever the guilt of the previous dissensions
may have rested, henceforward we need not hesitate to impute
it wholly to the Vatican.   Legates and mendicant emissaries*
continued to visit the country, and contend with the divines,
and tamper with the people.   Even Pius II., whose personal †
intercourse with the sectarians had not softened his ecclesiastical indignation at their disobedience, exhibited in his nego-

* The most celebrated among these papal missionaries was John Capistano,
a Franciscan, who had gained great distinction in a spiritual campaign against
the Fratricelli in the Campagna di Roma and March of Ancona, and had condemned thirty-six of them to the flames.   He is described by Cochlæus (lib. x.
ad finem) as a little emaciated old man, full of fire and enthusiasm, and indefatigable in the service of the Church.   The year of his exertions in Bohemia was
1451.   Such emissaries were in those days among the most useful tools of the
Roman hierarchy.

† It was in 1451 that Æneas Sylvius made his celebrated visit to Bohemia, as
imperial envoy.   His mission was merely political; but it deserves our notice
from the very interesting description which he has drawn of the manners of the
Thaborites, among whom he found an asylum when in some danger from bandits:
—" It was a spectacle worthy of attention.   They were a rustic and disorderly
crew, yet desirous to appear civilized.   It was cold and rainy.   Some of them
were destitute of all covering except their shirts; some wore tunics of skin; some
had no saddles, others no reins, others no spurs.   One had a boot on his leg,
another none.   One was deprived of an eye, another of a hand; and to use the
expression of Virgil, it was unsightly to behold

'————populataque tempora raptis
            Auribus et truncos inhonesto vulnere nares.'

There was no regularity in their march, no constraint in their conversation; they
received us in a barbarous and rustic manner.   Nevertheless, they offered us hos-
pitable presents of fish, wine, and beer.....   On the outer gate of the city were
two shields; on one of them was a representation of an angel holding *a cup :* as
it were to exhort the people to the communion in wine,—on the other Zisca was
painted; an old man, blind of both eyes, whom the Thaborites followed, not only
after he had lost one eye, but when he became a perfectly blind leader.   Nor was
there any inconsistency in this," &c.—(See his 130th Letter.)   In the mean time
these wild and unseemly sectarians nourished in their rude abodes opinions which
were the glory of the following age, but which were indeed pernicious to themselves.   Exactly seven years after the visit of Æneas Sylvius, the King of Bohemia, Pogebrac, willing to bring them to more moderate sentiments of reform,
summoned a General Council of Hussites, who condemned some of their tenets;
and then, on their refusal to abjure them, the King assaulted Thabor, and destroyed them (as it is related) with such scrupulous exactness, that not one was
left alive.

tiations with Pogebrac *, the king, an intolerant and resentful
spirit. And at length Paul II., his successor, once more found
means to light up a long and deadly war in the infected
country. It was considered, no doubt, as a stigma upon the
Church, which all occasions and instruments were proper to
efface, that a single sect should anywhere exist which dared to
differ from the faith or practice of Rome on a single article,
and which maintained its difference with impunity.

The Bohe-
mian
brothers.

It was in 1466 that Paul II. excommunicated and deposed
Pogebrac, and transferred the kingdom to the son of Huniades.
In that object he was not successful; but during the discords of
almost thirty years which followed, the offensive names of Thaborite, Orphan, and even Hussite, gradually disappeared, and the
open resistance to the Catholic predominance became fainter and
fainter. But the principles were so far from having expired in
this conflict, that they came forth from it in greater purity, and
with a show of vigour and consistency which did not at first
distinguish them. Early in the ensuing century, about the year
1504, a body of sectarians, under the name of the " United
Brethren of Bohemia," begins to attract the historian's notice.
Beausobre † affirms that this association was originally formed
in the year 1467; that it separated itself at that time from the
Catholics and Calixtines, and instituted a new ministry; that
it made application to the Vaudois, in order to receive through
them the true apostolical ordination; and that Stephen, a
bishop of that persuasion, did actually ordain Matthew, the
first bishop of the " United Brethren." It is unquestionable,
that those among the Thaborites, and the other more determined dissenters, who had escaped the perils of so many dis-

* Pogebrac was a moderate reformer, a Calixtine; he was extremely anxious
to be subject to the Church, on the condition only that it would leave him the
cup: he had been brought up, as he said, in that practice, and would never resign
it. His persecution of the Thaborites sufficiently proves how far he was from
any anti-ecclesiastical tendency. Yet he seems to have been as much hated at
Rome as if he had gone to the full extent of opposition, and he was certainly
much less feared. The Pope had still a powerful party among the aristocracy of
Bohemia.

† Dissertation sur les Adamites, Part I.

asters, continued with uncompromising constancy to feed and
mature the tenets for which they had suffered; and that many
of the leading articles of the Reformation were anticipated and
preserved by the " Bohemian Brothers." It is also true that
the evangelical principles of their faith were not unmixed with
some erroneous notions; but it is no less certain, that when
Luther was engaged in the accomplishment of his mission, he
was welcomed by a numerous body of hereditary reformers, who
rejected, and whose ancestors had rejected, the sacrifice of the
mass, purgatory, transubstantiation, prayers for the dead, the
adoration of images; and who confirmed their spiritual emancipation by renouncing the authority of the Pope *.

* Bossuet (in the eleventh chapter of his Variations) consumes his ingenuity
in endeavouring to show that the " Bohemian Brethren " were descended from
the Calixtines, not from the Thaborites, and had thus only one point of doctrinal
difference with Rome. But, at the same time, he admits their *disobedience*—
" Voilà comme ils sont disciples de Jean Huss. Morceau rompu d'un morceau,
schisme séparé d'un schisme—Hussites divisés des Hussites; et qui n'en avoient
presque retenu, que la désobéissance et la rupture avec l'Eglise Romaine.

CHAPTER XXVI.

History of the Greek Church after its Separation from the Latin.

Origin, progress, and sufferings of the Paulicians—They are transplanted to
Thrace, and the opinions gain some prevalence there—Their differences from
the Manichæans—and from the Church—Six specific errors charged against
them by the latter—Examined—Points of resemblance between the Paulicians
and the Hussites—Mysticism at no time extinct in the East—and generally
instrumental to piety—Introduction of the mystical books into the West—
Opinions of the Echites or Messalians—Those of the Hesychasts or Quietists
—who are accused before a Council, and acquitted—The mixed character of
the heresy of the Bogomiles—Controversy respecting the God of Mahomet—
terminated by a compromise—Points of distinction between the two Churches
—Imperial supremacy constant in the East—Absence of feudal institutions—
Superior civilization of the Greeks—They never received the False Decretals,
nor suffered from their consequences—Passionate reverence for antiquity—
Animosity against the Latins—Hopes from the foundation of the Latin kingdom of Jerusalem—Its real consequences—Establishment of a Latin Church
in the East—Influence of the military orders—Legates *à latere*—Latin conquest
of Constantinople—confirmed by Innocent III.—A Latin Church planted and
endowed at Constantinople—Tithes—Dissensions of the Latin ecclesiastics—
Increasing animosity between the Greeks and Latins—Secession of the Greek
hierarchy to Nice—Mission from Rome to Nice—Subject and heat of the controversy, and increased rancour—John of Parma subsequently sent by Innocent IV.—Extinction of the Latin empire—The Church does not still withdraw
its claims—Subsequent negotiations between the Emperor and the Pope—Confession of Clement IV.—Conduct of the Oriental Clergy—Ambassadors from
the East to the Second Council of Lyons—Concession of the Emperor presently disavowed by the Clergy and People—Subsequent attempts at reconciliation—Arllval of the Emperor and Patriarch at Ferrara—First proceedings
of the Council—Private deliberations by Members of the two Churches—The
four grand Subjects of Division—The Dispute on Purgatory—Doctrine of the
Latins—of the Greeks—First Session of the Council—Grand Disputation on
the Procession—The Council adjourned to Florence, and the same Discussions
repeated there—Suggestions of compromise by the Emperor, to which the
Greeks finally assent—The common Confession of Faith—A Treaty, by
which the Pope engages to furnish Supplies to the Emperor—The Union is
then ratified—The manner in which the other differences, as the Azyms, Purgatory, and the Pope's Primacy, are arranged—Difficulty as to the last—How
far the subject of Transubstantiation was treated at Florence. On the fate of
Cardinal Julian—Return of the Greeks—Their angry reception—Honours paid
to Mark of Ephesus—Insubordination of three Patriarchs—Russia also declares against the Union—Critical situation of the Emperor—The opposite
party gains ground—the prophetic Address of Nicholas V. to the Emperor
Constantine—Perversity and Fanaticism of the Greek Clergy—They open
Negotiations with the Bohemians—Tumult at Constantinople against the Emperor and the Pope's Legate—Fall of Constantinople—*Note.* On the Armenians
—and Maronites.

WHILE the jealousies which had so long disturbed the ecclesiastical concord of the East and West were ripened into open

schism by the mutual violence of Nicholas and Photius *, the Eastern Church was in the crisis of a dangerous contest with a domestic foe.   A sect of heretics, named Paulicians, had arisen The in the seventh century, and gained great prevalence in the Paulicians. Asiatic provinces, especially Armenia.   It was in vain that they were assailed by imperial edicts and penal inflictions. Constans, Justinian II., and even Leo the Isaurian successively chastised their errors or their contumacy; but they resisted with inflexible fortitude until at length Nicephorus, in the beginning of the ninth century, relented from the system of his predecessors, and restored the factious dissenters to their civil privileges, and religious liberty.

During this transient suspension of their sufferings, they gained strength to endure others, more protracted and far more violent.   The oppressive edicts were renewed by Michael Curopalates, and redoubled by Leo the Armenian ; as if that resolute Iconoclast wished to make amends to bigotry, for his zeal in the internal purification of the Church, by his rancour against its sectarian seceders.   The struggles, the victories, and the misfortunes of that persecuted race are eloquently unfolded in the pages of Gibbon : we shall not transfer the narrative to this history, for it belongs not to our purpose to trace the details even of religious warfare.   It may suffice to say, that the sword, which was resumed by the enemy of the Images, was most fiercely wielded by their most ardent patroness ; and that, during the fourteen years of the reign of Theodora, about 100,000 Paulicians are believed to have perished by various methods of destruction.   The conflict lasted till nearly the end of the century ; and at length the survivors either sought for refuge under the government of the Saracens, or were transplanted by the conqueror into the yet uncontaminated provinces of Bulgaria and Thrace.   But not thus were the doctrines silenced, or the spirit extinguished.   The fierce exiles carried with them into their new habitations the sectarian and proselytizing zeal ; and the errors of the East soon took root and flourished in a ruder soil.   During the tenth and eleventh

* We refer the reader to the 12th chapter of this History.

centuries the Paulicians of Thrace were sufficiently numerous
to be objects of suspicion, if not of fear ; and in the latter we
find it recorded that Alexius Comnenus did not disdain to
employ the talents and learning, with which he adorned the
purple, in personal controversy with the heretical doctors.
Many are related to have yielded to the force of the imperial
eloquence; many also resigned their opinions on the milder
compulsion of rewards and dignities; but those who, being
unmoved by either influence, pertinaciously persisted in error
and disloyalty, were corrected by the moderate exercise of
despotic authority *.

After this period we find little mention of the Paulician sect
in the annals of the Oriental Church. But we should remark
that Armenia, the province of its birth, was never afterwards
cordially reconciled to the see of Constantinople; and that,
though it no longer fostered that particular heresy, it continued
to nourish some seeds of disaffection, which frequently recommended it in later ages to the interested affection of the Vatican †.

It is generally much easier to describe the fortunes of a suffering sect than to ascertain the offence for which they suffered.
The resistance of the Paulicians, their bravery, their cruelty,
their overthrow, are circumstances of unquestionable assurance;
the particulars of their opinions are disputed. By their enemies they were at once designated as Manichæans—it was the
name most obnoxious to the Eastern as well as the Western
Communion: yet, if we may credit contemporary testimony ‡,

Opinions of the Pauli-cians. (margin)

* They were removed to Constantinople, and placed in a sort of honourable
exile in the immediate precincts of the imperial palace. Anna Comnena (Alexiad,
b. xiv.) describes with filial ardour her father's zeal and patience in converting
these *Manicheans.* Τοῖς μὲν ὅπλοις τοὺς βαρβάρους ἐνίκα, τοῖς δὲ λόγοις ἐχειροῦτο τοὺς
ἀντιθέους. ὥσπερ δὲ τότε κατὰ τῶν Μανιχαίων ἐξώπλιστο, ἀποστολικὴν ἀντὶ στρατηγικῆς
ἀναδειξάμενος ἀγωνίαν—καὶ ἔγωγε τοῦτον τρισκαιδέκατον ἂν ἀπόστολον ὀνομάσαιμι ....
ἀπὸ πρωΐας οὖν μέχρι δείλης ἑώας ἢ καὶ ἑσπέρας, ἔστιν οὗ καὶ δευτέρας καὶ τρίτης φυλακῆς
τῆς νυκτὸς μεταπεμπόμενος αὐτοὺς, &c. &c.

† See the Note at the end of this chapter.

‡ " Iidem sunt (says Petrus Siculus, page 764) nec quicquam divertunt à Manichæis Paulliciani, qui hasce recens a se procusas hæreses prioribus assuerunt,
et ex sempiterno exitii barathro effoderunt : qui, tametsi *se a Manichæorum im-
puritatibus alienos dictitant,* sunt tamen dogmatum ipsorum vigilantissimi cus-

they earnestly disclaimed the imputation. The truth is, that they are only known, like so many other sects, through the representations of their adversaries *. These have been investigated by Mosheim† with his usual care and impartiality, and the result of his inquiry may be received with as much confidence as is consistent with the nature of the evidence.

The obvious difference between the Paulicians and the Manichæans related to the ecclesiastical profession and discipline. The former rejected the government by bishops, priests, and deacons (to which the Manichæans adhered), and admitted no order or individuals set apart by exclusive consecration for spiritual offices.   Neither did the authority of councils or synods enter into their system of religious polity. They had, indeed, certain doctors, called *Synecdemi*, or *Notarii*; but these were not distinguished by any peculiar dignities or privileges, either from each other or from the body of the people. The only singularity attending their appointment was, that they changed, on that occasion, their lay for scriptural names. They received all the books of the New Testament, except the two Epistles of St. Peter; and the copies of the Gospel in use among them were the same with those authorized by the Church, and free from the numerous interpolations imputed to the Manichæans.

The peculiarities already mentioned may appear alone suffi- Six imput-
cient to have excited the animosity of the established clergy of ed errors.
the East; but these were by no means the only offences objected to the Paulicians by the Church writers. These last,

---

todes, &c." "Historia de Manichæis;" a Latin translation of which is published in the Maxima Bibliotheca Patrum Veterum; tom. xvi., ann. 860—900. The expressions of Photius are 'Μηδεὶς δ' οἴεσθω ῥίζης ἑτέρας βλάστημα εἶναι, παρ' ἣν ἐρρίζωσεν ὁ θεόμαχος Μάνης, τὴν παραφυάδα ταύτην τὴν δυσσεβῶν Σεργίου δογμάτων· μία γάρ ἐστι καὶ ἡ αὐτή," &c. (Διήγησις, &c., published in the Bibliotheca Coisliana (Paris, 1715), page 349.

* The books from which our best accounts of the Paulicians are derived are Photius'(Διήγησις τῶν νεοφάντων Μανιχαίων καταβλαστήσεως), and Petrus Siculus (Historia de Manichæis). By the account of Petrus Siculus we learn that, in the year 870, under the reign of Basilus the Macedonian, he was sent as ambassador to the Paulicians at Tibrica, to treat with them concerning the exchange of prisoners, and that he lived among them for nine months.

† Cent. ix., p. 2, chap. v.

without professing to give a perfect delineation of the monstrous
system of the Heretics, are contented to charge them with six
detestable errors : 1. That they denied that either the visible
world or the human body was the production of the Supreme
Being ; and distinguished their Creator from the most High
God who dwells in the heavens. 2. That they treated con-
temptuously the Virgin Mary. 3. That they disparaged the
nature and institution of the Lord's Supper *. 4. That they
loaded the cross of Christ with contempt and reproach.
5. That they rejected, after the example of the greatest part of
the Gnostics, the books of the Old Testament, and looked
upon the writers of the Sacred History as inspired by the
Creator of the world, not by the Supreme God. 6. That they
excluded Presbyters and Elders from all part in the administration of the Church †.

We are, of course, bound to receive these articles with suspicion, as the allegations of an enemy. Still they had, unquestionably, some foundation. The first and fifth are sufficient to
prove that the Paulicians maintained some opinions resembling
those of Manes. It seems, indeed, most probable that they were
descended from some one of the ancient Gnostic sects, which,
though diversified in many particulars, all professed one common characteristic. Again, whether or not they believed the
eternity of matter is questionable ; but it was seemingly their
opinion that matter was the seat and source of all evil; and
that, when endued with life and motion, it had produced an
active principle, which was the cause of vice and misery.   Re-

* The words of Petrus Siculus are —" Quod divinam et tremendam corporis et
sanguinis Domini nostri conversionem negent, aliaque de hoc mysterio doceant—
A Domino nempe non panem et vinum in cœna discipulis propinatum, sed figuratè
symbola tantum et verba, tanquam panem et vinum, data." In the article following—" Quod formam et vim venerandæ et vivificæ crucis non solum non
agnoscant, sed infinitis etiam contumeliis onerent." The six articles thus stated
by Petrus Siculus are given by Photius in the same order, and with no very important alteration or addition : only the patriarch increases the list by the charge
of the most abandoned obscenity and profligacy.

† The Sicilian elsewhere admits that the Paulicians professed the principal
Catholic doctrines; but *aliter ore, aliter corde.* These *mental* heresies, so gratuitously imputed where every outward proof is wanting, are the most wicked
invention of ecclesiastical rancour.

specting the third charge, it appears that, in their passion for
the allegorical interpretation of Scripture, they attached merely
a figurative sense to the bread and wine administered by Christ
at the last supper, understanding thereby a spiritual food and
nourishment for the soul.   The second and fourth evince their
freedom from some of the popular superstitions of the Greeks
—the adoration of the Virgin, and reverence for the fancied
relics of the Cross; and this, again, had alone been crime sufficient to arm against them, in the eighth and ninth centuries,
the intemperate zealots of the Oriental Church.   Add to this,
that they held the images of the Saints in no reverence, and
recommended to every class of the people the assiduous study
of the Sacred Volume ; not suppressing their indignation
against the Greeks, who closed the sources of divine knowledge
against all except the priests*. These various subjects of difference duly considered, we shall not wonder that the Paulicians
became the victims of the most deadly persecution which ever
disgraced the Eastern Church.   And since they were, in some
manner, the reformers of their time, and as their zeal was indiscriminately directed as well against the sacerdotal order as
against the corruptions introduced or supported by it, the
Schismatics of Armenia resembled, both in their principles
and their excesses, the Bohemians of the fifteenth age.   The
resemblance was increased by the violent means which were in
both cases adopted to crush them, and which were resisted with
the same ferocious heroism by both. Nor were their concluding

---

* A considerable proportion of the work of Petrus Siculus is consumed in describing the process, by which the mind of Sergius or Constantine, the founder of
the sect, was corrupted by the seductions of a Manichæan woman. The following
is an important specimen of the dialogue (page 761) : " Audio, Domine Sergi, te
literarum scientia et eruditione præstantem esse, et bonum præterea virum usque-
quaque. Dic ergo mihi, *cur non legis sacra Evangelia ?* Quibus ille ita respondit.
Nobis profanis ista legere non licet, sed sacerdotibus duntaxat. At illa—Non est
ita ut putas ; nec enim personarum acceptio est apud Deum. Omnes siquidem
homines vult salvos fieri Dominus et ad agnitionem veritatis venire. At sacer-
dotes vestri, quoniam Dei verbum adulterant et mysteria occulunt, quæ in Evan-
geliis continentur, idcirco, vobis audientibus omnia non legunt quæ scripta sunt,"
&c. It is related that Constantine received from a deacon, in return for some acts
of hospitality, the present of the New Testament. Thus it appears that, before
the middle of the seventh century, the Eastern clergy had effectually shut up the
sources of sacred knowledge.

destinies very different; for, though the sect of the Paulicians
was at length expatriated, and finally extinguished or forgotten
in the Bulgarian deserts, the Christians of Armenia never afterwards returned with any fidelity to the communion from which
they had been so violently dissevered.

Mysticism
prevalent
in the East.
Amidst the metaphysical disputes which agitated the Greeks
in the sixth and seventh centuries, that strong disposition to
Mysticism, which is peculiarly congenial with the Oriental character, gave frequent proofs of its activity, though it never
became the predominant spirit. It was principally cherished
in the monastic establishments ; and when free from the
strange notions into which it not uncommonly seduced irregular minds, it gave birth, without any doubt, to much genuine
and ardent piety. But in the course of ecclesiastical history,
through a painful necessity perpetually imposed upon its writer,
it is by the excesses of piety rather than its natural and ordinary fruits, by the abuses of religion rather than its daily and
individual uses and blessings, that attention is fixed and curiosity excited. In the civil and political records of nations the
exploits of patriotism and the deeds which throw dignity on
human nature, are proclaimed and celebrated, because they
were performed in the public fields of renown, with kings and
nations for their witnesses. But in a religious society the purest
characters are commonly those which shun celebrity and court
oblivion. The noblest patriots in the kingdom of Christ are
men who serve their Heavenly Master in holiness and in peace.
They have their eternal recompense; but it is rare that they
rise into worldly notice, or throw their modest lustre on the
historic page.

On this account it is that, while the absurdities of Mysticism
are commonly known and derided, the good effect which it has
had in turning the mind to spiritual resolves, and amending
the heart of multitudes imbued with it, is generally overlooked.
We cannot now recall the names, or publish the pious acts or
aspirations, which have been concealed or forgotten; yet may
we approach, in a spirit of benevolence, the follies which have
been so carefully recorded; and while we pursue with unsparing denunciation the crimes of ecclesiastical hypocrites—the

ambition, the frauds, the avarice, the bigotry of a secular hier-archy—we may pass with haste and compassion over the errors and extravagances of piety.

Mosheim* ascribes the introduction of the mystical theology into the Western Church to a copy of the pretended works of Dionysius the Areopagite, sent by the Emperor Michael Balbus to Louis the Meek. Whether this be true or not, it was cer-tainly in the East that those opinions were most prevalent, not in earlier only, but also in later ages. It is particularly recorded that, in the twelfth century, numerous fanatics dis-turbed the unity and repose of the Oriental Church by errors proceeding from those principles. It is said that they rejected every form of external worship, all the ceremonies, and even the sacraments of the Church; that they placed the whole essence of religion in internal prayer; and maintained that in the breast of every mortal an evil genius presided, against which no force nor expedient was availing, except unremitted prayer and supplication. One Lycopetrus is believed to have founded this sect, and to have been succeeded by a disciple named Tychicus; and their followers were presently known throughout the East by the denomination of Euchites or Mes- Euchites or salians †, *Men of Prayer.* The term was considered ignomi- Messalians. nious; and it presently came generally into use to designate all who were adverse to the persons of the clergy, or the system of the Church. The Churchmen of the West were at the same period beginning to employ the terms Waldenses and Albigenses with the same latitude and for the same purpose; and as, in the one instance, we are well assured that many holy individuals were involved in the indiscriminate scandal, so also may the seeds of a purer worship have lurked in the barren bosom of the Messalian heresy.

Two centuries afterwards, the eye of Barlaam, an inquisitive Hesy-ecclesiastic, sharpened by much intercourse with the hierarchy chasts or Quietists,

---

* Cent. ix., p. 2, chap. iii. The works of Dionysius, though long received as genuine, are a palpable forgery, probably of the fifth century.

† This was, in fact, only the revival of an ancient heresy, condemned, under the same name and probably for the same errors, by the Council of Antioch, held towards the end of the fourth age. See Fleury, l. xix., s. 25, 26, and l. xcv., s. 9.

of the West, detected, in the monasteries of Mount Athos, a
very singular form of fanaticism. A sect of persons was there
discovered, who believed that, through a process of intense
contemplation, they had attained the condition of perfect and
heavenly repose. The method of their contemplation is conveyed in the following instructions, handed down to them, as
it would seem, from the eleventh century*:—" Being alone in
thy cell, close the door, and seat thyself in the corner. Raise
thy spirit above all vain and transient things; repose thy
beard on thy breast, and turn thine eyes with thy whole power
of meditation upon thy navel. Retain thy breath, and search
in thine entrails for the place of thy heart, wherein all the
powers of the soul reside. At first thou wilt encounter thick
darkness; but by persevering night and day, thou wilt find a
marvellous and uninterrupted joy; for as soon as thy spirit
shall have discovered the place of thy heart, it will perceive
itself *luminous* and full of discernment." When interrogated
respecting the nature of this light, they replied that it was the
glory of God; the same which surrounded Christ during the
transfiguration. These enthusiasts were originally called
Hesychasts, or, in Latin, Quietists; they afterwards obtained
or Umbili- the name of Ομφαλόψυχοι, or Umbilicani, " men whose souls
cani. are in their navels." They were also known by that of Thaborites, from their belief respecting the nature of their divine
light.

It might seem beneath the dignity of history to waste a
thought or a sigh on such pure fanaticism. Yet such was it
not considered in the age in which it rose; it occupied, on the
contrary, the solemn consideration of courts and councils.
Barlaam officiously denounced the heresy to the Patriarch of
Constantinople. The Metropolitan was astounded, and instantly summoned the Hesychasts into his presence. As they
argued with confidence, a council was thought necessary to
decide so grave a controversy; but the emperor Andronicus
hesitated to convoke it, and strongly recommended to both
parties silence and reconciliation. Howbeit, the polemics per-

---

* It is found in a spiritual treatise of Simon, abbot of the monastery of Xero-
cerka, at Constantinople, and is cited by Fleury, l. xcv. s. 9.

sisted; the emperor yielded; and the council was assembled*.
The Archbishop of Thessalonica, Gregory Palamas, advocated
the cause of the Thaborites; and, what might astonish even
those most familiar with the triumphs of religious extravagance,
he succeeded. Nay, so signal was his success, that the accuser
thought it expedient to retire from the country and return to
Italy. The controversy was soon afterwards renewed, and became the occasion of other councils, which agreed without
exception in the condemnation of the *Barlaamites*. But the
question had now assumed a more general form; the Quietism
of the monks of Mount Athos was no longer the subject of dispute; it ascended to the mysterious inquiry whether the eternal light with which God was encircled, which might be called
his *energy* or operation, and which was manifested to the disciples on Mount Thabor, was distinct from his *nature* and
essence, or identified with it†? The former was the opinion
of the pious archbishop Palamas. It grew gradually to be
considered as the more reasonable tenet, and finally took its
place, after a series of solemn deliberations, among the dogmas
of the oriental Church.

We must notice one or two other disputes, of greater notoriety than importance, which occasioned some transient agitation in the East. A monk named Basilius was burnt in the
Hippodrome during the reign of Alexius Comnenus for opinions which he refused, on repeated solicitation, to renounce‡.
They are known to us only from his enemies. He is said to
have maintained that the world and all its inhabitants were
the creation of an evil and degraded demon, so that the body
was no better than the prison house of the immortal spirit;
wherefore it became man to enervate and subject it by fasting,
prayer, and contemplation, and thereby to redeem the soul

*The heresy
of the
Bogomiles.*

---

* It was held on June 11, 1341, and the emperor presided in person, together
with the Patriarch and many of the nobility of the empire.

† See Mosheim, Cent. xiv., p. 2, ch. v.

‡ "Ὁ δὲ πρὸς ἁπασαν τιμωρίαν καὶ ἀπειλὴν καταφρονητικὸς κατεφαίνετο. οὔτε γὰρ τὸ
πῦρ κατεμάλαξε τὴν σιδηρᾶν αὐτοῦ ψυχὴν, οὔτε αἱ τοῦ Αὐτοκράτορος πρὸς αὐτὸν διαπομ-
πιμοὶ διαμηνύσεις κατέθελξαν. The people demanded the execution of all his followers, but the Emperor was contented with a single victim. See the Alexiad.,
book xx.

from its degrading captivity. This Heresiarch had many followers, who were called Bogomiles—as it is said, from a Mysian word signifying " the invocation of divine mercy." These sectarians also denied, with the Phantastics, the reality of the body of Christ; while, with the Gnostics, they rejected the law of Moses. Upon the whole, it would seem that their creed was formed by an infusion of mysticism into the leading Paulician tenets—a combination which it was natural to expect in an age when the latter were still in some repute, and in a Church wherein the former never wholly lost its influence*.

The relative worship of images.

About the same time, the same Alexius Comnenus was compelled to apply to the exigencies of the state some of the figures which adorned the churches. Leo, bishop of Chalcedon, loudly exclaimed against the sacrilege, asserting that the images were endued with some portion of *inherent sanctity*. The monks re-echoed the charge, and a council was in consequence assembled at Constantinople. It decided that images had only a relative worship (σχετικᾶς προσκυνοῦμεν οὐ λατρευτικῶς τὰς εἰκόνας), and that it was offered not to the substance of the matter, but to the form and features, of which they bear the impression; that the representatives of Christ, whether in painting or sculpture, did not partake of *the nature* of Christ, though enriched by a certain communication of divine grace; and lastly, that invocations were to be addressed to the saints only as servants of Christ in their relation to their master. This moderate exposition of the doctrine did not, however, satisfy the bishops, who persisted in their lofty notions, until the secular authority interposed to repress them †.

Controversy regarding the God of Mahomet.

The curious learning of Manuel Comnenus gave birth, in the twelfth century, to several frivolous disputes. There is, however, one which deserves some notice, as well from the singularity of its subject as from the spirit in which it was con-

* Anna Comnena's expression is, τὸ τῶν Βὸγομίλων δόγμα, ἐκ Μασσαλιανῶν καὶ Μανιχαίων συγκείμενον. That orthodox princess vituperates in very strong language the persons, the practices, and the opinions of the Bogomiles, and relates how the heresiarch was one night stoned by demons while reposing in his cell. She also particularizes an error respecting the Eucharist, but is not otherwise very specific in her charges.

† Mosh., Cent. xi., p. 2, ch. iii.

ducted and concluded. The catechisms of the Greek Church
contained a standing anathema against the God of Mahomet.
Through the imperfect comprehension of an Arabic word, the
Greeks represented that Being as *solid* and *spherical**, and consequently not an object of spiritual adoration.   As this anathema
tended to add irritation to the subsisting animosity, and offended
especially such Mahometans as had embraced, or were disposed to embrace, the Christian faith, the Emperor ordered it
to be erased from the public ritual.   The doctors and dignitaries were scandalized at the rashness of the innovation; they
entered eagerly into the most abstruse inquiries respecting the
nature of the Deity; they condemned the imperial decree, and
the purple itself was an insufficient shelter against the imputation of heresy †.   But an imperial heretic will never be destitute of supporters; and the contest was carried on with the
accustomed vehemence and rancour.   In this, as in most
other controversies, a moderate party interposed and proffered
a project of conciliation; but in this, unlike the usual fortune
of theological conflicts, the moderate party prevailed.   A
council was assembled; and after an angry and protracted
struggle, the bishops at length consented to the following compromise:—" That the anathema should keep its place in the
ritual, but that its object should be changed from the God of
Mahomet to Mahomet himself."   On these conditions the
fathers retired, authorized to denounce the impostor, but compelled to spare the Deity.

In resuming, after so long an interval, the history of the
Oriental Church, it becomes necessary to recur to some of the
leading principles of its constitution, and to notice the material
feature by which it was early distinguished, as it is still distinguished, from its Roman rival.   And as we have before

Essential distinctions between the two Churches.

* Ὁλόσφαιρος.   The Arabic word, which bears that signification, also signifies
eternal.

† Hildebrand himself, in an earlier age, had made himself liable to the same
imputation.   In a letter to the King of Morocco, expressing thanks for the liberation of some Christian captives, he expressed his conviction that the King had
been moved thereto by the spirit of God; and that both he and the infidel worshipped the same God, though the modes of their adoration and faith were different.   This is mentioned by Mills in his History of the Crusades.

traced the connexion of those communions until the beginning
of the schism, and as we now propose shortly to describe the
principal attempts which were made to reunite them, it is proper
to observe the different ground on which they stood, that we
may truly estimate the difficulty of those attempts; for though
the matters of doctrinal dispute may be reduced to a few
articles, and though the differences on discipline and government might seem to be virtually absorbed in one—the supremacy of the Pope—nevertheless, the numerous diversities which
subsisted in all the principles, as well as the economy, of the
two establishments, threw impediments in the way of reconciliation, which, though not always in sight, were ever in active
operation.

In the first place, we may mention the firm, uninterrupted
maintenance of the imperial supremacy. While the pontiffs of
the West were first securing their emancipation, and then asserting their pre-eminence over every secular authority, the
Greek ecclesiastics were the subjects of the civil magistrate;
they were translated, deposed, or even executed, at his undisputed control; and whatever wealth or influence they may
have obtained, they were never able to withdraw themselves
from the temporal yoke, nor to establish, like their Latin
brethren, a distinct and independent republic*. Hence it
results that the individuals who composed the higher order of
the clergy were essentially different in the two communions;
different in their personal habits, in their private views, in their
public estimation of the sacerdotal character, and the true
polity of the Church.

How much more widely was this distinction extended by
the absence in the East of all feudal institutions, and of the
character which they so deeply impressed upon every order,
and almost every individual, living under them! That patri-
monial jurisdiction by which public justice became private
property; the secular pomp and appendages of baronial state;
and, above all, the practice of military achievement, were circumstances unknown to the hierarchy of the East. They
viewed with astonishment the temporal greatness of the apos-

* See Gibbon, chap. liii.

tolical successors; they condemned it with justice and seeming sincerity; and the envy which may have mingled with that condemnation rendered it the more severe and malevolent.

Notwithstanding the literary degeneracy and languor of the Greeks, their superstitious reverence for the ancient models, the servility with which they copied without daring to emulate —though it be true that " in the revolution of ten centuries not a single discovery was made to exalt the dignity or promote the happiness of mankind, not a single idea added to the speculative systems of antiquity"—yet was it something in those barren ages to admire, to copy, to praise, even to possess the noblest monuments of human genius. And though they lay fruitless in the hands of their possessors, and unproductive of any original effort or bold imitation, yet were they not without effect in diffusing light and information, and in raising the people, by which they were cultivated however imperfectly, far above the prostrate barbarism of the West*. Nor was it only that the education of the clergy embraced more subjects of useful instruction, but also that education was not wholly confined to the clergy, but extended generally to the higher classes in society. It was the same with theological as with profane literature. It was an object of very general interest and inquiry; and the industry to pursue it was kept alive among a disputatious race by the occasional appearance of domestic heresy, and by the long-protracted controversies with the rival Church. A superiority in literary discrimination will account for the circumstance that the forgery called the " false Decre-

(margin note: Superior cultivation of the people of Greece.)

---

* The eleventh age, for instance, produced, besides Alexius Comnenus, and others of less renown, Cerularius, Cedrenus, and the illustrator of Aristotle, Michel Psellus. Among the literary names of the twelfth (and thirty-six are enumerated by Dupin as *commendables* for their knowledge of theology, canon law, and history) are Cinnamus, Glycas, Zonaras, Nicephorus, Dionysius the geographer, and the celebrated commentator Eustathius, Bishop of Thessalonica. The industry of the Greeks seems ever to be most keenly excited by controversy; and this age was enlivened not only by some warm disputes with the Latins, but also by a contest between the systems of Plato and Aristotle. During the greater part of the thirteenth age the Latins were in possession of Constantinople; but in the fourteenth, the names of Nicephorus Gregoras, Manuel Chrysoloras, Nicephorus Callistus, are boasted by the Greeks; and the works of St. Thomas Aquinas, and other scholastic writers, were translated and studied. Yet Plato had still his followers.

tals" was at once rejected by the Eastern Church. There
were, indeed, other sufficient reasons to prevent a code, which
conferred supremacy almost unlimited on the Roman bishop,
from being acknowledged either by the court or the Church of
Constantinople; but it is also probable that the penetration of
the Greeks at once detected the clumsy imposture.

The mention of the Decretals recalls the consideration of the
papal polity, founded in a great measure upon them. We have
observed, that, after their promulgation, a system of government and a form of discipline unknown to earlier ages grew
up, and continued as it grew to deviate farther and farther
from the original canons and practices. We have traced the
gradual usurpations of the see of Rome, and the changes introduced by pontifical ambition into the very heart and vitals
of the Catholic Church. That powerful agency had no existence in the East; before it began to operate with any great
success, the separation of the Churches was so decidedly pronounced, and their animosity so strongly marked, that the introduction of a change into the one would have been reason
almost sufficient for rejecting it in the other.

It was not, indeed, that the Patriarchs of Constantinople
were exempt from the ruling passion of their Roman brethren,
nor that they failed to profit by any favourable occasion to extend their authority and curtail the independence of their
clergy. But such occasions were rare, because they could only
arise through the co-operation or connivance of the civil authorities; and what the caprice of one despot had bestowed, might
be as easily taken away by the opposite caprice of another.
In the mean time, there was one steady and unvarying principle, on which the ecclesiastical policy of the East was conducted—an inviolable reverence for antiquity. It was by this
standard that the excellence of every institution was measured.
The canons of the Seven General Councils, the precepts of the
early fathers, the practice of the primitive Church—these were
the unalterable rules and models for the guidance and government of the Church. It was not so with the worldly hierarchy
of Rome. They presently learned to subject antiquity to the
more flexible laws of expediency. When it countenanced the

(margin) Reverence for anti-quity.

purpose of the moment, they bowed to its venerable name.
But whenever its voice was unequivocally raised in opposition
to their schemes, then was it readily discovered, that all truth
and excellence were *not* communicated in the beginning; but
that something was reserved for more seasonable revelation, or
mere human discovery.   On the other hand, the Greeks were
the *bigots* of antiquity; their worship was blind, and therefore
both consistent and passionate.   Hence it happened, that the
least important among the modern opinions or practices* of
their rivals disgusted them at least as deeply as the most essential; and that, while they rejected the change, they detested
the innovator.   They were as intolerant in their feelings towards the Latins, as were the Latins towards their own heretics; and so general were those feelings and so carefully nourished by the clergy, and so continually rekindled by the continuance of schism and controversy, that if a sincere reconciliation, founded on compromise, could possibly have been
effected by the directors of the two Churches, it was scarcely
probable that it would be accepted by the inferior clergy and
people of Greece.

The foundation of the kingdom of Jerusalem at the end of *The Latin*
the eleventh century gave to the Latins a substantial footing *Kingdom*
in the East, and seemed to open the gates of concord.   In a *of Jerusa-*
lem.
close alliance against the common enemy of the Christian
name, there was hope that the less perceptible differences
among Christians would altogether vanish and be forgotten.
The harmony of so many sects and tongues united in adoration
of the same Saviour, at his birth-place and round his tomb,
might have afforded a spectacle of charity and a prospect of
peace.   If any circumstance of place or association, any reverence of sacred monuments, any brotherhood in holy enterprise,
could have quenched the fire of sectarian animosities, we might
have expected that blessing from the occupation of Palestine
and the redemption of the Sepulchre of Christ.   What was
really the result?   The very circumstances, which should have

---

* The Latin practice of Tonsure (κούρευμα) may be particularly mentioned, as
exciting the indignation and disdain of a bearded priesthood.

produced religious unanimity, seem to have had no other effect than to multiply the causes of discord, to exasperate its nature, and to aggravate its shame.

Establishment of the Latin Church.

The first act of the conquerors was to establish, throughout the narrow extent of their new kingdom, a numerous body of Latin clergy.   A Latin Patriarch was appointed at Jerusalem, a second at Antioch; and episcopal sees were multiplied under the jurisdiction of both.   Of the native population, those who followed the Christian faith were indissolubly attached to a different rite, and the authority of the Latin Prelates was confined to a precarious host of crusaders and colonists.   Nevertheless, their first care was to place on a solid foundation the temporalities of their Churches*; and since the feudal institutions were those on which the civil government of Godefroy was formed, so the bishops sought to attach to their sees cities, and fortresses, and baronies, according to the preposterous practice of the West.   Then arose the customary dissensions between the spiritual and secular authorities, on the extent of their prerogatives and the limits of their jurisdiction: and they were inflamed in Palestine, even beyond their usual violence, by the peculiar position and character of the Military Orders; for these were endowed with various privileges by the Roman See, and were not disposed to concede them.   Thence proceeded perpetual appeals to Rome, with all their train of pernicious consequences. legates *a latere* were profusely poured into the Holy City; and by their ignorance, their obstinacy, their arrogance, and their avarice, precipitated the downfall of the kingdom.

It was dissolved after the battle of Tiberias in 1187; and

* See Fleury's Sixth Discourse on Ecclesiastical History. " According to the spirit of the Gospel (says that writer) the Latin clergy should have attended principally to the instruction and correction of the crusaders ; to form, as it were, a new Christianity, approaching as nearly as possible to the purity of the early ages, and capable of attracting, by its good example, the surrounding infidels. Next they should have engaged in the reconciliation of heretics and schismatics, and the conversion of the infidels themselves: it was the only method of making the crusade useful.   But our Latin clergy was not sufficiently well-informed to have views so pure and exalted—as it was on this side of the sea, such was it in Palestine, or even more ignorant and more corrupted."

whatsoever contempt of their Latin brethren the clergy of the East may have previously and perhaps ignorantly entertained, it was not diminished by the nearer inspection of their character which was afforded by the conquest of Palestine. Thus it proved, that the advances towards conciliation, which were made during this century by the Emperors of the Comnenus family, led to no good result. Negociations were opened; but the demands of the Vatican were positive, and they amounted to nothing less than spiritual submission. Perhaps the Emperors, who had discovered the secret of their own political weakness, and began to tremble at the temporal influence of the Vatican, might have consented even to that condition. But the prelates of the East, who were swayed by different views and interests, indignantly rejected it; and the failure of the attempt only increased the asperity of both parties.

The reign of the Latins in Palestine was concluded in less than ninety years; their dominion in Constantinople had a still Of Constantinople. shorter duration: yet its effects on the ecclesiastical relations of the East and the West were more direct and permanent, without being in any respect more beneficial. The Capital of the East was stormed by the Crusaders in the year 1204. Innocent III. was at that time Pope; and in the first instance he strongly reprobated the treacherous achievement: but the conquerors were acquainted with a sure expedient to soften his displeasure. Already did Alexis, when raised to the purple which he so soon forfeited, greet the Pontiff with promises of spiritual obedience for himself and for his Church; and Innocent, in rejoinder, gave him divine assurance of prosperity should he observe his faith*, and of speedy reverse should he violate it. It was also one of the first acts of the Latin conquerors to tender the same submission to the Pontiff, to proffer the same promises, and likewise to solicit, with all humility, his confirmation of the conquest. Innocent professed some

---

* The express condition prescribed by Innocent to Alexis was, that he should engage the Patriarch to send a solemn deputation to Rome, for the purpose of recognizing the supremacy of the Roman Church, promising obedience to the Pope, and soliciting the *Pallium*, as necessary for the lawful exercise of his patriarchal functions.

embarrassment at this application; the perversion of the legitimate object of the crusaders was too scandalous—their excesses in the spoliation of the city too notorious—their motives too obvious—the offence too recent. Accordingly the pontiff expressed his disapprobation both of the enterprise itself and the circumstances attending it; and particularly condemned that sacrilegious violence which had exasperated the Greeks, and turned them away from "obedience to the Apostolic See*." Nevertheless, since the deed was perpetrated, he thought it expedient, after mature deliberation, not only with his cardinals, but with all his influential clergy, to vouchsafe it his sanction—because, forsooth, the designs of Providence were inscrutable; and it might be, that, in chastising the long-endured iniquities of the Greeks, a just God had employed the arms of the Latins as the instruments of the holy regeneration †.

In the year following, the pope applied himself more directly to reap the fruits of this unprincipled adventure. He excited the zeal of all the faithful for the defence of the new empire. He wrote a circular letter to the leading prelates of France, exhorting them to preach the indulgence for its defence, and at the same time observing, that Providence had transferred the sceptre from the proud, superstitious, and rebellious Greeks, to the humble Catholic and obedient Latins, to the end that his holy Church might be consoled by the reunion of the schismatics.

Establishment of the Latin Church.

In the mean time not a moment was lost in establishing the Latin Communion at Constantinople; in introducing the Latin Liturgy; in encouraging eminent ecclesiastics to emigrate to the East, and firmly to plant in the Churches and schools of

---

* " Ut jam merito Latinos abhorreant plus quam canes." Epistle to the Marquis of Montserrat.

† See the Epistle of Innocent to the Marquis of Montserrat, published by Raynaldus, ad ann. 1205. " Divinum enim videtur fuisse judicium, ut qui tamdiu misericorditer tolerati, et toties non solum ab aliis sed etiam a nobis studiose commoniti noluerunt redire ad Ecclesiæ universitatem, nec ullum terræ sanctæ subsidium impertiri, per eos, qui ad utrumque pariter intendebant, omitterent locum et gentem, quatenus *perditis malè malis* terra bona bonis Agricolis locaretur, qui fructum reddant tempore opportuno, &c."

Constantinople the doctrines, the discipline, the polity, and the learning of the West. That the nature of that encouragement was not wholly spiritual—that an establishment founded by Innocent III. held out no inconsiderable temporal allurements *—is a circumstance which will excite no surprise in us; though it did not, perhaps, increase the respect or affection of the Greeks towards their new instructors. A concordat was signed in 1206 by the Latin Patriarch on the one hand, and the regent, barons, knights, and people on the other, by which a fifteenth portion of all domains without the walls, of all cities, castles, villages; of corn-fields, vineyards, forests, meadows and other immoveables, was at once bestowed upon the Latin Church. At the same time, all the monasteries, even within the walls, appear to have been transferred to the ascendant establishment †. By another article it was regulated, that tithe should also be paid by all Latins—and " if (it was added) in process of time it should be found practicable to persuade the Greeks also to contribute their tithe, the laity shall offer them no impediment." We should here recollect, that this method of remunerating the clergy, so long familiar to the people of the West, had never been sanctioned by any law, or grown into any general use, in the Oriental Church.

If one of the earliest exhibitions presented by the Roman Catholic clergy to the schismatics of the East was that of their avarice,—another as early, as violent, and almost as revolting, was that of their dissensions. Before the storming of the city by the French and Venetians, a sort of convention had been made between those two nations, to this effect—that, if the empire should be vested in a Frenchman, the Church should

Dissensions.

* The following are the Pope's expressions, addressed to the Archbishop of Rheims and his suffragans :—" Exhortamur, quatenus tam clericos quam laicos efficaciter inducatis ut ad *capessendas spirituales pariter et temporales divitias* ad præfatum Imperatorem accedant, qui singulos vult et potest, secundum status suo &c., *augere divitiis et honoribus* ampliare...."

† It should be mentioned that the French and Venetians had entered into a convention, by which, after making a decent provision for the Oriental clergy, they proposed to divide between themselves the rest of the Church property. But Innocent took under his own protection the property even of a rival Church, and immediately annulled the convention.

be under Venetian superintendence. Accordingly the first patriarch, Thomas Morosini, was a native of Venice; and he immediately took measures so to fill the chapter of the Patriarchal Cathedral, as to secure a compatriot for his successor. Innocent vehemently remonstrated against this design. He sent his legates to Constantinople; and as they acted in opposition to the resident head of the Church, the schismatics were edified by witnessing the jealous disputes of two independent authorities. But it was on the death of Morosini (in 1211) that the struggle really commenced. The Venetian Canons entered the Church of St. Sophia, with arms in their hands, and proceeded to the choice of a Venetian successor. Other ecclesiastics of other nations, who also claimed their share in the election, nominated three other candidates, and the matter was referred to Rome. The pope commanded them to meet and deliberate in common, and the result was a second disagreement. The dispute was conducted with the customary violence; and as it lasted for about three years, during which space the highest office in the Church remained vacant, it furnished the schismatic spectators with another equivocal proof of the superior excellence of the Roman polity. In the mean time the sectarian antipathy continued to be so strongly manifested on their part, that there were many of their clergy who, before they celebrated the Communion, caused those altars to be washed which had been polluted by the ceremony of the Latins; and who likewise insisted on re-baptizing all who had received that sacrament from Latin hands. These proofs of insubordination are mentioned with censure in one of the canons of the Fourth Lateran Church.

While the Roman hierarchy was endeavouring to fix and extend its conquest along the western shores of the Bosphorus, the genuine pastors of the Oriental Church, the legitimate guardians of its apostolical purity, were assembled in honourable exile at Nice. They had witnessed the shame, the pillage, and the desolation of the metropolis of their faith; they had seen their churches despoiled, and their altars violated; the holy images trampled under foot, the relics of departed saints scattered in the dust, the sacred utensils desecrated, and the sanctuary of

St. Sophia profaned and plundered by lawless and *Latin* hands. Such assuredly was not the season for any dreams of reconciliation.   But after the lapse of one generation, when these bitter recollections were not quite so recent, an accident occurred which opened the way to a serious negotiation between the churches—if we should not rather say, the courts—of Nice and Rome.   Five Franciscan missionaries, in the discharge of their perilous duties among the infidels, were seized by the Turks, and on their liberation dismissed to Nice.   They were humanely received by the patriarch Germanus, who was edified by their poverty and their zeal ; and, in the communications of a friendly intercourse, the division of the two churches was mentioned and deplored by both parties.   The emperor (John Vataces) had strong political reasons for desiring an accommodation; and with his consent the patriarch addressed some amicable overtures, though not unmixed with untimely reproach*, both to the pope and the cardinals.

This took place in 1232, during the reign of Gregory IX.; and in the year following the pontiff sent four mendicants (two Dominicans, and two Franciscans) to conduct the negotiations in the east.   They presented themselves at Nice before the

Latin Mission to Nice.

---

* " To go to the bottom of the question (said the patriarch), many powerful and noble persons would obey you, if they did not fear your oppression, and the wanton extortions and undue services which you exact from your subjects.   Hence proceed cruel wars, the depopulation of cities, the closing of the churches, the cessation of the divine offices, every thing short of martyrdom, and some things not far short of that.   For there is now imminent danger that the tyrannical tribunal will be unclosed, and torments and bloodshed, and the crown of martyrdom proposed to us.   Is this the lesson which St. Peter teaches, when he instructs the shepherd to conduct his flock without constraint or domination ?"   In his letter to the cardinals he wrote with equal bitterness.   " Permit me to speak the truth to you.   Our division has arisen from the tyrannical oppression which you exercise, and the exactions of the Roman Church, which, from being a mother, has become a step-mother, and tramples upon others in proportion as they humble themselves before her.   We are scandalized to see you exclusively attached to the good things of this world; heaping up from all quarters gold and silver, and making kingdoms your tributaries."   That such reproaches, however just, should have broken forth in letters expressly conciliatory, might well have led those to whom they were addressed to despair of the success of the negotiation.   The original epistles are given by Matthew Paris, Histor. Major. ann. 1237; whose remark it is, that the animosity of the Greek Church was occasioned by the acts, more than the opinions, of its rival.   See also Raynaldus, ann. 1232-3.

emperor and the patriarch, in the January of 1234; and a
series of conferences then commenced, which did not finally
terminate, though occasionally interrupted, till the middle of
May.   It were needless to unfold the particulars of this controversy, though they are not destitute of interest and instruction
to the theological reader; nor shall we pursue the intricate ma-
nœuvres of the disputants, though the most practised polemic
might possibly peruse them with profit.   It is sufficient to mention that the dispute turned entirely on two points, the procession of the Holy Spirit; and the use of leavened or unleavened bread in the Eucharist. The Greeks urged the ancient
doctrine and practice; the Latins, without conceding their claims
to the authority of early writers, rested the weight of their defence on scripture.   The debates were broken off and renewed;
the same arguments and assertions were repelled and reiterated; and the ardour of the opposition increased as the contest was prolonged.

Compro-
mise pro-
posed by
the Empe-
ror.

At length the emperor, who was less heated by the theological zeal, and more sincere, as he was more interested, in his
desire for reconciliation, personally proposed to the envoys a
compromise.   " As in political (said this simple mediator) so
be it in theological negotiations.   When princes differ respecting a city or a province, each party relaxes somewhat of his
pretensions for the attainment of peace.   Our differences in
this matter are two, and if you sincerely wish for concord, concede one of them.   We will approve and revere your holy
sacrament; abandon to us your creed; say the creed as we say
it, effacing the offensive addition."   They replied—" Let us
tell you that the Pope and the Roman Church will not abandon one iota of its faith, or of any thing contained in its creed.
But the following proposal we may consent to make to you.
You must firmly believe and teach others, that the body of our
Lord may be consecrated with unleavened *as well as* leavened
bread; and you must burn all the books which your churchmen have written to the contrary.   And in respect to the Holy
Spirit, you must believe that it proceeds from the Son as well
as from the Father, and teach the people so; but the Pope
will not oblige you to insert the article in your creed—only all

books which have been written against it shall be burnt." On hearing this final declaration, the emperor resigned himself to despair *; but in his prelates it excited only feelings of indignation and revenge. One other violent conference followed, to which large multitudes of the people were admitted; and it was broken off by mutual charges of heresy, and confirmations of the ancient anathema. The legates then withdrew; having increased the evils which they had proposed to remove, and added fresh fuel and fierceness to the controversy.

We should observe, that throughout this dispute it was always assumed by the Latins that the result, or rather that the meaning, of the reconciliation would be the *obedience* of the Greek to the Roman Church; a return to that (supposed) submission which the former had shaken off. Now this assumption was not (as far as we can see) contested by the Greeks, certainly it was not made matter of argument. And yet that establishment of supremacy was, in fact, the point at which the Roman was ultimately aiming—as it was also that to which his pretensions were most slightly founded.

The failure of this enterprise did not prevent a similar attempt on the part of Innocent IV., which was conducted with more moderation, but with no better success, than the former. The agent, selected for the conduct of this mission, was of great dignity and reputation in the Church. John of Parma, general of the Franciscan order, and alike eminent for his theological erudition, and the austerity of his life, was a character well calculated to influence the prelates of the East. It is something to be enabled to assert that his sojourn at Nice (in 1249) produced no mischief; but the negotiations which

Similar attempt by Innocent IV.

---

* " De corpore Christi ita dicimus—quod oportebit vos firmiter credere et aliis prædicare quod Corpus Christi confici potest ita in Azymis sicut in fermentato ; et omnes libri, quos vestri scripserunt contra Fidem, condemnentur et comburantur. De S. Sancto ita dicimus ; quod oportebit vos credere S.S. procedere a Filio sicut a Patre, et istud necesse, ut prædicetur in populo ; quod autem cantetis istud in Symbolo, nisi velitis, non compellet vos Dominus Papa ; condemnatis et combustis omnibus libris, qui huic capitulo sunt contrarii. Quod audiens imperator graviter tulit, &c." The envoys wrote an account of their own embassy, addressed to the Pope, and contained *in Libro Censuum ;* whence Raynaldus (ann. 1232) has made extracts.

seemed likely to result from it were prevented by the deaths of
the Pope and the Emperor. In 1261 the sceptre of the Latins
was broken; and, upon the whole, we are unable to observe
that their conquest had any spiritual fruits, or any other consequences than bitterness and aggravated rancour*. And we
may here remark, that as the Latins on their expulsion from
the East did not resign their claims to ecclesiastical ascendency,
or abolish the titles of the dignities there conferred upon their
own clergy, so there continued long to exist about the Roman
court titular patriarchs, and titular bishops, of Constantinople,
Antioch, Jerusalem and other oriental sees, who, by the assumption of those empty names, offended the sensitive vanity of the
Greeks, and kept alive the mutual irritation.

Subse-
quent at-
tempts at
re-union.
Howbeit, for a short period after the restoration, the reunion
was negotiated with much more ardour than at any former time,
and even with a momentary show of success. The reason of
this eagerness on the part of Palæologus was the consciousness
of his weakness, and the terror of another crusade against his
still unsettled government. " I speak not now," he said, " about
dogmas or ceremonies of religion. If there is any difference
on that subject, we can arrange it more easily, after peace shall
have been concluded between us." The union desired by the
emperor was external and political: a perfect theological concord he might think hopeless, or he might not comprehend its
importance. Some Franciscans were once more sent to the
East by Urban IV.; and some articles were hastily drawn up.
But Clement IV. refused them his ratification, and composed
a more accurate formulary of faith, which he proposed for the
acceptance of the Greeks. This confession contained not only
the disputed tenet of the Holy Procession, but also expressed,
with great precision, the doctrine of Purgatory, and specified
the condition of souls after death, according to the degrees of

---

* Fleury goes so far as to consider the schism, properly speaking, to have *commenced* only at this period. Such, however, was not the opinion of people in those
days; in the account of the previous negotiations at Nice, we observe, that the
emperor, on some occasion, remarked, that the schism had *then* lasted three hundred years. On the other hand, the emperor did not date with accuracy—from
the breach between Photius and Nicholas, the space was above 360 years; from
the dispute between Cerularius and Leo IX., not more than 180.

their impurity.   Also, the doctrine and name of Transubstantiation were marked in it very particularly.   Moreover, the
plenitude of Pontifical power, and the duty of universal appeal
to that tribunal were carefully inculcated.   Clement could
scarcely have expected so much acquiescence from the
clergy of the East; but in a subsequent letter to the Emperor
he failed not to remind him, that the crown possessed power
sufficient, and even more than sufficient, to control the inclinations both of the clergy and the people.

In the earlier part of these negotiations, the clergy had preserved the appearance of neutrality; because they were un-
willing, without great necessity, to oppose any project of the
Emperor, and because they considered his present project as
wholly impracticable.   Probably they did not suppose that he
was himself sincere in so desperate a scheme.   Nevertheless,
as his political difficulties increased, he became more earnest in
his design; and when some of his prelates were at length
alarmed into resistance, he employed the secular authority to
repress them.

In the mean time, the second council of Lyons had been
called together, and one of its professed objects was the reconciliation of the churches.   It was still assembled, when (on
June 24, 1274) the ambassadors from the East arrived.   Several difficulties were still apprehended; and there were many
who reasonably trembled, lest that solemn meeting of the universal Church should be distracted by the passionate broils of
an endless controversy.   But the Emperor had arranged it
otherwise; and at the session which immediately followed, the
Western fathers were edified and astonished by the voice of the
prelates of the East, chanting the *Double* Procession, in unison
with the worship of the orthodox.   The policy, which had
dictated the humiliating concession, did not hesitate there;
probably there was no depth of spiritual submission to which
the Emperor was not then prepared to descend: for it seemed
to depend on the decision of that council, whether the arma-
ment, to which all Europe was contributing, should be directed
against Syria or against himself.   Accordingly, the Pope's
supremacy was acknowledged without any scruple; and a com-

Council of Lyons. Concessions of the Greeks.

munication from Palæologus was publicly recited, in which he professed, without any equivocation or cavil, every tenet laid down in the confession of Clement IV. The reunion of the churches was then officially announced; and the Pope pronounced the *Te Deum,* with his head uncovered, and his eyes suffused with unsuspicious joy.

Revoked immediately afterwards.

As long as the fears and necessities of the Eastern Empire continued, as long as the fragile vessel of state lay at the mercy of any tempest from the West, so long did this hollow truce subsist. But not quite ten years after its conclusion, Andronicus, having succeeded to the sceptre of his father, proceeded, without delay, to dissolve the union. A council was assembled at Constantinople; the hateful act of humiliation was repealed; and the revival of the schism was proclaimed amidst the acclamations of the clergy of Greece. One circumstance, indeed, is here particularly forced upon our attention. The motive which chiefly persuaded Andronicus to re-open that ancient wound was, that he might heal a still more dangerous disorder, which the reconciliation with Rome had inflicted upon his own Church. The power of Palæologus had secured the outward submission, but it had not changed the opinions, or the principles, or the passions of his prelates: the great majority remained adverse to the re-union; and in their importunate and pressing clamours, the fears of an ancient and distant rival were forgotten. Howbeit the domestic dissensions of the Greeks were not even thus allayed: there were some too strongly impressed with the policy of their late connexion to applaud its hasty dissolution; and there remained ever afterwards a party in the East which professed its adhesion to the Roman communion.

We shall not pursue the insincere and fruitless overtures which were so often defeated and renewed during the fourteenth century, and especially under the Popes of Avignon. The pontificates of John XXII., of Clement VI., of Innocent VI., and Benedict XII., were particularly marked by those vain negotiations *; and during this period we may remark

---

* It was on the last occasion that the emperor sent that Barlaam, whom we have already mentioned, (the same who instructed Petrarch in the rudiments of

that the motives of both parties were equally removed from any spiritual consideration. If political exigencies invariably actuated the one, the other was now chiefly moved by pecuniary necessities. The military succours, which the Pope might be the means of raising, would be recompensed by obedient contributions to the apostolical treasury. According to the approach or suspension of immediate danger, the zeal for reconciliation burnt fiercely, or subsided; but the characters were still sustained under all circumstances. " That old song respecting the Greeks (said the fathers of Basle) has already lasted for three hundred years, and every year it is chanted afresh." At length the progress of the Turks excited a permanent alarm, and a proportionate sincerity; and we shall now shortly trace the chief events to which it led.

After separate negotiations with Pope Eugenius and the Council of Basle, the Emperor of the East at length decided to accept the proposals of the former. An oriental despot might well be perplexed by the claims of two rival authorities, both professing to be legitimate and supreme, and both acknowledged by many adherents in their own communion. But whether his imperial prejudices inclined him towards the *Monarch* of the Church, or from whatsoever other motive, he embarked (in November, 1427) with his patriarch, and numerous ecclesiastics, on the galleys of Eugenius, and arrived in due season at the appointed city, Ferrara. A trifling difference first arose respecting the seats to be respectively occupied during the conference by its spiritual and temporal presidents. But this was arranged by a compromise, by which the Pope conceded a part of his claim, but retained his pre-eminence. They were placed on different sides of the Church, but the Pope was on the right, and his throne was one step higher than that of

Council of Ferrara, 1428, A.D.

Greek,) to the court of Avignon. Sufficient accounts of these various negotiations are given by Bzovius, ad ann. 1331, s. i. 1339, s. 22, 1345-6-9, and particularly 1356, s. 22. On one occasion (in 1339) great efforts were made to show that the Greek opinions had always been the *same* with the Latin (after so many mutual excommunications!) and this, as we all know, furnished Leo Allatius in a later age with a fruitful field for sophistry. The detestation which the Greeks still entertained for the Pope is strongly expressed by the Patriarch Gennadius in a document which is cited by Bzovius, ann. 1349, s. 14,

the Emperor. The next proceeding, and it might occasion some surprise, if not distrust, among strangers, unused to the discords of the West, was the promulgation of a solemn anathema against the Council of Basle. All public deliberations were then adjourned for some months; but it was arranged that, during this interval, a select number of doctors of the two Churches should frequently meet, and prepare the way by amicable discussions for a more speedy reconciliation.

Contro-
verted
questions.
Accordingly these deputies, who were, indeed, the leading members of both parties, did meet. On the one side was the celebrated Julian Cesarini, Cardinal of St. Angelo, and so lately the President of the rival Council; and with him were Andreas, Bishop of Colossus (or Rhodes), John, a Doctor of Spain, and some others. Marc of Ephesus, and Bessarion, Archbishop of Nice, conducted the disputations on the other. It was here agreed, seemingly without difference, that the articles by which the schism was entirely occasioned were four. (1.) The Procession of the Holy Spirit. (2.) The use of leavened or unleavened bread in the Eucharist. (3.) Purgatory. (4.) The Primacy of the Pope. It was further settled that the subject of the first discussion should be Purgatory.

Purgatory.
Accordingly, Cardinal Julian laid down the doctrine of his Church on that matter as follows :—that the souls of the just, which are pure and without stain, and have been exempt from mortal sin, proceed directly to heaven, to the enjoyment of eternal happiness; but that the souls of men who have fallen into sin after their baptism, unless they have fully accomplished the penance necessary to expiate that sin (even though they may have performed some penance), and also manifested fruits worthy of their penitence, so as to receive entire remission, pass into the fire of Purgatory; that some remain there for a longer, others for a shorter period, according to the nature of their offences; and that, being at length purified, they are admitted to beatitude. But that the souls of those who die in mortal sin are consigned to immediate punishment. To this Marc of Ephesus replied, that the doctrine, in the main, was that of the Greek Church; only that the latter did not admit the purification by fire, but held that sinful souls were sent into a place of

darkness and mourning, where they remained for a season in affliction, deprived of the light of God. He admitted that they were purified, and delivered from this desolate abode by sacrifice and alms; but he held that the condemned would not be wholly miserable, and that the saints would not be admitted to perfect beatitude until after the resurrection of their bodies. On this last point an unexpected difference arose between Marc of Ephesus and his colleague, Bessarion, as to what really was the doctrine of their Church; and this was pressed to dispute and altercation. In the mean time the season advanced, and these preliminary conferences were discontinued before the disputants had touched on any other subject, or arrived at any specific conclusion even upon that.

At length the formal deliberations of the Council commenced, and the first public session was held on the 8th of October; but there were some among the Greeks who, observing that the Fathers of Basle had shown, in the mean time, no indications of submission, began already to despair of any durable effect from their mission. However, the prelates assembled in considerable numbers; the same were recognised by both parties, as the important subjects of difference, and it was agreed that the *first* of them was that in which the whole difficulty of reunion was, in fact, involved. They prepared, in consequence, to argue the mystery of the Procession with becoming solemnity: and it was vainly hoped that a question which had employed the learning and wearied the ingenuity of the Christian world for about eight hundred years, would finally be set at rest by the eloquence of the Doctors of Ferrara. *Procession of the Holy Ghost.*

It must be admitted that the advocates of both opinions displayed on this occasion abundant talents, unwearied zeal, and resources almost inexhaustible, especially the Cardinal of St. Angelo *; who here exhibited, in defence of the doctrine of his Church, the same commanding faculties and energy with which he had urged, at Basle, the reformation of its discipline. Through fifteen tedious sessions the controversy was main-

---

* Tiraboschi (vol. vi. p. 1, l. ii.) cites the testimony of Sguropulos, who was present at all these discussions, and expressed his astonishment at the eloquence of Julian.

tained with unabated ardour; and though the point principally argued was only, whether the words *Filioque* were, properly speaking, an addition or an explanation, it might have been supposed, from the warmth and prolixity of the orators, that the very existence of the Christian faith was at stake. At length, as no immediate result seemed at all probable, and as Ferrara was found, on many accounts, inconvenient for so large * an assemblage, the Pope, with the consent of the Emperor, adjourned the Council to Florence.

The Council is removed to Florence.

The Council of Florence held its first session on Feb. 26, 1439; and it opened with some proposals on the part of the Emperor and Cardinal Julian, for arriving more directly at the practical object of these conferences—a public reconciliation. But no expedient was discovered for attaining that end, and the disputations were accordingly renewed. The results of the conferences at Ferrara had not been such as either to bring the Latins to retrench the contested expression from the creed, or the Greeks to insert it: thus the Procession became once more the subject of debate. For the seven succeeding sessions the same assertions were advanced and denied, the same arguments reiterated and confuted. At length, however, the Latins found a new and powerful champion in John, provincial of the Dominicans. This learned mendicant, by reference to ancient manuscripts of St. Basil, and other Greek Fathers, professed to demonstrate that those venerable Patriarchs had asserted the double Procession. This was an assault upon that point, on which alone the Greeks were very sensible. Every shaft of reason might be foiled or blunted by sophistry or prejudice; every other authority might be suspected or disavowed; but when the archives of their own unerring Church were cited against them, it was hard indeed to raise any defence, or reply with any confidence. It would appear, too, that Bessarion had

---

* About one hundred and fifty Bishops, besides numerous Abbots, are said to have been present. We should here mention that the Greeks lived at the expense of the Pope, receiving a regular stipulated allowance from the Apostolical Treasury. Notwithstanding, so great was their despondency as to the result of the embassy, that they betrayed from time to time a strong desire to return to Greece.

for some time taken little share in the disputes, and at length
even Marc of Ephesus withdrew from the conference. The
victory now appeared to rest with the Latins; when the Emperor, who possessed some skill in theology, and was sincerely
desirous of the reunion, discovered what he considered an equi-
table method of compromise. In a letter of St. Maximus, that
Father was found to have asserted that "the Latins, when
they declare that the Holy Spirit proceeds from the Son, do
not pretend that the Son is the cause of the Holy Spirit, since
they know very well that the Father is the only cause both of
the Son and the Holy Spirit—of the Son by generation, of the
Holy Spirit by procession—they only mean, that the Holy
Spirit proceeds *through* the Son, because he is of the same
essence." Soon after this proposal had been made, the public
sessions of the Council were suspended, and the Greeks held
several conferences among themselves, with a view to some
honourable accommodation.

The Greeks were now openly divided. Bessarion, gained,
as his adversaries assert, by the presents and promises of the
Pontiff, at once avowed his adhesion to the Latin dogma, and
defended it with confidence and eloquence. Of this same party
was the Emperor, through his anxiety to reconcile the Churches
on any terms, and at any sacrifice. Marc of Ephesus obstinately maintained his original opinions; he abhorred the *heresy*
of the Latins, and rejected every overture of compromise.
Nevertheless the conferences continued: several attempts were
made to devise some explanation of the Oriental doctrine which
might be satisfactory to the Latins; and the party of the
Unionists gained ground. The Emperor saw his advantage,
and pursued it by such means of persuasion as an Emperor TheGreeks
may always exercise. And at length, after more than two concedethe
months of discussion, the Greeks unanimously consented to Procession.
the terms of reconciliation, with the single honest exception of
Marc of Ephesus.

The confession of faith, on which this treaty of concord was Common
founded, was as follows:—"In the name of the Holy Trinity, Confession
of the Father, the Son, and the Holy Ghost, we, Latins and of Faith.
Greeks, agree in the holy union of these two Churches, and

confess that all true Christians ought to receive this genuine
doctrine : that the Holy Spirit is eternally of the Father and
the Son, and that from all eternity it proceeds from the one
and the other as from a single principle, and by a single production, which we call Spiration.   We also declare that what
some of the Holy Fathers have said, viz., that the Holy Spirit
proceeds from the Father through the Son, should be taken in
such a manner as to signify that the Son, as well as the Father,
and conjointly with him, is the principle of the Holy Spirit.
And since, whatsoever the Father hath, that he communicates
to his Son, excepting the paternity which distinguishes him
from the Son and the Holy Spirit, so is it from the Father
that the Son has received, from all eternity, that productive
virtue through which the Holy Spirit proceeds from the Son,
as well as from the Father."

Treaties of Union.   We should here mention that, while this spiritual negotiation
was in progress, another convention of a very different character
was also under consideration ; and the two treaties were brought
to their conclusion at the same time.   It was stipulated by the
latter that his Holiness should furnish the Greeks with resources
for their return; that he should maintain a standing military
and naval force for the defence of Constantinople ; that the
galleys carrying pilgrims to Jerusalem should be compelled to
touch at Constantinople; that, if the Emperor should require
twenty galleys for six months, or for a year, the Pope should
bind himself to supply them ; and that, if soldiers were wanted,
he should use his influence with the princes of the West to
procure them.   This convention having been officially ratified,
the Emperor announced the consent of his Prelates to the doctrinal accommodation ; and on the 6th of June, 1439, it was
announced, that the divisions of so many centuries were at
length closed for ever.   The Confession of Union was recited
in Greek and in Latin, and it was hailed by the acclamations
of both parties, who embraced with seeming warmth, and interchanged the salutation of peace.

It will have been observed that the public disputations had
been entirely confined to one of the four subjects of difference ;
and that the arrangement of that, as it was considered by far

the most difficult question, was held to be a sufficient pledge of agreement upon all. And so indeed it proved. The difference on the Azyms was removed by the confession of the Greeks, that the Eucharist might be celebrated with unleavened, as worthily as with leavened, bread. Respecting Purgatory, it was acknowledged on both sides that those souls which could neither, through some unatoned sins, be received into immediate beatitude, nor yet deserved eternal condemnation, were delivered into some abode of temporary durance and purification; but regarding the method of purification—whether it was by fire, as some thought, or by darkness and tempest, as seemed to be the opinion of others—it was held more prudent to abstain from any positive declaration. The question of the Pope's primacy occasioned somewhat greater embarrassment, because its practical consequence was more directly perceptible; and though the imperial eye might overlook the importance of doctrinal differences, it was not blind to any encroachment on imperial prerogative. And thus, though Palæologus readily assented to the *general* proposition of papal supremacy, he objected to its application in two cases. He would not consent that the Pope should call councils in his dominions without his approbation and that of the Patriarchs; nor would he permit appeals from the patriarchal courts to be carried to Rome. He maintained that the Pope should send his legates to decide them on the spot. The Pontiff insisted; but as the Emperor declared that he would prefer to break off the negotiations, even in that their latest stage, rather than yield those points, a method of verbal compromise was discovered, which satisfied the consciences of both parties.

To the attentive reader it will, perhaps, appear strange that in so many controversies between the two Churches no dispute had yet been raised on the subject of Transubstantiation. And it will thence seem natural to infer that, on that point, no difference existed between them. In a later age, when the Protestants were contending with the Roman Catholics for the spiritual adhesion of the Greeks, this important question was thoroughly investigated; and the result, as it appears to us *,

Question of Transubstantiation.

---

* This subject has been shortly treated by the Author of this History, in a work " On the Condition and Prospects of the Greek Church."

was not quite favourable to either party. For, if some of the ancient Fathers indulged in very lofty expressions on the nature of the Eucharist, yet the Latin dogma was never formally established among the Articles of the other Church. We shall now mention that, during the conferences at Ferrara and Florence, certain expressions fell from the Greek Doctors, which excited suspicions of their orthodoxy so generally, that the Pope deemed it necessary to demand of them a formal declaration on that point, before the "Decree of Union" should be finally ratified. Accordingly, Bessarion of Nice, on the part and in the presence of his brethren, made an affirmation to this effect:—"Since in the preceding congregations we have been suspected of holding an erroneous opinion touching the words of the Consecration, we declare, in the presence of your Holiness, . . . that we have learnt from our ancient Fathers, and especially from St. Chrysostom, that it is the words of our Lord which change the substance of the bread and wine into that of the Body and Blood of Jesus Christ; and that those divine words have the force and virtue to make that wonderful change of substance, or that Transubstantiation; and that we follow the sentiments of that great teacher." These expressions are, in themselves, sufficiently explicit: but, on the other hand, we are bound to recollect that the Greeks at Florence had by this time abandoned in despair every manner of resistance to the Emperor and the Pope; and also, that the Prelate who read the declaration, and whose motives are liable to very well-founded suspicion, was afterwards exalted to the dignity of a Cardinal in the Roman Church.

Fate of Julian Cesarini.

Bessarion, an Asiatic archbishop, ended his days in the peaceful enjoyment of a Roman dignity. His great antagonist, Julian Cesarini, Cardinal of St. Angelo, under a less auspicious influence, exchanged the field of controversial achievement for that of military dishonour. Let us here trace his concluding fortunes. Being appointed by the Pope to superintend, as his legate, the warlike operations against the Turks, he attached himself to the camp of Huniades. Under his sanction, and with his consent, (it was a reluctant consent,) a truce for ten years was signed, with religious solemnities, between the contending parties; and Amurat reposed in confidence on the shores of the Bosphorus, or employed his forces in some other enterprise. Suddenly some new circumstance came to light, which promised advantage to the Christians from the renewal of hostilities. Hereupon the Cardinal Legate, perceiving some hesitation among the generals, seized a favourable moment to counsel the violation of the truce. To this effect, he urged the impolicy of the secret engagement, the *infidelity* of the party with whom it was contracted. He pressed the injustice thereby offered both to the Pope and the Emperor; the prejudice done to their own reputation and to the interests of the Church. He maintained that the very compact with the Turk was in itself an act of perfidy to their allies. These and similar arguments he advanced with his customary power. But seeing that his unlettered hearers were not yet persuaded that a treaty so solemnly ratified could at once be violated without reproach, he proceeded more curiously to distinguish between the obligation due to a mere promise and that which is demanded by the public welfare, and to show the higher authority of the latter. Whenever these, forsooth, were at variance, the faith plighted to an infidel could have little solid weight. For though, in truth, an oath is binding when it is just and founded in equity, it is properly considered as null, and displeasing to God, when it leads to private or public calamity, &c. &c. !

The eloquence of the Cardinal so well enforced his fallacies upon minds which probably were only thirsting for conviction, that the whole assembly demanded with acclamations the violation of the truce. The army moved forwards, and immediately engaged in that campaign which was terminated by the battle of Varna. In that fatal encounter, among thousands of less illustrious victims, fell the Cardinal of St. Angelo. The nature of his death is uncertain. It is variously asserted that he was slain in the field, and in the rout; that he was drowned in the Danube; that he was plundered and murdered by Hungarian robbers. And it had been happier for his memory had the last struggle of his genius been wrapt in the same obscurity—could we forget that it was made for the purpose of corrupting the rude morality of Christian soldiers and statesmen, and leading them into that perjured enterprise which ended in his destruction and their disaster, and the infamy of all.

Return of the Greeks, and their reception.
After the last confession of Bessarion, the " Decree of Union" was signed and ratified; and the Greeks, their object accomplished, set forth, with various emotions perhaps, but with general satisfaction, on their return to the East. The voyage was favourable; and on the 20th of February, 1440, they were restored to the altars of Constantinople. With what feelings were these messengers of religious concord welcomed? What salutations hailed them on their arrival from that holy enterprise? The joy, the gratitude, the affection of their fellow-*Catholics?* Let us turn to the circumstances of their reception: through a general confederacy of the clergy, of the people, and particularly of the monks, who chiefly swayed the conscience and directed the movements of the people, the authors of the Union found themselves excluded even from their ecclesiastical functions. They were overwhelmed with insults. They were called azymites, apostates, traitors to the true religion; the sanctuaries which they entered were deserted; they were shunned, as if convicted of impiety, or blasted by excommunication; and in many of the churches, the spirit went so far, that the very name of the Emperor himself was erased from the Dyptics. On the other hand, Marc of Ephesus, who had fought without concession or compromise the battles of his Church, and persisted inflexibly in his repugnance to the reunion, was rewarded by universal acclamation. Marc of Ephesus had alone stood forth as the defender of the faith and of the honour of the Œcumenic Church.

Dissensions in the East.
The controversy was immediately renewed in the East. Marc placed himself at the head of the schismatics, and many compositions were published, as well by himself as by others, to press the repeal of the Union. Various polemical treatises were also put forth in rejoinder; and at the same time the Emperor exerted, on the same side, a more equivocal method of persuasion. He selected for the Patriarch of Constantinople a decided supporter of the Union, and caused the patronage of the see to be conferred exclusively upon ecclesiastics of that

party. Within the limits of his temporal sovereignty the Head of the Oriental Church received a reluctant obedience. But beyond those boundaries, under the Patriarchs of Jerusalem, of Antioch, and Alexandria, his spiritual subjects—for they were no more than spiritual—broke forth into undisguised rebellion. In 1443 those three Prelates united in publishing a Synodal Epistle, in which they pronounced the sentence of deposition against all those on whom their Brother of Constantinople had conferred ordination, and then added the threat of excommunication, in case this sentence should be neglected. At the same time, they addressed to the Emperor himself a similar menace, should he still continue to protect his Patriarch.

A Synod, which combined the authority of three of their Patriarchs, was reverentially regarded by a people already predisposed to embrace its edicts. Even the resolution of Palæologus appears to have been shaken by so bold an act of insubordination. At the same time, as if to increase his confusion, the clergy and populace of the Northern provinces of his Church, Russia and Muscovy, loudly declared themselves against the Union, and insulted and imprisoned a Papal Legate who was sent to publish it among them. Thus, after his sojourn under foreign dominion, after his personal exertions in allaying the heats of controversy, and conducting it, as he fondly fancied, to a lasting termination, the Emperor of the East discovered that his ecclesiastical influence was confined almost to the city and suburbs of Constantinople; and that the treaty from which he expected such advantage was received even there with a reluctant and precarious, even though it was an interested, submission.

It might have been supposed that some sense of political advantage would have moved the feelings of his subjects; that the prospect of a powerful alliance would have exerted some influence; that the sight of the advancing Turk would have inspired some moderation; or, if reason was, indeed, excluded from the controversy, that the passion of fear would, in some degree, have counteracted the passion of bigotry. Some mitigation of the first phrenzy might at least have been expected from time; and in the interval of eleven years, more charitable

[marginal note:] Universal outcry against the Union.

feelings and more provident considerations might gradually have gained prevalence under the imperial patronage. But the event was far otherwise: if the heat of either party relaxed during this critical period, it was that of the friends of the Union; its opponents increased in strength, and remitted nothing of their original rancour.

Prediction of Nicholas V., and fall of the Greek empire.

In the year 1451, Nicholas V., after engaging in some earnest endeavours to rouse the energies of Christendom against the common foe, issued a celebrated address to the Greeks. He exhorted them to pay some regard to their own safety, and not to paralyse the efforts which Providence was making to preserve them; to display their devotion in acts of penitence, and to receive, without delay, the decree of the Council of Florence. To the Emperor Constantine he addressed a menace, dictated, as some have thought, by a prophetic spirit. After complaining that the Greeks had now too long trifled with the patience of God and man, in deferring their reconciliation with the Church, he announced that, according to the parable in the Gospel, three years of probation would still be granted for the fig-tree, hitherto cultivated in vain, to bring forth fruit. But if it did not bear fruit in that season—if the Greeks, during the space which God still indulged to them, did not receive the decree of the Union—that then, indeed, the tree would be cut down even to its root—the nation extirpated by the ministers of divine justice.

This denunciation contemplated no improbable catastrophe; and the Emperor took such measures as were left to him to conciliate the dispositions of the Vatican. But what was the spirit which at this last crisis animated his subjects? It was during this very year that several Greek ecclesiastics addressed, in the name of the whole Church, a communication to the rebels of Bohemia. They praised the zeal of their brother schismatics; they applauded them for their rejection of the innovations of Rome, and their adherence to the true faith; and, finally, called on them to conclude a treaty of Union with themselves —not such union as that mockery of concord dressed up at Florence, from which truth was far removed, but union, founded on the respectable opinions of the ancient Fathers!....

And thus those precious moments which the Pope devoted to vows and exertions for the salvation of Greece were employed by her zealous theologians in courting the bitterest enemies of his government.

In the year following, the Emperor having received with honour the Papal Legate, and made him some fair promises, they proceeded to celebrate the Liturgy in St. Sophia. But as soon as mention was made, in the course of the service, of the names of the Pope and the Latin Patriarch*, the whole city rose in commotion, and the multitude, uncertain what course to take, rushed in a mass to consult a popular fanatic, named Gennadius. This man was a monk, and attached to the door of his cell they found a written rescript, denouncing the last inflictions against all who should receive the impious decree of Florence. Then it was that Priests and Abbots, Monks and Nuns, soldiers and citizens, the entire population, except the immediate dependents of the Emperor, shouted, as with a single voice—" Anathema against all who are united with the Latins!" The sanctuary of St. Sophia was proclaimed profane; all intercourse was suspended with all who had assisted at the service with the Latins; absolution was refused, and the churches were closed against them.

This was the madness of a falling empire—this was the heaven-inflicted delirium which prepared the path for destruction. The measure of fanaticism was at length filled up; the pontifical prophecy † hastened to its accomplishment. And while the frantic people of Greece were in the highest ferment of theological excitement—while their religious hatred against their brother Christians was burning most intensely—while partial differences were most exaggerated—while sectarian intolerance was most fierce and uncompromising, the banners of

* Gregory—then a voluntary exile at Rome, through his reluctance to preside over a rebellious Church.

† Constantinople was certainly taken in the third year (inclusive) after the prediction of Nicholas. The Pope wrote some time in 1451; the city fell on May 29, 1453. The coincidence, even with this latitude, was fortunate; but after the battle of Varna, no light from heaven was necessary to foreshow the speedy downfall of the Greek empire.

the Infidel were in motion towards the devoted city, and a
nation of Christians was consigned in bondage to the common
enemy of Christ.

Notes on Chapter XXVI.

NOTE (1) ON THE ARMENIANS.

Differences
between
the Arme-
nians and
the Greeks.
THE first occasion on which we can observe the Armenians to
have come into contact, as an independent communion, with
the Church of Rome, was the following:—In the year 1145,
while Pope Eugenius was resident at Viterbo, certain deputies
from their patriarch (also called their *Catholic*), arrived to
salute the Pontiff, and proffer every sort of respect and deference.   The particular object of their mission appears, however, to have been this—to appeal to the decision of the Pope
respecting their differences with the Greek Church.   The differences principally debated were two:—the Armenians did
not mix water with the wine in the eucharist; they made use
of leavened bread, excepting on the festivals of Christmas and
the Epiphany.   We do not learn that there were any lasting
results from this embassy; but it is carefully recorded* that
the Orientals assisted at the Latin mass celebrated by the Pope
in person; and that one of them beheld on that solemnity a
sunbeam resting on the head of the Pontiff, as well as two
doves ascending and descending above him in an inexplicable
manner—a marvel which greatly moved him to reverence and
submission.

Notwithstanding, the circumstances under which the Armenians next present themselves to the historian prove the futility
of the former overtures to Rome.   For we find that, in the year
1170, the *Catholic* Norsesis addressed a letter to Manuel
Comnenus, in which he mentioned some points whereon himself and the Greeks were not agreed, and expressed a strong
desire for reconciliation.   The Emperor intrusted the commis-

* By Otho Frisingensis, who was at that time at Viterbo.

sion to a philosopher named Theorian, who proceeded to Armenia, and conferred with the patriarch and another influential prelate. On this occasion much more important differences were advanced than those discovered at Viterbo; and that which was most prominent respected the nature of Christ. From the account of this controversy it would appear that, in the outset, the Greeks supposed the Armenians to be involved in the Eutychian heresy, while the Armenians imagined the Greeks to have embraced the opposite error of Nestorius. In the course of the conference both were undeceived. The Armenians did indeed admit that they held *one incarnate nature ;* but not by confusion, like Eutyches, nor by diminution, like Apollinaris, but in the " orthodox" sense of Cyril of Alexandria*. The Greeks cleared their own tenets from the charge of Nestorianism with equal perspicuity. The result was, that the Catholic acknowledged their orthodoxy, and undertook to bring over all his compatriots to the same opinion. Some other differences of inferior weight were also discussed; and these, too, the Armenian is related to have softened away with equal facility. At length, after an affecting interview, in which many tears were poured forth in pious sympathy by both parties, Theorian returned to Constantinople, and Narsesis prepared to communicate his own convictions to the Church over which he presided.

With what little success these negotiations were attended appears from the next glimpse that we catch of the ecclesiastical affairs of the Armenians. On the 23rd of May, 1199, Leo, their king, addressed an epistle to Innocent III., expressing his anxiety for the re-union of his Church with that of Rome. At the same time he disclosed the motive of his anxiety; for he deplored the ravages to which his kingdom was exposed by the inroads of the infidels, and proclaimed the absolute need

Overture to Rome.

---

* See " Theoriani Orthodoxi cum Catholico Armeniorum Colloquium," in the Maxima Biblioth. P.P., tom. xxii., p. 796—812, (Edit. Lugdun., 1677). " Dicimus in Christo naturam unam esse, non secundum Eutychen confundentes, nec secundum Apollinarem detrahentes, sed secundum Alexandrinum Antistitem Cyrillum, in Orthodoxia, quæ in libro contra Nestorium scripsit, unam esse naturam *Sermonis* incarnatam".... The controversy turned a good deal on the distinction (real or imaginary) between *Christus* and *Sermo,* in this question.

in which he stood of foreign succour. This application was accompanied by one from the Catholic, in which he professed his wish for reconciliation, and his readiness to make submission to the Vatican. The Pope sent, in reply, many civil expressions; and intended, no doubt, to confer a more substantial service on his militant fellow-Christians, when he presented them at the same time with the standard of St. Peter, as a safeguard against the sword of the unbeliever. Some negotiations succeeded: at length (in the year 1205), the king prevailed upon his subjects to acknowledge their spiritual allegiance to the Pope; and the Catholic publicly placed the act of his submission in the hands of the legate. He accepted the *pallium** from the same authority, and engaged to visit the Holy See, by his Nuncios, once in every five years, and to assist in person, or by deputy, at all councils which might be held in the West for the regulation of his interests. Greater objections appear to have prevailed among those Orientals against the introduction of the Roman code of Canon law; but it was arranged that some part of its institutions should be received at once, and the rest at some future time, after more mature deliberation among the Armenian prelates. Such was the general nature of the reconciliation then effected: but some dissensions presently arose between the king and one of the pontifical legates; and there seems no reason to believe that the above negotiation had any lasting consequences†.

As the amicable overtures from Armenia to Rome were entirely occasioned by the political necessities of the former, they were more frequent during the desolation of the East in the

* See the Letter from Leo to Innocent, published by Raynaldus, ann. 1205, in which he boasts that, with great labour, and through divine grace, he had at length brought about that obedience of the Armenians to the Roman Church, which his ancestors had so long attempted in vain.

† From the fragment of a Greek writer, named Nico (probably of the thirteenth century), translated and published in the Max. Bibliotheca P.P. (tom. xxv. p. 328), and entitled "De Pessimorum Armeniorum pessima Religione," it appears that they still retained all the errors imputed to them by *either* Church. Among a multitude here enumerated, it is one that "that they do not adore the venerable images, but, on the contrary, that their Catholic anathematizes those who do so. Neither do they worship the Cross, until they have driven a nail into it, and baptized it," &c.

fourteenth century. The interested obedience of that communion was tendered to John XXII., and accepted by him.
A few years afterwards (in 1341) we observe another king,
named Leo, soliciting temporal assistance from Benedict XII.
The Pope made answer in two letters, respectively addressed
to the King and to the Catholic. In the former, he made
mention of the errors entertained by the Armenians, and of the
exertions which he had made, both by personal inquiry from
those professing them, and by the examination of the authorized
books, to ascertain their nature and extent. In the latter, he
exhorted the clergy to assemble in council, to condemn and
extirpate the false opinions which they held, and then, for their
better instruction in the faith and observances of the Roman
Church, to receive the Decree, the Decretals, and other Canons
used in the West. He expressed a pious persuasion that when
the errors of the Armenians should once be removed, the
enemies of the faith would no longer prevail against them; and
concluded his address by the proposal of a conference.

The first of these epistles was accompanied by a memorial, *Imputed errors of the Arme-nians.*
in which the errors in question were enumerated. They were
expanded into a tedious catalogue of one hundred and seven-
teen ; but they may, without much inaccuracy, be reduced
under the following heads :—1. The Armenians were accused
of adhesion to the opinions of Eutyches, involving, of course,
the Monophysite heresy, the rejection of the Council of Chalcedon, the condemnation of St. Leo, and the secession from
both the Œcumenic Churches. 2. They were charged with
administering the sacraments of confirmation and the eucharist,
together with that of baptism—a practice which (as Fleury
observes) had very early prevalence in the Church. 3. They
mixed no water with the wine in the holy communion—which
again was an ancient usage. 4. They rejected Transubstantiation, and maintained that it was the figure only, not the real
body, that was received by the communicants—an opinion
which was then naturally considered as a consequence of the
Eutychian error respecting the nature of Christ—for if any
doubts were thrown on the reality of Christ's body on earth,
the same would extend in an equal (if not in a greater) degree

to the reality of his flesh in the sacrament of his supper. The
other imputations concerned some fabulous notions respecting
the resurrection, the last judgment, the place of punishment,
the earthly and heavenly paradise, the intermediate state, and
other questions of difficult determination.

In consequence of the pontifical remonstrances, the Patriarch
assembled his council, and condemned all the imputed errors ;
he then sent deputies to the succeeding Pope (Clement VI.),
charged with a general obligation to retract any other obnoxious opinions which might thereafter be discovered ; and
at the same time to acknowledge the Bishop of Rome as the
chief of the Church of Christ, and to solicit copies of the Decretals for the more faithful administration of his own subordinate
communion. The Pope engaged to send them, and in November, 1346, despatched two legates on a mission to the East.

Questions proposed by Clement VI.

Five years afterwards, the Pontiff, still dissatisfied with the
communications (perhaps equivocal) which he received from
his new subjects, and desiring a more express declaration of
their opinions on those points which most interested himself,
addressed the Catholic of Lesser Armenia in terms not sub-
stantially different from the following :—" Since we are unable
clearly to collect your opinions from your answers, we desire
distinctly to propose the following questions :—Do you believe
that all who at their baptism have received the Catholic faith,
and have afterwards separated from the communion, are schismatics and heretics, if they persist in such separation ? and
that no one can be saved who has renounced obedience to the
Pope ? Do you believe that St. Peter received from Jesus
Christ full power of jurisdiction over all the faithful ? that all
the power which the Apostles may have possessed in certain
provinces was subject to his ? and that all the successors of
St. Peter have the same power with himself ? Do you believe
that, in virtue of that power, the Pope can judge all the faithful
immediately, and delegate to that effect such ecclesiastical
judges as he may think proper ? Do you believe that the Pope
can be judged by no one, except God himself ; and that there
is no appeal from his decisions to any judge ? Do you believe
that he can translate bishops, and abbots, and other ecclesias-

tics from one dignity to another, or degrade and depose them, if they deserve such punishment? Do you believe that the Pope is not subject to any secular power, even regal or imperial, in respect to institution, correction, or destitution; that he alone can make general canons, and grant plenary indulgences, and decide disputes on matters of faith?" .... These interrogations were accompanied by the notice of some Armenian errors on the intermediate state, on the sacraments, and especially the Eucharist; and by some complaints, that promises hitherto made with facility had not been sufficiently observed. But they chiefly merit the historian's attention, as they prove the uncompromising severity with which Rome, even during the exile of her Pontiffs, exacted all her usurped ecclesiastical rights, and imposed the whole weight and pressure of her yoke even on the most distant and most reluctant of her subjects. Howbeit, after that period, we do not observe any proof of the continuance or renewal of friendly negotiation between Rome and Armenia, sufficiently important to deserve a place in this History.

NOTE (2) ON THE MARONITES.

MARO, or Maroun, from whom this sect derives its appellation, lived during the latter part of the sixth century on the banks of the Orontes; and in the disputes then prevailing between the Eastern and Western Churches, he exerted his influence, which was considerable in that part of Syria, in favour of the latter. About a century later, a certain John, surnamed the Maronite, was distinguished by his opposition to the Melchites Greeks; and it seems to have been under his guidance, that the Syrian "rebels" * settled apart in the secure recesses of Libanus and Antilibanus. There they formed a powerful association, formidable alike to the orthodox Greeks and to the Mahometan invader. The first crusades brought them once more into immediate contact with the Latins; but not always as allies, nor by any means as members of the same ecclesias-

---

* They were then called Mardaites—which means Rebels. The reader is familiar with the picture of the Maronites drawn in Volney's admirable "Travels in Syria."

tical communion. For it appears certain that the Maronites had imbibed, in the first instance, the opinions of the Mono-thelites, and that they long maintained them, together with some other peculiarities in rites and discipline. At length, how-ever, about the year 1182, they were induced to abandon their leading error, and were then received into the bosom of the Roman Church.

At the same time it was stipulated that the Pope should in no respect interfere with any of their ancient practices or cere-monies; consequently they continued to observe the discipline of the Greek Church, regarding the marriage of the clergy, and to administer the Eucharist in both kinds, and according to the manner generally in use in the East. They retained, too, in other matters, a much closer resemblance to their original, than to their adopted, communion. Nevertheless, they have faithfully preserved the name of obedience to Rome from that time to the present; and if the contributions, which they have continually received from the apostolical treasury, should occasion any suspicion respecting the motives of their fidelity, it is worthy, at least, of observation that the pecuniary current has invariably set in that direction, and that the more ordinary principles of the Vatican have never extended to the oppression of its Maronite subjects.

CHAPTER XXVII.

From the Council of Basle to the beginning of the Reformation.

The real weight of General Councils as a part of the Constitution of the Church —Circumstances preceding the accession of *Nicholas V.*—His popular qualities —Love of all the Arts—His public virtues—Recorded particulars of his Elec-tion—Concord with Germany—Celebration and abuse of the Jubilee—Death of the Cardinal of Arles—His recorded miracles and canonization—Efforts to unite the Christian States against the Turks—Dissatisfaction and Death of Nicholas—*Calixtus III.*—Crusading enthusiasm of Æneas Sylvius—Jealousy between the Pope and Alphonso of Arragon—Nepotism of the former—Æneas Sylvius justifies the Pope against the complaints of the Germans—His history —The circumstances of his elevation to the Pontificate—The Council of

Mantua, for the purpose of uniting Europe against the Turks—The project of
Pius II.—Failure of the whole scheme—Embassy to Rome from the Princes
of the East—Thomas Palæologus arrives at Rome—Canonization of Catharine
of Sienna—The Bull of Pius II. against all appeals from the Holy See to
General Councils—The Pope retracts the errors into which he fell, as Æneas
Sylvius—Probable motive of his apostacy—His speech in Consistory—Departure against the Infidels—Arrival at Ancona, and Death—His Character—
Compared to Nicholas V., and Cardinal Julian—Conditions imposed by the
Conclave on the future Pope—Remarks—*Paul II.* is elected, and immediately
violates them—A native of Venice—Principles of his Government—He diverts
the War from the Turks against the Hussites, and persecutes a literary society
at Rome—*Sixtus IV.* makes a faint attempt to rouse Christendom against the
Turks—Violent broil between the Pope and the Florentines—Otranto taken by
the Turks—Excessive Nepotism of this Pope—Institution of the Minimes—
Increased venality of the Court of Rome—The moral character, talents, learning of Sixtus—Elevation of *Innocent VIII.*—Violation of the oath taken in
Conclave—Preferment conferred on his illegitimate Children—His weakness
and his avarice—The great wealth, election, and reputation of *Alexander VI.*
—Distribution of his Benefices, &c., among the Cardinals who voted for him—
Great Festivities at Rome—Moral profligacy and indecency of the Pope—His
projected alliance with the Sultan Bajazet—He confers the possession of the
New World on the Kings of Spain—The Act contested by the Portuguese—
On what ground—His negotiations with Charles VIII. of France—History and
fate of Zizim, brother of Bajazet—Cæsar Borgia, Duke of Valentino, or Valentinois—His co-operation with his father—The object of their common ambition
—Probable circumstances of the death of Alexander VI.—Expressions of Guicciardini—*Pius III.* dies immediately after his election—Julian della Rovéra,
or *Julius II.* unanimously elected—His policy and character—His dispute with
Louis XII.—Ecclesiastical scruples of the latter—Julius resumes the possession
of the States of the Church, and extends them—His extraordinary military
and political talents—Encouragement of the Arts—Lays the foundation of
St. Peter's—A Council convoked by the Cardinals against the Pope—Its entire
failure—Julius convokes the fifth Lateran Council—Subjects discussed by it
till his death—Continuation of the Council under *Leo X.*—A number of constitutions enacted by it—Its edict to restrain the Press—Its abolition of the Pragmatic Sanction, through the co-operation of Francis I.—Dissolution of the
Council—Observations—On the gradual degeneracy of the See—Of the government of the successive Popes—their Nepotism—On the morality of the Conclave—Obligations undertaken there on Oath—Reasons of their perpetual
violation—Ignorance of Cisalpines respecting the real character of the Court
of Rome—Respectability ascribed to it through the merits of its literary Pontiffs
—The great use made by the Popes at this period of the dangers of a Turkish
invasion, in order to suppress the question of Church Reform.

THE Council of Basle, after its protracted and resolute struggle
with the Vatican, having at length dissolved itself, and Felix V.,
its creature, having resigned his ill-supported pretensions to
the Chair of St. Peter, the prospects of the Court of Rome
once more brightened, and its authority was again secure from

The real value of General Councils.

any immediate invasion. As a restraint on papal despotism, a
General Council was effectual, so long as the Council was assembled; and even its name and the menace of an appeal to it,
as a last resource, have operated, on more occasions than one,
with salutary influence on the fears of an arbitrary pope. But
the power of the Monarchy was continuous; its principles were
never suspended; its action was uniformly directed to the same
object—whereas the controlling body, the Senate of the Church,
had only an occasional and very precarious existence; and
even when it was most efficaciously in action, it was liable to
all the incidents which throw uncertainty into the deliberations
of very large assemblies. It is true that the Councils of Pisa,
Constance, and Basle had endeavoured, by express enactments,
to make their sittings periodical, so as to erect the Council
General into a permanent branch of the constitution of the
Church. But as the power of convoking it still remained with
the Pope; as the collecting together of so large a body of prelates from all parts of Europe must always have occasioned
many local evils; and as the general consent, and even private
inclinations, of the more powerful sovereigns were not, under
such circumstances, to be disregarded, it was easy for the Pontiff
to evade an obligation which he detested. So, in fact, it proved;
for when they had once shaken off the fetters that were forged
for them at Basle, the successors of Eugenius IV. carefully
abstained, for above half a century, from acknowledging any
power in the Church, except their own.

Accession
of Nicho-
las V.

The moment of the accession of Nicholas V. was even favourable to the unlimited supremacy (the high Papists called it
the independence) of the Court of Rome. The faithful children
of the Church had now, for seventy years, been distracted by
dissensions almost uninterrupted, The schism which had dissevered kingdoms, and dishonoured the Church, had been *seemingly* aggravated by the Council of Pisa; and no sooner was it
appeased, after many fierce disputes at Constance, than a third
assembly succeeded, which occasioned (to all appearances) a
new broil, and which ended by creating a second schism. The
spectacle of a Pope and a Council launching anathemas against
each other was not calculated to edify the devout Catholic, nor

even to conciliate towards the Council the affections of the un-
thinking, who form the majority of mankind.   But when the
Pope assembled his rival Council at Ferrara, and when the two
infallible antagonists interchanged the bolts of excommunication, we may fairly believe that the dignity of those venerable
bodies suffered much in popular opinion, and even that their
utility was made matter of serious question.   Wearied by continual dissension, and disgusted by endless exhibitions of ecclesiastical discord, many were disposed to acquiesce in the unrestrained licentiousness of the Vatican, as the lesser evil.

Again, the formidable successes of the Turks, and their near His ob-
approach to the capital of the East, diverted the attention of jects and
merits.
men from their spiritual grievances to a more sensible object
and the zeal which Nicholas displayed in that, the common cause
of all Christendom, reconciled many to an authority so earnestly
exercised in so holy a cause.   Above all, his personal character was of great use in conciliating the disaffected, and rallying
them under the pontifical banners.   His reputation, his talents,
his pursuits, were in accordance with the spirit, which, in Italy
at least, so peculiarly prevailed at that time, for the cultivation
of ancient literature.   His gradual ascent from an inferior origin to the highest dignity was truly ascribed to his literary
genius and accomplishments ; and having attained that eminence, he surrounded it—not with sensualists or sycophants—
but with men of study and erudition, whose society he loved,
and whose affection he obtained.   A multitude of transcribers
and translators were continually in his employment ; and the
learning of the Greeks was placed within the reach of an ordinary education.   He founded the Vatican library, and sent his
messengers into every country for the collection of rare and
valuable manuscripts ; and while he sought to amass the most
precious treasures of profane lore, he exerted even greater zeal
to multiply authentic copies of the sacred writings.

But neither was his polite taste, nor the profusion of his liberality, confined entirely to literary objects.   His patronage was
bestowed on the arts, and especially on that of architecture.
He embellished his capital with several superb edifices ; many
churches, which had fallen into ruins during the schisms and

disorders of preceding generations, were now restored to more
than their ancient splendour ; and the ground was prepared,
and the foundations traced out, on which the least unworthy
temple which man has ever dedicated to Omnipotence was
destined to rise. The talents of Nicholas were illustrated by
private as well as public virtues*. He discouraged the practice of Simony, so long habitual to the Court of Rome ; and the
records of his history permit us once more to associate the word
" charity" with the character of a Pope. Such were purposes
on which the revenues of the Church were honourably employed, and for which they were less reluctantly contributed ;
and such the character which, being raised at that moment to
the pontifical chair, conciliated minds already weary with dissension, and seduced them into a temporary acquiescence in
acknowledged abuses.

Circum-
stances of
his elec-
tion.

When the Cardinals went into conclave, on the death of
Eugenius, nothing was farther from their intention, or from
general expectation, than the election of Nicholas. Prosper
Colonna was the person on whom the choice was expected to
fall ; and though the common proverb was not then forgotten,
" that he who enters the conclave Pope, comes out Cardinal,"
(chi entra Papa, esce Cardinale,) still among the names at all
connected with success Thomas of Sarzana was not mentioned.
Eighteen Cardinals were present ; and, after two or three scrutinies, eleven were united in favour of Colonna ; one only was
wanting to give him the requisite majority. At that moment
the Cardinal of St. Sixtus is reported to have turned suddenly
to Sarzana, and said to him, " Thomas, I give my vote to you,
because this is the eve of St. Thomas !" It was, in fact, the eve

---

* We may be allowed to cite (from Platina) a part of his epitaph, because
the praises it offers were really well founded :—

Hic sita sunt Quinti Nicolai Antistitis ossa,
    Aurea qui dederat sæcula, Roma, tibi.
Consilio illustris, virtute illustrior omni,
    Excoluit doctos doctior ipse viros.
Abstulit errorem, quo Schisma infecerat orbem.
    Restituit mores, mœnia, templa, domos.
Attica Romanæ complura volumina linguæ
    Prodidit—en tumulo fundite thura sacro.

of St. Thomas Aquinas.   The rest of the College immediately followed the example, and Thomas of Sarzana was unanimously elected*.

One of the first acts of Nicholas was to sign a Concordat with the German Church.   Its provisions did not extend beyond the subject of patronage ; and it was arranged that the Pope should appoint to all great benefices of every description which should become vacant *in curia ;* to all vacated by Cardinals, or other officers of the Roman Court ; and to all inferior benefices which should fall during six alternate months of the year.   The rest appear to have been left at the disposal of the Ordinaries ; all (except the smallest) being liable to the payment of Annates, according to the tax of the Apostolical Chamber ; and all to papal confirmation.   This Concordat, properly considered, was the substantial effect produced by the Council of Basle upon the constitution of the Church of Germany ; it was for this end that the labours of so many pious prelates and learned doctors had been exhausted !   Yet even this result, as we shall presently see, was not such as to secure the satisfaction or bind the faith of the Court of Rome.

In the year 1450 the avarice of the Roman Clergy and people was again nourished by the celebration of the jubilee ; and so vast were the multitudes which on this occasion sought the plenary indulgence at the tombs of the apostles, that many are said to have been crushed to death in Churches, and to have perished by other accidents †.   Nevertheless, as there were still many devout persons, particularly in the more remote countries of Europe, who were precluded from reaping the promised rewards by personal disabilities, Nicholas, in imitation of the

Marginal notes: Concordat with the German Church. — Abuse of Jubilees.

---

* The Roman people were allowed to retain (in return, perhaps, for their long-lost share in the election) the licentious privilege of plundering the mansion of the Pope elect.   On this occasion it happened, that Prosper Colonna, as first Deacon, had the office of communicating the election from the window to the assembled populace.   Now the people knowing him to be the favourite, thought no other than that he had appeared to announce his own election.   Consequently they rushed, without further inquiry, to his magnificent palace, and stripped it bare.   After they had learnt their mistake, they proceeded to atone for it by plundering Sarzana also ; but he was a scholar, and had little to lose.

† Ninety-seven pilgrims, for instance, were thrown at once by the pressure of the multitude from the bridge of St. Angelo, and drowned.

abuse of his predecessors, afforded them facilities to redeem their omission. To the Poles and Lithuanians a private jubilee was accorded, on the condition, that every pious person should pay for his indulgence only half of the money which the pilgrimage to Rome would have cost him; but through some sense of shame, as is said, at the enormous sums which would thus have been raised, the proportion was finally reduced to one quarter. Of the proceeds, which were still considerable, half was consigned to the King of Poland, for the prosecution of the holy war, a fourth to the Queen Sophia, for charitable uses, and a fourth for the reparation of the Roman Churches. In this instance we have the unusual consolation of believing that the money thus levied upon superstition, and levied, too, chiefly upon the superstition of the poor, was applied, for the most part, to the purposes professed. There are shades in the colours of religious imposture; and the sin of deluding a credulous race would have been still blacker, had it been followed by perfidy, or had its fruits been expended in pampering the profligacy of the Court of Rome.

The Cardinal of Arles. In that year, also, died the Cardinal of Arles, the same who had succeeded Julian Cesarini as the President of the Council of Basle. But the history of that eminent ecclesiastic did not terminate at his death. On the interment of his body at Arles, many extraordinary miracles were performed at his tomb; and their fame spread so widely, and with such assurance of truth, that the partizans of the rival Council of Florence were struck with confusion. This Prelate had been excommunicated by Pope Eugenius, and stigmatized as the author of schism, the child of perdition, the nursling of iniquity; he had been condemned by two General Councils for rebellion against the Church, and degraded and deprived of all his dignities. He had continued, notwithstanding, in the exercise of his episcopal functions at Arles; and so lasting was the impression of his sanctity—founded on his charitable disposition, and other Christian excellencies—and so pressing was the importunity of his devotees, who had even anticipated in their prayers the determination of the Vatican, that at length Pope Clement VII. published (in 1527) the Bull of Beatification; and by that act exalted among the holy mediators the denounced, anathematized foe of Pontifical corruption and despotism.

If Nicholas V. had made some ineffectual exertions to preserve the Eastern empire, while there seemed yet some hope of its preservation, he redoubled his efforts when the shadow of a hope no longer existed. The fall of Constantinople, though long foreseen, fell like an unexpected bolt upon the nations of the West ; and it was quickly perceived that the capital of the ancient Empire, the throne of the Christian religion, the opulent palaces and cities of Italy, presented peculiar temptations to an ambitious, unbelieving depredator. Accordingly numerous religious persons began to preach a new crusade ; and while Æneas Sylvius was astonishing the Princes of Germany by his polished eloquence, a simple Monk, a hermit of St. Augustine, was exerting a more successful influence over the republics of Italy. His name was Simonet ; he was destitute of all acquirements ; but his natural address won the confidence of those who listened to him. He traversed the country, in repeated journeys, with unwearied activity. At Venice, at Milan, at Florence, he reiterated his counsels and his arguments. The orator was disinterested, and his object was the concord of his hearers. It was by such simple machinery that he prevailed in effecting an union among those powerful cities. Yet the practised statesmen of the day were confounded * when they learnt, that a humble undistinguished Monk, without rank, without wealth, without any worldly support, had accomplished an enterprise which the Pope, and his Court of Cardinals, had attempted in vain.

(marginal note:) Preaching of Simonet.

In the midst of his chivalrous designs to recover Constantinople, and expel the conqueror from Europe, and at a moment when there seemed some prospect of a partial co-operation for that purpose, Nicholas V. died. His complaint was gout ; and it is commonly asserted that its progress was hastened by the affliction with which he saw the triumphs of the infidel. It is at least certain, that during the two or three last years of

* " Visum est id omnibus monstri simile humilem et incognitum monachum Italiam pacavisse." Æn. Sylv. Hist. De Europa, cap. 68, p. 460, edit. Basil. See Platina, Vit. Nic. V. ad finem.

his life the natural suavity of his temper deserted him; that he became morose, and even cruel; fearful of his enemies and suspicious of his friends; querulous, and discontented even with the Chair of St. Peter. "No man (he once said) ever crosses my threshold who tells me a word of truth. I am confounded by the artifices of those who surround me; and if I was not restrained by the fear of scandal, I would resign the Pontificate, and become once more Thomas of Sarzana. Under that name I had more enjoyment in a single day than any year can henceforth ever bring me." Nicholas, however amiable in his domestic qualities, had been ever unable to recognize any political rights in the subjects of the state; and thus he had persecuted the patriots of his day with precipitate severity. In consequence, it is made a natural question by the author of 'The Italian Republics' whether it was not remorse, rather than commiseration, which embittered and curtailed his declining days.

Calixtus III. Alphonso Borgia, a native of Spain, was chosen as his successor, and assumed the name of Calixtus III. Scarcely was he established in his dignity, when Æneas Sylvius presented himself at Rome, the bearer of the most flattering assurances on the part of the Emperor, both respecting his own military preparations and the general eagerness for the Turkish war. In an animated address to the Pope and Cardinals, the orator depicted the dangers which impended over Europe: he then dilated on the great numerical superiority of the Christians—

Projected Crusade. that many Princes of Germany had taken the vow; that the King of Arragon was in readiness; that the Duke of Burgundy was ardent for the enterprise. Charles of France would not fail to emulate the zeal of his predecessors; the ancient courage of the English would not now desert them; the Castilians, the Portuguese, all nations, in short, awaited only the pontifical summons to arm for the defence of religion—if his Holiness would only second the vows of the faithful, by unlocking the treasures of the Church, and sending the labourers to the harvest. . . . These magnificent declarations were, for the most part, the spontaneous fruits of the orator's enthusiasm—that they had no result is not to be entirely ascribed to the lukewarmness of the Pope. Yet it is remarkable that, among the various Princes announced as forming that holy confederacy, the first who withdrew from it, and that, too, in consequence of personal dissension with the Pontiff, was Alphonso of Arragon. Borgia had been the subject of that monarch—more than that—he had been engaged in his domestic service, and owed his ecclesiastical advancement to the same patronage. On his elevation to the Chair, Alphonso sent ambassadors to inquire of his Holiness what terms were hereafter to subsist between them? Calixtus peevishly replied " Let him rule his kingdom, and leave the government of the Church, without any interference, to me." Some have considered the reply as too harsh, while others have discovered in the overture of Alphonso a want of due veneration for the Vicegerent of Christ. Probably the monarch had not forgotten, and perhaps the Pontiff could not forgive, the relation which had formerly subsisted between them; and their knowledge of each other's character may have been too deep and intimate to leave much room for reverence on either side.

Calixtus III. reigned only three years, and died in August, 1458, at a very advanced age. His pontificate was signalized by no striking incident, nor were his acts in any respect remarkable, unless, indeed, we should consider him as having introduced into the government of the Church the system of Nepotism. For though instances of that vice had occasionally occurred before, it was not till now that it became the practice of the Vatican. Calixtus exhausted upon his worthless nephews the riches of the Apostolical Treasury, and limited his ambition to the aggrandizement of his own family. It was to this that the aspirations of pontifical presumption sank at last! From that lofty spiritual arrogance which, in earlier ages, has extorted from us something approaching to admiration, the character of papacy first descended to the grasping after temporal power; its great object then became to enlarge the dominions of the See—to secure the obedience of the city. Avarice attended; still its fruits were, for the most part, applied to ecclesiastical objects—to maintain the interests of the Church, and extend the authority of the Vicar of Christ. In-

The system of Nepotism.

trigues and wars flowed from the Vatican, and deluged Europe
with blood; still they were designed to extend the power, to
augment the dignity, of *Rome*. It was for the declining years
of papal despotism that the last and lowest degradation was
reserved; it was not till the age of Calixtus III. and Sixtus IV.
that the ambition of St. Peter's successors degenerated into mere
family passion, and was confined to the narrowest circle of
selfishness.

Change in
the policy
of Æneas
Sylvius.

In the year preceding his death, Calixtus was accused by
the Germans of having raised exorbitant contributions, under
the pretext of a holy war, and violated the Concordat made
with his predecessor. There was considerable ground for both
these complaints. Nevertheless, it was on this occasion that
Æneas Sylvius, formerly the adversary of pontifical oppression,
more recently the advocate of the Imperial claims, came forward in defence of the Pope, and vigorously maintained his
rights and justified his conduct. In some letters, composed
during this dispute, he reproached the German Prelates for
deferring to any other authority, rather than the Chief of the
Church*. He asserted that their grievances, even had they
been real, should have been left to the remedial benevolence of
the Holy See; he applied himself to confute some arguments
against its authority, which were derived from the Councils of
Constance and Basle; he made mention of a sort of Pragmatic
Sanction, established by certain Prelate-Princes of Germany,
with a view to degrade the Holy See; and he reproached the
nation with an unnatural ingratitude in having resolved to
withhold contributions from Rome, to prevent appeals, to restore elections to the Ordinaries, to refuse Annates, and so, in
effect, to deprive the Sovereign Pontiff of the plenitude of his
power.

It is important to notice these particulars, because they indicate the secret working of that spirit, which, in the next

---

* He went to the utmost extent of papal orthodoxy, by asserting " that none
who had disregarded the authority of the Roman Pontiff could at any time enter
the kingdom of heaven, and that those who had spurned the commands of the
Apostolical See should not now have any occasion for exultation. Hos enim
Catholica veritas, nisi resipuerint ante obitum, ignis æterni mancipio sine inter-
missione deputat." Æn. Sylv. Epist., lib. i., Ep. 369, &c.

generation, broke forth with irresistible violence. Nor is it without a feeling of sorrow, mingled with shame, that we observe the most enlightened ecclesiastic of his age casting off the wise and generous principles of earlier life, as his ambition was warmed by a nearer prospect of gratification, and as his selfish interests became more closely associated with ecclesiastical corruption. Æneas Sylvius Piccolomini was born at Corsigni, near Sienna, in 1405, and his first laurels were gathered at the Council of Basle; he remained faithful to that Assembly, and promoted its objects, and advanced his own reputation in the conduct of some important missions which were confided to him. In the year 1442, he became secretary to the Emperor Frederic; but throughout the pontificate of Nicholas V. he was engaged in the service of the Holy See, and zealously exerted himself, as its Nuncio, in a cause which was always dear to him, to confederate the Christian powers against the Turkish aggressor.

He was raised to the dignity of Cardinal (of Sienna) by Calixtus III., and on the death of that Pope he entered into Conclave with his brethren. The first scrutiny was indecisive; but it was followed by a very effective intrigue, which seemed likely to terminate in the election of the Archbishop of Rouen, an ambitious and unprincipled Frenchman. Piccolomini exerted all his eloquence and influence against that choice; he addressed several of the Cardinals separately; he appealed to their consciences, to their interest, to their vanity; he exaggerated the vices of the Archbishop; he addressed the national jealousy of his compatriots; he threatened them with a second secession to Avignon, and painted the approaching shame and desolation of Italy. The College proceeded a second time to the scrutiny. The golden chalice was placed upon the altar, and the Cardinals of Rouen, of Rimini, and Colonna remained near it. The others took their appointed seats, and, rising in succession, according to seniority, they placed in the chalice the paper which expressed their suffrage. When Sylvius went up in his turn, the Cardinal of Rouen, who knew how bitter an enemy he was, hastily said to him " Remember me on this occasion." " What," replied Piccolomini, " do you address me, who am but a vile worm of earth!" He resumed his place; and when the scrutiny was finished, and the papers examined, it appeared that the Cardinal of Sienna had nine votes, and that of Rouen six only.

His election to the Pontificate. Three still were wanting to the former to make good his election; and the Cardinals then proceeded to the *accessit.* For some time they sat in profound silence. One of them at length arose, and gave his voice to Piccolomini; it was a thunderbolt for the Cardinal of Rouen. There was a second interval of silence, and during it those individuals who had any hopes for themselves, having penetrated the secret, that Piccolomini was on the point of being elected, left their places on various pretexts. Presently another Cardinal gave his vote to Sylvius; and only one more being now required, Prosper Colonna rose; and though the Cardinals of Rouen and Nice endeavoured to prevent his design by a charge of perfidy, he gave his decisive suffrage to Piccolomini. The latter was then saluted Pope by the whole College; and after replying, with great modesty, to the excuses and congratulations of the opposite party, tendered by Bessarion of Nice, he assumed the name **Pius II.** of Pius II., and went through the customary solemnities.

The object to which the exertions of Æneas Sylvius had been faithfully directed in all his subordinate offices equally distinguished his pontificate; and the gradual progress of the Turks, by increasing his apprehensions, fortified his zeal. Accordingly, he allowed not a moment to elapse before he convoked a Council for the promotion of a general crusade. **Council of Mantua, 1459 A.D.** Mantua was the place selected for that purpose; his call was obeyed by the greater number of the Italian Princes; and finally, though with more reluctance, by representatives from most of the European States. Many deputies from the East were also present—from Rhodes, from Cyprus, from Lesbos, from the Peloponnesus, Epirus, and Illyria—to express their sufferings or their fears, and pour out their supplications. Pius II. proceeded with extraordinary pomp to the opening of the Council. In various cities through which he passed he was received with the same ostentatious homage which is paid to a temporal Prince; and the religious motive which *may*

have animated the Pontiff was forgotten in the less questionable policy of his design.

Pius II. opened the Council of Mantua on the 1st of June, Project of
1459, just six years after the fall of Constantinople.   His first a new Crusade.
discourse was employed in rebuking the indifference of the
Christian Princes; in contrasting the devotion of the Turks for
their "execrable sect" with the apathy of the children of the
Gospel; and in expressing his own resolution never to abandon his project, but to sacrifice his life, if necessary, for the
people intrusted to him by God.   His earnestness, his activity,
his brilliant and commanding eloquence, produced an immediate, though it proved but a temporary, effect.   The Council
continued its sessions till the end of the January following: as
its deliberations proceeded, it increased in numbers and dignity; and it grew warmer in the cause, as it was more influenced by the ardour and genius of the Pontiff.   The methods
by which he proposed to effect his design contained nothing
that was impracticable—much that was reasonable and generous.   An army of 50,000 or 60,000 confederates was to be
immediately collected for the defence of Hungary and the adjacent provinces; the men were to be raised in Germany,
Bohemia, Poland, and Hungary.   The pecuniary means were
to be furnished chiefly by Italy; the clergy * were to contribute
a tenth of all their property, the Jews a twentieth, and the laity
a thirtieth part.   The Pope professed his readiness to conduct
the war in person, and to consecrate to that purpose all that
belonged to him.

The Council was then dissolved; and whatsoever may have
been the sincerity of its members, while they were awed by
the presence of the Pontiff, and animated by his eloquence, the

---

* The Venetians and Genoese were not included in this engagement. The
greatest difficulties were raised by the former, partly owing to their commercial
and other intercourse with the Infidel, and partly, perhaps, because they had been
accustomed to profit by crusades, not to contribute to them. Again, though the
Duke of Burgundy had given some reluctant promises of aid, neither the French,
Castilians, nor Portuguese had offered any hopes. " As to England (said the
Pope), we have nothing to expect from that kingdom, on account of the troubles
which divide it; nor from Scotland, hidden in the depths of the ocean. Den-
mark and Sweden, and Norway are too distant to send us soldiers, and, content
with their fish, they could not send us money, if they would,"

engagements they contracted were, for the most part, violated. The intestine dissensions of the Christian Powers were too deeply seated to permit any cordial or general co-operation; and so far was Pius II. from succeeding in his attempt to heal them, that he did not himself long escape their contagion, but presently became entangled in the malignant politics of Europe.

Embassy from the East.

In the same year (1460) a solemn embassy from the Princes of the East arrived at Rome: the respect which could not be claimed for their power was offered to their titles and pretensions, and to the object of their mission. The Envoys professed to represent David, Emperor of Trebizond, George, King of Persia, the Sovereigns of the Two Armenias, and many others. They advanced a profusion of hopes and promises—the Turks were to be assailed from the East by a powerful army, through the Hellespont, Thrace, and the Bosphorus; among their allies they numbered Bendis, King of Mingrelia and Arabia, Pancratius, King of the Georgians, Moüic, Marquis of Goria, Ismael, Lord of Sinope, and some others: it was the object of their mission to inform his Holiness of these preparations, and to render homage to the Vicar of God upon earth. Pius II. applauded their zeal, and accepted their homage; but assuring them that little could be done on his part, unless in conjunction with the Courts of France and Burgundy, he sent them forth to tell their pompous tale beyond the Alps. It may seem needless to add that this deputation had no result.

Reception of Thomas Palæologus.

The year following, Thomas Palæologus presented himself at Rome, and he was received with a munificence which did honour to the pontifical court. The Imperial Exile had passed from Corfu to Ancona, and brought to that city the relics of the Apostle St. Andrew. He bestowed the sacred treasure upon the Pope; and accordingly commissioners were appointed, who conducted it with great solemnity to Rome. It was deposited in St. Peter's with every mark of veneration : and though the reader is already familiar with such absurdities; though he has had frequent occasion to deplore the deference to popular superstition which has been paid by very intelligent, and even very pious, ecclesiastics, we may still record another humiliating act which it was the fate of Pius II. to perform. Catharine of Sienna had died above eighty years before in perfect odour of sanctity; continual miracles, certified by sufficient testimony, had been performed at her tomb; people were anxiously expecting her canonization. A Duke of Austria and a King of Hungary had successively solicited the Pontiff of the day to do that justice to her extraordinary qualities; but the ceremony had been deferred through the confusion of the Church and the disorders of the Holy See. It was reserved to the genius of Æneas Sylvius at length to perform that office; and one of the most extravagant enthusiasts that ever dishonoured the profession of Christianity* was enthroned among the Saints of the Church by one of the most enlightened Prelates who has in any age adorned it.

It may not here be out of place to mention that the first recorded Act of Canonization was performed in 993, by John XV., in behalf of Udalrig, Bishop of Augsburg. The right in the first instance was not exclusively vested in the Pope: councils, and even prelates of high rank, were qualified to perform it; till Alexander III. placed this among the more important acts of authority (Causæ Majores) to be executed only by the Pope †. Canonization.

From being the zealous advocate of the Council of Basle, we have observed Æneas Sylvius defending the usurpations and exalting the majesty of the Roman See. It was thus that he became qualified to occupy it; and the enjoyment of its power and prerogatives was not calculated to revive his ardour for its reformation. To have imposed limits on an authority exercised by himself had been a rare and difficult effort of magnanimity: and so far was Pius II. from harbouring the design, that he seized an early occasion to discourage those liberal principles of Church government, which were entertained by many ecclesiastics, and which had so lately been propagated by himself. During the Council of Mantua, shortly before its dissolution, Edict against General Councils.

* The exploits of this fanatic fill twenty-four folio pages in the works of St. Antoninus, Archbishop of Florence.—(Chronicorum, Tertia Pars, p. 692, et seq.)

† See Mosh. Cent. x., p. ii., ch. iii.

and at a moment when his influence over its members was probably the greatest, he published a celebrated Bull against all appeals from the Holy See to General Councils. "An execrable abuse, unheard of in ancient times*, has gained footing in our days, authorized by some, who, acting under a spirit of rebellion rather than sound judgment, presume to appeal from the Pontiff of Rome, Vicar of Jesus Christ, to whom, in the person of St. Peter, it has been said, 'Feed my sheep;' and again, 'Whatsoever thou shalt bind on earth shall be bound in heaven;' to appeal, I say, from his judgments to a future Council—a practice which every man instructed in law must regard as contrary to the holy canons, and prejudicial to the Christian republic." . . . . The Pope then proceeded to paint in vague and glowing expressions the frightful evils occasioned by such appeals; and finally pronounced to be *ipso facto* excommunicated all individuals who might hereafter resort to them, whether their dignity were imperial, royal, or pontifical, as well as all Universities and Colleges, and all others who should promote and counsel them.

Recantation of Pius II.

This Edict, published in January, 1460, was no unworthy prelude to the most remarkable act of the pontificate of Pius— his public retraction of his early opinions. Not contented to leave others to contrast his actual conduct with his former principles, and both were too notorious to escape such contrast, he boldly stepped forward as his own judge, and published the most unequivocal condemnation of himself. Before his departure for Ancona, in the year 1463, he addressed to the University of Cologne a bull to the following effect :—"That being liable to human imperfection, he had said, or written, much which might unquestionably be censured; but that, as he had sinned, like Paul, and persecuted the Church of God through want of sufficient knowledge, so he now imitated the blessed Augustine, who, having fallen into some erroneous expressions, retracted them; that he ingenuously acknowledged his former ignorance, lest what he had written while young

* "*Execrabilis* et pristinis temporibus inauditus" are the opening words, which give the title to the decree.

should lead to some error prejudicial to the Holy See; for if there were any one, whom it peculiarly became to defend and maintain the eminence and glory of the first Throne of the Church, it was assuredly that individual whom God, in his mercy and goodness, had raised to the dignity of Vicar of Jesus Christ. That, for these reasons, no confidence was due to those of his writings which offended, in any manner, the authority of the Apostolical See, and established opinions which it did not acknowledge. Wherefore (he added) if you find anything contrary to its doctrine, either in my dialogues, or my letters, or any other of my writings—despise those opinions, reject them, and follow that which I now proclaim to you. Believe me now that I am old, rather than then, when I spoke as a youth; pay more regard to the Sovereign Pontiff than to the individual; reject Æneas—receive Pius. The former name was imposed by my parents—a Gentile name,—and in my infancy: the other I assumed as a Christian in my Apostolate *." In conclusion, the Pope, anticipating the natural suspicion of ambitious motives as the occasion of his change, took some pains to remove that notion, by recounting the circumstances of his introduction to the Council, and recurring to the seductions which misled his tender inexperience. If that change, of which the first indication was so nearly coincident with his personal advancement, had been a change to a wiser, from a rash and inconsiderate opinion; had the adopted principles of the convert been calculated to advance the permanent interests of the See better than those which he rejected, the historian might have listened with some attention to his assurances of sincerity. But when we have the soundest reasons to convince us that the counsels of his youth were sage, and provident, and generous, those of his riper years narrow, and at the same time selfish, there is scarcely space to doubt what the motives really were which determined his apostasy.

In the mean time the Turkish arms were making progress in all quarters, and the tide of war was rapidly descending to

His exertions against the Turks,

---

* " Æneam rejicite, Pium recipite—illud Gentile nomen parentes indidere nascenti; hoc Christianum in Apostolatu suscepi."

the Adriatic. Italy lay next in its course; and her contentious children seemed, for the moment, disposed to suspend their intestine animosities. The Pope renewed his exertions. "Life itself (thus he spoke in Consistory) must be laid down for the safety of the flock intrusted to us. The Turks are wasting the provinces of Christendom in succession. What expedients remain to us? To oppose arms to their invasions? We have no means to provide them. What then? Shall we exhort the princes to confront and expel them? This has already been attempted in vain: it is in vain that we tell them to go! Perchance they would listen better, if we should say to them— *Come!* This, then, shall be our next experiment: we will march in person against the Turks, and invite the Christian monarchs to follow us; not by words only, but by example also. It may be, when they shall behold their master and father—the Roman Pontiff, the Vicar of Christ Jesus—an infirm old man, advancing to the war, they will take up arms through shame, and valiantly defend our holy religion. . . Not that we propose to draw the sword—a task incompatible with our bodily feebleness and sacerdotal character,—but after the example of the Holy Father Moses, who prayed on the mountain, while Israel was fighting with the Amalekites, we shall stand on some lofty galley or mountain's brow, and holding before our eyes the Divine Eucharist, which is our Lord Jesus Christ, we shall implore Him to grant safety and victory to our contending armies*."

These were not vain expressions; a numerous force was already assembled at Ancona, and the Venetians had at length engaged to furnish maritime succours. The pontiff departed to assume, in person, the conduct of the expedition. He was preceded by the Cardinal of St. Angelo—an old and venerable prelate, remarkable for his zeal against the infidel; he followed at slow journeys, borne in a litter, and debilitated by sickness; and on his arrival at the camp, he was received by a multitude imperfectly armed, without resources, without discipline, and, for the most part, without enthusiasm. Such were the cham-

---

* Raynaldus, ann. 1463, sect. 25.

pions of the Cross; such the human instruments to which the care of Christendom seemed at that moment to be confided! Many of them Pius immediately dismissed with his pontifical benediction, and a profusion of indulgences, which they no longer affected to value. Those who remained he still proposed to lead against the enemy, and only awaited the arrival of the Venetian galleys. They arrived; but scarcely were their white sails visible from the towers of Ancona, when the Pope expired. On this event the whole expedition immediately and death. dispersed; and it seemed as if so many spectators had assembled, from such various and distant regions, for no other purpose than to witness the death of their chief, and swell his funeral procession.

The treasure which was found in his chest was sent, by his express command, to Corvinus, King of Hungary: but it bore no proportion to the sums which had been placed at his disposal for crusading purposes; and there was reason to believe that much had been diverted by the pontiff for the establishment of Ferdinand on the throne of Naples. And thus Pope Pius II., who was fortunate in many circumstances of his life, may not have been least happy in the moment of his departure; at least, it is manifest that he had engaged with very slender resources, and little promise of support, in a dangerous enterprise, which could scarcely have terminated otherwise than in defeat and dishonour.

Nevertheless, Pius II. was the most accomplished, the most liberal, perhaps the most enlightened, individual of his time. Like Nicholas V. he obtained his ecclesiastical advancement by his literary powers, by the acquisition of learning, and the useful application of it. Like Cardinal Julian, he was intrusted with the conduct of difficult negotiations; he influenced the counsels of courts; he swayed the deliberations of ecclesiastical assemblies. Like both those eminent churchmen, he displayed unremitting zeal for the defence of Christendom against the Turkish aggression. And herein he imitated the merit of the former, that it was his strenuous exertion in this cause which gave the colour and character to his pontificate; and in one respect he accomplished, in some manner, the destiny of the latter, that he died in the heart of a Christian camp, prepared to move, under his own personal direction, in a hopeless enterprise, against the armies of the Infidel.

Conditions imposed in Conclave. It was now so common for the Cardinals, while in conclave, to bind themselves to the observance of certain stipulations, in case of election to the pontificate, and so invariable for the cardinal elected to violate his engagement, that we have ceased to notice acts of habitual—it might almost seem authorized— perjury. But the articles which were imposed by the college, on the death of Pius II., were such as to require attention, from their own importance. The following were, in substance, the principal:—" That the Pope shall continue the war with the Turks, re-establish the ancient discipline of the Roman Court, and assemble a Council General within three years. That he shall not augment the number of cardinals to more than twenty-four, nor create any one who is less than thirty years of age, or deficient in the knowledge of civil and canon law and of the Holy Scriptures; nor more than one from among his own relatives. That he shall condemn no cardinal, except according to the legal and canonical forms; that he shall enter into no war, nor sign any treaty without the consent of the college; that he shall leave to the subjects of the Roman court entire liberty to make their wills; that he shall establish no new imposts, nor increase those existing; that he shall take the votes of the cardinals aloud, and not in a whisper, so that the result of their deliberations may be faithfully expressed; and lastly, that the cardinals shall assemble twice a year, apart from the Pope, to examine whether these conditions have been observed."

From these stipulations we perceive that it was no light or lenient yoke to which the courtiers of Rome, with all their outward show and pomp of licentiousness, were, in fact, subjected; and if they had indeed acquired the efficacy of laws, the constitution of the Vatican would have undergone an entire change:—from a slightly-limited despotism, it would have assumed much more of the oligarchical character. It may be questioned whether the Catholic Church would have gained any advantage by that alteration—whether the dominion of the

Sacred College would not have been at least as oppressive, as despotic, as fruitful in abuses, as hostile to reformation, as that of the Pope. But the experiment was not made; the oath was indeed administered with great solemnity, and accepted by all. One among those who had taken it (the Cardinal of St. Marc) was immediately raised to the pontificate; and his first official act was to confirm his obligation. But Paul II. Election of (he assumed that name), alike imperious and vain, pompous Paul II. and frivolous, was not so constituted as to sacrifice any interest to the sanctity of any engagement. He presently expressed his contempt for the laws imposed by the conclave; he enacted others on his own authority; he demanded the approbation of the cardinals, and after a very feeble resistance, partly by menaces, partly by promises, partly by granting them some childish indulgences *, he obtained it. He then proceeded to administer the Church according to the established maxims of government †.

Paul II. was a native of Venice, and his election was, in His abo- some measure, occasioned by that circumstance; for it was minable policy, manifest that no Italian confederation could act with any vigour against the Turkish power, unless Venice should place herself at its head; and it was hoped that her co-operation would be effectually secured by the choice of a Venetian pontiff. Italy was now at peace; the impulse towards the East had been given by Pius II., and all circumstances seemed favourable to the enterprise. Much unquestionably depended at that moment on the character and policy of the Pope. Now

---

* He permitted them to wear mitres of silk, such as had hitherto been confined to the pontiffs alone; he forbade their use to all other prelates. He likewise allowed them to adorn their horses and mules with trappings of a scarlet colour.

† One of his first acts was to dismiss from their offices all the *abbreviators* appointed by his predecessor. The biographer Platina was one of them. And when he remonstrated with the pontiff, and threatened to bring the case before the judges of the *Rota*, Paul regarded him fiercely, and said,—" Nos ad judices revocas? Ac si nescires *omnia jura in scrinio pectoris nostri collocata esse ?* Sic stat sententia. Loco cedant omnes ; eant quo volunt; nihil eos moror; pontifex sum; mihique licet arbitrio animi aliorum acta et rescindere et approbare." Platina, notwithstanding, was contumacious, and the Pope placed him, for some months, in rigorous confinement. See his Life of Paul II.

the measures taken by Paul II. during his whole pontificate were precisely those which a council of Mahometans assembled at Constantinople would have dictated. He began his reign by a nefarious attempt to embroil the states of Italy in civil confusion. He failed; and then he engaged in a different project, which has made him more hateful, because it was for the moment more successful. Corvinus, the son of Huniades, was defending the frontiers of Christendom with courage and honour. He had gained several advantages over the enemy, which he might with efficient succours have converted into substantial triumphs. Let us mark the policy of Paul II.

external

Thirsting, as it would seem, for *Christian* blood, that Pope proposed to divert the war from the Turks, and turn it against the Hussites. He professed a Catholic ardour to punish the priests who fostered those errors, to reduce the rebels to obedience to the Apostolical See, and to extirpate every heresy. Accordingly, he offered to Corvinus the crown of Bohemia on those terms, and the boon was accepted. For the space of seven infamous years, those arms, which might have chastised the foreign aggressor, were fiercely directed against the kings of Bohemia; and it is no alleviation of the pontiff's guilt, that those reiterated efforts were finally defeated. While he pursued the principles of Innocent III., his conduct was even more revolting, because he pursued them under circumstances of greater danger to Christendom, and in an age in which the increase of knowledge left less excuse for crime.

and internal.

If it was the object of this pontiff to make his internal government as detestable as his external policy, he took an effectual measure to accomplish it. We have observed with what ardour the taste for polite learning was cultivated in Italy at this time, and what great encouragement it had received from two recent pontiffs. In furtherance of those objects, a literary society was formed at Rome during the reign of Paul II. But Paul affected to discover in that institution a dangerous conspiracy against the safety of the Pope and the peace of the Church. The stupid jealousy which suggested that suspicion was supported by the cruelty usually inherent in narrow and passionate minds; and, as if the blood of the

Bohemians flowed in too scanty profusion, the Pope commenced the work of inquisition at Rome. Several innocent individuals, of great literary* and moral reputation, suffered on the rack; one in particular, Agostino Campino, died under the torture. Paul persevered in his persecution, but he did not succeed in eliciting any confession, or discovering any shadow of heresy or conspiracy, in excuse for so much barbarity; nor did it produce any other result, than to create one additional motive for execrating his name. He died in 1471, in possession of treasures which he had hoarded through the mere love of gold; and in the very year preceding his death, he increased an ecclesiastical abuse (in the belief, no doubt, that he should personally reap the fruits of his change †), by reducing once more the intervals between the celebrations of the Jubilee from thirty-three to twenty-five years.

Sixtus IV. (a Franciscan Monk) commenced an unusually Sixtus IV. long pontificate, of thirteen years, by professing the policy and affecting the designs of Pius II. He called for the enforcement of the decrees of Mantua; he promised indulgences to all who should march against the Turk in person, or find efficient substitutes, or contribute to the expense of the expedition; he sent letters and legates to all the Courts of Europe. All disregarded his solicitations, some through apathy, others, perhaps, through suspiciousness; others through the nearer occupation of civil dissension. The Pope was easily diverted from an object on which he may never have been sincerely bent. His boiling zeal presently evaporated; his clamours were silenced by the first repulse; and he appeared to resign his daring projects, and subside into the ordinary channel of papal misgovernment, without a sigh or a struggle.

In the year 1478, during some disturbances between the His dispute with Flo- Medici and the Pazzi at Florence, the Archbishop of Pisa rence. suffered an ignominious death at the hands of the former. There is little doubt that he had promoted a sanguinary

---

* A long account of this affair is given by Platina (himself a sufferer) in his Life of Paul II. That Pope's hatred for learning was so great, that he held the terms *studious* and *heretical* to be synonymous, and carefully impressed upon his subjects the advantages of ignorance. The historian died in the year 1481.

† Thus the year 1475 became a year of jubilee.

tumult—nevertheless, this was an outrage upon the prerogative of the hierarchy, which, in an earlier age, would have been visited with signal vengeance, and which even Sixtus IV. was not prepared to overlook. He placed the offending city under an interdict, excommunicated Lorenzo de' Medici*, and published a declaration of war. The Florentines, even the ecclesiastics, defended the cause of their compatriot; they treated with scorn the pontifical menaces; they continued to celebrate the divine offices in defiance of the interdict; they assembled a Synod of the Bishops of Tuscany, in order to appeal with greater solemnity to a General Council. At the same time, they retorted all the blame of the original offence upon the Pope himself, and called upon France and Milan to aid them against his oppression.

Soon afterwards, Louis XI. held an Assembly at Orleans, principally for the purpose of restoring the Pragmatic Sanction, which he had previously and hastily annulled. But an embassy, subsequently sent to Rome, was likewise charged to exhort the Pontiff to make peace with Florence, and to assemble, without any delay, a General Council. These solicitations were seconded by certain menaces, to which Louis could have given efficacy, had he so chosen. But he had either no serious intention of enforcing his demands, or he allowed it to melt away before the temporizing policy of the Vatican†. In the mean time, the Pope persevered in measures of hostility, and the blood of the Archbishop cried so loudly for vengeance, that all external dangers were forgotten, and the hosts of Mahomet II. approached unheard to the gates of Italy. The same Pontiff who had so lately preached the blessings of union to the Christian Courts, even while the danger was more remote, persisted in hostility against a Christian State, when it was already impending over his head. At length he relented;

---

* The Bull is given at length by Roscoe, Life of Lorenzo de' Medici. Appendix, No. xxvi.

† The advice tendered to the Pope on this occasion by the Cardinal of Pavia, the most accomplished politician in his Court, affords an excellent illustration of the great principle of ecclesiastical statesmanship—*not* to remove the grounds of complaint, but to gain time, to preserve the abuse, to *defer* the hour of danger, rather than avert it altogether by timely concession.

but it was not till the city of Otranto had been stormed by the Infidel that the conditions of peace were dictated*, and the Florentine ambassadors admitted to receive their absolutions at the entrance of St. Peter's; and even then they appear to have been subjected to more than the customary circumstances of humiliation.   The Pope was presently relieved from imme-diate apprehension by the death of Mahomet, and he then had leisure to return to what had been, indeed, the favourite object of his pontificate, the aggrandizement of his nephews.

The nepotism of no former Pontiff had been indulged with so scandalous a sacrifice of the interests of the Church as that of Sixtus IV.   One of his nephews, Leonardo della Rovera, he married to a natural daughter of Ferdinand of Naples; and on this occasion he abandoned to that monarch some estates and fiefs which his predecessors had spared no toil to acquire and retain.   Another, named Julian, the same who was after-wards Julius II., was enriched with several ecclesiastical bene-fices.   For a third, named Jerome Riario, the principality of Imola was purchased from the resources of the Apostolical Treasury.   But it was on Pietro Riario, the youngest, that the profusion of his fondness was principally lavished.   Without talents, without virtues, from a simple Franciscan Monk, Pietro was immediately elevated to the dignity of Cardinal. He was made titular Patriarch of Constantinople; he was raised to the Archiepiscopal See of Florence; he received, be-sides, two other Archbishoprics, and a multitude of inferior benefices.   In the mean time, his splendid prodigality, the pride of his attendants, his equipage, and his sumptuousness, kept pace with the abundance of his resources, and he ex-pended on the pomp of a single ceremony, or the festivities of a single night, sums which exceeded the revenues of kings.

His nepo-tism.

The same Pope, as if to atone for the laxity of one extreme of the ecclesiastical establishment by the austerity of the other,

The Minimes.

---

* This scene is described at length by Machiavel, Stor. Fiorent., lib. viii.   The particulars of the dispute are detailed by Paul Jovius, in the First Book of his Life of Leo X.   This connexion of Pope Sixtus with the history of Florence has procured for him a peculiar, and not very enviable, celebrity.   " Di grossi conti (says Muratori, Annal. v. 9) avrà avuto questo Pontefice nel tribunale di Dio."

gave his confirmation to a new religious body, called the Minimes—*the least* among the servants of Christ. They were founded by one Francisco of Paula; and to the usual monastic obligations they added a fourth vow, of perpetual fast and abstinence from all nourishment, except herbs and roots. The popular appetite for such extravagance was not yet wholly satiated; and though the Minimes never acquired the celebrity which would certainly have attended them in the thirteenth age, there were still not wanting devotees to swell their numbers, and recompense their vain enthusiasm by reverence and by gold.

When we shall come to examine the spiritual condition of the Roman Catholic Church during this period, and the character of the papal edicts which were more particularly directed to that object, we shall find that no one descended more deeply into superstition than Sixtus IV. At present we shall only mention the singular venality introduced into his government by the creation of certain new offices, which he publicly sold, and which he created for the purpose of selling. This was a new scandal in the history of the Vatican; and when the same Pontiff raised to the dignity of Cardinal a youth named Jacopo di Parma, his own valet, he may seem to have offered the last insult to his Court and his Church. The deeper outrage which was now continually cast upon the religion of Christ has almost ceased to be matter of mention with us—because the name of Christ was now seldom appealed to, unless in support of some monstrous ecclesiastical pretension; and the rulers of the Apostolical Church had for some time learned to dispense, both in their morals and their administration, even with the semblance of holiness, even with a decorous affectation of religious motives.

Character of Sixtus.   Sixtus IV. was not deficient, as a political character, in quickness and sagacity, and even grandeur of conception. But his character (as Sismondi has well observed) corrupted his talents, and stained his noblest projects with falsehood and perfidy. As he could discern no distinction between virtue and crime, he employed the basest means to attain the best ends, and dishonoured his own designs by the instruments

with which he chose to accomplish them.   His private life has
not escaped the suspicion of the foulest enormities—it cannot,
at least, pretend to the praise of piety or innocence.   His
learning, the exertions which he made, and the funds which
he appropriated to enrich the Library of the Vatican from
every quarter; his architectural labours, and the noble buildings* with which he adorned his capital; these are the only
monuments by which he is honourably known to posterity.
His capacity was considerable, and it was enlarged and enlightened by literary accomplishments.   But if these were
unable to infuse into his soul any disinterested virtue, or generous principle of action, they failed to accomplish the only purpose for which they are really valuable, and they left the pos-
sessor the more dangerous and the more detestable, from the
authority which they added to his talents, and the aid which
they lent him to abuse them.

Sixtus IV. died in 1484, and the election of his successor **Election of Innocent VIII.**
was attended by some circumstances more scandalous than any
which had yet polluted the recesses of the Conclave.   Julian
della Rovera, Cardinal of St. Peter *ad Vincula,* had undertaken the negotiations requisite, and the price of every vote
was already arranged, when the College proceeded to invoke
the Holy Spirit.   The terms are expressly specified by a contemporary writer †; they were faithfully observed by the successful candidate; and they might be ascertained from the
various castles and benefices, which he immediately bestowed
on his supporters.   John Baptist Cybo, a native of Genoa, was
the individual thus elevated to the throne of the Church, and he
assumed the name of Innocent.

Notwithstanding the recent perfidy of Paul II., defended by **His perfidy,**
the constitution of Innocent VI.‡, and countenanced by the

* The *Ponte Sesto* was his great work. His literary monuments were of a less
durable construction; for, indeed, the subjects which he chose were not always
the most favourable to their perpetuity.   One treatise he composed on The Blood
of Jesus Christ; another on Indulgences accorded to Souls in Purgatory; another
on the Conception of the Holy Virgin, &c. &c.   Such, however, were the controversies of the day.

† The letter of Guidantonio Vespucci to Lorenzo de' Medici on this subject, is
given entire by Roscoe, Append. No. xliv., and without suspicion of its truth.

‡ Published in 1353. See Chapter XXII., vol. iii., p. 21.

example of so many Pontiffs, the members of the Conclave once more attempted to bind the future Pope by a similar engagement. It was tedious to repeat the stipulations which were accepted in the name of God, on his holy altar, and which were even then intended for immediate violation. Their object was ever the same—to increase the power of the Cardinals at the expense of that of the Pope—and it was ever frustrated by the most deliberate perjury. On the day of his installation, Innocent VIII. confirmed and repeated his oath, and bound himself, on pain of anathema, neither to receive nor *give* absolution from it—for the Pontiff possessed exclusively the power of self-absolution. Howbeit, he no sooner felt his strength, and the independence of his despotism, than he cancelled the treaty and annulled both his oaths.

and contemptible character.

If Sixtus IV. had wasted the resources of the Church upon his profligate nephews, Innocent introduced a still more revolting race of dependants, in the persons of his illegitimate offspring. Seven children, the fruits of various amours, were publicly recognized by the Vicar of Christ, and became, for the most part, pensioners on the ecclesiastical Treasury. This was yet a new scandal for the Apostolical Church! Again, if Sixtus IV. was bold and unprincipled, Innocent was, at least, destitute of any positive virtue; and the extreme weakness which distinguished him was, in his circumstances, little less pernicious than wickedness. With power so vast and arbitrary, in a Court so utterly depraved, the personal excesses of a vigorous character might even have been less hurtful to the Church, than the unrestrained licence of so many masters. Fewer crimes would, perhaps, have been perpetrated, had the Pontiff resolved to be the only criminal. But with all his weakness, Innocent was animated by a spirit of avarice, which attracted observation even in that age of the popedom. And he performed at least one memorable exploit, as it were, in the design to surpass his predecessor by a still bolder insult on the sacred College—he placed among its members a boy, thirteen years old, the brother-in-law of his own bastard *. But

* This boy was John, the son of Lorenzo de' Medici, the same who became Leo X. It should be observed, that Innocent, on making the creation, stipulated

the Court of Rome did not resent the indignity—it was sunk even below the sense of its own infamy.

The Pontiff sounded, like most of his predecessors, the trumpet of a general crusade against the Infidel; in his addresses to the European ambassadors he set forth, in eloquent expressions, the blessings of concord, and the calamities of international warfare; and he preached with the usual inefficacy. Some Italian States did, indeed, exhibit a slight disposition to support him, owing to the greater proximity of the danger, and Innocent persisted to the end of his reign in pressing his first solicitations. But the only effects proceeding from them were those which flowed into the Apostolical Treasury, and which the Pope consumed, partly in his own personal expenses, partly in family hostilities against the King of Naples. He died in 1492.

In the downward progress of pontifical impurity, from Paul II. we descend to Sixtus IV.; from Sixtus to Innocent VIII.; from Innocent to Alexander VI.: and here, at length, we are arrested by the limits, the utmost limits, which have been assigned to papal and to human depravity. The ecclesiastical records of fifteen centuries, through which our long journey is now nearly ended, contain no name so loathsome, no crimes so foul as his; and while the voice of every impartial writer is loud in his execration, he is, in one respect, singularly consigned to infamy, since not one among the zealous annalists of the Roman Church has breathed a whisper in his praise. Thus, those who have pursued him with the most unqualified vituperations are thought to have described him most faithfully; and the mention of his character has excited a sort of rivalry in the expression of indignation and hatred. *Alexander VI.*

The College assembled for this election amidst the tumults of the Roman people, who were venting their curses against the avarice of the deceased Pontiff; and it was not till the Conclave had been garrisoned by soldiers, and fortified by cannon, that the Cardinals ventured to proceed to their deliberations. *Circumstances of his election.*

that the boy should not take his seat in Consistory till he was sixteen. Some state the age of creation at fifteen, that of admission at eighteen. See Raynaldus, ann. 1489.

It was presently discovered that the candidates who had any prospect of success were two * only. One of them was Roderic Borgia, who was nephew of Calixtus III.; the other was Julian della Rovera, nephew of Sixtus IV. Nepotism now formed so conspicuous a feature in the pontifical policy, that we shall not be surprised to see the popedom disputed by the nephews of Popes. Roderic was far advanced in years; he abounded in wealth, accumulated in the service of the Church; he was at the same time in the enjoyment of three archbishoprics in Spain, besides numerous other benefices in other quarters of Europe. All these would be vacated by his elevation, and falling into his patronage would be bestowed, of course, according to the measure of private services. Borgia was moreover a man of some abilities, of great address and versatility in negotiation and intrigue, and of morals which opposed no impediment to any means of compassing any purpose. Julian possessed more powerful talents, and, though his habits had been chiefly military, a much less exceptionable character. But he was younger; his preferment was not nearly so valuable, and the private wealth at his disposal bore no proportion to that of his competitor. The College was principally composed of the creatures of the two last Popes, Sixtus and Innocent, educated in those principles on which the morals of the Roman Court were at this time founded. Accordingly the election was not long doubtful; indeed, Borgia had taken a sure precaution to preclude hesitation, by placing two mules laden with gold † at the disposal of a faithful Cardinal, to be bestowed as occasion might require.

Alexander VI. immediately proceeded, after the example of his predecessor, to fulfil the conditions privately stipulated with the Cardinals, who had simoniacally elected him. On Ascagna Sforza he conferred the profitable dignity of vice-chancellor; to Cardinal Orsini he ceded his palace at Rome, together with two other mansions; to Cardinal Colonna he gave an

---

* Ascagna Sforza, who appeared at first to possess some claims, very soon resigned them in favour of Borgia.

† Some say, four mules laden with silver. The difference, in a moral point of view, is not important.

abbey, with numerous dependencies; to the Cardinal of St. Angelo, the bishopric of Porto, together with his furniture and a cellar of delicious wines; to others, churches or towns; to others, undisguised gold.   Five only in the whole college— one of whom was Julian, his rival—are believed to have resisted all these varieties of corruption.   In the mean time, the Roman people, as if they gloried in the iniquity of their rulers, hailed the decision of the Conclave with unusual expressions of satis- faction.   On no other occasion had the holy city arrayed her- self in such festive splendour, or descended to such loathsome- ness of adulation *, as on that, when she placed in the aposto- lical chair the most profligate of mankind, and offered the last insult—we say not to the name of Christ, for *that* had long been scorned—but to a Church which still called itself Chris- tian, and to the nations which still recognized that Church.

In early life, during the pontificate of Pius II., Roderic Borgia, already a Cardinal, had been stigmatized by a public censure for his unmuffled debaucheries.   Afterwards he pub- licly cohabited with a Roman matron named Vanozia, by whom he had five acknowledged children.   Neither in his manners nor in his language did he affect any regard for morality or for decency; and one of the earliest acts of his pontificate was, to celebrate, with scandalous magnificence, in his own palace, the marriage of his daughter Lucretia.   Those cardinals, who had conspired for his elevation, could not pretend either surprise or offence at this outrage.   But Julian della Rovera refused his countenance to those festivities, and shut himself up in the fortress of Ostia.

His profli- gate cha- racter.

---

* The following distich was published on this occasion:—
>   Cæsare magna fuit, nunc Roma est maxima; Sextus
>   Regnat Alexander: ille vir, iste Deus.

This was the serious flattery of the day: some other verses, published after some little experience of the Pope's *divine* administration, are less discreditable to the city of Cæsar and Pasquin:
>   Vendit Alexander Claves, Altaria, Christum.
>   Emerat ille prius: vendere jure potest.
>   De vitio in vitium, de flammâ transit in ignem;
>   Roma sub Hispano deperit imperio.
>   Sextus Tarquinius, Sextus Nero, Sextus et iste—
>   Semper sub Sextis perdita Roma fuit.

At this period in the annals of papacy, the spiritual exertions of the See were so very insignificant, compared with its struggles for temporal objects, and these struggles were now so interwoven with the general politics of Europe, that to trace, with any accuracy, the exploits of Alexander, or Julius II., would be to transcribe the civil history of Italy, France, and Germany. Such a task is consistent neither with the limits of this work, nor its design; and since the various vices, which peculiarly distinguished this Pope, are chiefly exemplified in his political transactions, we must refer the reader to the circumstantial narrative of Sismondi, or Guicciardini *—contented in our more contracted course to mention such incidents as are more closely connected either with the religion of Christ, or the economy of the Church, or the pretensions of the Apostolical See. Thus shall we not pass unnoticed the celebrated project of alliance against Charles VIII. of France, which was proposed by Alexander VI. to Bajazet, emperor of the Turks. The Pope appeared, on this occasion, as the Suzerain Lord of Naples; and in his overtures he represented to the Sultan, that that kingdom was menaced by foreign invasion; that it was the design of Charles to subject it to his authority, and then to turn his arms into Thrace, against the walls of Constantinople; that the French king was full of ambition, and careless about the means of indulging it; while for himself he had nothing more at heart than the repose of the Turk, in consideration of the good-will and mutual friendship subsisting between them. The nature of the engagements into which Bajazet consequently entered does not certainly appear, but when the crisis arrived, he took no measures to fulfil them; and the

His negotiations with Bajazet.

---

* We shall cite the words in which this author has drawn the character of Alexander VI. " In Alexandro Sesto fù solerzia e sagacità singolare, consiglio eccellente, efficacia a persuadere maravigliosa, e a tutte le faccende gravi sollecitudine e destrezza incredibile—mà erano queste virtù avanzate di grande intervallo da' vizii—costumi oscenissimi, non sincerità, non vergogna, non verità, non fede, non religione, avarizia insaziabile, ambizione immoderata, crudeltà più che barbara, e ardentissima cupidità di esaltare in qualumque modo i figliuoli, i quali erano molti; e tra questi qualcuno... non meno detestabile in parte alcuna del padre.' Storia d' Itali, lib. i. Guicciardini was ten years old when Borgia was raised to the pontificate, and his history begins with that year.

Vicar of Christ, after having invoked the Mahometan arms into the heart of Europe against a Christian prince, was pursued by the additional, and to him more bitter reflection, that he had incurred that infamy in vain.

On the return of Columbus to Spain, Ferdinand and Isabella announced to the Pope, their compatriot, the success of his expedition. Alexander VI. hastened to avail himself of so magnificent an occasion to exhibit the plenitude of his authority: accordingly, he conferred upon the crown of Castile the full right to possess all that had been discovered, and all that might hereafter be discovered, whether islands or continents, whether situated in the Indies or in any other region. In a succession of bulls published on this subject, in the year 1493, at a season when the power of the See bore no proportion to its ancient grandeur, and when the character of the prelates who administered it was not certainly such as to redeem its degradation, Pope Alexander drew a line along the map, from the north to the south, and gave away, by a stroke of his pen, half the habitable world. And so much seriousness did he affect to attach to his donation, that he descended to specify the exact distance from his line at which the rights of Spain should begin, and those of other nations end. *Donation of the newly-discovered regions.*

It is proper to add, that the Portuguese contested the validity of the act. Let us inquire, then, on what ground did they rest their opposition? Did they dispute the authority by which the edict had been issued? Far otherwise; only they maintained that, by a similar act, Eugenius IV. had previously bestowed the same rights upon themselves. It was no contest between the king of Portugal and the See of Rome, but only a question whether a Pope could confer upon one prince what a preceding Pope had already bestowed upon another. And in this dispute between a living and a departed pontiff, after many assemblies had been held, and new boundaries delineated, and great violence displayed, Alexander persisted and succeeded, in defiance of every right and every semblance even of pontifical justice. In the year following, Africa became the subject of a very similar dispute; but on this occasion the Pope showed thus much respect to the authority of Pius II., who *The Pope's right acknowledged by both parties.*

had conferred the contested provinces upon Portugal, that he confined the conquests of Ferdinand and Isabella to the kingdoms of Algiers and Tunis, leaving Fez and the contiguous regions to the possession of Portugal. We may smile at the arrogance of a declining despotism; nor shall we be astonished by the obsequiousness of those who found their interest in obsequiousness. At the same time, if the right of the See was not disputed, the motives which it pretended were certainly such as to justify the exercise of its right. For it was expressly stipulated in the act of donation, that holy and pious missionaries should be dispatched forthwith, for the conversion of the newly-conquered tracts and the extension of the kingdom of Christ and of the Catholic Church.

Charles VIII. at Rome.

When Charles VIII. entered Rome in the year 1494, Julian della Rovera (as well as some other cardinals) was in his suite, and shared in his councils*. From the determined hostility of Julian; from the wish for reformation, which had so often been manifested by the court and people of France; from the undue estimate then formed of the character of the actual king, Alexander felt reason to apprehend the accomplishment of the menace so frequently repeated—the assembly of a General Council; and he easily foresaw that the first act of that Council would be to depose himself. From the castle of St. Angelo he opened negotiations with the conqueror; but whether it had never been the intention of Charles to press the Holy See to any extremities, or whether, as is believed by the best writers, Alexander found means to corrupt the most intimate advisers of the king by largesses and promises, the designs of Julian were frustrated, and the dignity of the Pope was preserved by a favourable convention. He returned to the pontifical palace; he resumed his former state; he gave the king a formal reception at St. Peter's, with the usual solemnities; and the king did not disdain to submit to the

---

* Guicciardini (lib. i., cap. iii.) does not hesitate to ascribe the accomplishment of Charles's designs against Italy to this Cardinal—" fatale instrumento è allora, è prima, è poi de' mali d' Italia."—The King at one moment certainly relaxed in his zeal, and was reanimated by the authority and vehemence of Julian.

usual humiliation. He bent his knees, and kissed the pontiff's foot and hand; and, subsequently, on the celebration of the pontifical mass, took his seat below the first cardinal, and ministered water to the hands of the Pope*. Such were the marks of deference which had long been exacted by Popes, and paid by Sovereigns; but never, till now, had they been prostituted so gratuitously—never, till now, had they been tendered in the place of chastisement and infamy, by a powerful and victorious prince, to a pontiff as destitute of strength as he was notoriously polluted with crime.

There was one article in the above treaty which leads to the mention of a singular episode in papal history. The Sultan Bajazet had a brother named Zizim, or Jem, (like himself, the son of Mahomet II.,) whose popularity, courage, and ambition made him dangerous to the throne. The morals of the Seraglio permitted the destruction of such rivals; and Zizim, fearing that fate, had escaped to Rhodes, and placed himself in Christian hands. From Rhodes he was carried to France, and thence he passed into the custody of Pope Innocent VIII. It was then that Bajazet, availing himself of the avarice of the vicars of Christ as the means of preserving the concord of an empire hostile to the Christian faith, engaged to pay to the See a yearly sum of forty thousand ducats—nominally, for the keeping and entertainment of his brother; really, to make it the interest of the Vatican to secure the prisoner at Rome, and not to resign him to any enemy of the empire†. The money was faithfully paid, and Zizim remained a safe and profitable captive at the apostolical court. Charles VIII., who seems at that time to have really harboured some ulterior designs against the Turkish power, stipulated with Alexander

Zizim, the brother of Bajazet.

---

* Guicciardini mentions that the Pope, to preserve the memory of these ceremonies to all posterity, caused them to be represented in painting, in one of the chambers of the castle of St. Angelo. It is to be remarked that they were the formal ceremonies following the reconciliation of the parties. On their first meeting, which was not thoroughly official, some of the most humiliating were dispensed with. The " Capitula Conventionis Papæ et Regis Franciæ, &c.," are cited from the " Diary of Burchard," by Roscoe, Life of Leo X., Appendix, No. xxxv.

† Guicciard., lib. i., cap. iii.

for the possession of Zizim.   The pontiff observed his engagement; but the prisoner carried with him from his confinement the seeds of a mortal disorder.   He died very soon afterwards; and there seems some reason to believe that the cause of his death was a slow and subtle poison administered under the superintendence of Alexander *.

The Duke Valentino.

Cæsar Borgia was the second, and favourite, and worthy son of Alexander VI.   He commenced his career as an ecclesiastic; but in 1498 he found it more politic at once to throw off that profession; and he then received the title which he has rendered one of the most infamous in history.   As Duke Valentino, or Valentinois, he took the field in Romagna, the temporal champion of the Holy See, for the destruction of its enemies, the confirmation of its authority over the city, and the enlargement of its territories.   Supported by the talents and resources of his father, he succeeded in these designs to an extent attained in no preceding age, and by means which are known to every reader.   But in seeking thus to advance the interests of the Church, Alexander had, in truth, no other design than to aggrandize his son; nor did Valentino toil through such a mass of crimes with any more distant object than to erect a principality for himself †.   To this end he had

* Of course this fact is not, nor could it well have been, undisputed.   Raynaldus (ann. 1495, s. 8, &c.) refers to Burchardus to prove that the captive died from a change of diet.   The words of Burchardus are—" 15 Feburier, le fils du grand Turc mourut à Naples—ex esu sive potu non convenienti naturæ suæ et consueto——."   At the same time, Raynaldus mentions the vulgar account, which is affirmed by Guicciardini.   See Roscoe, Life of Leo X., chap. iv.

† " Yet what he did (says Machiavel) turned to the Church's advantage; which, after the death of the Pope, and the removal of the Duke, became the heir of all his pains."   The partiality of this writer to the *public* character of the Duke (with whom he was personally acquainted) is known to every one.   Yet there is a passage (in the Prince, chap. vii.) which is worth citing.   " Having thus collected all the Duke's actions, methinks I could not well blame him, but rather set him as a pattern to be followed by all those who, by profane and other means, have been exalted to an empire.....Whoever, therefore, deems it necessary, on his entrance into a new principality, to secure himself from his enemies, and gain his friends; to overcome, either by force, or by cunning; to make himself beloved or feared of his people; to be followed and reverenced by his soldiers; to root out those that can hurt him, or owe him any hurt; to change the ancient orders for new ways; to be severe, and yet acceptable, magnanimous, and liberal; to extinguish the unfaithful soldiery, and create new; to maintain to himself the amities of kings and princes, so that they shall either with favour benefit, or be

calculated, as seemed to him, every possible contingency; by much daring, great address, and an entire contempt of every scruple, of all faith, and of all shame, he had already accomplished much: and, to secure the stability of his power, he had employed every expedient within the reach of human foresight—when the realization of his schemes was put to an unexpected trial by the death of his father and his own dangerous sickness.

The following are the circumstances relating to the death of Alexander, which stand on the most extensive evidence:— The Duke Valentino, being greatly in want of money to pay his troops, applied to his father for assistance; but the apostolical treasury was exhausted, and neither resources nor credit were then at hand to replenish it. On which the duke suggested to the Pope an easy, and, as it would seem, not very unusual method of supplying their wants. The Cardinal Corneto, as well as some others of the sacred College, had a great reputation for wealth; and it was then the practice at Rome for the property of cardinals to devolve, on their decease, to the See. He proposed to get rid of this Corneto. The Pope consented; and, accordingly, invited the cardinals to an entertainment, which he prepared for them in his vineyard of Corneto, for it was near the Vatican. Among the wines sent for this occasion, one bottle was prepared with poison; and instructions were carefully given to the superintendent of the feast respecting the disposal of that bottle. It happened that, some little time before supper, the Pope and his son arrived, and, as it was very hot, they called for wine. And then, whether through the error or the absence of the confidential

Various circumstances related respecting the death of Alexander VI.

wary how they offend him—cannot find more fresh and lively examples than in the actions of this man." In a separate narrative, usually published in the same volume, Machiavel relates at length (what is, no doubt, one of those lively examples) the methods which the Duke employed to rid himself of certain enemies —Vitellozzo Vitelli, Oliverotto of Fermo, Paul, and the Duke of Gravina; and a more black and scandalous tissue of perfidy, cruelty, and villany cannot possibly be imagined. That he was the author of the assassination of his elder brother, the Duke of Gandia, is believed by most historians; and that the motive was an incestuous jealousy respecting their common sister is a further imputation advanced by many, and not rejected by Sismondi: but there is no sufficient evidence to establish either of these charges.

officer, the poisoned bottle was presented to them. Both drank of it, and both immediately suffered its violent effects. Valentino, who had mixed much water with his wine, and was, besides, young and vigorous, through the immediate use of powerful antidotes *, was saved. But Alexander, having taken his draught nearly pure, and being likewise enfeebled by age, died in the course of the same evening.

It is proper to add, that there are two other accounts of this transaction, differing from that which is here given on the general agreement of numerous authorities. One is that of Pietro Martiri d'Angleria, a councillor of Ferdinand, of whom an epistle is extant, in which the Pope is exculpated from all participation in the crime, and the whole guilt thrown upon the duke. And this has been received by some writers as the more probable, through consideration of the general hatred then subsisting against Alexander, and the prevalent disposition to propagate and believe any evil rumour respecting him;

---

* He is said to have been inclosed in the belly of a living mule, and so preserved. The following is the brief account given by Paul Jovius of this transaction, in the beginning of lib. ii., De Vita Leonis X. " Nam Pontifex inopiæ metu rapax atque illo immani ingenio sævus, ut Cæsari filio magnos alenti exercitus et regio luxu liberalitatem passim ostendenti pecuniam suppeditaret, ditissimum quemque Cardinalium veneno sustulerat, haud dubie in reliquos aulæ sacerdotiis atque opibus insignes hæreditatis spe sæviturus, nisi admirabili deorum providentia homo in religionis causa probrosus et quod omnium fortunæ interfuit, ad exitium Italiæ natus, sibi mortem, supremam vero Cæsari filio calamitatem, peperisset—hilariori scilicet in cœna dum ad umbrosum Vaticani fontem venenum bibunt, lagena pocillatoris errore commutata, quam dira fraude opulentis aliquot senatoribus honoris specie paravissent. Mortuo Alexandro, et Cæsare exquisitis antidotis vel in ipso juventæ robore veneni impetum vix sustinente, Comitia sunt habita," &c. &c. The same author describes the same event (De Vita Magni Consalvi, lib. ii.) with little variation, but with the following addition :—" Accepi ego ab Adriano Cardinale Cornetano, in cujus villa cœnabatur, se eodem mortifero poculo petitum ita exarsisse eo subito viscerum fervore, ut obortæ caligines oppressis sensibus sibi rationem excuterent, sese in solidum frigida plenum mergere cogeretur, neque prius perustis interaneis ad vitam rediise, quam ei extrema cutis in exuvias abiens toto corpore decideret." Raphael Volaterranus, in his Life of Alexander VI., likewise mentions the illness of the cardinal, simultaneous with that of the Pope. Voltaire disbelieves the whole story, owing to its extreme improbability; while he allows that the father and son were " les deux plus grands scélêrats parmi les puissances de l' Europe." Is the story, then, so very improbable ? But if it were, mere probability is a very faithless test of historical truth. Things contrary to all calculation are happening every day, and have always happened.

but we are not aware that it rests on any other original testimony. The other account is extracted by Raynaldus (ann. 1503, sect. xi.), from a manuscript journal of the house of Borgia*; and herein we are entertained by a circumstantial description of the last natural illness of Alexander, the character of the fever, the practice of the physicians, the piety of the departing pontiff, the reverence with which he received the last sacrament, the demeanour of the cardinals and others who were present at the edifying scene. But this family narrative, being at variance with the less partial accounts of the same transaction, may be rejected without much hesitation.

Such, then, was the probable end of Alexander VI.; he was poisoned by the cup prepared for his own guest by his own hand, or, at least, by the hand of a beloved son, whose notorious crimes he had long endured and fostered, and whom he seems to have loved for those very crimes; so that, in respect to his general character, it imports not very much whether he was an accomplice or not in that last offence, of which he was the deserving victim. " All Rome (says Guicciardini) rushed to St. Peter's to behold his corpse with incredible festivity; nor was there any man who could satiate his eyes with gazing on the remains of a serpent, which, by his immoderate ambition and pestiferous perfidy, and every manner of frightful cruelty, of monstrous lust and unheard-of avarice, trafficking indiscriminately with things sacred and profane, had impoisoned the whole world." Yet the world still continued to acknowledge the vicegerent of Christ, and to bow before the throne of St. Peter. The cup was not yet full; some few remaining iniquities were still to be accomplished; the arm of vengeance was still suspended, and Luther, the destined instrument, had not yet commenced his noviciate among the Augustinian Mendicants.

After the funeral honours had been duly paid to the departed pontiff, eight and thirty cardinals entered into Conclave

---

* Sismondi likewise refers to the " Letters of the Ambassador of the House of Este," and to Muratori, Annali d'Italia, tom. x., p. 15. According to Guicciardini (lib. vi.), the death of Alexander took place on August 17, 1503,—" e il giorno seguente è portato morto secondo l' uso dei Pontifica nella Chiesa di San Piero, nero, infiato e bruttissimo—segni manifestissimi di veleno."

Election
and Death
of Pius III.

to choose a successor. The unusual number of the electors may be one reason why the present election was not charged with simony; but it presented a scene of treacherous intrigue, scarcely less shameful, in which Julian della Rovera was the principal actor—for as no man was more daring in warfare, so was not any one more astute in duplicity, than he. By the success of his machinations, a sick and feeble old man, the nephew of Pius II., was raised to the pontificate on September 22, 1503; and scarcely had he received the ordination to the priesthood, (which, though a cardinal, he had not previously received,) and undergone the ceremony of coronation, and assumed the name of Pius III., when he died—six and twenty days after his election. Great expectations were excited by his reputed virtues and piety, and his ardently expressed desire for a reformation of the Church; and it may be fortunate for his memory that they were disappointed by his death, rather than by some act of apostacy, by which he might not improbably have imitated so many of his predecessors.

Accession
of Julius II.

Julian celebrated the mass at his obsequies; and scarcely was that office performed when he re-opened his former intrigues in the design, on this occasion, of procuring his own election. He gained the leading cardinals; he gained the Duke de Valentinois, who directed the Spanish party in the Conclave, by magnificent promises, and the confidence that they would be observed. On the very first scrutiny, Julian della Rovera was unanimously raised to the chair of Alexander VI. We should here mention that, before the election of Pius III., the Cardinals in conclave had bound the future Pope, among other conditions, to convoke a Council General for the reform of the Church, within two years from the time of his election, and to make the assembly of such Councils hereafter triennial. It appears that Julian on his elevation gave his assent to the same stipulations *.

* The form of the oath deserves to be cited in its very words. " Præmissa omnia et singula promitto, voveo et juro observare et adimplere, in omnibus et per omnia, purè et simpliciter et bona fide, realiter, et cum effectu perjurii et anathematis, a quibus nec me ipsum absolvam, nec alieni absolutionem committam. Ita me Deus adjuvet, &c." It appears in Beausobre, Hist. Reform. liv. i.

He took the name of Julius II., thereby intending, as many His milita-
suppose, to avow his preference of the military to the sacer- ter.
dotal character, and to declare his greater disposition to imitate
the glories of Pagan, than of Christian Rome. Assuredly his
whole pontificate was directed by such motives; and if the
ten years through which it extended are not wholly destitute
of events properly appertaining to ecclesiastical history, those
events did scarcely ever originate with the Pope, and were unconnected with the principles of his government. It was not
that he neglected, in the progress of his negotiations and campaigns, to carry on his lips the name of St. Peter, to whet the
material upon the spiritual sword, and to thunder forth bulls
and anathemas with all the majesty of former days; but it was
in this respect only that he was distinguished from the *other*
temporal sovereigns, with whom he leagued or contended.

After so long a course of pontifical degeneracy, in the hands Remaining
of a Pope so absolutely secular as Julius, it might have been for the See
expected that those bolts had lost their force and their terrors; of Rome.
and that the Bishop of Rome, having descended to the policy
of a secular prince, would have been treated by his brother
princes with no superior reverence. Yet was it otherwise; the
fetters of the inveterate prejudice were not yet wholly unloosed,
and the spiritual weapon was still an object of apprehension
even to the king of France. So late as the year 1510, Louis
XII.*, being deeply embroiled with the Pope, and struck with
the sentence of excommunication, assembled a council of his
clergy at Tours, and formally demanded their opinions on
such points as these:—" Whether the Pope had a right to
make war, when neither the interests of religion, nor the domains of the Church were in danger? Whether a prince might
seize the ecclesiastical states, in case the Pope were his declared
enemy, and keep temporary possession of them, until he should
have humbled his adversary? Whether under the same circumstances a subtraction of obedience under certain restrictions were lawful? Whether a prince might defend another

* The same who caused a coin to be struck bearing the inscription *Perdam
Babylonis nomen.*

prince—his ally—against the pontifical arms?" Such were the scruples which still were felt even in the court of France. They were removed by the loyalty of the episcopal assembly: nevertheless, even after their removal, enough remained to distinguish the apostolical from all other governments; and as those distinctions were founded on popular opinion, fostered by priestly influence, it was not very easy to counteract their effect, or foresee their termination.

The triumphs of Julius II.

Julius II. knew better than any one the advantage which he thus possessed, and he likewise knew the precise extent of it, so that in using it constantly he seldom abused it; and thus it proved that he was successful beyond all expectation in the accomplishment of his most difficult designs. When he ascended the throne, he found the Duke de Valentinois in possession of many cities in the Romagna, which the latter had usurped during the reign of Alexander, and of which he appropriated the revenues. Him, the most dissembling of men, Julius in some measure supplanted by dissimulation*. From another nobleman (Paolo Baglioni) he recovered the city of Perugia by singular audacity; he suddenly entered the hold of his enemy with his Cardinals only, attended by no escort, and in such guise reclaimed and recovered his rights of sovereignty. He compelled the Venetians to restore several places which they had conquered from the Holy See—Rimini, Faenza, Ravenna, Cervia; and before the end of his pontificate, he had established a direct authority over all the cities which constitute the ecclesiastical states. Even in Milan he was almost paramount, while Modena, Reggio, Parma, Piacenza, were held in the name of the Church†. And some have supposed, that, had his reign been prolonged for a very few years, the whole extent of Italy would have been united under the *sceptre* of St. Peter.

* Alexander VI., who detested Julian, always admitted that he had one, though only one, redeeming quality: it was veracity. This reputation, Guicciardini says, gave him great opportunities of lying with advantage. Nevertheless, in this case, having the Duke's person entirely in his power, he certainly did not treat him so ill as the principles of his enemies, and even of his age, would have justified, nor nearly so severely as many expected and hoped.

† See Denina, Rivol. d' Ital., lib. xix. cap. vii. and lib. xx. cap. i., ii., iii.

The object, however, which he more openly professed, and which was at least honourable to his patriotism, was the expulsion of all foreigners (Barbari) from the soil of Italy. The measures by which he pursued that object belong to civil history, as well as the splendid reputation which they acquired for him. The talents and the qualities of Philip and Alexander are described by the panegyrists of Julius as combined in him : even in their vices he resembled them—anger and intemperance. Respecting the particulars of his policy, it is recorded that he never would listen to any proposal of peace, so long as war, with any promise of success, was open to him ; yet that he so conducted war as to be in perpetual negotiation. Enemies, as well as friends, were made to serve his designs, and distant, as well as neighbouring, powers. He was so fierce and indefatigable a warrior, that at an age almost decrepit he did not shrink, when necessary, from sharing the severest toils of the meanest soldiers ; but, at the same time, no one ever wielded the spiritual weapon with more imposing authority than Julius. His energy in the Vatican was scarcely surpassed by his bravery in the field ; and he dictated a bull with the same energy with which he commanded an army. It was, moreover, particularly remarked, that he directed the ecclesiastical functions, and mingled in the holy services, with wonderful decorum and solemnity ; thus under no circumstances forgetting the advantages to be derived from his sacred office, nor ever failing to make it the means of raising his personal dignity, or advancing his political purposes. *His extraordinary character.*

Another proof of the expanded mind of Julius II. was his patronage of the arts of peace, which had suffered in the general degradation of the preceding pontificates. Many celebrated masters flourished during his reign, and his encouragement was never wanting to animate, nor his liberality to support them. The foundations of St. Peter's, after being designed by Nicholas V., were finally laid by Julius ; and to prove the value which he attached to that undertaking, he placed the first stone with his own hand. The accumulation of so many and such various qualities in one character leaves no space to doubt his extraordinary capacity. And could we be contented to con- *His patronage of the Arts.*

sider him only as a secular prince—could we forget that he was
really the chief of the Church of Christ, and that he professed to
be His vicegerent—the homage which is extorted by his genius,
his audacity, and the ambitious grandeur of his spirit, however
qualified by his political immorality, would be offered with less
reluctance.

Some Cardinals convoke a Council at Pisa, 1511, A.D.

But the Popes, even during this their season of licentiousness,
had not wholly forgotten the lessons inculcated at Constance and
Basle; and among the various dangers to which they were
liable, the name which ever filled them with the deepest apprehension
was that of a General Council. And thus, when Julius
engaged* to convoke such an assembly within two years from
his election, nothing was farther from his intention than to keep
his faith, and in effect he constantly eluded every proposition
tending to that end. The King of France saw the advantage thus
given him; and as there was also a party in the Sacred College,
which, through an honest regard for the Church, or a personal
displeasure against the Pope, (for Julius II., by an ungracious
and disdainful manner, frequently offended even those whom he
intended to oblige,) boldly clamoured for the redemption of his
pledge, Louis at length prevailed upon them to summon the
Council on their own authority. They were nine in number;
and the city which they appointed for the assembly was Pisa;
it was a place convenient to the French and Italian prelates,
and it contained, in its own history, the precedent of a General
Council, summoned by Cardinals. The Emperor Maximilian
gave only a cold assent to these proceedings. Julius exerted
every nerve to crush the project: nevertheless, the prelates met
together, and the Council was formally opened on the 1st of
November, 1511. Presently some tumults between the French
and Florentine soldiers alarmed the fathers; and after the third
session they retired to Milan, where they were entirely under
French protection. During that winter and the following spring
they held five other sessions; and then, as the German Bishops

* Raynaldi, Annales, 1503, s. i., &c. It should, perhaps, be mentioned, that
Julius published, in 1506, a severe edict against the simoniacal election of Popes.
He pronounced Popes so elected to be Heresiarchs, and consequently degraded
and deposed. The decree was confirmed in the Lateran Council which followed.

had never joined them, and as the Emperor had at length withdrawn even the equivocal countenance hitherto vouchsafed to
them, they retired for the second time from Milan to Lyons.
But on this last removal, notwithstanding the efforts of Louis
to give dignity and power to the refugees, the Council became
virtually extinct.

It is unnecessary to particularize the respective acts of the
eight Sessions of that assembly, not only because they were
never carried into effect, but because they were entirely directed
to one subject—the relative authority of the Council and the
Pope. Julius, on his side, thundered from the Vatican; he
excommunicated all the members; he degraded and deprived
the Cardinals. They on their part, after some verbose declarations, summoned the Pope into their presence, declared him
contumacious, and finally suspended him. But this was their
last effort, and the signal as it were for their extinction; and
the blow thus impotently dealt by the expiring assembly was
not felt on the Throne of St. Peter*.

Nevertheless, this short-lived Council in some measure The Fifth
achieved its professed purpose. Julius, in the first instance, Lateran
really feared it; and he then saw no effectual method of crush- 1512, A.D.
ing it, except the convocation of a rival council. He therefore
issued a summons to the Catholic hierarchy, to assemble at
Rome, in April, 1512, for the celebration of the fifth Lateran
Council; and on the 3rd of May he opened it in person, with
extraordinary dignity and solemnity. Fifteen Cardinals and
about eighty Archbishops and Bishops were present; but it
must not be forgotten that almost all were Italians. During
the nine following months five sessions were held, in which no
subject of any ecclesiastical importance was proposed†, except

* The contest, literally speaking, did not cease here. Julius pursued his adversaries into France, and laid the kingdom which harboured them under an interdict. But though some fresh controversies then arose on the old subject—the
comparative *auferibility* of a council and a Pope,—it was clearly the king who was
now fighting the battle, and not the council.

† The confirmation of Julius's former decree against the simoniacal election of
Popes should, perhaps, be considered as important, though there could be no great
hope of its efficacy—not, at least, till the constitution of the Sacred College should
be wholly changed.

the Pragmatic Sanction; and this was treated in a spirit of such undisguised hostility to the French court and Church, as to show very clearly what were the uses to which Julius intended to turn his Council. But he was interrupted by a fatal sickness. On the night of February 20, 1513, he died; and it was the last recorded act of his life to refuse the Cardinal's hat to an undeserving claimant. When the Pope was on the point of death, the boon was earnestly solicited by a very near relative,—a woman, for her own brother. Julius coldly replied, "That the person was unworthy," and then turned his head away, and expired.

Leo X.

He was succeeded by Leo X.—a name which belongs to the history of the Reformation, and with which, in this work, we are no further concerned, than as we propose to follow the Council assembled by his predecessor through its remaining deliberations. Before the end of the year it held three more sessions, under the presidency of the new Pope: the sixth and seventh produced no memorable enactments, but the eighth was somewhat more important. On this occasion the King of France at length announced his adhesion. A bull was likewise published for the purpose of establishing the separate existence and immortality of the soul against the dangerous and, as it would seem, prevalent theories of certain philosophers; and at the same time an edict of safe-conduct was granted to the Bohemian schismatics, with an invitation to assist at the Council: for their heresy was again rising into formidable attention. These measures were followed by a decree, directed against the *officers* of the apostolical court, for the diminution of their

Canons of Reformation published by the Council.

fees or salaries. On the 5th of May, 1514, the prelates proceeded from the abuses of their dependants to the consideration of their own; and on this occasion they published an imposing body of regulations for the reformation of the Roman court, and the general discipline of the Church. It was enacted, that only persons of worth and morality be appointed to benefices: to bishoprics, at an age not earlier than twenty-seven years; to abbeys, not earlier than twenty-two; and that care be taken to ascertain their merit before their names should be proposed in Consistory. That deprivation be inflicted only after due examination. That monasteries and abbeys be not held *in commendam,* unless for the better preservation of the authority of the Holy See, and by cardinals or other persons qualified; and that cures and dignities of little value (less than 200 ducats a year) be not so held even by cardinals. That there be no separation or union of Churches, unless for a reasonable cause. That no dispensation be granted to hold more than two incompatible benefices, unless to persons qualified, and for sufficient reasons. That persons possessing more than four benefices, cures, or dignities, be obliged, within two years, to reduce them to the number of four by resigning the rest.

It was likewise ordained that the cardinals should lead an exemplary life,—celebrating mass in their chapels, observing perfect sacerdotal modesty in their house, furniture, and tables, to the exclusion of all secular pomp; treating with honour and respect those about them; attentive to the interests of the poor, no less than to those of princes; visiting in person, or by deputy, their titular churches; providing for the prosperity of the monasteries, or benefices, which they might hold *in commendam;* avoiding every show of luxury, and every suspicion of avarice in their attendants. Respecting the inferior members of the court of Rome, a number of laws were published against blasphemy, concubinage, and simony. It was strictly prohibited to all kings, princes, and lords, to seize or sequestrate the ecclesiastical property, *unless by permission of the Pope.* All the laws concerning the exemption of ecclesiastical persons and goods from lay jurisdiction were confirmed. And lastly, the Inquisitions were stimulated to proceed zealously against heretics* and Jews; especially against those who had relapsed, from whom every hope of pardon was withheld. . . . . On the above regulations, which formed the substance of the most important decree of this council, it is scarcely necessary to observe that they touched very ineffectually even those few among the multifarious corruptions of the Church, which they touched at all; that, in respect to the Court of Rome, as no attempt was

* "How ill, alas! (says Raynaldus) these most holy laws were observed, appears from the hydra-birth of the Lutheran heresy, which came so soon afterwards." Ann. 1514, sect. 31, &c.

made to reduce one fraction of its power and wealth, it was
superfluous to publish general exhortations to modesty and
humility; and, besides, that the principal points in dispute
with France and Germany were entirely overlooked in this reformation of the Catholic Church.

A year afterwards, (on May 4, 1515,) the Council held its
tenth session. It then published a decree to restrain some of
the abuses of Chapters; to moderate, though very slightly, the
granting of exemptions; to refer the decision of trifling suits
respecting the smaller benefices to the Ordinaries; and to
encourage provincial Councils. Another decree peremptorily
cited the ecclesiastics of France to appear at the Council, and
show sufficient reasons why the Pragmatic Sanction should
not be wholly abolished. Another, promulgated on the same
occasion, was levelled against the presumed abuses of the press.
The Pope (an enlightened and literary Pope) pronounced to
the effect "that, though knowledge was acquired by reading,
and though the press much facilitated such acquirement, the
cultivation of the mind, the instruction of Christians, and the
consequent propagation of the faith and the Church; yet, as
it had reached the ears of his Holiness how some printers had
published many Latin translations from the Greek, Hebrew,
Arabic, and Chaldean, which contained false and pernicious
dogmas, and offended the reputation of persons in dignity, he
was bound to ordain, in his desire to remedy that evil, that no
book should be hereafter printed at Rome, or in any other
city or diocese, until it had been examined—at Rome by the
vicar of his Holiness, and the master of the sacred palace—in
other dioceses by the bishop, or some doctor appointed by him,
or by the inquisitor of the place, on pain of immediate excommunication*.

The next session was not held till the 19th of December,
1516. The Pope found himself at the head of a very tractable

Decree against the abuses of the Press.

---

* This was not the first effort of the Popes against what they considered the
abuses of the press. In 1501, Alexander VI. ordained, under the severest penalties, that no books should be printed in any diocese, without the sanction of
the bishop. (Raynaldus, 1501, s. 36.) But Sixtus IV. has the distinction of being
the first who established that inquisition.

assembly, still consisting almost entirely of Italian prelates, and yielding obsequious approbation to decrees dictated from the Vatican.   Thus, without any display of impatience, he steadily pursued that which seems to have been the only object of his predecessor in this matter, and which was clearly the leading one with himself,—the abolition of the Pragmatic Sanction.   In the present session he accomplished that design; and the bull which he published on the occasion is worthy of the proudest days of pontifical despotism.   He began by asserting the implicit obedience due by divine authority to the Holy See, and afterwards took occasion especially to confirm and renew the constitution *Unam Sanctam* of Boniface VIII.   He showed the illegality and schismatic nature of the " Sanction," by disparaging the councils of Bourges and Basle, and proclaimed the unlimited control of the Pope over such assemblies; and finally, by his certain knowledge, by the plenitude of his power, and with the approbation of the holy Council, he annulled all the decrees, statutes, and regulations contained in the offensive enactment.

Abolition of the Pragmatic Sanction.

The bull received the assent of the council, with only one dissentient voice.   The bishop of a small diocese in Lombardy had the boldness to express his veneration for the Councils of Bourges and Basle, and his reluctance to disturb their inviolable decisions.   But he was immediately overborne; the authority of the present (it was argued) was not inferior to that of preceding assemblies; and in ancient times St. Leo had revoked at Chalcedon what had been too rashly ordained at Ephesus.   Yet such arguments might not effectually have served the Pontiff, had not Francis I. conspired to betray the liberties of his Church.   The abolition of the Sanction was immediately followed by the publication of a Concordat, which tacitly restored the possession of *Annates* to the Pope *, and

---

* The Annates were not expressly mentioned in the Concordat. But as the Pragmatic Sanction, which had alone abolished that payment, was itself abolished, the right to the payment was restored; at least, it was left on the same footing on which it stood before the Sanction, and then it was commonly levied by the Pope. In fact, in the ecclesiastical writers on this subject, the words *pragmatic sanction* and *annates* are so constantly connected, as to make it very clear that the recovery of that contribution was a great object with the Popes in their enmity to the

openly transferred a valuable portion of the ecclesiastical patronage to the king.   During the same session certain restrictions were imposed upon the license of preachers, and generally
upon the discipline of the monastic orders; but these last were
compensated by some privileges, which, though of no great
apparent importance, offended the jealousy of the bishops, and
roused some opposition in the Council.   The assembly divided,
but the majority was in favour of the papal measures.

Dissolu-
tion of the
Council.

On the 16th of the following March (1517), the Council met
for the twelfth and concluding session, and after prohibiting
the popular practice of pillaging the mansion of the Pope elect,
and ordaining an imposition of tenths for the service of the
Turkish war, it was dissolved.   The bull of dissolution announced the accomplishment of every object of the assembly:
peace had been re-established among the princes of Christendom; the schismatic synod of Pisa abolished; and above all,
the reformation of the Church and court of Rome had been sufficiently provided for!   There were, indeed, some fathers who ventured to argue that every abuse had not even yet been removed,
and that the lasting interests of the Church would be better
promoted by the further continuance of the Council—but the
majority supported the Pope; and the last universal assembly
of the Western Church, after having deliberately regulated all
matters requiring any attention, and restored the establishment
to perfect health and security, separated with complacency and
confidence!   And here we may mention (for the coincidence
is remarkable) that in the very same year, almost before the
assembled prelates had concluded their mutual congratulations
on the peace, and unity, and purity of the Apostolical Church,
Luther commenced, in the schools of Wittenberg, his public
preaching against its most revolting corruption.

Sanction, as the exemption from it may have been a great cause of attachment
to their liberties with the clergy of France. The question continued where it was
then placed, till the arrangement brought about by Bossuet, in 1682. The arguments by which the conduct of Francis has been defended are—that many of the
sees and monasteries were of royal foundation; that much confusion was occasioned by the popular method of election; that when subjects intrust the sovereign with the government of the state, that of the Church is therein included,
&c. &c.

Though it is not strictly true that the history of the Popes, Increasing degeneracy of the See of Rome.
from Nicholas V. to Leo X., presents, so far as their personal
characters are concerned, a series of uniform degeneracy ; yet
the principles of their government being bad, and not being
corrected, became gradually and necessarily worse. And thus,
though the name of Julius II. fills us with much less abhorrence than that of Alexander VI., the policy of the Apostolical
See was never so directly opposed to every spiritual object, as
when guided by the former : ends purely temporal were never
pursued with such undisguised vehemence, or by means so
sanguinary ; the keys of St. Peter, though not wholly cast
away, were never before so merely subsidiary to the sword of
St. Paul*; insomuch, that the hand of a retributive Providence
might almost seem to be traced in this circumstance—that the
long succession of spiritual usurpers, who were the chiefs of a
religion of peace and the professed vicegerents of the God of
love, should terminate at length in a *military* Pontiff. The
patience of angels and of men was exhausted by this last
mockery ; and the more daring the exploits of the soldier, and
the more splendid the conquests of the prince, the more awful
was the bolt which was even then descending to rend his spiritual empire.

We should also observe, respecting the Popes described in
this chapter, that there was scarcely one whose government
did not deteriorate as it proceeded. Almost all began their
reign with some promises of religious practice, or ecclesiastical
reform, or broad European policy; and some, for the first year
or two, observed such promises. But their reigns, upon the
whole, much exceeded the usual duration of pontifical power,
and they had space to imbibe the corruption which surrounded

* The popular story, that Julius II. actually threw the keys into the Tiber,
and drew the sword of St. Paul, seems to be founded (at least so thinks Bayle)
on the following *ut fama est* of an obscure poet, Gilbertus Ducherius Vulto:—
    In Gallum, ut fama est, bellum gesturus acerbum,
        Armatam educit Julius Urbe manum.
    Accinctus gladio Claves in Tybridis amnem
        Projicit, et sævus talia verba facit—
    Quum Petri nihil efficiant ad prælia Claves,
        Auxilio Pauli forsitan ensis erit.

them; so that even those who carried with them into the Vatican the ordinary principles of human conduct, presently forgot them in the society of debauched parasites, in the iniquities of a simoniacal court, in the administration of a system full of every impurity. Thus are we in no manner surprised, when we observe these sovereigns engrossed by the temporal interests of their states, and engaged in securing their power within the city, and extending their sway without it : this was merely to govern like secular princes, and to pursue the policy which some of the greatest among their own predecessors had bequeathed to them. But the vice peculiarly characteristic of this race, and 'that which reduced them below the level of former pontiffs, was Nepotism*. It was for this that the keys and the sword co-operated; that benefices were publicly sold, and the Pontificate all but publicly bought—that the nephews and bastards of a profligate Pope might be enriched and aggrandized. Many fiefs of the Church were alienated for that purpose; and what was of worse consequence than this, the chief of the Church thus acquired a new motive for attachment to its abuses, and repugnance to any serious reformation. If Julius II. was less tainted with this vice than those who immediately preceded him†—for Julius mingled some magnanimity with his worldliness—it was presently restored to honour by Leo X., and resumed its dominion over the councils of the Vatican.

The degradation of the Sacred College.   Another circumstance that strikes us, in the consideration of this period, is the utter debasement to which the Sacred College.

* (1.) Eugenius IV. was nephew of Gregory XII.; (2.) Paul II., of Eugenius IV.; (3.) Alexander VI., of Calixtus III.; (4.) Pius III., of Pius II.; (5.) Julius II., of Sixtus IV.; (6.) and finally, Leo X. was brother-in-law of the bastard of Innocent VIII. We should remark, however, that the thirst for aggrandizing their own families was not peculiar to the Popes, though peculiarly disgraceful to them. It was connected with that general struggle for supereminence among private families which distinguished the history of Italy during this century.

† "Julius designed to make himself master of Bologna, and extinguish the Venetians, and chase the French out of Italy; and these projects all proved fortunate to him, and so much the more to his praise, in that he did all for the good of the Church, and in no private regard." Machiavel (Principe, cap. xi.) is no great eulogist of Julius.

lege finally descended. The influence which the most wicked Pope invariably acquired in consistory may be ascribed to the less direct operation of his power and patronage. But the secrets of the Conclave, which have been transmitted by contemporary writers, abound with the particulars of intrigue and undisguised perfidy, and unblushing venality. Such was the mutual consciousness with which the Pope and his senate assembled to govern the Church of Christ! such the councils, from which edicts were issued for the suppression of simony and the correction of the morals of the clergy!

Again, it was now become almost the practice of the Conclave to bind the future Pope by a solemn obligation, intended to influence the nature of his government. The Cardinal, while on the point of being elected, voluntarily took this oath, in common with his colleagues; and immediately after his election he confirmed it. In a similar manner, restrictions were at that time not uncommonly imposed by the elective body on the emperor of Germany, and the king of Poland, and they were found effectual. But at Rome the result was so far otherwise, that among the many who undertook such engagements, there seems not to have been one, who faithfully observed what he had sworn, first as Cardinal, next as Pope. This distinction, so shameful to the Court of Rome, confirms the charges of super-eminent immorality commonly brought against it: it proceeds, however, from the singular principles of the Papal hierarchy. In the first place, the Pope, who enjoyed power unlimited over the obligations of others, might reasonably claim the right to dispense with his own. In the next, he had means of influencing those who might release him from his engagements, or connive at his contempt of them, such as the crown did not possess, either in Germany or Poland. The immense extent of his patronage, his authority over the property and persons of the Cardinals, and his prerogative of creating others, gave him irresistible instruments both of seduction and terror. He exercised them unsparingly; and the result was, that among the various crimes of the Vatican, that which became, as it were, peculiarly pontifical, was perjury.

While the crimes of the Vatican were indeed so various, as

(margin note: and perfidy of many individuals.)

to embrace almost every denomination of ungodliness, there was not one among the Popes of this period, who made even the slightest pretension to piety ; scarcely one, by whom decency, as well as morality and religion, was not grossly outraged. Indeed, when we consider the enormity of the scandals permitted and perpetrated by Popes and Cardinals during the latter years, it seems a matter of wonder that the whole Christian world did not rouse itself, as by an earthquake, and destroy them. But here it must be observed, that however notorious was the infamy of the Roman court to the nobles, and even to the people of Rome ; however generally it might be related and credited, even throughout Italy, that country profited too extensively by the tribute of foreign superstition, to feel any desire to close their sources : besides which, Italy, having long exhibited less regard than any other land for the spiritual treasures and censures of Rome, was less disgusted by the spectacle of her vices. But beyond the Alps, where a just indignation would really have been excited, the private arrangements of the Conclave, and even the secrets of the Pontifical palace did yet rarely or imperfectly transpire—a sacred veil still continued to conceal the impurities of the Fathers of the Church, nor was it raised, until the barriers were at length broken by Charles VIII., and the natives of every country were admitted to a nearer view of the pontifical mysteries.

Literary Popes.

Another circumstance, which made men less disposed to rebellion against the Holy See, was the literary character of some of the later Pontiffs. The genius and accomplishments of Nicholas V., of Pius II., and even of Sixtus IV., threw a light round the chair of St. Peter, which dazzled, and for a while deceived, the Transalpine nations. Besides, the vices of the court were really less general during those reigns. For if the example of the Pope did not necessarily influence all his cardinals, at least his own character directed him in the choice of those whom he created ; so that it is not uncommon, during this period, to find respectable authors*, as well as patrons of

---

* Some of these—for instance Cardinal Bessarion, who died under Sixtus IV. —were the creations of an earlier period—the turbulent times of Constance and Basle, when the Roman Court was obliged, in self-defence, to adopt men of some

learning, among the members of the Sacred College.   But in
the example of Sixtus evil upon the whole predominated ; and
those who next succeeded presented models of flagitiousness
almost unqualified, so that the effect produced upon the Christian world by the brilliancy of those former reigns gradually
faded away ; and when Leo X. restored the image of a splendid
pontificate, it was too late to prevent the out-breaking of settled,
deliberate discontent.

The period described in this chapter was also marked by
one other feature very deserving of attention ;—the hostility of
the Turk, and the consequent clamour for a grand Christian
confederacy.   In former ages the calamities of the Holy Land
and the pollution of the tomb of Christ were motives sufficient
to arm the indignation of the West.   As time proceeded, and
knowledge slowly advanced, and wisdom still more slowly followed it, that rage at length evaporated : but not till the Popes
had turned it, in various manners, to their own profit, to enrich
and aggrandize their See, and to *unite* the Catholic Church.
Precisely after the same fashion, as far as the altered principles
of the age would allow, did the Vatican treat the question of
the Turkish conquests.   In this case, there was more of reason
in the outcry, and proportionably less of superstition ; the danger was sometimes imminent ; it was never very remote ; and
the projected crusade was virtually defensive.   It is not that
some Popes were not very sincere, especially in the beginning
of their reigns, in their exhortations to arm against the infidel
—and some had been equally earnest in former ages, in their
exertions for the liberation of Palestine—but many more were
not so : yet these raised the same outcry, and repeated as loudly
the same arguments and declamations.   One of them, indeed,
Paul II., so closely imitated the worst exploit of Innocent III.,
as to divert the course of war from its purposed channel, and
direct it against Christian heretics.   But the others, when not
absolutely threatened by invasion, had, for the most part, two

Efforts against the Turks.

learning and talents. The works of Bessarion are enumerated and described by
the Continuator of Fleury (p. 113, s. 126). His defence of Platonism (in Calum-
niatorem Platonis) against George of Trebisond is the most celebrated of his
writings.

x 2

objects in their vociferations : the one, to bring money into the
apostolical chamber ; the other, to drown the reviving demands
for Church reform, and turn the thoughts of men to any subject rather than a General Council*.   In both these objects
they, for a time, succeeded—unhappily for the age in which
they lived, unhappily for the permanence of their own empire.
But it was God's providence which ordered this—to the end
that the reformation should be more full and perfect, owing to
the very blindness which had retarded it, and to the very bigotry
which thought to withhold it for ever.   For, however various
the opinions prevalent at the moment, there can now be no
question, that if the court of Rome had zealously employed
itself, during this period of seventy-four years, in removing its
scandals, in amending its morals, in retrenching its more extravagant claims, in reducing its expenses, and moderating its exactions, it might have continued, according to all human calculation, to sway for some time longer the spiritual destinies of
Europe.

* Sixtus IV., when pressed, in 1472, by the king of France, to call a General
Council, openly pleaded, as an objection, the urgency of the Turkish war. " It
was out of season (the Pope replied) to demand the convocation of a Council, which
required considerable time, when the evil was pressing, and the progress of the
Turks rendered the slightest delays prejudicial to religion ; the other Christian
princes had either kept their engagements, or were on the point of keeping them ;
and the king of France should rather join them in so holy a work, and *permit the
levying of tenths, and other charitable contributions,* throughout his kingdom, &c."
See Contin. Fleury, l. 113, s. 145.

CHAPTER XXVIII.

PRELIMINARIES OF THE REFORMATION.

SECTION I.—*On the Power and Constitution of the Roman Catholic Church.*

(1.) Origin, progress, and prosperity of the Pope's secular monarchy—Character and policy of Julius II.—Excuse for the union of the two powers in the Pope —Evils proceeding from it. (2.) The spiritual supremacy of Rome—its rise, character, and extent—Usurpation of Church patronage—pretensions to personal infallibility—control over the general morality—in Penance, Purgatory, and Indulgences—decline of the power—not of the pretensions. (3.) Claims of Rome to universal temporal supremacy—as advanced by Gregory VII.—on what founded—by what means supported—use and abuse of this power. (4.) Constitution of the Church. Origin and gradual aggrandizement of the Cardinals—to the rank of kings—The capitulations sworn in Conclave, and invariably violated—Relative interests and influence of the Pope and the Sacred College—to the advantage of the former—its usual co-operation with the Pontiff—General Councils—subordinate machinery of the Church—highest dignities accessible to all ranks—Good and evil of this—Envoys and emissaries—Mendicants—Inquisition—Moral extremes permitted—Maxims of policy —Methods of securing the obedience of the lowest classes.

SECTION II.—*On the Spiritual Character, Discipline, and Morals of the Church.*

(1.) Conservation of the most essential doctrines—Various innovations—Original system of penance—the Penitential of Theodore, Archbishop of Canterbury—subsequent abuses—The intermediate state—Purgatory—Original object and gradual abuse of indulgences—in nature and in object—Translation of an indulgence published by Tetzel—Prayers for the dead—Masses, public and private. The mystery of the Eucharist—The elevation of the Host—use of the bell—worship of the Host—Communion in one kind only—its object and impolicy—Prohibition of the Scriptures—Miraculous impostures—Saints, relics, &c.—More recent disputes and superstitions—on the ring of St. Catharine—and her Stigmata—on the Immaculate Conception—on the Worship due to the blood of Christ—the inscription on the Cross—the reed and sponge. (2.) Discipline and morals—Concubinage of the Clergy—Influence of the Laity—Perpetual acknowledgment of Church abuses from St. Bernard downwards—Cardinal Ximenes—Benefits conferred by the Church—in ignorant ages—Truce of God—Exercise of charity—Law of asylum—penance, &c.—Original character of Monachism—Merits of the Mendicants—chiefly as Missionaries—their success in the thirteenth and fourteenth ages—Morality in the fifteenth century comprised in the Mystics and the lower Clergy—Progress and preservation of Mysticism in the Western Church—Great, though obscure, virtues of many of the inferior Clergy.

Section III.—*On various Attempts to reform, or to subvert, the Church.*

(1.) Attempts at self-reform—The era of Boniface VIII.—subsequent decline—Necessity of some reform generally admitted—Designs of the Church reformers, as compared with the real nature of the corruptions—confined wholly to matters of revenue and discipline—very imperfect even in that respect—and never really enforced—Learning and blindness of the Papal party—their momentary success—Progress of improvement and knowledge to final and certain triumph—Tardy reformation in the Roman Catholic Church. (2.) Attempts of Protestants to trace their Church to the Apostolic times—how far successful—where they fail—Vaudois and Albigeois—Bohemian Brethren—*Note* on Bossuet—Errors of those Dissenters—On the Paulicians—On the Mystics—Real value and merit of the sects of the twelfth and following centuries. (3.) Treatment of heretics by the Church—Canon of Innocent III.—its fair explanation—consequence—Inquisition—Unity of the Church—A more moderate party—Principle of intolerance adopted by the Laity also—Conduct of the Church in the fifteenth age. (4.) On some individual witnesses of the truth—John of Wesalia—Wesselus—Jean Laillier—Savonarola—his history and pretensions—Erasmus. (5.) Particular condition of Germany—Great scene of Clerical licentiousness and Papal extortion—Political hostilities of Rome and the Empire—Violation of the Concordats—" The hundred Grievances"—Thirst of the people for the Bible—Character of Leo X.—Conclusion.

Section I.—*On the Power and Constitution of the Roman Catholic Church.*

On the temporal possessions of the See of Rome.

I.—In retracing the steps by which Papacy descended to that ground whereon it received its effectual overthrow, we shall observe in most of its elements signs of increasing corruption and decay ; but there was one circumstance, in which its singular prosperity ran counter to the general current. The temporal monarchy of the Pope was at no former period so extensive and so secure as at the accession of Leo X. At no time had the limits of the Ecclesiastical States been so widely stretched, or the factions, which alienated the capital from the government of its Bishop, so depressed and helpless as then. We have shown, in former chapters, how the Pope's political authority originated under the Exarchs of Ravenna, through the neglect or weakness of the Eastern empire; and how it was rivetted by the vigour and the virtues of some who then occupied the Chair. Soon afterwards the domains of the See were formed and enlarged by Pepin and Charlemagne, though still held by the latter as a dependent portion of his empire.

We have mentioned the donation of Matilda to Gregory VII., and the exertions afterwards made to secure those various possessions.   In this struggle, Innocent III., and some other Popes of the thirteenth century, obtained partial, though never permanent, successes; and the territories of Boniface VIII. were more respectable in magnitude, than united in allegiance and fidelity.   But the secession to Avignon was the signal for general insubordination; on every side the Barons rose and seized whatever lay within their grasp; and the patrimony of St. Peter was torn in pieces by their petty ambition and rapacity*.

The Schism followed; and if the residence of an Antipope recovered some portion of that authority which had been forfeited by the absence of the Pope, yet it was not much that was resumed, nor was it held with firmness or confidence. But when the Schism had ceased, and a Bishop of undisputed legitimacy became again resident, though Martin, Eugenius, Nicholas, and Sixtus† even then had some storms and reverses to encounter, the machine of temporal power upon the whole moved onwards; and at length, under the guidance of Alexander VI. and Julius II., it reached those ample boundaries from which it has never since receded.

---

* " Je regarde Rome (says Voltaire, Pyrrhonisme de l'Histoire) depuis le temps de l'Empereur Leo. III. l'Isaurien, comme une ville libre, protégée par les Francs, ensuite par les Germains, qui se gouverne tant qu'elle put en république, plutôt sous le patronage que sous la puissance des Empereurs, dans laquelle le souverain Pontife eut toujours le premier crédit, et qui enfin a été entièrement soumise aux Papes." It is observed, that no Pope ever assumed the title of King of Rome. This subject is remarkably well treated by Gibbon, in his 49th chapter.

† Gibbon has remarked, that Eugenius IV. was the last Pope expelled by the tumults of the Roman people (in 1434); and Nicholas V. (in 1447) the last importuned by the presence of the Emperor. The same writer places the last disorder of the Nobles of Rome under Sixtus IV., and considers the papal dominion to have become absolute about the year 1500. Machiavel (Principe, cap. xi.) has observed, that the great difficulty in crushing the two rival factions in Rome arose from the short reigns of the Popes, and the inconstancy of their policy: for when any Pontiff had succeeded in humbling one of those families, his successor might, very probably, raise it up again and depress the opposite. On the other hand, the existence of this feud accounted, in a great degree, for the temporal weakness of the Popes. At length, Alexander VI. and his son overthrew the Barons from motives of *family* ambition, and Julius II. reaped the fruits of their victory for the advantage of the Church.

The dangerous feuds of the Colonna and Orsini were extinguished; the usurpations on the states of the Church were extorted from the nobles who had made them; even the turbulence of the Roman people was worn down by severity, or softened by luxury and licentiousness; and a compact and fruitful kingdom bowed in secular servitude before the sceptre of St. Peter.

The Emperor Maximilian designed himself as the successor of Julius II., and solicited the votes of several members of the college, some little time before the death of that Pope. He did not strongly press his project; but the very attempt may show how little necessary any pretensions to the spiritual character were then thought for the enjoyment of the loftiest spiritual dignity. Julius was, in all essentials, a temporal prince; and had he not been so, he could scarcely have crowned his ambition with such extraordinary triumphs. Yet the spectacle of a secular and military Pope* was not well calculated to conciliate to the See, in the most critical moment of its history, the affection or respect of any description of Christians. The deep penetration of Julius may possibly have foreseen the approaching downfall of the spiritual supremacy, and for that reason he may have laboured the more zealously to give strength to the temporal fabric. If he did so, it was a wise and salutary providence; for in that controversy so often raised—whether the secular dominion of the Pope has tended, upon the whole, to increase or to diminish his general influence—there is ample room for difference, in respect to early times; but after the first movements of the Reformation, it is quite clear that it produced to him nothing but advantage; and from that moment the question rather becomes, whether any shred or fragment of his ghostly authority could have been saved without it.

The enjoyment of secular power and pride by the Vicegerent of Him whose kingdom is not of this world, is justified on the

* A plausible precedent was afforded by the personal expedition made by that simple, pious Pontiff, Leo IX., against the Normans, who so signally overthrew him. But it should be recollected, that Leo never repeated the experiment—his military thirst was satisfied by a single enterprise.

ground of his independence. It is plausibly maintained, that the Chief of the Œcumenic Church, scattered throughout so many nations, ought to stand unconstrained by any earthly potentate, and owe no other allegiance than that to heaven. The principle which would prevent him from being a subject, compels him to be a monarch—no other condition can be conceived, which could secure him from the control of the temporal sceptre. The above argument acquires some confirmation from the decline which did, in fact, take place in the pontifical domination during the exile at Avignon, though the Pope was there resident rather as a guest than as a subject, free from the direct authority of the prince, and liable only to his influence. In truth, the Catholic, after he has *assumed* the divine establishment of one spiritual universal monarchy, wants not sufficient plea for the maintenance of the temporal government, as secondary and subsidiary. But the Protestant, thoughtfully surveying the perplexities, the intrigues, and the crimes in which a Christian Prelate is thus necessarily involved—the armies which he levies, the contributions which he extorts, the blood which he sheds—receives from the sad spectacle only fresh reason to doubt whether the family of Christ has really been consigned to the rule of *one* who can scarcely rule it in innocence.

And this remark is the more striking, because, when we reflect on the different wars which the Popes have waged in Italy, it really appears that they had, for the most part, the plea of justice. It was generally their object (notwithstanding some deplorable exceptions), not to make conquests in the dominions of others, but to defend or to recover their own. There was no province in Europe so harassed by rebellions and usurpations as the states of the Church. We need not pause to account for this circumstance; but it is unquestionably true that no other prince was so commonly liable to depredation and insult as the Pope. Accordingly, his wars were usually defensive, and (it may be) necessary; but that very necessity annihilated the pastoral character, and dispiritualized the Vicar of Christ.

Again, these contests were not carried on without great ex-

The insults to which he was liable.

The
tributes
which he
levied.

pense; and the Holy See, despoiled of its patrimony, was at the same time deprived of its natural resources. Thence arose an obligation to seek supplies in other quarters*; and with an obedient clergy and a superstitious people, it was not difficult to make the whole of Christendom tributary. Once in possession of this ample treasury, and of the keys which unlocked its innumerable chambers, the Pontiffs explored and ransacked it without restraint, without decency, without discretion. Their emissaries were dreaded as the tax-gatherers of the Christian world. Their name was associated with donations, fees, contributions, exactions—with every thing that is most vile and unpopular in secular governments. And thus, besides the great scandal thereby reflected upon themselves, they exhausted the affection, the endurance, and almost the credulity of the faithful. It is not that the monies thus levied were applied *entirely* to the defence of the Ecclesiastical States, or even that they were generally levied under that pretence; but in the first instance, during the thirteenth century, and afterwards, more especially under the Avignon succession, a very large proportion was certainly absorbed by the temporal exigencies of the See, and the increasing demands and extravagance of the Court of Rome. The same system was continued through the Schism and the century which followed it, as far as the Popes had power to continue it; and therefore, when we admire their final success in erecting a permanent principality, we shall, at the same time, recollect the methods which they had so long and so vainly employed on that object, and the deep disaffection towards their government which those methods had every where created.

The spiritual supremacy of Rome.

II. It is not necessary to retrace the process by which the spiritual supremacy of Rome was engendered and nourished. We have observed, with sufficient distinctness, how equivocal and circumscribed it was in nature and dimensions, when it entered into the ages of gloom and ignorance—how it grew

---

* This system no doubt began soon after the eleventh age, when the Popes were so commonly expelled from Rome to Orvietto, Viterbo, Anagni, &c., and obliged to look to all parts of Christendom for their resources.

and dilated in its mysterious passage through them;—how portentous in magnitude and majesty it emerged from the cloud. We have followed it through its meridian course of disastrous glory; and we have seen that, even in its decline, it did not suddenly lose either its fierceness or its ascendancy. Indeed, however strange it may seem that an authority, so predominant in its power, so universal and searching in its influence, so extravagant in its pretensions, should have been at all created, and out of materials seemingly so incongruous; it would have been much more strange had it been easily or hastily extinguished. An authority which claimed the sanction of Heaven, and which stood on human imposture; which pleaded the holiness of antiquity, and which innovated every hour; which combined in its composition learning with fanaticism, the use of reason with its grossest abuse, extreme austerities with lawless licentiousness, much true piety with much vulgar and impious superstition—and which so applied those various qualities as at length to acquire an influence in the policy of every Court, in the institutions of every Government, in the morals of every people, in the habits of every family, in the bosom of almost every individual—an authority so constructed, supported, acknowledged, and felt, could not possibly fall in pieces without a protracted struggle and a final convulsion. It was impressed by the perseverance of fraud upon credulous, abject ignorance; but so deeply impressed, that, before it could be effaced, the substance whereon it was engraven must first change its nature: so that ages of gradual improvement were required to repair the mischief which ages had conspired to inflict.

For if we examine the extent of this power with respect to the objects on which it was more immediately exerted, shall we find any department, religious or moral, into which, in its triumphant days, it did not penetrate? In the first place, the Pope was the fountain of all ecclesiastical legislation. All the Canons and Constitutions of the Church were subject to him *.

Its unlimited prevalence.

---

* Immediately after burning the Pope's bull, Luther published several propositions, extracted from the Decretals, among which are the following:—" That the successors of St. Peter are not subject to the commandment of the Apostle to obey

He could enact, suspend, abrogate, as might seem good to him, and that not only with the advice or consent of the Consistory, or (as it sometimes happened) merely in its presence, but in the plenitude of his power, and by his own spontaneous movement*. At the same time, while he was supreme in his dominion over the laws, he claimed an entire exemption from their control, and found a powerful party in the Church to support his claim.

In the next place, he was the source of all pastoral jurisdiction. The final determination of every spiritual cause rested with him. He was the object of appeal from all the episcopal Courts; and he delivered, confirmed, or reversed decisions, according to the arbitrary dictates of his justice or his interest.

The apostolical character of the ministry, perpetuated by the uninterrupted communication of the Holy Spirit, was held to centre in the successor of St. Peter; and thus not only did all

the temporal powers; that the power of the Emperor is as much below that of the Pope as the moon is below the sun; that the Pope is superior to councils, and can abolish their decrees; that all authority resides in his person; that no one has a right to judge him or his decrees; that God has given him sovereign power over all the kingdoms of the earth, and that of heaven; that he can depose kings, absolve all oaths and vows; that he is not dependent on Scripture, but, on the other hand, Scripture derives all its authority, force, and dignity, from him," &c. (See Beausobre, Hist. Reform., liv. iii.) It is unnecessary to repeat, that the above propositions were either drawn from the False Decretals, or were of subsequent origin. Till the time of Valentinian III., neither the Eastern nor

Ancient codes of Canons.

Western Church had any other collection of canons than the "Code of Canons of the Universal Church," compiled by Stephen, Bishop of Ephesus. In the first year of Justinian, the "Collection of Dionysius the Little" was published. He was a monk, living at Rome—the same who introduced the practice of computing time from the birth of Christ—a friend, fellow-monk, and fellow-student of Cassiodorus. His collection contained the fifty Apostolical Canons, the Canons of Chalcedon, Sardica, and the African Councils; and the Decretals of Pope Siricius (who died in 398); and it had authority in the West under the name of "Codex or Corpus Canonum." Some other collections, of little repute, or only partial authority, were published soon afterwards. (See Giannone, Stor. Napol., lib. iii., c. v.) Then came the forgeries of the eighth age, and the pretensions—first proceeding from them, presently surpassing them—though it was scarcely till the twelfth century that the new maxims and principles came into full operation.

* De motu proprio. It appears that Bulls proceeding *de motu proprio* were received with great hesitation in France. But they were held by the high Papists to be as valid as any other Decrees or Canons.

sacerdotal sanctity emanate from him, but all the offices and dignities of the Church were vested in his See. We may observe, however, that there was not one among his pretensions which cost him so much toil and conflict to substantiate as this. In his earliest attempts to usurp the ecclesiastical patronage, he was contented to proceed by simple recommendation; and as he had already great power, his applications were seldom despised. Hence arose the practice; and from the practice the right. The prerogative of institution, of which he had gradually despoiled the Metropolitans for the augmentation of his own dignity, was serviceable as an instrument of further encroachment. The fierce and protracted contest respecting investitures between the See and the empire was inflamed by the same design in the former; and when it terminated, the Pope found himself in legal possession of that power of occasional interference in the collation of benefices, which it needed no great address to improve and extend. Still, time and boldness were required to complete the usurpation; and the merit of achieving that work is perhaps justly attributed to Innocent III.* Soon afterwards, the Pragmatic Sanction of St. Louis was levelled against it; and in later periods it has been obtruded so commonly upon our attention, as almost to convert the records of Christ's Church into a detail of disgusting squabbles about its temporalities. A new vocabulary was introduced into the history of religion; and as the magnificence of the Court of Rome kept pace with the majesty of the monarch, and as its avarice emulated his ambition, the field of *Reservation* and *Provision*† was enlarged with no limit,

Usurpation of Church patronage.

---

* See Mosheim, Cent. xiii., p. ii., ch. ii. It was probably at this time that a new pretext for this extension of the papal authority was discovered: viz., that through the Pope's vigilance, the gates of the Church might be secured against the intrusion of any Heretic.

† Even by the more moderate and acknowledged claims of the Popes, all benefices in the possession of Cardinals, or any of the officers of the Court of Rome; those held by persons who happened to die at Rome, or within forty miles from it; and all such as became vacant by translation, were *reserved*. The invention of mental reservation demanded the more refined ingenuity of the sixteenth century; it is ascribed to Leo X., or at least to his predecessor. Respecting Provisions, we may refer to the history of our own Church, to see with what pertinacity the battle was fought, and how the statutes enacted against them were

and the whole patronage of the universal Church seemed to be absorbed by the cupidity of one man.

The same power which thus created Cardinals and Bishops, and all other dignitaries, presumed by the same right to confirm, censure, suspend, or depose them*; so that the whole hierarchy of the West was placed at its arbitrary disposal †. And though this inordinate despotism was continually resisted and restrained by the princes and parliaments of Europe, it had no effectual check within the Church, nor was there any country in which it was not sometimes practically felt.

On the personal infallibility of the Pope.

It is more difficult to determine how far the Pope was held at any particular period to be personally absolute in matters of faith. No doubt, disputed points were perpetually referred to his decision, and the decision was considered as final. But,

perpetually confirmed, or perpetually eluded or violated. We may observe, however, that the Kings of Europe were not uncommonly neutral or lukewarm in this quarrel; the Pontiffs were sometimes found more tractable than the Chapters, and a concession seasonably made to the former might become the means of reciprocal advantage. Again, we sometimes find the Universities on the side of the Pope—not from any abstract conviction of his right, but because his appointments were often more judicious, more encouraging to the hopes of learned men, than those of the Ordinaries, who usually chose their own relatives or dependents. The Popes had *procurators* established in England, and probably in all other countries, to look after their interests; and the fury with which they pursued them during the fifteenth century is strongly depicted by Giannone, lib. xxx., cap. 6.

* The Council of Sardica in 347 (not a General Council) allowed a bishop, deposed by his neighbouring prelates, to appeal to the Bishop of Rome—it likewise permitted this last to send legates, to re-examine the case together with those prelates. These decrees (if they be genuine, which Mosheim sees reason to doubt) prove that the power of deposition was not then exercised by the Roman bishop, but by the provincial synods; but they also indicate a disposition in the Western clergy even thus early to distinguish the prelate of the Imperial City, and to confer greater power on him than on any of his brethren. This inference no one can reasonably dispute, neither can any one reasonably infer more than this from the canons in question. See Dr. Cook, Historical View of Christianity, book iii., chap. ii.

† The object of the "Oath of Fidelity" to the Pope, taken by the higher clergy on their admission to benefices, was to bind them—that henceforward they would be faithful and obedient to St. Peter, the Apostle, and to the Holy Roman Church, and to the Pope and his successors; that he should suffer no wrong through their advice, consent, or connivance; that they would maintain and promote all his rights, honours, privileges, and authorities, and resist and denounce all attempts against him.

on the other hand, there have been Popes at various times who have incurred the charge of heresy from very faithful Catholics. Now the very suspicion of error presumes the fallibility of the person suspected, at least in the opinion of the accusers ; and in the affair of John XXII. and the process against Boniface VIII., we have not observed that the friends of those Popes denied their liability to error. Again, in somewhat later times, in the Councils of Pisa, Constance, and Basle, we find it a principle admitted by both parties, that a Pope might be deposed on conviction of heresy ; whence we may draw the same inference respecting other periods of papal history. The claim of infallibility was not preferred in the deliberations at Florence, though conducted in the presence of the Pope and his Court, and entering very deeply into the subject of papal authority; nor was it advanced at any later period in the same century. So that, however clearly it might be deduced from the general expressions of various bulls and constitutions, and even though it should have been asserted by some individuals and acknowledged and maintained by others, yet it would be too much to account it among the authorized pretensions of the Roman See *. Howbeit the doctrines which proceeded from the chair (ex cathedrâ) were seldom disputed ; and the Pontiff might forget the possibility of error in the reverence which awaited and embraced his most questionable decisions.

Again, in the regulation of the moral duties of the faithful, the same searching hand interposed with the same rigorous inquisition. A general power of dissolving obligations was claimed by the successors of St. Peter, and they applied it in various manners, as suited their policy, or, it might be, their

---

* The claim to infallibility is not contained in the Creed of Pius IV., compiled out of the Canons of Trent, which Roman Catholics consider as the most accurate summary of their faith ; and the Universities have generally opposed it. But it has been maintained (as a matter of opinion, however, not of faith) by many distinguished individuals, among whom the most notorious is, perhaps, Bellarmine. It is mortifying to humanity to observe the genius of Pascal stooping to draw elaborate distinctions between infallibility in matters of *faith* and in matters of *fact*, and exhausting itself to prove that, though the Pope does really possess the former, it does not follow that he is also invested with the latter—that is, that though he cannot err in judgment, he may possibly be deceived by falsehood !

conscience—sometimes in divorcing a prince from his queen, sometimes in separating a nation from its monarch. The most sacred oaths were annulled with the same ease which dispensed with the slightest promise; and as there were many who profited, or might hope to profit, by that papal prerogative, and as it was made familiar by constant exercise, so were there few who cared to question it, however shameful the ends to which it was sometimes applied.

Roman Catholic doctrine of Penance and Purgatory.

It is the doctrine of the Roman Catholic Church that, besides the eternal punishments denounced against sin, there are also temporal penalties attached to it, which are still due to the justice of God, even after he may have remitted the former; and that those penalties may consist either of evil in this world, or of temporal suffering in the next and intermediate condition of purgatory. It is also an article of faith that a satisfaction in their place has been instituted by Christ, as a part of the Sacrament of Penance, and that the jurisdiction of the Church, as exercised by the Pope, extends to the remission of that satisfaction. The act of remission is called an Indulgence; it is partial or complete as the indulgence is for a stated time or plenary, and the conditions of repentance and restitution are in strictness annexed to it. Through this doctrine the Popes were, in fact, invested with a vast control over the human conscience, even in the moderate exercise of their power, because it was a power which overstepped the limits of the visible world. But when they proceeded, as they did soon proceed, flagitiously to abuse it, and when, through the progress of that abuse, people at length were taught to believe that perfect absolution from all the penalties of sin could be procured from a human being; and procured, too, not through fervent prayer and deep and earnest contrition, but by military service, or by pilgrimage, or even by gold—it was then that the evil was carried so far, as to leave the historian doubtful whether any thing be any where recorded more astonishing than the wickedness of the clergy, except the credulity of the vulgar.

Gradual decline of the spiritual power.

We shall recur to this scandal, for it was the immediate cause of the Reformation; but it is proper to remark that, in the general picture which has been drawn of Rome's spiritual despotism and pride, some features had already been effaced before the approach of Luther. From the death of Boniface VIII., the colours had been gradually, though insensibly, fading away. The dependent Popes of France sustained the character of Gregory VII. and Innocent IV. with feebleness and degeneracy. The profligacy and rapacity of their Court began to dissolve the hereditary spell, and withdraw the sacred veil, which had hitherto concealed their real weakness. During the Schism, the rival Antipopes railed against each other, while they covered themselves with crimes; and the nations who were appealed to, as arbiters of the dispute, could scarcely fail to detect the unworthiness of both parties. In the Councils which followed, some principles were advanced and established which, though still too narrowly limited by inveterate prejudices, were at least subversive of the absolute monarchy of the Pontiff. When the Councils were dissolved, and the duty of convoking others successfully eluded by the Popes, the Court of Rome, liberated from that terror, once more plunged into debauchery, more shameless, yet more notorious, than the abominations of former days; and the various scandals of the tenth century were surpassed by Innocent VIII., by Alexander, and Julius, in an age of comparative civilization. It is true, that in its pretensions the See had abated nothing of its ancient arrogance, and we have observed what awe it was sometimes capable of inspiring even in its decay. But the light had broken in; the slow, yet irresistible hand of knowledge had commenced its labours; and the basis of opinion, on which alone the spiritual despotism rested, was already shaken and shattered.

III.—The effect of successful usurpation is to aggravate ambition, and the more disproportionate the success to all reasonable hope and calculation, the wilder are the schemes which take their rise from it. The spiritual despotism of the Pope transcends any exhibition of human power described in any history, until we approach the surpassing magnitude of his temporal pretensions. The design of Gregory VII. was the most daring imagination of human ambition. To establish the Chair of St. Peter as the source of *all* power, secular as well as

The claims of Rome to universal temporal supremacy.

pastoral, civil as well as ecclesiastical—to subject all kings and all governments to the crosier of an unarmed, aged priest—to regulate the politics of the world by the annual meeting of a Senate of Ecclesiastics, under the eye of that autocrat—to dispose of all countries and of all thrones—to create monarchs and then to suspend or depose them—to sport, as it were, with all that is sublime and mighty in earthly things—such was a scheme beyond the boldest conception of secular pride; and it was engendered, where alone it could have found any nourishment, in the breast of a monk.

The temporal supremacy of the Pope was projected *not* in the darkest moment of superstition and barbarism; it was promoted during a period more enlightened than that in which it originated; it reached the height of its triumph during the latter part of the thirteenth century, when Frederic II. had given an impulse to literature, when Dante was earning immortality; and, but for that French intrigue which transplanted Papacy for a season into a foreign soil, it might have advanced still farther; it would not, at least, have receded so soon. Yet its fate must naturally have followed the decline of the spiritual authority of the See, since it had absolutely no other foundation than that; and as it was of later origin, and more obviously insulting to every man's reason, so was its overthrow more rapid and more complete. Yet its latest pretensions were not unworthy of its ancient insolence; and the presumption with which it distributed, in the fifteenth century, kingdoms and oceans and continents, is recollected with astonishment even by the Catholics themselves—since the Catholics now for the most part admit that that branch of the pontifical authority was an indefensible usurpation.

Countenanced by the secular power.

Nevertheless, it found much support in the temporary interests of the great; it held forth a plausible pretence in the pacific objects which it professed, and it was really instrumental in conferring some benefits on mankind. Probably there is no Court in Europe in which the Papal right to dispose of thrones has not at some time been virtually recognized. It was never disputed by any prince, who found his immediate profit in its acknowledgment—when the crown was *offered* by the Pontifical hand, the validity of the donation was never questioned; and thus did sovereigns sharpen for the chastisement of their rivals a weapon which was so easily turned against themselves.

In the worst periods of feudal government a mediatory in- *Its opera-* fluence over the various chiefs of the European Republic, vested *tion on hu-* in the head of the universal religion, if exercised with mode- *piness.* ration, with disinterestedness, with discretion, according to the rules of Evangelical charity, might have conferred the most substantial blessings on society; and since the Papal inter- ference was sometimes so regulated, it had not been wholly destitute of advantage. Divisions have been healed, wars have been prevented, crimes have been punished, justice has been honoured, tyranny has been checked, by the arbitrary decrees of the Vatican—the Popes were, upon the whole, as wise and as virtuous as the princes around them; and when we consider the holy ground on which their government professed to stand, it is very shameful that they were not much more so. But the good which they conferred was confined to evil times, and even then it was alloyed with much mischief. The motives of their mediation were at least as commonly found in anger or am- bition, as in religion or philanthropy; and it may be questioned whether the political benefits which proceeded from it, such as the establishment of a liberal party in Italy, and occasional restraints on kingly despotism, were not rather the consequence than the design of their policy. The means employed by their ambition were sometimes lower than the ordinary level of political immorality. To rouse subjects against their sove- reigns is a detestable method of effecting even a beneficial pur- pose—yet it is common and human; but to arm the hands of children against the thrones and lives of their parents is a policy suggested by the counsels of Satan.

IV.—It was a position advanced by Pierre d'Ailly, that a *The Con-* Council General had no power over the Pontifical dignity, *stitution of* which was of divine authority, but only over the abuse of that *theChurch.* dignity. "And on that account (he adds) the monarchical system of the Church is tempered by an admixture of the aris-

tocratical and democratical principle*." In the balance of the
Roman Catholic polity, the Papal despotism was, in fact, mitigated by two restraining powers—whatever may be the political
denominations properly belonging to them—the College of
Cardinals and General Councils; by the former as the electors,
the constitutional counsellors and coadjutors of the Pope; by
the latter as the states-general of the Universal Church.

Rise and
progress of
the Cardi-
nals.

Until the edict of Nicholas II. in 1059, the name of Cardinal † possessed little dignity or distinction, and the body had
no existence, as an acknowledged branch of the Ecclesiastical
system. The important share which it then received in the
election of the Pope was confirmed and extended by the further
regulations of Alexander III. The consent of two-thirds of the
body was made sufficient for a legal choice; and the College
was at the same time enlarged by some considerable permanent additions. To conciliate the higher class of the clergy,
the priors of some of the principal Churches were enrolled
among the electors—the acquiescence of the inferior orders

* "Et idcirco status monarchicus Ecclesiæ regimine aristocratico et democratico
temperatur." A position laid down by Gerson on the same subject is not at
variance with this—" Ecclesiastica Politia ita est monarchica, ut non mutari pos-
sit in aristocraticam aut democraticam."

† The sixty-first dissertation of Muratori treats " De Origine Cardinalatus ;"
and he arrives, through much learning, at the probable conclusion, that the term
was in Italy originally applied to all, whether bishops, priests, or deacons, who
were immoveably, and in perpetuity, established in a cure or dignity, in contra-
distinction to the Vicarii, or temporary and occasional ministers. Parochial
churches (originally called Baptismal) and Diaconiæ (pious houses for the reception of the poor, mendicants, infirm, and strangers) were respectively administered by the priest and deacon; and when he was fixed therein for life, he was
called Cardinal. The term implied the *stability* of the office—its dignity and
superiority were associated with that, and were secondary accompaniments. So
of Bishops. Vacant Sees were, originally, often *commended* to some one in the
interim, " donec ibi constitueretur proprius et *titularis.*" But when the permanent prelate was appointed, he was said to be *incardinated* (incardinari) in the see,
and became cardinal.... Respecting the subsequent aggrandizement of the Sacred College, we may mention, that Nicholas IV., in 1289, divided the Roman
revenues equally between the Pope and the Cardinals (Pagi, Vit. Nic. IV., s. xxii.);
and that they profited by the ultra-papal Decretals of Gregory IX. The title of
Eminence, in the place of Illustrissimus, was given them by Urban VIII.; but it
is an observation of Fleury (Discours 4me. sur la Discipline), that their frequent
appearance in the character of Legates *a latere*, on which occasions they took
precedence of all ecclesiastical dignitaries, and ruled as the representatives of the
Pope, contributed more than any other cause to their exaltation.

was secured by the admission of the cardinal deacons—and the civil authorities, who represented the interests of the people, were appeased by the elevation of the seven Palatine judges to the same office.   Indeed it is from this time, more properly than from the decree of Nicholas, that we should date the foundation of the Sacred College.

That event marks an important epoch in the history of the Church; not only because it secured the more peaceful election of the Popes, and prevented those perpetual broils and schisms which restrained the flight and dimmed the eye of Papacy; but also because it introduced a new element into the ecclesiastical polity, which gradually expanded, and acquired in process of time a great and unforeseen preponderance.   We observe an edict published by Honorius III. in 1225, for the especial protection of the Cardinals from all personal assaults and offences; and other proofs are afforded of the tenderness with which the monarch popes had begun to regard the *Court* of St. Peter. But the first public occasion, which was turned to the aggrandizement of the College, and which raised its members to an ideal level with mere worldly princes, was the first Council of Lyons, held (in 1245) by Innocent IV.   From that moment they became essentially distinguished from the rest of the clergy in rank and in pride; and the counsellors and associates of that Power which overshadowed the majesty of kings* looked down with disdain upon the *petty* bishops † who occupied the inferior regions of the hierarchy.   But their prosperity was not favourable to their virtue or their concord.   In the discharge of that very duty which gave birth to their dignity, they disgraced themselves and scandalized the church by their dissen-

First Council of Lyons, A.D. 1245.

---

* Louis II. seems, from Pagi (Vit. Nicolai, s. iii.) to have been the first emperor who held the Pope's bridle; and Nicholas I. (858—867) the first Pope who exacted that proof of inferiority—" humillima illa Imperatoris Ludovici erga Nicolaum Pontificem obsequia refert Anastasius Bibliothecarius."

† *Episcopelli* was the term by which the Cardinals loved to designate prelates who had not received the hat—according to Nicholas of Clemangis.   About the same time, Pierre d'Ailly in his Discourse *De Ecclesiæ Auctoritate* (Opera Gersoni, vol. i. p. 901) takes some pains to make out, that the Cardinals are the legitimate representatives of the Apostles, the Council of the representative of Christ. We should never forget that Pierre d'Ailly was a reformer, and decidedly opposed to the high-papist party.

sions; and instead of promptly repairing her loss, they frequently allowed long intervals to elapse, in which she remained
without a head, and Christ without a vicegerent upon earth.
This had been particularly the case before the election of Gregory X.; and that excellent Pontiff accordingly undertook to
remedy the evil which had touched himself so closely. And
then followed (in 1274) the institution of the Conclave.

The Cardinals, after some ineffectual attempts to shake off
the constraint thereby imposed on them, presently turned their
attention to lay such restrictions on the Pontifical authority, as
might still further enlarge the privileges and interests of the
College; and they proposed to make their right of election
subservient to this end *. The Conclaves of Avignon were the
first in which the *future* Pontiff was invited to bind himself by
that sacred oath which he never hesitated to take, which he
never omitted to confirm, and which he never failed to violate.
The introduction of that practice demonstrates the power of the
Sacred College, as well as its ambition; but in tempting the
morality of its masters, and exhibiting itself as a fruitful nursery
for Pontifical perjurers, it did not well consult either its own
interests, or the honour of the holy See, or the stability of the
Church. It is true that the mysteries of the Conclave were
not in those days very generally divulged, nor did they descend perhaps to the knowledge of those ranks in society
which are most sensible to the scandal of great crimes. But as
knowledge gained ground, and as the reformers of the Church
multiplied, while its enemies grew more powerful, those secret
iniquities were brought to light, and the tales of former days
were accredited by the deeds of the existing generation. In

*Oath im-
posed in
Conclave.*

* The professed object of the oath taken in Conclave previously to the election
of Eugenius IV. was "ad conservandum statum ecclesiæ Romanæ et monarchiam
ecclesiasticam cum cardinalium dignitate; qui cum sint lumina et ornamenta
prope Papam, Sedem Apostolicam illustriantia, et columnæ firmissimæ sustentan-
tes ecclesiam Dei, cum Romano Pontifice eadem, ut membra suo capiti, concordia
insolubili debent esse conjuncti." On the same occasion it was stipulated that
the formula "de consilio fratrum nostrum" should be changed to "de consensu;"
that the Pope should not create new cardinals without the consent of the old; that
half the revenues of the Church should be paid to the College, &c. See Pagi,
Vit. Eugenii IV.

truth it would seem, that, in the general corruption of the hierarchy of Rome, the disorders of the Court excited louder and more general indignation, even than those of the monarch of the Church.

The relative situation and reciprocal influence of the Pope and the Sacred College were such, in appearance, as to promise a moderate government under a limited monarchy: they were such, in reality, as to present, under that show, an imperious and oppressive despotism. According to ancient Canons, and the Constitutions of later Councils, the Consistory was the permanent Senate of this Church; and its sanction was, in strictness, required to give force to all the decrees of the Vatican*. It was likewise restricted by the same laws to a fixed and moderate number—none were to be admitted into it except men of mature age, acknowledged learning, approved piety; and its morality (the surest source of ecclesiastical power) was provided for by severe injunctions. These regulations were, indeed, for the most part disregarded; nevertheless the body did in fact contain many elements of strength. It consisted of individuals, most of whom were in the flower of life, practised in the affairs of the world, familiar with courts, possibly connected with princes; subtle in the conception of their designs, unscrupulous in the pursuit of their interests. On the other hand, the Pope was commonly enfeebled by age †. His election was placed entirely in their hands; and by their perseverance in attempts to make this power the means of abridging his authority, they sufficiently manifested their inclination to do so.

Where then was the point of their weakness? How was it that their design was so effectually frustrated? Of the reasons which may be mentioned for their failure, the first was the corruption of the College itself; for without that all the various resources of the Pope could not have upheld his predominance. The second was the power which he possessed over the persons and property of the Cardinals, which reached to imprisonment,

Note in margin: Relative Power and Interests of the Pope and Cardinals.

* The Cardinals were the *Brothers* of the Pope, and edicts were published by their *counsel.*

† The average reign of the Popes during the first fifteen centuries was of about seven years.

spoliation, torture, and even death, and which was not uncommonly exerted. But this required at least a pretext for its exercise; whereas that to which we next come was of easy and universal operation. The patronage of the Church was placed to a great extent at his disposal; and where menaces might not prevail, the most certain method of persuasion remained to him. Lastly, he enjoyed the prerogative of multiplying the members of his refractory senate, and thus creating a majority subservient to his views—for the laws, which had been enacted to restrain that power, do not appear at any time to have been seriously observed. By the dexterous application of these various means, the Pontiff was enabled to command with great certainty the suffrages of the Consistory.

Notwithstanding the restraints which the Cardinals endeavoured to impose upon the Papal Authority, they were zealously united in its defence, whenever it was assailed from any other quarter; because their own dignity was essentially involved in the majesty of the See. This was sufficiently proved by the proceedings of Constance and Basle : and on the same principle it became the object of those two Councils to reform the Court, no less than the Chair, of St. Peter. The real extent of the lawful power possessed by those august bodies was furiously contested both in that and succeeding ages; nor has it yet ceased to be a matter of speculative difference among Roman Catholics. Again, the decrees which they published for the reformation of the Vatican were, for the most part, eluded, or openly outraged. But the effects which they really produced on the destinies of Papacy, though less immediate, were more durable, and far more extensive, than their authors had contemplated. The association of powerful and learned laymen in ecclesiastical deliberations, the habit of free discussion, the popular constitution of the assemblies, especially that of Basle, the public promulgation of anti-papal principles, and the practice of contending with Popes and deposing them, produced a deep impression in every quarter of the Catholic world. Rome alone might fail to comprehend the warning, or affect to despise it; and she reaped the fruits of her blindness or perversity. For the truth is, that the springs which were then opened, had they

Effects of General Councils.

been allowed by the Papal policy to take the course originally marked out for them, would but have cleansed away some of the corroding abuses of the See, and thus increased its strength; but being dammed up and diverted by a short-sighted opposition, they were indeed repressed for the moment—yet they presently broke forth in another quarter with redoubled violence, and finally swept away the mansion, which they were at first intended to purify.

The sketch which is here presented of the general constitution of the Roman Catholic Church, and of its tendency to decline during the two centuries which preceded the Reformation, should be filled up by some of the less perceptible portions of the fabric, that we may not wholly overlook the subordinate machinery, which alone enabled it to subsist so long. First, then, let us mention that popular principle in its construction, by which it threw open its benefices and dignities, even the Apostolical Chair, to every rank in society. It appealed to the ambition of all mankind: nor was this any faithless lure, to excite the industry of the faithful, and then to elude their hopes; so far otherwise, that several of the most eminent and honoured among the Pontiffs were of ignoble and even unknown origin. As long as the level of ecclesiastical morality approached at all near to the pretensions of ancient purity; as long as virtue and piety were held requisite for high offices, no less than talents and learning—so long the emulation awakened among Churchmen was serviceable not only to the prosperity of the Church, but to the general welfare of society, and the general interests of religion. But when, in the first stage of sacerdotal corruption, other paths were discovered of ascending the spiritual pyramid*; when the bigot or the parasite was found to reach the summit more surely than the man of holy and humble, yet upright, industry—then it became probable that men so promoted would throw scandal on the Church; and it was certain that they would confer no benefits on mankind. But

Various Principles and Instruments of the Roman Church.

---

* It is said, that the tops of pyramids are accessible only to two descriptions of animals—the eagle and the serpent. Both have found their imitators in the history of the Roman Catholic Hierarchy.

when at length, in days of deeper iniquity, the most odious
vices formed, as it were, the morals of Rome, ecclesiastical ambition became very closely connected with anti-Christian principles, and avarice, licentiousness, and perfidy too frequently
prepared the way to the throne of St. Peter. Howbeit, the
talent and ingenuity of men were still stimulated by the splendid
prospect, and all the energies of the mere intellect * were still
exercised and abused in the service of the Church. Nor yet
were they always abused—the love of letters was sometimes a
passport to the most elevated dignities, and the instrument
which was destined to overthrow the See was sometimes employed to illustrate and support it. Nicholas V. and Pius II.
eminently proved the great advantage which the democratical
principle *might* confer upon the Church, even in its worst age.
But the occasional success of genius, of even learning, was insufficient for the support of a religious establishment. The
springs of morality were poisoned. The vices of the ecclesiastics were those least pardonable, and least pardoned, in the
ecclesiastical character. The contrast between the demeanour
of the Hierarchy and its professions and purposes was too violent and too manifest. The tutelary spirit of piety had deserted
the temple, and its gates were thrown open to invite the invasion of the Reformer.

Pope's
Legates.
Mendi-
cants.

The hand of arbitrary power must sometimes be seen as well
as felt, in order that its commands may always be obeyed.
And the Bishop of Rome soon discovered the policy of visiting
the more distant communities of the faithful by envoys and
emissaries. In earlier ages, the pomp and haughtiness of his
Legates sufficiently represented the pontifical presence. They
awed the assemblies of the great, and insulted the dignity of
princes. In succeeding times, when reason and heresy raised
their heads, and it became necessary to exert a more direct and
searching influence over the people, the Mendicants started
into existence, and spread like a cloud over the face of Europe.

* The great mass of business, carried from all quarters to Rome, so as to make
it for such matters the school of Europe, drew thither men of talents and ambition, and gave them occupation, and consequently engaged them in the defence
of the system by which they profited.

These men were zealous and indefatigable ministers of a master whom, if many served from interest, many revered with honest enthusiasm. They practised great austerities; they preached with fervour, sometimes with eloquence; above all, they eagerly embraced and appropriated the scholastic erudition of the day: and thus it was that by feeding the false appetite for fallacies and subtleties, they converted learning, which was the natural enemy of Papacy, into its useful instrument. Among the accidents (if accident it can properly be called) which conspired to prolong the dominion of Rome, the most fortunate was assuredly this—that the first efforts of reviving reason were so perplexed and tortuous as to be capable of serving falsehood no less effectually than truth.

The Scholastic system was in due season supplanted by a better—but the influence of the Mendicants fell still earlier into decay; because they insensibly departed from the show of moral excellence which had recommended them to popular favour; because the Pope had gradually converted them into the instruments of his cruelty and the representatives of his avarice. It was thus that they lost their hold on the affections of the vulgar. For the lowest classes of mankind, though they may sometimes judge wrong, will always feel right; their principles may be shaken by the example of their superiors, but they will always tend to rectitude; and if they ever show favour to any crime or baseness, it is because they are deceived, not because they are depraved.

The discipline of the Church of Rome *practically* permitted the utmost latitude of rigour and laxity. In the same community, under the same government, within the walls of the same monastery, licentiousness was tolerated and austerity encouraged. The lordly Prelate transcended the pomp of secular luxury; the genuine disciple of St. Francis disclaimed all right even to the *use* of earthly possessions. The Cardinal and the Carmelite were united by the same ministry, by devotion to the same master, by the same professional hatred of heresy. But this startling inconsistency was not without its use, nor, perchance, without its design. For since, in the diversity of the human character, the vulgar may either be dazzled by

pageantry, or moved to reverence by mortification and humility, so also the exhibition of the one was a guarantee against
contempt, that of the other against envy and reproach.   So
that the Church, in this respect truly universal, had space and
occupation for every character and every faculty; whilst it
nourished a multiform and incongruous progeny, who confuted
(while at the same time they confirmed) the most opposite
accusations.   The poverty of the Mendicant and the piety of
the Missionary redeemed in public estimation the wealth and
vices of the Hierarchy.

The gene-
ral policy
of the
Vatican.

We pass over the maxims of policy usually ascribed to the
Vatican—to confound the marks of filial and feudal obligation;
to accept respect as obedience, and offer counsels as commands;
to obscure the limits of temporal and spiritual jurisdiction*; to

---

* Though, in the progress of this work, the author has purposely abstained
from any particular notice of the ecclesiastical affairs of England, in the belief
that they are intended to form the subject of a separate history, yet the following
remarks on the nature of one branch of spiritual jurisdiction, as exercised in this
kingdom, having been kindly furnished him by a legal friend, are too valuable
not to be accepted and inserted with gratitude.

" It is asserted in several of the old law books, that the spiritual jurisdiction
within the English realm is derived from the king, and that such jurisdiction,
when exceeded, is subject to the control of the king's temporal courts. The latter
assertion is of course true at present; the former, perhaps, relates to a question
of words rather than of fact. If the Church in early times claimed the authority,
and the king assented to the claim, the result might be stated as an act either of
obedience or of favour on the part of the Crown.

" With respect to one particular subject-matter of ecclesiastical jurisdiction,
the wills of deceased persons, and the disposition of the goods of those who died
intestate—its origin has been the occasion of much controversy. The question
relates simply to personal property. A freehold interest in land was in early
times, with a few exceptions, not subject to the will of the dying owner. The
superior lord's rights, as they existed during the vigour of the feudal institutions,
would have been prejudiced by permitting such a power of devising. The
restriction was only to be evaded by a transfer of the property, during the owner's
life, to a person who was to hold it subject to particular purposes to be declared
by will; and the courts of equity, by a proceeding which seems to have originated
with the ecclesiastical chancellors, compelled the party so holding to apply the
estate as the will directed, treating the matter as a question of conscience. The
statute passed in the thirty-second year of the reign of King Henry VIII. first
gave the direct power of devising freehold interests in land. But a devise,
deriving its validity from the provisions of this statute, has been always considered as a conveyance of the property, not a designation of the heir. It prevents
the land from being inherited *at all*. This distinction, although it may appear
rather technical, leads to many practical results of importance; and it is a point

keep all disputed rights in suspense and perplexity, so that the greater craft might never want pretexts for encroachment;

in which the English law differs from the Civil law. But it is here sufficient to state that devises of freehold estates are in no way the subject-matter of ecclesiastical jurisdiction. Even where a will contains a disposition of both realty and personalty, the authority of the spiritual courts operates only so far as the will affects the personalty.

" The present authority of the spiritual courts over the personal property of deceased persons amounts to this. If there be a claim to establish a will, it is to be proved before the spiritual court; that is, the spiritual court determines whether it be a valid will of the deceased. The recognition of the validity is technically expressed by saying that the executor proves the will, or obtains Probate, which is granted by the court. The authenticity of the will, as to personalty, cannot be directly questioned in the temporal courts, after probate has been granted; nor can it be asserted there before probate is granted. If there be no executor named in the will, or if the executor named will not or cannot act, the spiritual court gives the administration (or disposal) of the effects to an administrator, who is to administer according to the directions of the will. Again, if there be no will, the spiritual court invests an administrator with the power of administering.

" This jurisdiction of the spiritual courts is certainly very ancient. Authorities have been produced to show that, by the Saxon laws, the probate of testaments (a) was given by the old county courts. The bishop and the sheriff sat together in these courts, as presidents. A charter of William the Conqueror separated the ecclesiastical court from the civil; giving to the former the cognizance of suits prosecuted *pro salute animæ*. But testamentary questions are not expressly mentioned. In the second year of the reign of Richard the Second, the law of William the Conqueror was established and confirmed; and it was directed by the king's charter that no matters of ecclesiastical cognizance should be transacted in the county courts. This re-enactment seems to furnish evidence of the spiritual authority having fallen into desuetude, so far as regarded the courts. Whether or not it had been originally understood, at the time of William's charter, that wills were matter of spiritual jurisdiction, it is clear that the question had been raised before the time of Richard the Second. For by a charter of King Henry the First, the King's tenants (who were the suitors in the county courts) were enabled to dispose of their personalty for the good of their souls. It can scarcely be doubted that this was effected by the activity of the clergy; and even if we could believe that they had been at first unconcerned in the matter, it was quite certain that they would instantly apply such an enactment to their own purposes. Probably, therefore, the charter of Richard the Second was at once interpreted to apply to testaments. And, on the whole, it seems that this is the epoch to which we ought to assign the undisputed jurisdiction of these courts in testamentary matters. This history of the origin of the power explains and accounts for the opinions of most of our old lawyers, that the probate of wills came to the ecclesiastical courts, not by ecclesiastical law, but by devolution from the temporal law of the realm, or, as they express it, by the custom of England.

" (a) Originally, the form of bequeathing personal property extended only to a part; the law regulated the distribution of the remainder."

to crush the obstinate and gain the mercenary; to plunder
the subject without offending the vanity of the prince; to

And it receives strong confirmation from the fact that, by the local custom of
some particular manors, acknowledged by the English law, the probate of wills
and the granting of administration belongs to the court baron or manor court.
And a power of the same sort belongs, in some boroughs, to the mayor, as to
the goods of the burgesses.

"That the disposal by will of a dying man's goods is a matter relating to the
good of his soul, is a truth in no other sense than that in which *every* earthly act
has a relation to the spiritual welfare of the agent. But a will, being frequently
an act performed shortly before death, might, by a natural association, be connected most closely with the eternal destiny of the testator. Besides which, the
Roman Catholic doctrines asserted the dependence of the fate of the departed
soul upon the intercession of the living. Now this intercession might be purchased from the clergy by an application of the goods of the deceased. From
these causes, the will was asserted by the ecclesiastics to be a matter of *peculiarly*
spiritual interest. When this was acknowledged, it must have been, according to
priestly logic, a very plain inference that the disposal of the goods of a man who
left no will was a matter in which the clergy, for the sake of his eternal interests,
were bound to interfere. It was beyond the skill of the priests, or at any rate of
those whom they had to influence, to distinguish between the motive and the
result; so that a man whose property had been applied to pious purposes without
his own consent was thought to derive some merit from the application. Again,
it was thought highly important that a part of the property should be applied to
the performance of religious rites, for the good of the soul of the deceased; the
clergy were the persons most fitted to ensure such an application. Hence the
Ordinary (or spiritual judge) had the absolute disposal of the intestate's property;
and this, according to Lord Coke, was a power previously exercised by the kings
of England. But in the thirteenth year of the reign of Edward I., a statute
was passed (commonly called the statute of Westminster the Second), by one of
the provisions of which the ordinary was bound, as far as the goods extended, to
satisfy the debts of the intestate ([b]). Hence, says Lord North, what was formerly found very beneficial to the Ordinaries, began to be very troublesome,
which obliged them to put the administration into other hands, taking security
to save them harmless from suits. This, however, did not entirely put an end
to the Ordinary's trouble; for the persons named by him were considered merely
as his servants or attornies. But a statute, passed in the thirty-first year of the
reign of Edward III. provided that the Ordinary should depute the next and
most lawful friends of the intestate to administer his goods; and it gave the
minister so appointed power to act in his own right. A statute, passed in the
twenty-first year of Henry VIII., enacted similar provisions for the case of a

" ([b]) Cum post mortem alicujus decedentis intestati, et obligati aliquibus in
debito, bona deveniant ad ordinarium disponenda, obligetur de cætero ordinarius
ad respondendum de debitis quatenus bona defuncti sufficiunt, eodem modo quo
executores responderе tenerentur si testamentum fecisset. Cap. 19. Lord Coke
says that this was only an affirmance of the common law (2nd Inst. 397). It
however was so far a new enactment, that it put a decisive end to any question
on the point. Many enactments of the same statute are clearly intended to settle
disputed rights."

manage by treaties those who had been insulted by bulls; to provoke war and mediate peace—such were the ordinary rules of its government, and they are best exemplified in the exploits of its most honoured champions. But there is one peculiarity in the construction of its power, to which sufficient attention is not always directed. Every one has perceived how it towered above all earthly principalities, and veiled its sublime front in the most inscrutable mysteries of the spiritual world; but few have observed the real secret of its strength, which lay in the devotion of the lowest ranks of mankind. This general conquest over the affections of the vulgar was no doubt greatly facilitated by the general ignorance: but it was achieved through the zeal of the inferior clergy; and if in some degree ascribable to the peculiar character assumed by the Romish priesthood, it was no less effectually advanced through their plebeian condition and humble manner of life.

According to the literal interpretation of the New Testament, Christ is the only sacrificing priest, as he is also the only sacrifice; thus, likewise, is he the only mediator between God and man. Hence it followed that the proper character of the ministers of his religion is essentially different from that of the Jewish or Pagan priests. The prerogative of the latter

Mediatorial character assumed by the Romish priesthood.

will, where the executor should refuse to act. The power of the ordinary was thus limited to deputing an administrator; but he had still some choice in the selection; for he was entitled to elect as he pleased where persons of equal proximity to the deceased made claim. The ordinaries are said to have availed themselves of this power by appointing such as they expected to find most obsequious; and they further derived an advantage from calling the administrator to account for the overplus, which they insisted upon his applying to pious uses for the good of the deceased's soul. At last the temporal courts of law decided that the ordinary, after granting administration, could not exercise any authority over the administrator in his disposal of the property. This shifted the dangerous power to the hands of the administrator absolutely. In the twenty-second year of the reign of Charles II., a statute was passed to prevent this mischief. By this act, the method in which the administrator is to distribute the personalty is pointed out. By these successive steps, the power of the spiritual authority has been almost reduced to the exercise of a limited discretion in the appointment of a deputy, who is to act according to prescribed rules. The Ecclesiastical courts have ceased, for some ages, to be any instruments of power to the Church, for good or for evil. Their share in the distribution of justice is very limited; but they are still characterized by the peculiarity of their forms of process; and by their total departure from the rules of evidence which prevail in the courts of Common law."

was to offer the sacrifice to God, and to intercede with him for
the sins of the people. It is the office of the former to inter-
pret and dispense his word, to be the *stewards* of his mysteries,
and to point out the only path through faith to salvation—and
such were the earliest ministers of the Christian Church. But
it was not very long before the *elder** insensibly assumed the
loftier office of the Hiereus, or Sacerdos, and affected the ex-
piatory, and, at the same time, the mediatory character. Such
were the priests of the Eastern Church—μεσίται, Mediators—
no less than those of the Western; and we are at no loss to
perceive what an access of reverence and authority accrued to
them through the change. They were supposed to be alone
initiated in the mysteries of the faith—they were supposed to
be in more immediate communication with its divine founder
—they were supposed to influence, if not actually to administer, the judgments of Heaven. But we must also observe,
that if such a character was well calculated to overawe an
ignorant age, or the ignorant classes in any age, it was sure to
be stripped off whenever any intellectual independence should
be exercised, and to be accounted among the impostures fabricated by an artful priesthood for the delusion of mankind.

Advan-
tages of a
plebeian
clergy.

We shall readily acknowledge that all sacerdotal influence is
vicious and dangerous, except that which is acquired by the
religious and moral excellence of the priest: yet even the
highest qualities will often miss that end, when the condition of
the pastor is very far removed above that of his flock. And
thus was it the profoundest policy of the Roman Church to
maintain a faithful ministry of the same origin, the same language, almost the same habits with the people. The ecclesiastical chain extended through every gradation of society, till
it was folded round the Apostolical throne; but it was that
lowest link which, being fixed in a substantial support, gave
firmness and tenacity to the rest. To possess some habits of
familiarity with those intrusted to his guidance; to approach
them without constraint, to be received without diffidence; to

* The original meaning of the word Priest (Presbytes) is " Elder." This
subject is very well treated by Archbishop Whately, in his " Errors of Roman-
ism,' book i'.

have the same thoughts, the same expressions, the same sympathies; to observe the birth of sin; to watch the workings of remorse; to distinguish the moments proper for censure, or consolation; to be near at hand in times of doubt, or sickness, or domestic calamity—these, and such as these, are advantages peculiarly belonging to a plebeian clergy. Such an order of pastors, under the superintendence of a vigilant hierarchy, may at all times be made serviceable to the best purposes of religion; and it diffused many spiritual blessings, even in the most secular ages of Rome. But to the Church — the external and human establishment—it was the very origin of strength, and principle of vitality: it was the root which spread underground in secrecy and silence; while nations and their princes worshipped under the golden branches, and gathered the bitter fruit which sometimes fell from them.

The very corruptions in the ecclesiastical system were for a season serviceable in rivetting its influence. Auricular confession, the various abuses of penance, the adoration of the Host, and the *attributes* ascribed to it, all furnished additional instruments to the clergy; and as long as they were used with moderation extended their dominion. But it is ever the mistake of the usurper to despise the people whose confidence he has deceived or insulted; and the error is seldom discovered till the moment for correcting it has passed by. It was thus with the Hierarchs of Rome. They increased the measure of degradation and imposture, till they exhausted the affection, and then the patience of mankind. And it was the last excess of their wickedness and folly to make the inferior clergy their accomplices, and thus to poison the only wholesome fountain of their own authority. *Serviceable abuses.*

The above outline of the constitution of the Roman Church represents it not such, perhaps, as it is sometimes painted in the theories of its advocates; but such as it really and long existed in its practical operation on society. Nor will it seem strange to any reflecting mind that that Government, which was, in appearance and in fact, the most perfect despotism ever conceived by the mind of man, should be found at the bottom to rest on a popular basis. Even in civil governments *Popular foundation of the Roman despotism.*

there are instances of the same anomaly; but in an empire, essentially and peculiarly the empire of opinion, the support of the multitude was not so much the only source of strength, as the only principle of existence. If the Roman Church had been more evangelical in doctrine, more consistent in discipline, more moderate in pretension, it might have appealed with greater safety to the reason of mankind. But as it appealed to their ignorance, to their earliest and deepest prejudices, so was it that it urged the irresistible predominance of authority —the inviolable holiness of antiquity,—all those principles and all those motives which awe, when they do not irritate, the human understanding. Nevertheless, the appeal, howsoever insidiously made, was still an appeal to the mind; and thus was it seductive and universal. And so long as it found hearers and believers; so long as it retained its hold, by whatsoever means, on the devotion of the people; the dominion of Rome was not less substantial, and more secure, than if the sword had raised or upheld it. But from the moment that the spiritual bond was loosened, the mere worldly fabric, having no longer any element of coherence, subsided in progressive decay and dissolution.

SECTION II.

On the (I.) Spiritual Character, (II.) Discipline, and Morals of the Church.

The doctrine of the Roman Church.

I.—The Roman Catholics assert with great truth, that their Church has preserved, through the most perilous times, the essential mysteries and tenets of the Christian faith. It is with reverence that we have received them from her hands, and with gratitude that we acknowledge the inestimable obligation. Yet the most zealous Catholic must be contented to share that praise with the schismatics of the East. The same treasure has been guarded with the same fidelity by the Church of Greece; and would thus have been equally perpetuated, if the purity of the Roman creed had been corrupted by the barbarian conquest. But while those rival Churches

may divide the merit of having transmitted the apostolical doctrines to the latest generations, there is this difference in the
manner of that tradition—the one has transmitted them such
as she received them from the highest antiquity, not daring to
violate by any important innovation the integrity of the pristine
faith ; the other augmented her confession by some articles
which were left by the discretion of early times to the liberty of
private judgment. We have endeavoured (in the Thirteenth
Chapter) to indicate the sources whence many of those innovations proceeded. We shall now remark upon one or two
others, which, though of distant origin also, did not acquire
any general, or at least any very perceptible, prevalence till a
later age*.

According to the original system of penance, it was incul- Gradual
cated that transgressions could be expiated by prayer, fasting, changes in
and alms—there was no period in the history of the Church, tential
in which *pious works* were not held efficacious to redeem sin, and system.
were not imposed for that purpose, either directly, or by a partial substitution for bodily mortifications. To this circumstance
many holy structures owed their origin, many poor-houses and
hospitals—the Xenodochia, Nosocomia, Gerontocomia, &c., of
the ancient establishment; and these works were considered
satisfactory to God. This system was gradually corrupted,
and fell, especially in the Western nations, into great disorder;
when Theodore of Tarsus, Archbishop of Canterbury, pub- Theodore
lished, about the year 680, his celebrated Penitential. By the of Tarsus.
instructions herein delivered, the clergy were taught to distinguish sins into various classes, and to judge them according to
their nature, to the intention of the offender, and other circumstances. The Penitential likewise pointed out the penalties
proper for every sort of offence; prescribed the forms of consolation, exhortation, absolution, and set forth the duties of the
Confessor. (Mosh., Cent. VII., p. ii., ch. iii.) This new disci-

* It was a general, but not quite correct, opinion of the early reformers, that
the Scholastics had invented the new Dogmas, and the Monks the new practices.
But it is quite certain that the immediate causes of the insurrection against Rome
were the *later* corruptions in her doctrine—just as most of the edicts of Constance
and Basle were levelled against the later innovations in her discipline.

z 2

pline, though of Greek origin, was eagerly embraced in the
Latin Churches, and it was immediately corrupted.   The
method of redemption of penance was presently reduced to a
regular system : in the place of so many days of fasting, so
much alms was to be given, or so many psalms sung, or so
many masses celebrated, *by others,* who were to be rewarded
for the office; or so much money to be paid down.   The number of the Penitentials was increased, and their character
altered, according to the caprice of individual confessors ; and,
in spite of some attempts * to repress the abuse, pecuniary redemption became more and more common, and presently
almost every sort of penance had its fixed price in gold.   It
may seem needless to add that the clergy (the *Servi Dei*)
easily proved themselves to be the properest objects of these
eleemosynary contributions, and that a great proportion of the
wealth, so expended, flowed almost directly into the treasuries
of the Church.

Indul-
gences.
    These, however, were only corruptions of the ancient peniten-
tial system, they did not effect its entire destruction ; but that

---

    * Muratori (Dissertat. 68), from whom several of these remarks are borrowed,
cites the following as the 26th Canon, Concil. II. Cloveshoviensis, A.D. 747.
"Sicuti nova adinventio, juxta placitum scilicet propriæ voluntatis suæ, nunc
plurimis periculosa consuetudo est, non sit eleemosyna porrecta ad minuendam
sed *ad mutandam satisfactionem* per jejunium et reliqua expiationis opera à Sacer-
dote Dei indicta," it is ordained that alms are to be so offered, that the person of
the Penitent may not be wholly spared.   The vicarious recitation of Psalms was
at the same time prohibited, as well as other abuses.   This Council was held by
the Archbishop of Mayence, not forty years, perhaps, after the death of Theodore.
About twenty years earlier, Gregory II. (Epist. 13) addressed to Leo the Isaurian the following vigorous description of ecclesiastical, as contrasted with civil,
discipline.   " Ubi peccaverit quis et confessus fuerit, suspendii vel amputationis
capitis loco, evangelium et crucem ejus cervicibus circumponunt, eumque, tanquam in carcerem, in secretaria sacrorumque vasorum æraria conjiciunt, in Ecclesiæ Diaconia, et in Catechumena ablegant, ac visceribus eorum jejunium occulis-
que vigilias et laudationem ori ejus indicunt.   Cumque probè castigaverint probe-
que fame afflixerint, tum pretiosum illi Domini Corpus impartiunt et sancto illum
sanguine potant; et cum illum vas electionis restituerint ac immunem peccati,
sic ad Deum purum insontemque transmittunt.   Vides, Imperator, ecclesiarum
imperiorumque discrimen," &c.   (The passage is cited by Giannone, Stor. Ital.,
lib. iii., cap. vi.)   It was not till the eleventh age that the practice of flagellation
became common, and it was then that St. Dominicus, surnamed *Loricatus,* the
friend of Peter Damiani, acquired his celebrity.   He could discharge by stripes
in six days the penance of a hundred years.

result was afterwards brought about by the abuse of Indulgences. An indulgence, as a mere relaxation of canonical
penance, existed as early as the days of Cyprian ; and it was
not till the Council of Clermont that the discharge of a single
duty was substituted for all that was due, or might hereafter
be due, to the penal authority of the Church. When people
thenceforward found it so easy to release themselves at once
from the ancient burden of redemption, they became clamorous
to receive what the Pope, on sufficient consideration, was never
reluctant to grant. We shall recur to this subject immediately:
in the mean time, it is very true that there existed from time
to time many ecclesiastics, even in the worst age of the Church,
who exclaimed against the *abuse* of that papal prerogative,—
against the indiscriminate distribution and open venality of indulgences. But we have not perceived that any argued on the
false *principle* on which they were founded; it was not then made
a reason for their condemnation that they disparaged the efficacy of Grace ; and perverted, if they did not wholly overthrow,
the doctrine of salvation through the merits of Christ alone.

The existence and nature of an intermediate state naturally The doc-
awakened the speculations of the early Christians; but the trine of
Purgatory.
subjects were long left open to the curiosity, the vanity, or the
piety of contemplative individuals—these were not restrained
by any ecclesiastical edicts, and impunity yet attended the profession of opposite doctrines. Among the Greeks the question
was not afterwards pressed to any practical system or inference.
It is true, indeed, that a certain opinion was selected and sanctioned as that most probable, and was apparently inscribed
among the authorized tenets : but it was at no time recommended to the peculiar reverence of the faithful; still less was
it converted into an engine of ecclesiastical government. But
during the iron ages of the Roman Church, the same inexplicable question assumed a much more definite and durable
shape. Differing from the Greeks, who considered the immediate abode of the departed to be one of obscurity and discom-
fort, the Latins boldly lighted the penal fire of purgatory, and
gave a substance, a locality, and an object to the timid and
distrustful speculations of the early Christians.

It is the modern doctrine of the Roman Catholic Church*
"that there is a purgatory; and that the souls imprisoned
there are aided by the prayers of the faithful, and the acceptable sacrifice of the altar." But in this matter it is not so important to ascertain what has been, at various times, the outward *profession* of the Church, as to remark the consequences
which have practically flowed from the dogma, and influenced
the happiness and morality of mankind. For the history of
the Church is not a lifeless record of its Canons and Confessions, but a display of their operation, whether for good or
for mischief, whether in their use or in their abuse, upon the
Christian community. The consequence which presently followed from the establishment of a place of temporary punishment, or purification, for departed souls, was that the successor
of St. Peter assumed, through the power of the keys, unlimited
authority there. By indulgences, issued at the discretion of
the Pope, the sinner (in the theory, the repentant sinner) was
released from suffering, and immediately passed into a state of
grace. As long as these indulgences were granted with discrimination and reserve †, the ill effects which they occasioned
do not often meet the eye of the historian. But as soon as
they were turned into mere instruments of papal ambition, and
as such were not only promiscuously scattered over the world,

* Founded on the Canons of Trent.—It is frequently asserted to be the doctrine
of that Church, that the *fund* whence the above forgiveness is drawn is composed
of the supererogatory merits of the saints (added to those of Jesus Christ), which
are inexhaustible; and such, indeed, it is clearly laid down by St. Thomas Aquinas (see Mosheim, Cent. XII., p. ii., c. iii.). Modern divines disclaim this opinion,
as at variance with the great doctrine of justification—and this is not the only
instance of salutary change which has purified the bosom of the Roman Catholic
Church during the last three centuries.—May such changes be multiplied!

† Baronius (Ann. 847, s. iv.) boasts the moderation of the indulgences granted
in those days, and instances one (trium annorum et trium quadragenarum) given
under Leo IV. Even as late as the eleventh age there are proofs (as Muratori
observes) of similar discretion in the directors of the Church. And it is proper to
mention that Gregory the Great, in his Chapter on Purgatory (Dialogorum, lib. iv.,
cap. xxxix.), expressly limited its operation to venial and very trifling offences
(de parvis minimisque peccatis hoc fieri posse credendum est), such as mere vain
and leisurely discourse, immoderate laughter, or an error in unimportant matters
proceeding from ignorance. He adds, moreover, that thus much is certain—that
no one will obtain any purgation, even from the least offences, unless he merit,
by his good works here, to obtain such remission there.

CH. XXVIII.]   A HISTORY OF THE CHURCH.   343

but also extended in character to a plenary remission, they became simple, manifest means to poison the morality of the faithful.

Thenceforward their *nature* could scarcely be further corrupted; for the only proof which was now required of the sinner's spiritual mortification and amendment was his willingness to perform a single act. But on the character of that act, that is, on the *object* of the indulgence, it still depended whether the subversion of the principle of evangelical repentance was to be made subservient to the seeming advantage of the world, or obviously instrumental in aggravating its misery.

The object of the indulgence was changed repeatedly; yet never so changed as to take the guise of philanthropy. First, it was the recovery of the Holy Land and the extirpation of the Infidel. Then from the general foe of Christ it was turned against the spiritual adversaries of the Catholic Church; from the spiritual adversaries of the Church it descended to the temporal enemies of the Pope. It next assumed a more innocent shape (if superstition could ever be innocent), and summoned the obedient pilgrims to enrich, on stated Jubilees *, the apostolical shrines of Rome. Lastly, it degenerated into a mere vulgar, undisguised implement for supplying the necessities of the pontifical treasury †,—and it was in this last form that it at length aroused the scorn and indignation of Europe.

Various objects of papal indulgences.

The profane and even blasphemous expressions by which the emissaries of the Vatican recommended their treasures to

---

* In the Jubilee of 1300, "Papa (Boniface VIII.) innumerabilem pecuniam ab iisdem recepit; quia die et nocte duo Clerici stabant ad altare Sancti Petri tenentes in eorum manibus rastellos, rastellantes pecuniam infinitam."—*Gulielmus Astensis Ventura* (an eye-witness) *Chronicon Astense*, cap. 26, ap. Muratori. Again, in the Bull of Clement VI. for the jubilee of 1350 are these words—"Et nihilominus prorsus mandamus Angelis Paradisi, quatenus animam illius a Purgatorio penitus absolutam in Paradisi gloriam introducant." See Giannone, lib. xvii., cap. 8.

† It should be recollected that the sale of indulgences was faintly countenanced by the corresponding enormities of civil legislation, according to which, in somewhat earlier times, every crime had its price. The Church in every age should, *in some degree*, be judged according to the principles of that age,—yet in such wise that we never lose sight of that one great and unchangeable standard, by which the actions of a Christian ministry must, in every age, be measured.

popular credulity were tacitly permitted by the authorities of the Church; yet we shall not detail them here, nor impute them to any others than the individuals who uttered them— they may repose in the same oblivion. But it is proper to transcribe a specimen of the indulgences which were publicly sold in the beginning of the sixteenth century, because they were the authorised productions of the Church. The following is the translation of that which was circulated by Tetzel:—

Indulgence circulated by Tetzel. " May our Lord Jesus Christ have mercy upon thee and absolve thee, by the merits of His most holy passion. And I, by his authority, that of His blessed Apostles, Peter and Paul, and of the most Holy See, granted and committed to me in these parts, do absolve thee first from all ecclesiastical censures, in whatever manner they have been incurred; and then from all thy sins, transgressions, and excesses, how enormous soever they may be, even from such as are reserved for the cognizance of the Apostolical See[*]. And as far as the keys of the Church extend, I remit to you all punishment which you deserve in purgatory on their account; and I restore you to the Holy Sacraments of the Church, to the unity of the faithful, and to that innocence and purity which you possessed at baptism; so that, if you should die now, the gates of punishment shall be shut, and the gates of the Paradise of delight shall be opened. And if you shall not die at present, this Grace shall remain in full force when you are on the point of death. In the name of the Father, and of the Son, and of the Holy Ghost." This indulgence, in spite of the ambiguity of one or two expressions, is nothing less, when fairly interpreted, than an unconditional permission to sin for the rest of life; and as such it was assuredly received by those classes of the people for which it was chiefly intended, and whose morality is peculiarly confided to the superintendence of the clergy. And thus was it that the destiny of the Church was accomplished.

Private masses. However easy the acquisition of pardon (for the moderate price of indulgences placed them within the reach of the lowest

---

[*] The translation given by Beausobre (Hist. Reform., liv. i.) here differs slightly from that published by Dr. Robertson (Hist. Charles V., b. ii.); but not so as to make any important change in the sense of the whole passage.

orders), still many neglected to profit by the facility, and were accordingly consigned to the penal fire. Yet even thus they were not removed beyond the power and mercies of the Church *. It was inculcated that the prayers of the living were efficacious in the purification of those departed souls; but that their release was most speedily secured by the sacrifice of the altar. Hence arose in early times† the practice of offering masses, both public and private, for that purpose; and, as these too had subsequently their price in gold, the piety of the survivors was taxed to redeem the transgressions of the dead— so various were the devices of the Church to render tributary the weaknesses, the virtues, even the natural affections of the faithful. The sale of private masses was a fruitful source of revenue to the clergy, especially to the monastic orders, and that likewise was one of the abuses first proscribed by the eloquence of Luther.

When Innocent III. gave the sanction of a General Council to the Roman doctrine of the Eucharist, and distinguished it by the name of Transubstantiation‡, he not only secured its universal reception in the West, but also countenanced the superstitious practices which flowed from it. It appears to have been during his pontificate that the custom was introduced of elevating the Host after consecration. The use of the bell to

The elevation of the Host.

---

* Gerson, however, (De Indulgentiis, vol. ii., p. 351,) admits that it is a question *ad utramque partem probabilis,* whether the keys have such power in purgatory as to remit the punishment of a venial fault or excommunication, committed or incurred during life. This doubt of the Chancellor must have made him unpopular in the monasteries. He asserts, in the same place, without any hesitation,—" Indulgentiæ ad pœnas ex corruptione naturæ non extendunt."

† We find it proclaimed by the Protestants at Augsbourg (1530), that there is no instance of private masses in ecclesiastical history earlier than the time of Gregory the Great. Mosheim is contented to assert that manifest traces of them may be found in the eighth century, though it be difficult to decide whether they were instituted by public law, or introduced by private authority. We are not aware of the existence of any earlier public regulation on this subject than the 43rd Canon of the Council of Mayence, held in 813, and this is expressly prohibitory,—" No priest shall say mass alone."

‡ The following is a part of the celebrated Canon (Can. i., Lat. Concil. IV.) in question—" Una est fidelium Universalis Ecclesia, extra quam nullus omnino salvatur. In qua idem ipse sacerdos et sacrificium Jesus Christus; cujus corpus et sanguis in sacramento altaris sub speciebus panis et vini veraciter continentur, *transsubstantiatis* pane in corpus et vino in sanguinem, potestate divina," &c. &c.

signify to the people to prostrate themselves while the Holy
Sacrament was passing, is ascribed to an ordinance published
in 1201, by Guy Paré, the legate of the same at Cologne. And
that it may be shown how early this practice was supported
by the direct authority of the See, and how widely it was
thought expedient to extend it, we may mention that Honorius,
the successor of Innocent, addressed an epistle to the Latin
prelates of the East, in the Patriarchate of Antioch, in which he
instructed them to oblige the people to *incline* on the appearance of the Host*. In that age, and at that distance from the
centre of orthodoxy, it was not held advisable to inculcate the
necessity of absolute genuflexion. A simpler act of devotion
was deemed sufficient to recognize the divinity of the consecrated elements.

The re-
trenchment
of the cup.
The sufficiency of the Sacrament administered in one kind
only is by many considered as an immediate inference from
the doctrine of transubstantiation, since the bread, when converted into the body of Christ, of necessity contains his blood;
so that the object of the sacrifice being thus satisfied, the communication of the cup may be safely retrenched, as a vain and
superfluous ceremony. At what precise period this change in
the *practice* of the Church (it was maintained to be no more
than that) was introduced we cannot pronounce with certainty†;
but its antiquity was pleaded by its defenders at Constance
and Basle, and it may be ascribed, without any great error to
the beginning of the thirteenth century. We may consider it
as completing the list of those peculiar observances which the
Church of Rome has thought proper, on her own infallible authority, to impose upon her adherents. Probably the motive
for this innovation was to add solemnity to the mystery, by

* Fleury, l. lxxviii., s. 24. The Institution of the Festival of the Holy Sacrament or body of Christ, another early consequence of the universal establishment
of Transubstantion, is generally ascribed to Robert, Bishop of Liege—who is
said to have been moved thereto by the pretended revelations of a fanatical
woman named Juliana. The event took place in the year 1246. Mosh., Cent.
XIII., p. 2, chap. iv.

† We have not observed that it was formally and universally established by
the highest ecclesiastical authority, till it attracted the attention of the Council of
Constance.

excluding the profane from perfect initiation, and at the same
time to exalt the dignity of the priesthood, by giving them
some exclusive prerogative, even in communion at the Lord's
table. Nevertheless, even with that view, its policy was extremely questionable; it was founded on the ignorance of preceding ages; it had no foresight of the character of those which
were to come. And thus it proved that, after the lapse of some
few generations, men were rather shocked by the public, practical disregard of one of the plainest instructions delivered in
the Gospel, than edified by the spectacle of sacerdotal usurpation. The innovation was too rash, too openly at variance with
an express command, intelligible to the lowest classes of the
vulgar, and sacred with all who thought their Bible more
venerable than their Church. Accordingly we have observed
that the deprivation of this privilege, so clearly granted by
Christ to all believers, was the grievance which united the dis-
cordant sects of the Hussites—the restoration of the cup was
the manifest, incontestable right round which they rallied. To
this extent, too, they were successful; and their success afforded
the first example of any usurpation having been wrested from
the hands of Rome by the open rebellion of her subjects.

Neither was there any one among the peculiar tenets or Prohibi-
observances of Rome which so taxed the ingenuity of her ad- tion of the
Scriptures.
vocates, as the retrenchment of the cup. This perplexity is
attested by the records of Constance and Basle; and it deserves
particular remark that Gerson, in his very elaborate treatise
against the Double Communion, discloses the source of his
difficulty in this simple complaint. "There are many laymen
among the heretics who have a version of the *Bible in the
vulgar tongue*, to the great prejudice and offence of the Catholic faith. It has been proposed (he adds) to reprove that
scandal in the committee of reform." That scandal was as old
as the heresy of Peter Waldensis; but the practice which it
offended certainly grew up in much more distant ages, nor was
it peculiar to the Church of Rome. As early as the seventh
century the appropriation of the Scriptures to the use of the
priesthood was a practice generally established throughout the

East*, and the Latins speedily adopted (if they had not already enforced) a precaution so necessary for preserving the unity of the Church and concealing its abuses. It was authorised by the Council of Toulouse in 1229; but the spirit of independence nevertheless gained ground. From the time of Wiclif the unhallowed veil was gradually withdrawn; curiosity was more keenly excited, as it had been more tyrannically repressed; the invention of the press increased the facility of possessing the sacred oracles; and before the preaching of Luther, the *scandal*, which had been deplored a century earlier by the orthodox reformer of the Church, had made very general progress amongst the educated classes in almost every nation in Europe.

False miracles.

Those prodigious impostures which, in the eyes of Laurentius Valla †, surpassed the impiety of the Pagans, and which were ascribed by Gerson to the phantastic somnolency of a decrepit world, were continued with unrestrained temerity, even to the days of Erasmus. The impostures were the same which had so long been employed to delude the people of Christ— but the people were changed. A spirit of inquiry was spreading over the surface of Europe, and it was seen and felt by all, except the monks and bigots, to whom alone it was dangerous. But these persevered in the same blind path of habitual fraud and momentary profit, which at length conducted them to the precipice whither it had always tended.

Certain other unscriptural practices, long inherent in the Romish system, never had flourished with greater luxuriance than at the beginning of the sixteenth century. The abuse of images had been carried at no period to a more unpardonable

* See Chapter XXVI., p. 211, vol. iii.

† *De Donatione Constantini.* "Nostri Fabulatores passim inducunt Idola loquentia; quod ipsi Gentiles et idolorum cultores non dicunt, et sincerius negant, quam Christiani affirmant." The passage of Gerson is,—"Mundus senescens patitur *phantasias* falsorum miraculorum, sicut *homo senex phantasiatur in somno;* propterea sunt habenda miracula valde suspecta." Both these passages are cited by Semler. The detection of the artifices practised upon Jetzer at Berne, for the confirmation of the Dominican opinion respecting the immaculate conception, created a notorious scandal, which assisted in preparing the path for Zuinglius.

extent. The popular adoration of the saints had never deviated farther from the professed moderation of the Church *—relics had never been approached with a reverence more superstitious, or one more directly encouraged by the priesthood †. The pomp and order of the ceremonies had been at no time more entirely at variance with the character of a spiritual religion. Indeed, some of the festivals which were instituted or revived during the fifteenth century, seem designedly established to turn away men's minds from the substance of Christianity to vain formalities, or wicked fables. And in this place it will be proper to instance more particularly in what manner the highest ecclesiastical authorities were supplying the spiritual necessities of the faithful at the very moment when the cry for reformation was resounding (in various notes indeed, but general accord) from one end of Europe to the other.

The first regulation for the "Exposition of the Holy Sacrament" was published in 1452 by the Pope's Legate in Germany, at a Council held at Cologne; and the expressions of the edict ‡ are entirely worthy of its object. If a comet appeared (as in 1456), or the country was ravaged by inundation or pestilence (as happened twenty years later), the Pope of the day immediately pressed to offer his indulgences to all who should celebrate the feast of the Holy Sacrament, or of the Immaculate Conception—to all who should thrice repeat the Lord's Prayer, or the Angelic Salutation. About the end

Later festivals, disputes, controversies, &c.

---

* The following is the doctrine of modern Roman Catholic Divines:—" That the saints reigning with Christ offer up their prayers to God for men : that it is good and useful suppliantly to invoke them and to have recourse to their prayers, help, and assistance, to obtain favours from God, through his Son, Jesus Christ, our Lord, who is alone our Redeemer and Saviour." Alas! ask the peasant of Romagna or the Sicilian mariner for *his* explanation of the doctrine!

† We refer the reader to Beausobre's account (Hist. Reform., lib. iv.. p. 243) of the holy contents of the Church of All Saints at Wittenberg, which had been most profusely enriched by the bulls of Julius II. and Leo X. The whole number of relics exceeded 19,000, divided into twelve classes, according to the dignity of the saints. There were bulls to the effect, " that all who visited this Church on certain days might retain all property dishonestly acquired, to the amount of twenty-five golden ducats; and that any one who doubted the validity of such indulgences was *ipso facto* excommunicated, without power of absolution, even by the Pope himself, and *in articulo mortis.*"

‡ See the continuator of Fleury, lib. cx., s. 97.

of the year 1480, Sixtus IV. was invited to settle a dispute between the inhabitants of Perugia and Sienna, on a very remarkable subject. The former were accused of having obtained fraudulent possession of the nuptial ring of St. Catharine, the hereditary property of the latter, her compatriots. The object was holy; and its sanctity was enhanced (as a grave historian* informs us) by its various virtues, frequently experienced by the faithful, especially that of reconciling conjugal differences. This quarrel was prolonged for some time under Sixtus and his successor.

The stigmata of St. Francis and St. Catharine. In the "Book of Conformities" between the life of Jesus Christ and that of St. Francis, the fanatic is exalted to the level, if not above the level, of the Saviour. To complete the resemblance, the former carried about with him the marks of the five wounds of Christ; and the belief in these *stigmata* was enjoined to all the faithful by Alexander V. But in the age following St. Francis, the same miraculous impressions were claimed, on the same authority, by the female impostor of Sienna†. And when Catharine was at length canonized by Pius II., an office was instituted in her honour, of which the hymns affirmed that she had received the stigmata. This was to offer an unpardonable indignity to the Franciscans—for they were jealous of the glory of their patron‡, and asserted his exclusive pretension to that intimate sympathy with Christ. Immediately the Dominicans rose in defence of St. Catharine. The office was, nevertheless, denounced to Sixtus IV.; and that Pope presently published an edict, prohibiting any one, under severe penalties, from representing the stigmata of St. Catharine in painting; but he seems afterwards to have

* Raynaldus, ann. 1480, n. 44. See Semler, cent. xv., cap. ii., and Bzovius, ann. 1480.

† It is perhaps proper to mention that the Dominicans likewise claimed the stigmata for their patron; but they were compelled to admit that his extreme humility had prevented him from disclosing them.

‡ Earlier in the same century, an opinion was propagated " that those who die in the habit of St. Francis, and making profession of the third order, remain only one year in purgatory; because the saint descends thither once a year, and takes away all those of his order to heaven with him." This proposition was not beneath the notice of the Council of Basle—on the contrary, it was solemnly condemned (May 19, 1443) in the forty-fourth or forty-fifth session.

retracted his prohibition. These matters took place about the year 1483—it was the same which gave birth to Luther.

About the year 1050, a daily Office was instituted to the blessed Virgin, distinguished by seven canonical hours, in a form anciently used in honour of divine majesty; and in the course of the next hundred years the reverence so paid grew into worship. Among the attributes early * ascribed to her was exemption from original sin; but this opinion was for some time confined to the breasts of a few individuals—it had no place in ecclesiastical ceremonies, or the arguments of the learned. At length, however, about the year 1136, the Canons of Lyons ventured to introduce it into the offices of their Church. St. Bernard immediately opposed that innovation, and attacked the indiscreet zeal of those ecclesiastics. But in the following age, the subject was found to open too large a space for disputation to escape the polemical zeal of the scholastics—it became, on the contrary, their favourite field of controversy. And since the Dominicans ranged themselves on the one side and the Franciscans on the other†, the contest was heated and perpetuated by monastic jealousy. But it was reserved for the Council of Basle to establish the doctrine, and to excommunicate all who should preach the contrary. A feast was then instituted in honour of the Immaculate Conception, and it received in 1446 the official confirmation of Sixtus IV.‡ Yet not thus was the controversy composed, nor even the show of concord restored between the contending orders.

Without closely pursuing the inexhaustible subject of monastic dissension, we may mention that a violent dispute arose in this age between the Canons regular and the Hermits of St. Augustine, respecting the *dress* assumed by the original

The Immaculate Conception.

---

* As early as the ninth century—some ascribe the origin of the opinion to Paschasius Radbertus. See Padre Paolo, Hist. Concil. Trident., lib. ii.

† Semler (Sec. xiv., cap. 1) mentions 1384 as the year in which the controversy on the Immaculate Conception broke out between the rival orders at Paris. In 1387 the faculty censured John de Montesono for maintaining the less exalted opinion—that is, the opinion of St. Bernard and the Dominicans. Nevertheless, the war continued to rage.

‡ The bull of Sixtus is given by the Continuator of Fleury, lib. cxv., s. 102.

monks of that father. The clamour ascended to the Apostolical Chair, and commanded the attention of Sixtus IV. He
published a Bull, in which he wisely enjoined peace to both
parties—wisely, but vainly;—for the controversy (as it was
called) continued for some time longer to disturb the harmony
of those holy brethren.

On the
blood of
Christ.

A difference respecting the kind of worship which is due to
the Blood of Christ first arose at Barcelona in 1351, between
the Dominicans and Franciscans. It was renewed at Brixen*
in 1462. James à Marchia, a Franciscan, publicly maintained that the blood which Christ shed on the cross did not
belong to the divine nature, and consequently was not an object of worship. The Dominicans were roused to fury by an
assertion so derogatory to the Redeemer; and the preacher
was immediately summoned before the Inquisition. Pius II.
made some ineffectual attempts to suppress the controversy;
but finding his authority insufficient for that purpose, he at
last submitted the question to a commission of divines. Howbeit, both parties were so highly inflamed, that the doctors
were unable to arrive at any decision. At length the Pontiff
published a reasonable decree, " that both opinions might be
lawfully maintained, until Christ's vicegerent should find leisure and opportunity for examining the question"—and so the
matter rests at this moment.

In 1492, some labourers, repairing the foundations of the
Church of the Santa Croce at Rome, discovered what was immediately proclaimed to be the original Inscription on the
cross of Christ. The belief was propagated that it had been
sent to Rome by St. Helena, mother of Constantine; and
though there was no authority for this tradition, and though

* Semler, Cent. xv. cap. ii. While such were the subjects on which monastic
absurdity was exhausted, a very different description of nonsense was in vogue,
proceeding more directly from the scholastic method—the following may serve
as a specimen. One Jean de Mercœur was condemned in 1346 for errors, among
which were the following: " (1) Jesus Christ, through his created will, may
have willed something, which has never come to pass. (2) In whatsoever
manner God wills, he wills efficaciously, that it come to pass. (3) God wills,
that such a one sin and be a sinner, and he wills it by his will, at his free pleasure. (4) No one sins in willing otherwise than God wills, that he will," &c.
More may be found in Fleury, lib. xcv., s. 37.

the pious Catholics of Toulouse pretended to have possessed the true inscription undisturbed for many ages, Alexander VI. pronounced (four years afterwards) the authenticity of the Roman title, and recommended it by particular indulgences to the devotion of the faithful. On the 29th of May in the same year, an ambassador from Bajazet arrived, bearing, as a present to the Pope, the head of the true lance. All the clergy went forth in procession to receive it, and the Pontiff assisted in person at the miserable mummery. Raynaldus likewise assures us (on the authority of Jacobus Rosius) that the sponge and the reed were presented on the same occasion: such were the offerings with which the Infidel insulted the superstition of Christendom, and found his ready agent and most zealous accomplice in the Pope.

But while the spiritual guides of the faithful were thus de-gradingly employed—while absurdity and imposture seemed triumphant in the Church, and monks and seculars were lend-ing, in rivalry, their aid to nourish them—a far different spirit was growing up among those who had sought their instruction elsewhere. Many pious Laymen had already explored the forbidden treasures of Scripture. They had long ago abhorred the vices of the ecclesiastical system; they now discovered that whatever in it was wicked was likewise unfounded in truth. They advanced with increasing confidence towards evangelical perfection, just as the Churchmen were rushing most wildly in the opposite direction, and casting wisdom and piety, as if in scorn and detestation, behind them. Yet was there some reason even in this their madness. The superstitions of Rome were closely connected with her authority, and these exerted on each other a reciprocal and potent influence. The super-stitions enslaved the consciences, and thus commanded the *riches* of the faithful; and so they ministered to the Papal power—while, on the other hand, that power established and canonized the abuses: and it had so long been efficient in protecting them, that to many it seemed capable of sustaining them for ever.

II.—*On the Discipline and Morals of the Church.* The

Celibacy of
the clergy.

severe edicts of Gregory VII. against the concubinage of the clergy, and the disorders which followed them, in no very dissolute age of the Church, sufficiently prove that a law which offended the principles of nature could not command observance, even though professional zeal and worldly interest and morality itself pleaded against its violation. And if the severity of that Pontiff for the moment abated the scandal, it was never wholly removed, but continued sometimes to elude, and sometimes to defy the unremitted exertions of Popes and Councils. Insomuch that, considered only as an instrument of ecclesiastical policy, it would seem that the celibacy of the clergy has produced less advantage to the Church of Rome by the exclusive spirit which it encourages, and the popular influence of which it facilitates the acquisition, than it has done mischief by the reproach and shame to which it has given unceasing occasion*.

General
demorali-
zation of
the Church.

Early in the twelfth age, the general relaxation of discipline and morals was deplored by St. Bernard, and it increased in despite of his eloquent denunciations. From that time forward the Reformation of the Church, in its head and its members, became a subject of frequent mention, and of constant hope or apprehension, according to the sanctity or the worldliness of individual Churchmen. At the Council of Vienne, the particulars of ecclesiastical corruption were boldly exposed, but imperfectly remedied. During the exile at Avignon the pesti-

* The following Canons of a Council held at Toledo in the year 400 sufficiently show the practice of the Church of Spain, nearly 80 years after the Council of Nice. *Canon I.* " Married deacons or priests who have not preserved continence with their wives shall not be promoted." *Canon VII.* " If the wife of a priest has sinned, he may bind her in his house, and make her fast and chastise her.... he should not, however, eat with her until she has done penance." *Canon XIX.* " If she be the *daughter* of a bishop, priest, or deacon," &c. And again, " the widow of a bishop, priest, or deacon, who marries again, shall not receive communion, except on her death-bed." On this subject Guizot has remarked that the necessity of recruiting an unmarried clergy from the ranks of the laity was one reason for the failure of the Papal scheme of universal monarchy. To have secured its success (he adds) the clergy ought to have been a distinct caste, bringing up their own children to their own profession. But there is much to be said against this opinion. A caste producing itself is a much more separate and distinguishable object for an enemy's aim than a body which is incessantly recruiting itself from the mass.

lence increased; it was inflamed by the schism which succeeded; till at length, whatever still remained of learning and excellence in the Church, combined against its further progress. It is superfluous to repeat the names or transcribe the indignant expressions of those Reformers. The truth of their testimony has never been disputed *; and one of the few circumstances in the history of the Roman Catholic Church, which has escaped all controversy, is that of its demoralization. The fathers of Constance and Basle having failed to repair the discipline of the Church, it received no improvement during the interval which succeeded; nor were the examples of Innocent VIII., Alexander VI., or Julius II., well calculated to re-establish the authority of the Canons, or restore the model of ancient purity.

If there was any country, which at that time had escaped the general degradation, the exception may have been formed by Spain: and Spain is chiefly indebted for that distinction to the morose, monastic austerity of Cardinal Ximenes. That haughty Churchman revived the image of the spiritual champions of early days. Under the habit of a Franciscan, he nourished unbounded ambition, and more than pontifical insolence †. As regent of the kingdom, he possessed great secular authority; but his religious profession was ever nearest to his heart, and it was his favourite boast, " that he could bind the grandees to their duty by his *cord*, and crush their pride with his sandals." The object, on which he was most ardently bent, was the conversion of the vanquished Moors. His impatience permitted no method, except compulsion; and no fewer than fifty thou-

Margin: Cardinal Ximenes.

---

* " La discipline ecclésiastique (says Bossuet) s'étoit relâchée par toute la terre: les désordres et les abus portés jusqu'aux environs de l'autel faisoient gémir les bons, les humilioient, les pressoient à se rendre encore meilleurs—mais ils firent un autre effet sur les esprits aigres et superbes." Histoire des Variations, lib. xi., s. 294. We might also refer to the celebrated avowal made (in 1522) by Adrian VI. at the diet of Nuremberg.

† On one occasion Ximenes opposed the levy of tenths in Spain, though commanded by Leo X., under the pretext of a Turkish war. The Cardinal (should we not rather say the Regent?) informed the Pope, that, unless on the urgency of some very pressing occasion, he would never allow the clergy of Spain, under his government, to *become* tributary. See Beausobre, Hist. Reform. liv. i. It should be mentioned that Ximenes published a Polyglott Bible. Cont. Fleur. l. 119, s. 142.

2 A 2

sand are related to have submitted to baptism, and made their
faithless professions of conformity. The triumph was applauded ; the tyrant was feared and imitated ; and his severe
court presented a remarkable contrast to the licentiousness of
Rome. In the opposite extremities of the moral scale the
evangelical Christian will discover, perhaps, an equal departure
from the will of the Saviour. That selfish arrogance, which
swells and hardens under the garb of religion, is scarcely less
at variance with the spirit of the Gospel, than positive sensual
sin. Yet both were the inevitable produce of an ecclesiastical
system, which was compelled to maintain its hold on the
affections of men, by offering, at the same time, encouragement
to their fanaticism, and impunity to their vices.

Benefits
conferred
by the
Church.

Yet should we be very unjust to the Roman Catholic Church,
if we should allow it to be supposed, that she opened no recepta-
cles for the nurture of true excellence—that in her general institutions, especially in her earlier ages, she has overlooked the
moral necessities of man—the truth is far otherwise. We have
repeatedly observed, how commonly in seasons of barbarism
religion was employed in supplying the defects of civil government and diffusing consolation and security. The *Truce of
God* mitigated the fury of private warfare, by limiting the
hours of vengeance, and interposing a space for the operation
of justice and humanity. The name of the Church was associated with peace *—and it was a prouder position, than when
she trampled on the necks of kings. The emancipation of the
Serfs was another cause, equally sacred, in which her exertions were repeatedly employed. In her interference in the
concerns of monarchs and nations, she frequently appeared as
the advocate of the weak, and the adversary of arbitrary power.
Even the much abused law of Asylum † served through a long

* The " Peace of the Church" was first proclaimed early in the eleventh century. The particular edict, which was more formally promulgated at the Council
of Clermont, prohibited all private warfare from sunset every Wednesday till sun-
rise on the Monday following, so that four days a week were sanctified from acts
of violence. On this occasion, we cannot, perhaps, give the Pope much credit for
his motives; but our question is not with motives, but with facts.

† This subject was made a matter of legislation in the Theodosian and Justinian
codes. It drew a decree from Boniface V. in the seventh century ; and in the

period as a check on baronial oppression, rather than an encouragement to crime.

The duty of charity, during the better ages of the Church, was by no means neglected by the secular clergy, while it was the practice and office of the monastic establishments. And even the discipline so strictly inculcated by the earlier prelates, however arbitrary in its exercise and pernicious in its abuse, was not unprofitable in arresting the first steps and restraining the earliest dispositions to sin. Confession and penance, and the awful censures of the Church, when dispensed with discretion, must have been potent instruments for the improvement of uncivilized society.

The original principles of monachism were entirely guiltless of the evils which flowed from it in later ages. In the East, it was the passion for retirement and contemplation which chiefly contributed to people the mountains and wildernesses with holy recluses. In the West, it was rather a desire of association for useful purposes, which caused the construction of so many monasteries—schools were connected with their establishment, and whatever impulse was given to the human understanding proceeded from them. In both, they were effectual in drawing off from the virtual exercise of paganism those nominal proselytes, extremely numerous in all ranks of the laity, who concealed, under the profession of Christianity, a lingering affection for the hereditary superstition. It is, indeed, true, that such an institution could not have originated, except in a very peculiar and unhappy condition of society; that it took root and flourished in general demoralization, and public and private misery. But on the other hand, it is equally true, that it operated for some ages with great efficacy in abating the evils out of which it sprang.

The rule of St. Benedict was well calculated to improve the generation to which it was delivered; and the retreats which he opened gave security and employment to multitudes, in the

Original principles of Monachism.

eighth the Lombard Kings passed some laws to deprive the worst description of criminals of such protection. The Abbots and Bishops were commanded, under severe penalties, to give up such fugitives into the hands of civil justice. Consult Giannone, lib. v., cap. vi.

most calamitous period of Christian history.   No self-torture
or maceration was] prescribed to his disciples by that reasonable legislator—those were the inventions of the later and more
depraved ages of the Church, when the fanaticism of some was
found requisite to counterbalance the profligacy of others.
These changes insensibly took place, as the monks departed
step by step from the independence of their original profession;
first throwing off the character of laymen, and obtaining admission into the ranks of the clergy, by which they became
subject to severe oppression from the bishops*; and then gradually escaping from that yoke to the more indulgent, but not
less arbitrary, despotism of the Pope.   Nevertheless, even
during the decline of the monastic principles, some sparks of
former virtue were revived by the frequent reformation of the
old orders and the establishment of new—some remains of
pristine excellence were very long preserved amid the ruins of
the system.

Mendicants distin-
guished as Mission-
aries.

As we have been compelled on many occasions to notice the
vices of the Mendicant orders, and to observe how soon they
became the zealous agents of the Holy See in all its worst practices and projects, so should we not forget, that the same were
for some time the most active ministers of the Church, in the
discharge of its holiest offices.   It is not without reason, that
Roman Catholic writers vaunt the disinterested devotion of the
early Mendicants—how assiduous they were in supplying the
spiritual wants of the poor, how frequent in prisons and in hospitals, how forward to encounter the fire or the pestilence; how
instant on all those occasions where the peril was imminent,
and the reward not in this world.   They were equally distinguished in another, and not less righteous, duty, the propagation of Christianity among remote and savage nations.   We
have noticed in a former Chapter the method, by which the
Gospel was introduced into the North of Europe, before the

---

* See Guizot (Hist. Moderne, Leç. 14. and 15.), from whom some of the above observations are borrowed. The distinction, such as it now exists, between monks and
lay brethren, was first established as late as the eleventh age; but it seems probable, that the greater part of the monks were already ecclesiastics, and that the
lay brothers were introduced, for the discharge of the inferior and secular offices.

middle of the eleventh century. In the twelfth, we observe Boleslaus, Duke of Poland, opening the path for its reception in Pomerania by the sword; and in like manner, both the Sclavonians and Finlanders were prepared for conversion by conquest. Again, Urban III. consecrated Mainhard, an unsuccessful missionary, Bishop of the Livonians, and proclaimed a holy war against them; the Bishop conquered his See, and promulgated at the head of an army the tidings of evangelical concord. The same methods were pursued by Innocent III. But from that time forward we find much more frequent mention of pious missionaries, whose labours were directed to accomplish their great work by legitimate, or, at least, by peaceful means. It may be true, that some of them were satisfied with mere nominal conversions, and that others had chiefly in view either their own advancement, or the extension of the papal sovereignty. But there were likewise many, who were animated by the most admirable motives, and whose exertions, if they failed of complete success, failed not through any want of disinterested devotion.

The missions of the thirteenth and fourteenth centuries were principally directed to the North of Asia. In 1245, Innocent IV. sent an embassy composed of Dominicans and Franciscans to the Tartars; and a friendly communication was so maintained, that the envoys of Abaca, their king, were present in 1274 at the second Council of Lyons. Nicholas III. (in 1278) and Nicholas IV. (in 1289) renewed those exertions. John of Monte Corvino, a Franciscan, was distinguished during the conclusion of the century by the success of his labours *; and in 1307, Clement V. erected an Archiepiscopal See at Cambalu (Pekin) which he conferred upon that missionary. Seven other Bishops, also Franciscans, were sent to his support by the same Pope; and this distant branch of the hierarchy was carefully nourished by succeeding Pontiffs, especially John XXII. and Benedict XII. It is certain, that the number of Christians was not inconsiderable, both among the Chinese

Missions into Asia; China.

---

* He is recorded to have translated the Gospels and Psalms into the language of the Tartars.

and Moguls, as late as the year 1370,—and they were still increasing, when they were suddenly swept away and almost wholly exterminated by the Mahometan arms *.   Howbeit, the disastrous overthrow of their establishment detracts nothing from the merit of those who constructed it; and it must not be forgotten that the instruments in this work were Mendicants, and, for the most part, Franciscans.   But during the following age (the fifteenth), there are no discoverable traces of the same spirit; nor can we refer with any satisfaction to the compulsory proselytism of the Moors of Spain, or to those spiritual conquests which immediately followed the discoveries of the Portuguese and Spaniards.

When we reflect on the various excellencies ascribed in the preceding paragraph to the Papal system, we cannot fail, however unwillingly, to make two observations; first, that they had declined and almost disappeared before the conclusion of the fifteenth century; next, that the greater part of them were only adapted to times of civil anarchy or general ignorance. But are we therefore to suppose, that, even during the reign of Alexander VI., the great Christian community of the West was wholly destitute of religious instruction, or of examples of sacerdotal piety? that the practice of moral justice, or even of Evangelical righteousness, was entirely confined to the sectaries of Bohemia, or of the Alpine valleys?   The prospect is not quite so gloomy; the destinies of man were not thus abandoned by his Creator.

Mysticism a source of piety.

(1.) Under the respectable name of Mysticism much genuine devotion was concealed, and many ardent and humble aspirations poured forth before the Throne of Grace.   Since the introduction of the supposed works of Dionysius into the west (in the ninth century), the flame has ever continued to burn with more or less of intensity or languor, of purity or the contrary, according to the principles of the age, the policy of the Church,

* It is certain (says Mosheim) that we have no account of any members of the Latin Church residing in Tartary, China, or among the Moguls, later than the year 1370; nor could we ever learn the fate of the Franciscan missionaries, who had been sent thither from Rome.   Yet some doubtful records may seem to prove, that there were Nestorians in China as late as the sixteenth age.

and the character of the prevalent literature.   In the tenth and
eleventh centuries, we may search, indeed, almost in vain for
any useful records of the piety of the Mystics—in the latter,
some traces, which they have left, are strongly marked by
visionary enthusiasm, and bear no comparison with the more
rational devotion of Anselm.   In the twelfth, the age of Abe-
lard and his scholastic disciples, they faintly * opposed the progress of that barren system of speculative morality, which grew
out of the theology of the Schoolmen, and which spread with
such freezing prevalence in the succeeding century.   Yet, while
those heartless teachers (the " Patriarchs of Pedantry") were
classifying the duties of man, distinguishing moral from theological virtues, minutely subtilizing and dissecting, and subdi-
viding their subdivisions—while they were creating subjects
for angry dispute, rather than holy meditation, and labouring
in vain to resolve the difficulties which themselves had created,
the Mystic Moralists formed an opposite, and not inconsiderable, party in the Church.   They ventured openly to combat
the positions of the Scholastics; and they were followed by
those with whom religion addressed the affections, rather than
the reason, and who more willingly abandoned themselves
to an ardent emotion, than engaged in an intellectual controversy.   Thus numerously supported, they commanded the respect of their adversaries; and some of these even deigned to
write commentaries on the Book of the Areopagite.

Though not less opposed to the fashionable " casuistry" of
the fourteenth age, they were then less active, or at least less
prominent; it is probable that they employed that interval in
the purification of their own system, and in cleansing away
those fanciful absurdities which had covered it with dishonour
and ridicule.   At least, in the fifteenth century, they again
came forward with the show of a far more rational piety than
had heretofore distinguished them: insomuch, that the Platonists of the day strove to reconcile the warm devotion of the
Mystical scheme with the plausible ingenuity of the Scholastic,

* Mosheim (Cent. xii. p. ii. chap. iii.) mentions the names of a few of their
works.

and thus to construct a new and more perfect method of moral theology. It is unquestionable that they comprehended, together with the Platonists, many individuals of deep and ardent, though it might be misdirected, piety *, and of the purest simplicity of moral conversation. Yet the age in which they flourished was defective in expositions of Scripture; the Oracles of Truth were insufficiently consulted, or injudiciously interpreted, even by the best among the servants of the Church; and the Book †, by which her pretensions were so soon to be tried, was studied most successfully by her enemies. The merits of the Mystics were not sufficient either to reform, or to preserve, the declining establishment. Their sublime aspirations after the Divine presence removed them too far from the ordinary sphere of human action. In the abstract contemplation of the attributes of the Deity they lost the power of influencing the counsels of men; and their warm imagination was not controlled by that firm and temperate judgment, which is as essential for the good government of Churches, as of empires.

Virtues and piety of the inferior Clergy. (2.) The real heroes of Ecclesiastical history are those whose belief and life are regulated by the laws of Christ; and the very circumstance which constitutes their excellence ensures their obscurity. They are not without their reward even in this world—but it is not in the enjoyment of renown, or in the hope of worldly immortality. It is in silence that they perform their offices of charity; it is in secrecy that they fulfil the commands of their Master; it is in humility that they exalt their fellow-creatures; and as soon as their peaceful course of usefulness is over they disappear, and leave no sort of trace or record of their virtues. It is to the proud, the turbulent, the ambitious, to the fanatic or the hypocrite, that the pages of the annalist are principally consecrated; and those whose life has

* Among the Mystics, Mosheim places Thomas à Kempis, Laurentius Justinianus, Vincent Ferrier, Savonarola, Bernard of Sienna. Among the Platonists, John Gerson, Nicholas Casanus, Dionysius the Carthusian, and others.

† The Bible Divines, who had been declining from the thirteenth century, were now become nearly extinct. Books of Sentences and Sums of Schoolmen were the principal objects of study; and when, in 1515, Erasmus published his edition of the New Testament, and thus "laid the egg which Luther hatched," the clergy exclaimed against the act as dangerous if not impious.

been an insult to their religion stand far more prominent in
the Ecclesiastical picture than those who have loved and obeyed
it.   It is not that many have not existed, even in the worst
ages of the Church, whose almost spontaneous piety has supplied its laws and corrected its abuses, and repaired, as far as
their private influence extended, the ruins of its discipline—
under whose sacred guardianship the treasures of life have
been faithfully dispensed, and whose example has given sanction
to their instructions.   It is not that even monastic depravity
has not been redeemed by thousands of instances of monastic
excellence.   But it is that the vices have been registered and
blazoned, while the opposite qualities have either attracted no
notice, or have generally been so exaggerated, as to revolt our
reason and belief.   Among the numerous progeny of saints, so
venerated by Catholics, so proscribed by Protestants, there
have been some examples of pure Evangelical holiness ; there
have been some cardinals who have dared to deviate from the
rule of profligacy ; there have been many prelates, eminent for
learning and integrity, as the History of National Churches
and General Councils sufficiently demonstrates.   But such characters were far more common among the humble and undistinguished pastors, who were free from the vanity, the enthusiasm, or the ambition, which so often lurks beneath the garb
of *celebrated* sanctity.   Yet the eye of the historian is fixed by
the austere and wonder-working Saint, by the pompous Prelate, and the intriguing and rapacious Cardinal, while it over-
looks the plants which flourish in the lower regions of serenity
and fruitfulness.   Notwithstanding, it is scarcely too much to
affirm, that it was the zeal and piety of the inferior clergy
which so long supported the cumbrous machinery of the Court
and Prelacy of Rome.   It was their virtues which sustained
the vices of their superiors; it was their humble piety which
enabled mitred apostates so long to outrage the name of Christ.
And it was not till the poison had descended to the extremities of the system, and communicated even to the village-pastor
some portion of its hierarchical malignity, that the Church of
Rome reeled to its foundation, and by its weakness and depravity invited and justified the rebellion of its children.

Section III.

On various Attempts to reform, or to subvert, the Church.

I.—An attentive consideration of the facts and remarks advanced in the preceding sections will show that, in almost every particular, whether of internal polity, or ghostly authority, or doctrinal purity, or discipline, or morals, the Church of Rome stood lower at the end of the fifteenth century than at any preceding period. There was one circumstance only in which it had gained ground: the temporal power of St. Peter had been exalted into a durable monarchy, and the limits of the sacred patrimony extended and secured, during the last decay of the spiritual fabric. The era of Boniface VIII. was probably that in which the various pretensions of the See combined with the greatest effect for its aggrandizement. Its territorial domains were then respectable; its clergy were generally exempt from civil jurisdiction; its divine right to worldly power was not universally disputed; its abuses were comparatively inoffensive; its domestic enemies were almost harmless. Then commenced its downfall; and it was precipitated through two centuries of progressive calamity and disgrace. Its constitution, which, by the co-operation of the Pope with the Cardinals and General Councils, presented the means of regeneration, was suspended and perverted by Eugenius IV. and the succeeding pontiffs. In the pageantry of its ceremonies, in the character of its festivals, and its controversies, it receded farther and farther from the soberness of reason and the simplicity of the Gospel: and its moral degeneracy kept pace with its other depravations. On the other hand, the general principles of society were improved, and the laity had begun to shake off the deep slumber of obedience and conformity. The corruption was universal, the danger imminent; many even among the prelates of the Church were not insensible to either; and some, who might perhaps have tolerated the scandal, were moved by the peril. Thus there grew up a large party within the Church who proclaimed the necessity of Reform.

The necessity of *some* reform having aroused the wisest and most virtuous among the churchmen, questions might naturally have grown up among them, to what extent, and on what principles their work ought to be conducted? Yet on this subject no important difference appears to have arisen. A sacred barrier was placed before them which separated that which might be touched from that which was inviolate; and it was guarded by irresistible prejudices. On this side lay the field of discipline and temporalities—on the other were the mysterious regions of Faith, embracing all that mass of mingled truth and superstition, which the Infallible Mother had imposed with equal rigour, as equally holy, upon her believing children. Into the former space the Fathers of Constance and Basle entered with some boldness of upright determination; but it had been sacrilege and heresy to have invaded the latter. Hence it arose that the most dangerous wounds were not examined, perhaps not even suspected. "In a mortal disease lenitives were administered and oil applied*;" and if some outward impurities were feebly remedied, their inward causes were purposely covered from all inquiry with a venerable veil. Thus, while all the genius and learning of the Church were combined to repress the abuses of Pontifical power—while the Pontiff was essaying every art in defence of those abuses—while anathemas were interchanged, and the contending parties seemed to be emulating each other's rancour—no question was for a moment started as to the legitimacy of that power. It was thought much to deny the infallibility of the Pope, to contest his absolute despotism; but his supremacy was as sacred as the Church itself, and the Church was identified with the religion. In this delusion both parties were equally sincere; and though the high Papists were certainly the farthest removed from any consideration of Gospel truth, it must be admitted that their opponents were almost equally destitute of evangelical principles. The *Church* was the exclusive object to which their education, their interests, their prejudices, their

> Nature and extent of the reform attempted by the churchmen.

* The Bishop of Segovia addressed this expression to the Fathers of Trent, who, under still more dangerous circumstances, were following the same policy. See Padre Paolo, b. vi.

enthusiasm, their very piety attached them. Within it whatever was holy and righteous was concentrated. Without it all
was blindness and rebellion and blasphemy; and their belief
was not so much that the Church was founded on the Bible,
as that the Bible was comprehended in the Church.

From men with such principles, it was to be expected that
those who pleaded Scripture as an independent testimony of
truth—that those who spoke even of truth as independent of
ecclesiastical authority, would meet with no sympathy, and
little mercy.   Accordingly, their advances towards reform
were made in the very bosom of orthodoxy. The most frivolous
superstitions were rather encouraged than restrained; no innovation was introduced which could have startled the bigotry of
the most rigid Romanist. Nothing was even remotely intended
for change, except the discipline. Yet even this department
presented ample employment for the hand of the reformer, had
he entered upon his work honestly and fearlessly. Howbeit,
even on this ground, unhallowed as it was by any spiritual
prejudices, those fathers did not penetrate, in their boldest
attempts, to the roots of the evil. They confined their hostility
to the abuses which were of modern origin. Their veneration
for antiquity, that professional reverence for established practices, which so strongly characterized the clergy of that Church,
forbade them to search very deeply or very generally. They
endeavoured, indeed, to correct some disorders which had notoriously grown up during the two or three preceding ages; it
was a specious object to abolish the corruptions of Avignon, to
repair the ruins of the schism! But they are awed by the
holy obscurity of earlier times; and the clumsy forgery of a
monk of the eighth century arrested the most enlightened
among the doctors of Constance and Basle.

The failure
of their
projects,
Nevertheless, the schemes of the reformers, though bearing
no proportion to the real emergencies of the Church, were
wise as far as they went, and calculated to prolong the existing
system. Had they been cordially carried into effect, some
useful improvements would have been introduced, some unpopular scandals removed; the most distinguished ecclesiastics
would have rallied round the Pope, and the laity would have

respected, for a certain time, the concessions and the union of the clergy. But even this imperfect result did not take place. It has been shown with how great pertinacity the Pope and his profligate adherents fought the battle of corruption, and defended every abuse which was fraught with present profit, and future and early destruction *. In the struggle which divided the Church the policy of the hour prevailed. The unity of power and design, the keen sense of personal interest, the tyranny of inveterate prejudice, gave the triumph to the less virtuous, the less provident, even the less numerous party; and after the fathers of Basle had reluctantly dispersed, and their creature Felix V. resigned the name of Pontiff, the bark of St. Peter was urged forward by a gale of unruffled prosperity, until suddenly, and soon, and in the moment of most exulting security, it was dashed against the rocks and shattered irreparably.

A circumstance, which may have suspended the downfall of the Church was the elevation of two Popes (Nicholas V. and Pius II.), whose reputation and pursuits were in harmony with the popular passion for reviving letters. Their personal qualities concealed for a moment the vices of the system, and substituted in public observation the splendour of a literary court. Again, the overthrow of the Eastern Empire, and the danger of Turkish invasion, became powerful instruments for diverting attention from ecclesiastical grievances : and the clamour for reform was, for a while, drowned in specious appeals to the policy of princes, and the enthusiasm of their subjects— *and its consequences.*

---

* It might seem unnecessary to fortify this position by any authority. Yet the opinion of one of the most clear-sighted prelates who have ever adorned and defended the Roman Catholic Church, may not by some be thought superfluous. "C'est ainsi (says Bossuet) que dans le quinzième siècle le Cardinal (Julien), le plus grand homme de son temps, en déplorait les maux, et en prévoyait la suite funeste : par où il semble avoir prédit ceux, que Luther allait apprêter à toute la Chrestienté, en commençant par l'Allemagne ; et il ne s'est pas trompé lorsqu'il a crû, que *la Réformation méprisée, et la haine redoublée contre le Clergé allait enfanter une secte plus redoutable à l'Eglise que celle des Bohémiens.* Elle est venue cette secte sous la conduite de Luther ; et en prenant le titre de Reforme, elle s'est vantée d'avoir accompli les vœux de toute la Chrestienté, puisque la réformation étoit desirée par les peuples, par les docteurs, et par les prélats Catholiques." Histoire des Variations, liv. i.

but for a while only. The spirit of the age, when once decided
and pronounced, can neither be long eluded, nor safely resisted.
A little time may be gained: the progress of improvement may
be slightly retarded; but it will presently spring forward the
more rapidly, as it has been the longer held back. Now the
preceding century (the fourteenth) was one of mixed and conflicting principles ; it had not assumed any marked or definite
character; and thus the Church marched safely through it,
with all its depravity on its head. But in the fifteenth, the
principles of society were fixed; the general voice of Christendom proclaimed the necessity of reformation; the high-church
dominant party presumed to disobey, or, with equal impolicy,
descended to evasion; and through their own perversity they
fell. And whether it was that they were too blind to see their
danger, or too obstinate to sacrifice their vices, they fell by a
fate which few will affect to deplore, and which none can deem
undeserved.

Howbeit, since the secession of the Protestant communities,
a gradual though tardy reformation has been virtually accomplished in the bosom of the Roman Catholic Church. Its most
extravagant pretensions have been generally withdrawn; and
if no important change has been introduced into the body of
its doctrine, yet the abuse of some of its tenets has been in
some places mitigated; and its discipline has been every where
amended and purified. When it had lost the half of its dominions, it turned itself to improve and preserve the rest—from
the blow which cleft its triple crown it first began to learn the
wisdom of moderation; and to discover in sackcloth and ashes
that its wisest counsellors and truest friends had ever been
those who had warned it to repent and amend.

Attempts
to trace the
continuity
of the Pro-
testant opi-
nions to the
apostolical
times.

II. Several learned and pious Protestants have attempted
to trace the uninterrupted descent of their doctrines, or at least
of some essential portion of them, even from the apostolic
times. Great ingenuity and research have been employed for
this purpose, partly to make it thus manifest that the Almighty,
while he permitted so much iniquity to be perpetrated in his
name, did still nourish in secret his true and everlasting Church;

partly, that the perpetual succession of the ministry might not seem wanting to the reformed communities; partly, because the reverence for antiquity, especially in ecclesiastical matters, has a powerful, perhaps an undue, influence on the greater part of mankind. For these reasons very much has been written about the " Lutheranism which was prevalent before Luther;" the unbroken series of " Witnesses of the truth;" the unceasing *protestations* which have been silently breathed in all ages, against the abuses of Rome *.

It is unquestionable, that, so early as the beginning of the Various precursors

---

* This subject has been treated by Bossuet, in the eleventh chapter of his *Variations*, eloquently, learnedly, and of course not impartially : and thus, while he has unquestionably established many of his positions, he has advanced others which are untenable. (1.) Respecting the *Albigeois*. He has established that they were wholly distinct from the Vaudois : and that they held many opinions which are condemned by all Protestants. But he has failed in proving their Manichean origin—still more their Manichean doctrines—for to make out this identity he has invented so many *marks* or *characters* of Manicheism, wholly unconnected with its original and only true mark, the doctrine of the two principles, as to embrace under that name errors entirely dissociated from it. He calls them indeed *new* Manicheans, and admits that " they had softened some of their errors." But they had parted with *the* characteristic error, or, in fact, they had never held it. For the same reason he has failed in confounding them with the Catharists, Bulgari, &c., who were the real descendants of the Paulicians. (2.) Respecting the *Vaudois*. He shows the great uncertainty, perhaps the entire vanity, of their claims to a separate descent from the Antenicene Church. He shows that, at their first appearance, their differences with Rome were less numerous and important than they became afterwards : that they adopted some new opinions after their union with the Protestants : that they were the same with the *Leonists* and the *Insabbatés*. But he does not establish his assertion, that they were founded by Peter Waldo of Lyons. (3.) Respecting the *Bohemian Brethren*. He rightly supposes, that the Hussites were not descended from the Vaudois ; and that the " Brethren" made some doctrinal concessions on their union with the 'Lutherans. But when he asserts that Huss had no doctrinal difference with the Church, except on the single communion ; and that the same was the *only* subject of disaffection with the Calixtines ; he has not fairly represented either the one or the other. The " heresies" of Huss were less bold and numerous than those of Wicliff; those of the Calixtines than those of the Thaborites ; and that respecting the cup was the most publicly professed ; but it was associated with others less notorious. In the mean time, we must admit, that he has, in our opinion, established his two leading positions, viz., that the Protestants fail in their attempts to prove an uninterrupted succession ; and that those whom they claim as their ancestors differed from them in numerous points of doctrine. We might notice some rash assertions on less important points—but our readers are aware that they should be cautious in following Bossuet on his own unsupported assertion—on that *parole*, " toujours éloquente" (as Voltaire truly says of it) " et quelquefois trompeuse."

of the Re-
formation.
twelfth century, some of the Protestant opinions were openly professed, and atoned for by death.   And it is equally certain that, from the preaching of Peter de Bruis to that of Luther, there have subsisted in some quarter or other of the western community various bodies of Sectaries*, who were at open or secret variance with the Church of Rome—who rejected, according to their respective principles, in part or in whole, her tenets, or her ceremonies, or her ministry.   It may be doubted, whether the Albigeois, in spite of the crusades of Innocent, and the Inquisition of Toulouse, were ever entirely extirpated.   The Vaudois were certainly preserved through the perils of four centuries of oppression.   The ashes of Wicliff were not lost in their rough descent into the ocean; and the spirit, which rose out of the funeral flames of Huss, survived to expand in the bosoms of his compatriots.

From this short catalogue we have purposely excluded innumerable denominations of heresy, of which there were scarcely any which did not, in some one respect, or in more than one, anticipate the Confession of Augsbourg.   The various forms of Mysticism were universally opposed, in their progress as in their origin, to the outward pageantry of the Roman Church. The spiritual Franciscans, who questioned the omnipotence of the Pope, and denounced the corruptions no less than the wealth of the Clergy, are even placed by Mosheim among the forerunners of the Reformation.   At least, it is certain, that their continued insubordination, combined with such high pretensions to sanctity, had its effect in preparing the downfall of Papacy; and thus they may properly be numbered among the instruments appointed to divide its strength, and betray its fortress by intestine discord to the foe without.

---

* It might seem scarcely necessary to remark, that we have frequently, in the course of this work, used the word *Sect* in its original and proper sense—of a body of men united by certain tenets,—the sense in which Tertullian used it (Apol. cap. v.) when he called the whole Christian community *hanc Sectam.*   Only it is a common error to connect with this term the idea of *cutting off*, and thus to attach a degrading notion to it.   In the same manner, the term Heresy (in its origin equally inoffensive), we have commonly applied to those, whom the church has denounced as heretics—without any reference whatever to the nature of their opinions.

Again, among the sects, which we have mentioned as the more genuine precursors of Luther and Zuinglius*, there was not one which furnished in all respects a faithful model for *their* more perfect reformation. There were points on which they differed from each other. There were points on which they differed both from Roman Catholics and Protestants. There were even points in which they agreed with the former, and fell far short of the subsequent doctrine of the latter. But there were also many articles of essential importance, on which they opposed, with premature independence, their reason and their Bible to the abuses, and even to the authority, of the Church.

Such were the sects, from which the Protestants claim their descent, and to which they are justly grateful for having prepared their path, and set the example of non-conformity. But they sprang up before their season; their imperfect lights were unable to preserve them from error ; curiosity and knowledge were yet too scantily distributed among the mass of the people to give them a substantial footing *there ;* and thus they fell before the established despotism, and shed their precious blood, both as an eternal testimony against the Church, and as the seed of more enlarged principles in a more enlightened age.

In our journey back towards the apostolical times, these separatists conduct us as far as the beginning of the twelfth century; but when we would advance further, we are intercepted by a broad region of darkness and uncertainty. A spark of hope is indeed suggested by the history of the Vaudois. Their origin is not ascertained by any authentic record; and being immemorial, it *may* have been coeval with the introduction of Christianity. Among their own traditions there is one, which agrees well with their original and favourite tenet, which objects to the possession of property by ecclesiastics. It is this—that their earliest fathers, offended at the liberality with which Constantine endowed the Church of Rome, and at the

The Vaudois.

---

* Semler (Secul. xv. cap. iv. p. 218) enumerates a variety of opinions hostile to the Church, in the design to show that Luther was not so much the first who came into the design of vindicating the public Christian religion, as that he trod in footsteps clearly traced before him— so that those are in error, who consider the Reformation as a political, rather than a religious, movement.

worldliness with which Pope Sylvester accepted those endowments, seceded into the Alpine solitudes; that they there lay
concealed and secure for so many ages through their insignificance and their innocence.   This may have been so—it is not
even very improbable, that it was so.   But since there is not
one direct proof of their existence during that long space; since
they have never been certainly discovered by the curiosity of
any writer, nor detected by the inquisitorial eye of any orthodox
bishop, nor named by any Pope or Council, or any Church record, chronicle or memorial, we are not justified in attaching
any historical credit to their mere unsupported tradition.   It is
sufficient to prove, that they had an earlier existence than the
twelfth century; but that they had then been perpetuated through
eight or nine centuries, uncommemorated abroad, and without
any national monument to attest their existence, is much more
than we can venture, on such evidence, to assert.   Here then
the golden chain of our apostolical descent disappears; and
though it may exist, buried in the darkness of those previous
ages, and though some writers have seemed to discern a few
detached links which they have diligently exhibited, there is
still much wanting to complete the continuity *.

* The claims of the Protestant Mountaineers in Dauphiné appear to be somewhat stronger than those of the Vaudois; because (as has been mentioned) neither
the worship of images, nor the pontifical jurisdiction was established in France, so
early as in Italy—probably not till the middle of the ninth century. Now, as soon
afterwards as the year 1025 we have records of the existence, at Arras, of certain
erroneous opinions, which were supposed to have proceeded from "the Alpine
borders of Italy."   In this case, the interval of silence is reduced to rather less
than two centuries: and though this space will seem to many sufficient to destroy
all historical ground for asserting an uninterrupted succession, nevertheless upon
the whole, we are disposed to consider it as very probable, that on the sides and
under the brows of those desolate mountains there may have existed in every age a
few obscure peasants, whom all the innovations of Rome have never reached.
Different persons will attach different degrees of importance to this result—we
therefore refer the curious reader, with great pleasure, to Mr. Gilly's "Memoirs of
Neff," where the subject is argued with learning and earnestness.   At the same
time it is proper to mention what those opinions really were which were condemned
at Arras in 1025 ; lest it should be supposed, that they were at variance only with
the Roman Catholic Church, and strictly in accordance with apostolical truth.
(1.) It was asserted, that the sacrament of baptism was useless, and of no efficacy
to salvation. (2.) That the sacrament of the Lord's Supper was equally unnecessary. (It would seem that the objections of the heretics on this point went beyond

When we turn to the history of the Albigeois, we find there The
still less to flatter our hopes, or encourage our pursuit. For ^{Albigeois.}
if we adopt the more probable opinion respecting the origin of
that sect—that it was engendered by the contrast, so perceptible even to the least instructed, between the character of the
Church and the first principles of Christianity—its birth must
at least have succeeded the manifest corruption of the Church;
nor is there any evidence to prove it more ancient than the
twelfth or perhaps eleventh century. If, on the other hand, we
should identify those Dissenters (as some have done) with the
Cathari, the Gazari, Paterini, Publicani, and others of the same
age, who were collateral branches of the Paulician family, we
are not, indeed, any longer at a loss to trace the succession to
very high antiquity. It is also true, that the contempt of
images, the disbelief in transubstantiation, and some other protestant principles, were faithfully perpetuated in that heretical
race. But these attractive characteristics were tainted, more
or less deeply, by the poison of Manicheism : and since it is
our object to establish a connexion with the primitive Church,
we shall scarcely attain it through those, whose fundamental
principle was unequivocally rejected by that Church, as irrational and impious.

If the claim again be reduced from a succession of sects to a Mysticism.
series of pious individuals, who in every age of the Church

the mere denial of the change of substance.) (3.) That there was no peculiar
sanctity in churches, (4.) nor holiness in the altar. (5.) That the use of bells,
&c., to summon the people to worship, was objectionable. (6.) That the sacred
orders of the ministry were not of divine institution. (7.) That the Church rites
of sepulture are to be ascribed to the avarice of the clergy. (8.) That penance
was altogether inefficacious. (This appears to have been an inference from their
denial of the efficacy of baptism.) (9.) That alms, vicarious penance, &c., are
of no use to the dead (which involved the denial of purgatory.) (10.) That marriage in general was contrary to the evangelical and apostolical laws. (11.) That
saint-worship is to be confined to the apostles and martyrs—not extended to the
confessors, *i. e.*, holy men, not martyrs. (12.) That ⸱ hurch music is reprehensible.
(13.) That the cross is not an object of worship, (14) nor the Saviour's image on
the cross, nor any other image. (15.) That the orders of the hierarchy are objectionable. (16.) That the doctrine of works (Justitia) supersedes that of divine
grace, and every man's hope of salvation lies in his own deserts (see Labbæi
Concil. tom. xix. p. 423. Ex Dacherii Spicileg. 2d ed. vol. i. p. 607.) So mixed
and various is the substance of those opinions, to which learned writers on the
subject appeal with so much satisfaction.

may have secretly protested against its abuses and its worldliness, it becomes equally impossible to prove its existence, and
to deny its probability. The aspirations of mysticism, sometimes degraded into absurdity, sometimes exalted into the purest
piety, have unquestionably pervaded and warmed every portion
of the ecclesiastical system, from the earliest æra even to the
present. Its perpetual existence alone shows, that in private
bosoms, and especially in the abstractions of the monastery, a
disaffection towards the ceremonies, towards the grosser abuses,
and perhaps towards some of the sacraments of the Church,
has been unceasingly nourished, even within its own precincts.
But the names of these contemplative and unambitious individuals are, for the most part, lost in oblivion; and even if they
were not so, the truth of the Protestant principles would gain
little assurance, and their dignity little increase, from so slender, imperfect and precarious a connexion with the apostolical
purity.

Upon the whole, then, it seems impossible to establish on
historical ground the theory of an uninterrupted transmission
of the original faith from the primitive times to those of Luther.
Indications of its occasional existence may be discovered, but
no proof of its continuity. Yet is this no disparagement to
those faithful witnesses who were called into existence in the
iron days of the Church. They bequeathed to their more fortunate successors their principles and their example. Nor
were they in their own times without influence, nor even without peril to the pontifical predominance. Innocent III. did
not despise their infancy: he beheld it, on the contrary, with
such anxious apprehension as to divert the engine with which
he was armed for other purposes to their destruction. He
knew the real character of his own despotism, and the secret of
its weakness; and while, by his clamour for the crusades, he
subdued the understanding of mankind, his own deeper penetration taught him from what quarter the storm must really
issue, which would finally overthrow his throne: and in that
little cloud which raised its prophetic hand in the horizon of
heresy, he read the denunciation of future wrath, and heard
the distant murmur of advancing reason.

III. It was not till the Popes had established their authority On the treatment of heretics by the Church. in most of the Courts of Europe, that the principles of persecution were displayed in their full extent, or the practice attended with much barbarity. The previous efforts of Alexander III. and Calixtus II. betrayed the disposition and showed the sting —but it was not yet armed and poisoned. The execution of the mystics of Orleans, at a still earlier period, was perpetrated by the king and the bishop, without any excuse of pontifical interference. In fact, the unity of the Church was not protected by the authorized use of the sword until the reign of Innocent III. His great power enabled him not only to turn a casual storm against a particular sect of the heretics of the day, but to engage the temporal weapon, by a general and perpetual edict, in the service of the spiritual.

The third Canon of the Lateran Council, held by that Pontiff, contained an injunction to the effect " that temporal lords The third Canon of the Fourth Lateran Council. be admonished, and, if necessary, compelled by censures, to take a public oath to exterminate heretics from their territories. If any one, being thus required, shall refuse to purge his land, he shall be excommunicated by the Metropolitan and his suffragans; and if he shall give proofs of still further contumacy, the Pope shall absolve his subjects from their fealty *."

. . . Of Roman Catholic writers, those who would willingly cleanse their Church from the stain of blood, and those who disapprove of its claims to temporal authority, are equally perplexed by this edict. But while there are some who affect to doubt its genuineness; while others affirm that it was directed only against feudatories, not against the supreme Lord; others that it was dictated by Innocent to a council so servile, as even to impeach its authority; others, again, that it was only levelled against the contemporary heretics, whose detested Manicheism

---

* The words are these ;—" Si vero Dominus Temporalis requisitus et monitus ab ecclesia terram suam purgare neglexerit ab hac heretica fœditate, per metropolitanos et cæteros episcopos comprovinciales excommunicationis vinculo innodetur. Et si satisfacere contempserit infra annum, significetur hoc summo pontifici : et extunc ipse vassallos ab ejus fidelitate denuntiet absolutos, et terram exponet catholicis occupendam...salvo jure domini principalis, *dummodo* super hoc ipse nullum præstet obstaculum, nec aliquod impedimentum opponat : eadem nihilominus lege servata circa eos, qui non habent dominos principales.' See Labb. Concil. Collect., tom. xxii., p. 981, et seq., et supra chap. xviii., p. 349.

deserved the sentence—a more plausible excuse may be alleged in the consent or silence of the princes and ambassadors who were present at the council. In fact, on Innocent's death, which followed soon afterwards, Honorius, his successor, applied to Frederic II. to insert the Canon among the constitutions of the empire. He did so. And having thus embarked the State in the same conspiracy with the Church, and degraded it, besides, to be the mere executioner of the sentences of its accomplice, he loaded the former with ignominy, and shared, without in any respect diminishing, the guilt of the latter.

Henceforward, the ecclesiastical and civil authorities legally and systematically co-operated in the destruction of many bold and virtuous spirits, who for three successive centuries asserted, under different forms and names, the private right of reading and interpreting the Gospel. Henceforward, the secular arm was ever in subservient attendance on the decisions of sacerdotal barbarity; and it was in this subordinate ministry of an independent power, that the real executioners found a pretext to proclaim their own unsullied charity—that *their* hands, at least, were undefiled; that the Church was merciful and long suffering, and that the penal flames were lighted by the vengeance of the temporal powers!

The unity of the Church.

The Inquisition embodied the principles and practice of persecution: and notwithstanding the abhorrence which it raised in some places, it was an engine of good service in protecting the Unity of the Roman Catholic Church. That fatal principle, of which the name at least, and even the seeds may be traced to the earliest ages, occasioned more than half the crimes that stain the ecclesiastical annals. Every hope of salvation was confined to the bosom of the Church; should any dare to abandon that exclusive sanctuary, their heritage was eternal perdition—if, then, by the fear or endurance of mere temporary torture, men could be preserved from eternal inflictions, was not the office salutary? was not the duty peremptory? Alas! for the presumption of those who were sincere in this profession. But if any there were who falsely joined the cry with no further object than to support the system by which they profited, there may be pardon reserved for them in the mercy of God, but there is no term in the vocabulary of crime which can express their guilt.

It would be an insult on human nature not to suppose that among the ministers of the Roman Church there were many who individually abhorred the practice, and softened by their private tolerance the rigour of the ecclesiastical code. But the high and dominant party in the Church was always that which stretched the principle of its "Unity" to its extreme length, and pursued the victims of that principle with as much severity as the policy of princes and the endurance of the laity would permit. As in the thirteenth century, so was it in the fifteenth; as in the Lateran, so was it in the halls of Constance; as with Innocent, so with Gerson and Clemangis, and the reformers of Innocent's abuses*. The spirit *possessed* the Church: thence it emanated and swelled the bosoms of its ministers; and the more devoted was the individual to the service of that Church, the more thoroughly was his soul impregnated with the venom.

It was not that even these ecclesiastics were necessarily destitute of private virtues, or that they lost, in the exercise of official barbarity, all sense of justice and all feeling of mercy. They might be compassionate, they might even be charitable.

* It must not be understood that Innocent III. deliberately corrupted, or even relaxed, the ecclesiastical discipline; on the contrary, he published many excellent decrees for its severer observance; only, by unduly aggrandizing papal authority, he rendered those decrees in effect nugatory. Thus, for instance, respecting the abuses of pluralities and non-residence—the fourteenth canon of the *Third* Lateran Council (held by Alexander III.) denounces both those practices in very strong terms, as in direct violation of the ancient canons, and then adds—" Cum igitur ecclesia, vel ecclesiasticum ministerium committi debuerit, talis ad hoc persona quæratur, quæ residere in loco, et curam ejus per seipsum valeat exercere"—on the penalty of deprivation to the minister, and loss of patronage to the patron. Innocent III., thirty-six years afterwards, published a canon (the twenty-ninth) in the *Fourth* Lateran, on the same subject. Herein he referred to the law of Alexander, mentioned the little fruit which it had produced, and decreed in confirmation of it, " ut quicunque receperit aliquod beneficium habens curam animarum annexam, si prius tale beneficium obtinebat, eo sit jure ipso privatus: et si forte illud retinere contenderit, alio etiam spolietur." He added, moreover, that no one should hold two dignities in the same church, even without cure of souls. But then he concluded with a *salvo*, which Alexander had not interposed, in favour of the Pope's dispensing power; " Circa sublimes tamen et literatas personas, quæ majoribus sunt beneficiis honorandæ, cum ratio postulaverit, *per sedem apostolicam poterit dispensari.*"

It might be that they were only cruel and unjust, and uncharitable, in as far as they were imbued with the high ecclesiastical
principle—in as far as they identified the religion of the Gospel with their own modification of it—in as far as they mistook
the interests of their order for the honour of Christ.

General
spirit of intolerance.

A practice sanctified by the authority and enforced by the
zeal of the sacred body, found innumerable advocates among
the laity, and it was never in more general favour than at the
end of the fifteenth century. Even the philosophers of that
age were hostile to the exercise, or perhaps ignorant of the
name, of tolerance. The Popes pressed with unrelenting rigour
the hereditary usage; and the arm of the Inquisition was
lengthened, and its ingenuity sharpened and refined. In the
rarity of Christian * victims—for the Hussites were not victims,
but enemies and warriors—attention was turned to the perversity of the Jews; and Sixtus IV., Innocent VIII., and Alexander VI. added to their other offences the crime of persecution. Persecution was, indeed, at this time almost the only
proof which the Court of Rome affected to exhibit of its attachment to religion. It was become the apparent object of the
spiritual government; and the perpetrator of every enormity
sought atonement for his guilt in the blood of the misbeliever.
It was become a part of ecclesiastical morality; and it was
now founded not so much on hostility to any particular opinion, or any bigoted belief in the opposite, as on the determination that no new opinion should be broached with impunity.
It was not against the results of thought, but against the liberty
of thinking, that the bolts were now really levelled. The rebellion was more detestable than the heresy; and the wretches
who dared to plead their Bible against their Church were

---

* It should not, however, be forgotten that the Vaudois suffered several severe
outrages during this period. In 1400 they were attacked in the Valley of Pragela
and driven to the summits of the mountains, where many died from starvation.
In 1460 the Separatists in the Val Fressinière (on the French side) were persecuted by a Franciscan, under the authority of the Archbishop of Embrun. Every
thing that fraud and calumny could invent seems on that occasion to have been
practised against them. In 1487 and 1488 fresh bulls were issued, followed by
military violence. Albert de Capitaneis, Archdeacon of Cremona, was deputed
by Innocent VIII. to command the attack. But the fortune of war appears for
this time to have favoured the oppressed. See Milner, Cent. xiii., chap. iii.

marked out not for conversion, but for massacre*. The end, being holy, sanctified the means; and in pursuing the details of religious warfare, we shall commonly observe, that if the deeds of pure atrocity are equally balanced, the superiority in fraud, perfidy, and perjury, is without any comparison on the side of the Catholics.

IV. It is needless here to repeat the names of the anti-papal adherents of Louis the Bavarian, or of the more eminent reformers of Constance and Basle. Nor shall we recur to the premature, but not fruitless, efforts of Wiclif and Huss. But it is proper to make some mention of those individuals who were distinguished for their opposition to ecclesiastical abuses during the latter part of the fifteenth century. These were the immediate precursors of Luther; and though differing on many matters from each other and from him; and though his inferiors in evangelical wisdom, in intellectual power and personal character, they were not without their use in preparing the path for his triumph. *Some individual Reformers of the Fifteenth century.*

In 1479, John of Wesalia incurred, by some opinions unfavourable to the pretensions of the hierarchy, the indignation of the Monastic Orders. He pronounced indulgences to be of no avail—that the Pope, Bishops, and Priests were not instruments for the obtaining of salvation. He spoke with disparagement of the fasts, of the holy oil, of pilgrimages, of the Pope and his Councils. He advocated the Greek doctrine on the procession of the Holy Ghost. Moreover, he was a zealous *John of Wesalia.*

---

* " On ne voulait point convertir les Bohémiens (says Sismondi), on voulait les traîner sur le bûcher." We may plead the authority of that historian for the justice of some of these last remarks. See likewise Semler, Secul. xv., cap. iii., p. 51, &c. &c. Still it should be observed that a certain latitude of private judgment, on certain subjects, was generally indulged to the members of the Church, as, for instance, to many Mystics; but this was either when the " Latitudinarians" were in themselves deemed harmless, or when the opinions touched none of the essentials of the ecclesiastical system, none of the sources of dignity, revenue, &c. Thus, for example, in the dispute between Luther and Cardinal Carvajal, there were two grand subjects of difference, indulgences and justification. Luther was disposed to attach by far the highest importance to the latter; but the Cardinal assured him, that if he would retract his error respecting indulgences, the other affair could be easily arranged.

Nominalist at a moment when the violence of the rival scholastics equalled any recorded display of theological rancour.
He was brought to trial; among his judges Monks and Real-
ists preponderated; " if Christ (said he) were now present,
and ye were to treat him as ye treat me, He might be condemned by you as a heretic." He was pronounced guilty; and
in spite of a tardy retractation, was committed to penitential
confinement in a monastery, where he presently died.

John Wes-   John Wesselus, of Gröningen, was more eminent in genius
selus.   and learning, and more fortunate in the circumstances of his
fate, since he enjoyed the friendship of Sixtus IV., and died in
peace (in 1489) in his native city.   His general attainments
were such as to acquire for him the title of the " Light of the
World;" and among the numerous witnesses of the truth*, it
is he who has been more peculiarly designated the Forerunner
of Luther.   The resemblance between them was, indeed, remarkable, not only as to the conclusions at which they arrived,
but as to the steps by which they reached them.   Insomuch,
that Luther himself, in a preface, in which he recommended
to more general attention some of the works of Wesselus, used
the following expressions: — " It is very plain that he was
taught of God, as Isaiah prophesied that Christians should
be; and as in my case, so with him, it cannot be supposed
that he received his doctrines from men.   If I had read his
works before, my enemies might have supposed that I had
learnt every thing from Wesselus, such a perfect coincidence
there is in our opinions.   As to myself, I not only derive pleasure, but strength and courage from this publication.   It is
now impossible for me to doubt whether I am right in the
points which I have inculcated, when I see so entire an agree-

---

* The " Catalogus Testium Veritatis," by Flacius, is intended, we presume,
to contain every name and thing which has in any age and by any means done
any ill to Papacy.   Out of the various particulars of this Catalogue (which
begins with *Sacra Scriptura* and ends with *Concilia XV. Seculi*), we select as
specimens the following names:—Constantine, Gregory the Great, Bede, Charlemagne, Claudius of Turin, Hincmar, Paschasius Radbertus, Otho Frisingensis,
Nicholaus Orem, Scotus, Occam, Dante, Petrarch, Wiclif, Gerson, Ziska, Peter
of Luna, Æneas Sylvius, Platina, Trithemius, Wesalia, Wesselus, Savonarola,
Machiavel, and above all, *Germaniæ vulgus*.   Reasons are alleged under each of
these names for its insertion in the honourable list.

ment in sentiment, and almost the same words used by this eminent person, who lived in a different age, in a distant country, and in circumstances very unlike my own. I am surprised that this excellent Christian writer should be so little known—the reason may be that he lived without blood and contention, for this is the only thing in which he differed from me. . . . ." This was written in 1522, when Luther had made some progress towards evangelical perfection. His testimony makes it unnecessary to particularize the opinions of Wesselus; but we may relate one anecdote respecting him, which proves that the humble, unambitious spirit of the Gospel had penetrated to his heart, and influenced his conduct under powerful temptation.

When Sixtus IV. was raised to the chair, not forgetful of his ancient friendship with Wesselus, he offered to grant him any request. Wesselus replied by a solemn exhortation to the Pontiff faithfully to discharge his weighty duties. " That (replied Sixtus) shall be my care : but do you ask something for yourself."—" Then (rejoined Wesselus) I beg you to give me out of the Vatican library a Greek and a Hebrew Bible."— "You shall have them (said Sixtus); but is not this folly? Why do you not ask for some Bishopric, or something of that sort ?"—" Because I want not such things." It is recorded that the Hebrew Bible which was given in consequence of this dialogue, was long preserved in the library at Gröningen*.

John Laillier, licentiate in theology, advanced at Paris in July, 1485, various offensive petitions, derogating from the power and primacy of St. Peter; asserting an equality of ranks in the ecclesiastical hierarchy, the uselessness of even pontifical indulgences, and the human institution of confession. He

John Laillier.

---

* " Hæc nobis erunt curæ ; tu pro te aliquod pete. Rogo, ergo, inquit Wesselus, ut mihi detis ex Bibliotheca Vaticana Græca et Hebræa Biblia. Ea, inquit Sixtus, tibi dabuntur—Sed tu stulte ; quare non petis episcopatum aliquem, aut simile quidpiam ? Respondit Wesselus, quia iis non indigeo." See *Vita Wesseli* inter *Vitas Professorum Groningens.* The story is there related as one that was frequently told by Wesselus himself. Some valuable abstracts from the writings of this reformer are given by Milner, History of the Church, end of Cent. xv., and Semler, Cent. xv., cap. iv., p. 212-219. Bayle calls him " un des plus habiles hommes du quinzième siècle."

argued that the decrees and decretals were mere mockeries, that the Roman Church was not the key of the other Churches, with other matters of a like nature, and he defended his opinions in public disputation against the doctors of the Sorbonne. We find nine of his propositions expressly specified, together with the censure affixed to each of them, and we shall here insert two or three of the most curious :—*Proposition* (III.) " Rich saints are now canonized and poor saints abandoned ; wherefore I am not obliged to believe that such are saints. If the Pope receives money, though he should mount on twenty scaffolds to canonize a saint, I am not bound to believe him such ; nor is he, who disbelieves, in sin." *Censure.* " This proposition is false, offensive to pious ears, injurious to the Holy Apostolical See, contrary to the piety of the faithful,— and the third part of it, according to the sense which it presents, is heretical." *Proposition* (V.) " The priests of the Eastern Church do no sin in marrying; and I think that we, in the Western Church, should be equally free from sin, if we were to marry." *Censure.* " The first part of the proposition in the sense which it presents, viz., that the Eastern priests marry after taking orders, is false. The second, which is the profession of the author's faith, makes him guilty of error ; if he adds obstinacy, of heresy." *Proposition* (IX.) "One is no more obliged to believe the legends of the saints than the chronicles of the kings of France." *Censure.* " This proposition is false, and capable of offending pious ears ; it derogates from the authority of the Church, and, if taken universally, is even heretical."

Sentence of condemnation was passed in the following year, and the offender was commanded to retract. He did so with perfect humility. The Bishop of Paris immediately granted him full and unconditional absolution. But the faculty, less placable, prohibited him from proceeding to his doctor's degree, and appealed from the bishop's decision to the Pope. Innocent VIII. seems even to have surpassed the hopes of his petitioners ; for he issued an order that Laillier should be thrown into prison. But whether the sentence was executed, or whether the protection of the bishop availed to preserve him

from it, does not appear from the records of this transaction*.
They are sufficient, however, to show us that the theological
faculty of Paris, notwithstanding the boasted *Liberties* of the
Church, was very little disposed to encourage, or even to
endure, any evangelical truth which might endanger the spiritual despotism of Rome. Nor is this wonderful; since Paris
was the very centre and nursery of the scholastic system.

Such were the principal Cisalpine † "witnesses" of that age; Jerome Sa-
and their obscurity may be ascribed to their own timidity or to vonarola.
the overwhelming power of the hierarchy. But Italy, at the
same time, produced a far more celebrated champion of reform;
such a man, so enthusiastic in his piety, so wild in his enthusiasm, so daring in his spiritual pretensions, as might have
been expected to rise up in that country, where the vices of
the Church were best known, and among that people which
has seldom tempered religious zeal with any discretion; which
loves to be addressed through the imagination rather than the
reason, and whose emotions, if strong, are always violent and
generally transient. Jerome Savonarola was born at Ferrara
in 1452, the descendant of an illustrious family. His early
years gave indications of a profound religious feeling, and he
presently assumed the habit of a Dominican. In 1483 he first
felt those impulses which gave the peculiar character to his
mission; he began to preach on prophecy, and himself assumed
the mission of a prophet. His first effusions were delivered
at Brescia; but in 1489 he desired a more extensive field for
his powers, and proceeded to Florence.

Most of the Italian cities were distracted by political factions, The objects
and none, perhaps, so fiercely as Florence. These agitations and charac-
reached down to the lowest classes, and in the bosom of the preaching.

---

* This account is taken from the continuator of Fleury (liv. cxvi. s. 30–38)
who refers to *D'Argentré Collectio. Judic.*, tom. i., p. 308, ann. 1484.

† Lest Spain should seem to have had no candidate for admission into this
venerable host, we should mention that one Peter of Osma, professor of theology
at Salamanca, published some anti-papal and anti-ecclesiastical opinions in the
year 1479. It is remarkable that the Pope, in condemning, refused to specify
them, on account of their enormity—"to the end that those who already know
them may the sooner forget them; and that those who know them not may learn
no new sin." See the continuator of Fleury, lib. cxv., s. 2, 3, &c.

meanest citizen there was a nerve exquisitely sensible to all
appeals respecting his public rights.   Thus, whether in the
design to enlarge the range of his influence, or because he
really shared the popular passion, Savonarola combined the
politician's with the prophet's character *, and made each, as
the circumstances of the moment required, subservient to the
other.   Reform was the subject on which he preached, reform
and penitence—reform in the discipline of the Church, in the
disorders of the clergy, in the morals of the people—reform,
instant and immediate, ere the tempest of divine vengeance,
which was already impending over Italy, should descend and
overwhelm it.   He made no appeals to reason, none to the
ordinary principles, or even passions of men—it was in the
name of heaven that he commanded them to amend; it was
inspiration from above—the unerring prescience of imminent
calamities—which filled him with eloquence, and armed his
eloquence with authority and terror.   It was no dew of persuasion that fell from his lips—it was the word of an offended
God, clothed in thunder and hail, announcing the approach of
desolation.

At the same time he promised the divine protection to the
republican party.   He denounced the usurpation of Lorenzo
de' Medici, and refused to acknowledge his power, or show
deference to his person.   He pursued with fierce anathemas
the luxury and despotism of the aristocracy; and his genius
was so extraordinary and his enthusiasm so resistless, as almost
to give a colour to his claims of supernatural communications.
At least we need not discredit the accounts we read of his controlling influence over the people, and of the various acts by
which their devotion was displayed.   Multitudes believed in
his heavenly mission†; and the effect of his moral exhortations

---

* "Il vouloit (as a French writer observes) jouer à la fois le rôle de Jérémie et
de Demosthènes." We may recollect that Arnold of Brescia, who, like Savonarola, was an Italian, a reformer, and a martyr, like him also denounced, in the
same breath, political and ecclesiastical abuses.   And we should remind the
reader that Sismondi compares the sort of mixed influence, acquired by Savonarola
over the people of Florence, to that exercised by Calvin at Geneva.

† It seems probable that the enthusiasm for this man—we may even call it
the belief in him—was not confined to the lowest classes. The story of his inter-

was speedily perceptible throughout the city. "By the modesty of their dress, their discourse, their countenance, the Florentines gave evidence that they had embraced the reform of Savonarola; and it was easy to foresee (says Sismondi) that the political lessons of the preacher would not produce less impression on his audience than his moral instructions."

The political impression was more violent, and proportionably less beneficial. Savonarola had promised the citizens of Florence—or they understood him to have promised—that a pure theocracy should be substituted for their actual government, and that Christ himself should deign to rule over them. On this the popular fury rose beyond all restraint. It was in vain that the Pope thundered from the Vatican. It was in vain that the clergy refused to bury the bodies of any who believed the announcement of the prophet. The people thronged to listen to his sermons; and not unfrequently, when the harangue was concluded, rushed forth from the churches and assembled in the squares and public places, with tumultuous cries of *Viva Christo!* They would then dance in circles, formed by a citizen and a friar placed alternately, and commit every kind of absurdity*.

In 1494 Savonarola conducted the Florentine embassy to Charles VIII. at Lucca. It was in Charles that his prophecies (as he confidently declared) were accomplished—Charles was the promised minister of vengeance, commissioned to chastise the crimes of Italy. The monk presented himself before the victorious monarch, as the ambassador of a suppliant city

His interview with Charles VIII.

view with Benvieni, (told by Nardi, Stor. Fiorent., lib. ii., and cited by Roscoe,) proves, at least, his authority over those in command. Nardi likewise mentions the hesitation, and even apprehension, with which the inquisitors themselves made the first application of the torture.

* Roscoe (whom we have consulted with profit on the subject of Savonarola) cites from Girolamo Benvieni, who composed songs for these occasions, the following specimen (it can scarcely be a fair specimen) of the popular effusions:—

"Non fù mai più bel solazzo
Più grande, nè maggiore,
Che per zelo è per amore
Di JESU—divunter pazzo—
Ognun gridi, com' io grido,
Semprè pazzo, pazzo, pazzo."

—but he did not lose in the character of the monk or of the envoy the consciousness of his heavenly mission : he did not forget that the man whom he addressed was the mere instrument sent to fulfil *his* predictions, and accomplish the work of Providence. Himself was the prophet of the Lord—he maintained the superiority communicated by a nearer intercourse with God, and preserved his customary tone of admonition and command*.

In the mean time, the enemies of Savonarola, if less numerous and enthusiastic, were more constant and determined than his friends. The aristocracy of Florence, supported by the Pope and all the superior clergy, were patiently watching for the moment to destroy him. A ready weapon was furnished by monastic dissension : the Franciscans, already jealous of the fame of a rival, were eager to enter the lists against him. At the proper season they commenced their attack—and the object, of course, was to withdraw from their adversary the only foundation of his strength, the confidence of the people.

It was not by assailing him from the pulpit that this could be effected ; his great powers and irresistible authority forbade any hope of overthrowing him in a field which was peculiarly his own. Accordingly, the Franciscans proceeded by a very different method ; against the popular impostor they made their appeal to the grossest popular superstition. A Franciscan challenged Savonarola to go through the trial by fire, together with himself. The prophet reserved his own person for greater occasions ; but a faithful Dominican undertook the ordeal in his place : and had he not thus anticipated the general devotion, a multitude of citizens, of women, and even of priests, would have pressed to the flames with eagerness, as the substi-

---

* "Come, come with confidence, come with joy and triumph; for the Being who sends thee is even he who, for our salvation, triumphed on the cross. Nevertheless, listen to my words, most Christian king, and engrave them in thy heart. The servant of God, to whom these things have been revealed by divine communication, warns even thee, who art sent by the Majesty of heaven, that, after his example, it is thy duty to show mercy everywhere," &c. Such were the opening sentences of the prophet's harangue. Sismondi (who displays even more than his usual eloquence in his account of this enthusiast) has translated the whole address, chap. xciii.

tutes of Savonarola. The government gave its sanction; the day (April 17, 1498) was fixed for the trial; the necessary Trial, preparations were made; and the entire population of Florence and the neighbouring towns and villages thronged to the spot, in devout expectation of some visible sign of the divine interposition. The two parties presented themselves; the flames were kindled—but even then, in the presence of the chiefs of the Republic and the impatient multitudes, a dispute arose which finally prevented the exhibition. The people dispersed, disappointed and irritated. It also happened that the subject of the dispute had been such as to raise a prejudice against Savonarola. The Dominican, his substitute, had, in the first instance, required to enter the flames in his sacerdotal habits, to which the Franciscans reasonably objected. The former then expressed his readiness to enter naked, on the condition only that he should carry the host in his hand. The Franciscans again refused their consent; and, as Savonarola persisted in that condition, the ordeal did not take place. Now, besides the appearance of some secret design in his perseverance in his last demand, the people were easily taught to believe that it contained no slight mixture of impiety. To commit the body of Christ, under any human guarantee for its security, to the raging flames, was to treat with irreverence, to profane, nay perhaps to expose to destruction, the most holy of all things. Savonarola was not, indeed, without his advocates; but it was clear that the popular current had turned. The advantage was instantly pursued; the prophet was seized, imprisoned, tortured; and immediately on the arrival of two legates from Alexander VI. he was condemned to death, and executed. His and execution. ashes, according to the usual precaution, were cast into the Arno—and it does not appear that his exertions, either religious or political, extraordinary as they certainly were, and for the time successful too, impressed any lasting trace of any description even on the history of that city, to which they were exclusively confined.

John Reuchlin (or Capnio, as he was called), a German of Reuchlin great reputation and integrity, lent his indirect assistance to and Erasmus. the cause of religion by his labours for the restoration of

2 c 2

learning*. He died in 1522, and received his *apotheosis* from the pen of Erasmus, who had entered on the same career with still higher powers and greater celebrity. Of Erasmus much need not here be said, since his merits and weaknesses are generally known and not improperly estimated. His writings rendered the highest service to the first reformers: he had already stigmatized numerous abuses; he had rejected the Scholastic divinity, and recommended and facilitated the study of the Bible and the Fathers; he had covered with ridicule and contempt the vices of the monks, and their love for the ignorance in which they grovelled. By such means as these he had contributed to the success of the Reformation, even more, perhaps, than he had himself designed: for his predominant passion was that for literature; and though by no means indifferent to the interests of religion, he was fearful of all great practical changes, and could never shake off that irresolute timidity so commonly associated with literary habits.

The abuses of the Church especially displayed in Germany.

V. If the oppression of Rome was now generally felt and acknowledged throughout Europe; if the scandals of the court were now becoming every where notorious, and the vices of the monks and clergy had inflamed the general hatred of Christendom,—there was no country in which either the tyranny or the licentiousness of the Church was so shamelessly exhibited and so deeply detested as in Germany. While the first Othos imitated the policy of Charlemagne in exalting the sacred order†, they even exceeded his generosity; and some of the leading German ecclesiastics became at the same time bishops and powerful princes. Nor was there any region more pregnant with popular superstition, and with the fruits so diligently gathered from it by a worldly priesthood. From these causes, the wealth of the German Clergy had grown to

* It was Reuchlin (in the representation) who threw down the straight and crooked billets, which Erasmus tried in vain to accommodate: then came Luther, and set fire to the crooked ones, &c. Reuchlin was honoured by the hatred of the monks, who would willingly have fixed upon him the imputation of heresy.

† Their motive, too, was the same, to counterpoise the power of the barons; and it is a deed for which they are almost invariably praised by ecclesiastical, and condemned by civil, historians.

an inordinate excess; and their secular habits and vulgar vices* are stigmatized in every age of history. The proceedings of the Council of Vienne—the remonstrance of the Emperor Charles IV. to the Archbishop of Mayence, and, above all, the *prophetic* denunciations of Cardinal Julian at the Council of Basle, display at the same time the immorality and the insecurity of the German Church.

From the time of Gregory VII., the political interests of the empire and the Popedom had been at perpetual variance. And not only was Italy divided between their conflicting parties, but even the internal concord of Germany had been incessantly disturbed by pontifical interference. Its emperors had been insulted and deposed; Italian intrigues had distracted all its provinces; children had been raised up against their parents; and the battles and miseries of four centuries had been inseparably associated with the name and enmity of Rome. It was the consequence of this inveterate hostility, not only to nourish public animosity, but also to raise up private opponents against the See, who had at various times uncloked its abuses and denounced them to the people. So that, when the appointed season at length arrived, the prejudices of the lower classes had been in a great degree removed; and they listened without repugnance, and frequently with intense satisfaction, to any thing that reflected upon the See or Court of Rome.

The Germans had endeavoured to protect their Church against the pontifical depredators by the Concordats of Constance and Aschaffenburg; and however narrow the field of amendment which they comprehended, still, had they been strictly observed, some advantage would have been produced, and some irritation allayed. But so far were the Popes from any desire to correct usurpation by timely concession, or sincerely to conciliate those whom they had injured, and whom

Concordats violated.

---

* The Bavarian ambassador, addressing the Council of Trent in 1562, asserted, respecting the morality of his clerical fellow-subjects, that there were not more than three or four in a hundred who were not either secretly or openly married, or living in a state of concubinage (P. Paolo, Hist. Conc. Trident, lib. vi.) The saying of Pius II. on this subject, that if there were good reasons for enacting the law of celibacy, there were better for repealing it, was now in every man's mouth.

they ought to have feared, that they made it their policy to elude the conditions which they had reluctantly accorded, and to resume in substance the spoils which they had in semblance restored. By this conduct they not only nourished without any remission the prevalent animosity against them, but they inflamed it still further, when they aggravated former oppressions by recent perfidy. There was, indeed, no part of Christendom wherein the whole machinery of the apostolical chancery* had worked with such pernicious efficacy as in Germany. The privileges of the Jubilee, so fruitful to the See which granted, so expensive to the districts which enjoyed them, were dispensed during the schism principally to that country; the fathers of Constance and Basle published, though they failed to remove, its complaints and the circumstances of its oppression; and the " Hundred Grievances †" which were afterwards presented to the Diet of Nuremberg (in 1523) formed only a catalogue of hereditary wrongs, the subjects of perpetual remonstrance, and of remonstrance which was perpetually despised.

The people of Germany. The papal usurpations enumerated in that celebrated document are severally placed under three heads—such as tended to enthral the people; such as impoverished and despoiled them; such as withdrew them from the secular jurisdiction. Thus the interests of the people were become the foundation of the remonstrances of their rulers: thus, too, was it in *their* affections that the Reformer had fixed his surest asylum ‡. At

---

* About the time of the Diet of Augsbourg (in 1518) an archbishop of Mayence declared, during his last moments, that his greatest regret in dying was to leave to his poor subjects the burden of buying the *pallium* of his successor. About 27,000 florins appear to have been advanced on these occasions, and it was chiefly levied upon the poor. Robertson asserts (Hist. Charles V.) that companies of merchants openly bought the benefices of different districts from the Pope's agents, and retailed them at advanced prices.

† The *Centum Gravamina* comprehended the following abuses:—Payments for dispensations and absolutions; sums of money drawn by indulgences; appeals to Rome; reservations, commendams, annates; exemptions of ecclesiastics from the legal punishments; excommunications and unlawful interdicts; secular causes tried before ecclesiastical tribunals; great expenses in consecrating churches and cemeteries; pecuniary penance; fees for sacraments, burials, &c. P. Paolo, Hist. Concil. Trident., lib. i., n. 65.

‡ On Aug. 23, 1520, Luther wrote to Spalatin, " that he dreaded neither cen-

a somewhat earlier moment (on April 1, 1520), Frederic, Elector of Saxony, addressed to his Envoy at Rome the following remarkable expressions :—" Germany is no longer such as it has been; it is full of accomplished men in all the sciences. The people exhibit an extraordinary passion for reading the Scriptures*; and if the Court of Rome shall obstinately persist in rejecting the offers of Luther and in treating the affair with haughtiness, instead of replying to his arguments, she must prepare herself for troubles which will hardly be appeased, and for revolutions which will be no less fatal to herself than to others." To this wise admonition Leo X. addressed a reply, in which he designated Luther " as the most wicked and detestable of all heretics—a man who had no other mission than that which he had received from the Devil !"

The condition of Germany being such as the Elector represented it, and the disposition of the Vatican such as is betrayed in the answer of the Pope, it is not difficult to comprehend the nature or the result of the conflict which followed. On the one side, we are led to expect a succession of just demands commencing in moderation, and rising in exact proportion to the contempt with which they were rejected—on the other, a fierce and selfish determination to maintain the established system in its full integrity, without distinction of good or evil, of use or abuse, of truth or falsehood, of divine or human authority; and the conclusion was such as must certainly follow, sooner or later, from collision between such principles.

When the train is thus prepared, the moment of explosion Conclusion. will commonly depend on what is called accident; and thus it will frequently arrive when it is least expected. Thus was it with the beginning of the Reformation. Never was the

---

sures nor violence ; that he had a safe asylum in the hearts of the Germans, and that his enemies should beware, lest, in destroying one adversary, they should give birth to many." Beausobre, Hist. de la Réformation, liv. ii.

* " The world (said Erasmus in 1521, in his Advice to the Emperor) is weary of the ancient theology, which is only a mass of useless questions and vain subtleties, in which the sophists exercise their ingenuity. *The people are thirsting for the doctrine of the Gospel, and if it shall be attempted to close the source against them, they will open it for themselves by force.*" This letter is translated by Beausobre, Hist. Réf., liv. iv.

Court of Rome more confident in the sense of security than at that instant. The various heresies which had so long disturbed the Church were, for the most part, dismayed and silenced; the complaints and petitions of the faithful had long been rejected with insolent impunity; the Council, which had last been held, had effaced by its subservience the memory of Basle and Constance; and the warnings of Julian Cesarini were despised or forgotten. The temporal monarchy of Rome was more firmly established than at any former period, and her power and influence were still considerable in every part of Europe—her ecclesiastical agents were never more numerous or more zealous in her service. The pillars of her strength were visible and palpable, and she surveyed them with exultation from her golden palaces; but she did not so readily discern the moral causes which were combining for her dissolution, and slowly and secretly sapping the foundations of her pride.

The qualities of Leo X., though not despicable, were not calculated for that crisis. Fond of letters, devoted to pleasure, contemptuous of morality; ignorant of the science, careless of the duties, neglectful even of the decencies, of religion; vain, extravagant, necessitous and venal, he had not the character which could prevent the rebellion, or crush the rebel. Tempered in the schools of courtly negotiation, the weapons of the Vatican were of no service against a popular enemy; and the Pope himself at length condescended to complain*, that " the present disease was not in the princes and great prelates, with whom familiarity and interest prevailed; but in the people, with whom it was necessary to use reality, and make a true reformation." In that people, so long the object of pontifical contempt and spoliation, new energies had insensibly replaced the incurious and servile ignorance of former days. An occasion and an instrument were alone required to bring them into action. The former was furnished by the vices and blindness of the Church; the latter was raised up by Providence in the

---

* Padre Paolo, Hist. Concil. Trident., liv. i.

person of Luther. Yet Luther himself, endowed as he was with great and ardent qualities, was but the voice that called the labourers to their office. The abuses were so ripe and pregnant, and the perception of them so deep and so general, that, even had Luther never been born, the harvest could not long have needed bold and holy ministers to gather it. " I do not doubt (they are the words of the Reformer himself addressed to Melancthon) that if we are unworthy to bring this work to its conclusion, God will raise up others, worthier than we are, who will accomplish it."

ANALYTICAL TABLE OF CONTENTS.

VOLUME III.

PART V.

CHAPTER XXII.—*Residence at Avignon.*

SECTION I.

CHAPTER XXIII.—*Grand Schism of the Roman Catholic Church.*

CHAPTER XXIV.—*Attempts of the Church at Self-Reformation.*

CHAPTER XXV.—*History of the Hussites.*

CHAPTER XXVI.—*History of the Greek Church after its Separation
from the Latin.*

CHAPTER XXVIII.—*Preliminaries of the Reformation.*

SECTION I.

2 D 2

A CHRONOLOGICAL TABLE

OF

EMINENT MEN, AND OF THE PRINCIPAL COUNCILS.

Popes.	Died.	Eminent Persons connected with Ecclesiastical History.	Important Councils.
Linus . . .	78		
Anacletus . .	91		
Clement . .	100	Pliny the Younger.	
Alexander . .	116	Ignatius. Tacitus.	
Sixtus . . .	126		
Telesphorus . .	137		
Hyginus . .	141	Justin Martyr.	
Pius . . .	157	Polycarp.	
Anicetus . .	168	Montanus.	
Soter . . .	177		
Eleutherus* . .	192	Pantænus.	
Victor . . .	196	Irenæus.	
		Ammonias Saccas.	Carthage (217.)
Zephrynus . .	219	Clemens Alexandrinus	
Callistus . .	224	Tertullian.	
Urban . . .	231	Origen. Celsus.	
Pontianus . .	235		
Anterus . .	236		
Fabianus . .	251	Sabellius.	A Synod at Rome
Cornelius . .	253	Cyprian.	against Novatian
A Schism between Cornelius and Novatian.			(251).
Lucius . . .	255		Synod at Carthage
Stephen . .	257		(256), by Cyprian,
Sixtus II. . .	259	Paul of Samosata.	on the Baptism of
Dionysius . .	271	Manes.	Heretics.
Felix . . .	275	Porphyry.	Synod at Antioch
Eutychianus . .	283		(269), against Paul
Caius . . .	296		of Samosata.
Marcellinus . .	304		Cirta (305), respecting
Marcellus . .	309	Lactantius.	Traditors.
Eusebius . .	311	Hosius.	Council of Eliberis
Melchiades . .	†314	Constantine. Eusebius of Cæsarea. Arius. Eusebius of Nicomedia. Athanasius.	(305), against the Lapsed, &c. Arles (314), against the Donatists.

* The succession of the earliest Bishops of Rome and the duration of their government are involved in inexplicable confusion. We have followed Spanheim.

† The *Indiction* was a cycle of three lustres, or a revolution of fifteen years. It was instituted by Constantine soon after his victory over Maxentius (September 24, 312), and the financial accounts for the payment of tribute were regulated by this term. At the Council of Nice the method of Indiction was substituted for that of Olympiads. The year of the first Indiction began January 1, 313 ; consequently, to find this Indiction,

Popes.	Died.	Eminent Persons connected with Ecclesiastical History.	Important Councils.
Sylvester . .	335		I. (*General* *.) *The Council of Nice* (325.)
Mark . . .	336	Constantius.	Synod of Tyre (335), against Athanasius.
Julius . . .	352		Council of Sardica (347), against the Arians.
			Council of Milan (355), by Constantius, against the Catholics.
Liberius . .	367	Julian. Ammianus. Marcellinus.	Council of Seleucia (359), held by the Semi-arians.
A Schism between Liber and Felix.		Chrysostom. Gregory Nazianzenus.	Council of Rimini (360). Catholic.
		Basil. Gregory of Nyssa.	Laodicea (370), on various matters of Church discipline.
		Priscillian. Epiphanius.	St. Martin of Tours. Synod of Saragossa (380), against Priscillian.
Damasus . .	385	Theodosius the Great. Ambrose of Milan.	II. *First of Constantinople* (381), on the Divinity of the Holy Ghost.
Schism between Damasus and Ursicinus		Jerome. Jovinian. Vigilantius. Rufinus.	Council of Milan (398) against Jovinian.
		Augustin. Donatus.	
Siricius . . .	398	John Cassian, author of the Institutions (350—433).	The Fourth Council of Carthage (398) prohibited secular studies.
Anastasius . .	402	Pelagius and Celestius.	
Innocent . .	417	Sulpicius Severus.	Conference at Carthage, against the Donatists (411).
Zosimus . .	418		
Boniface . .	423	Socrates.	
Schism between Boniface and Eulalius		Sozomen. Paulinus of Nola (died 431.)	
		Nestorius.	III. *Council of Ephesus* (431) against Nestorius.
Celestine . .	432	St. Prosper. Mamertus Claudianus. Theodoret.	
Sixtus III. . .	440	Zosimus.	Second (*False*) Council of Ephesus (449).

subtract 312 from the given year, or add three to it ; divide the difference, or sum by 15, and the remainder, if any, will be the year of the Indiction. The Popes still use this cycle in their bulls and diplomas.

* The italics designate the Councils held General by the Latin Church.

Popes.	Died.	Eminent Persons connected with Ecclesiastical History.	Important Councils.
Leo the Great .	461	Eutyches.	IV. *Council of Chalcedon* (451), against Eutyches.
Hilary . . .	467	Sidonius Apollinaris	
Simplicius . .	483	(Bishop of Clermont.)	
Felix II. . .	492		Arles (452), on various matters of discipline.
Gelasius . .			
	496	Clovis.	
Anastasius II. .	498	Vigilius Tapsensis.	Rome (494), on the canonical and apocryphal Scriptures, and other works to be read, or prohibited.
Schism between Symmachus and Laurentius			
Symmachus . .	514	Boethius.	Orleans (511), convoked by Clovis, chiefly on Discipline. Others held there, on the same subject, in 538, 541, and 549.
Hormisdas . .	523		
John . . .	526	Benedict of Nursia.	
Felix III. . .	530	Justinian.	
Boniface II. . .	532		
A schism between Boniface and Dioscoras.			
John II.	535		
Agapetus . .	536		
Sylverius . .	540		
Schism between Sylverius and Vigilius.			V. *Constantinople* (553), against Origen and others. On the Resurrection of the Flesh and Pre-existence of the Soul.
Vigilius . .	555	St. Gregory, Bp. of Tours (544—599).	
Pelagius . .	559	VenantiusFortunatus.	
John III. . .	573	Isidore of Seville.	
Benedict . .	577	John the Faster, Ph. of C. P.	
			Council of Toledo (589), against the Arians.
Pelagius II. . .	590	St. Columban. Euagrius.	
Gregory the Great .	604	St. Austin, Apostle of England.	
Sabinianus . .	605		
Boniface III. . .	606		
Boniface IV. .	614		
Deodatus . .	617	Mahomet. Heraclius.	
Boniface V. .	625		
Honorius . .	638		
Severinus . .	639		
John IV. . .	641	St. Eligius, Bishop of Noyon.	
Theodore . .	648		
Martin . . .	665	Fredegarius, of Burgundy.	A Lateran Council (649), against the Monothelites.
Eugenius . .	656		
Vitalianus . .	669	Theodore, Archbishop of Canterbury.	

Popes.	Died.	Eminent Persons connected with Ecclesiastical History.	Important Councils.
Adrodatus . .	676		Council of Hertford
Domnus . .	678		(673).
Agatho . .	682		VI. *Constantinople* (680), against the Monothelites.
Leo II. . .	684		Council of Toledo
Benedict II. . .	685		(682), deposed Vamba,
John V. . .	686		King of the Visigoths.
Conon . . .	687		Constantinople, in
			Trullo (692) (Quini-
Sergius . . .	701		sextum) *, on the
John VI. . .	704		marriage of the
John VII. . .	707		Clergy, &c.
Sisinnius . .	707	The Venerable Bede.	The last Council of
Constantine . .	714	St.Boniface, the Apos-	Toledo (696).
Gregory II. . .	731	tle of Germany.	
		Luitprand.	
Gregory III. . .	741	Leo the Isaurian.	
Zachary . .	752	Charles Martel.	
Stephen II. . .	752	ArchbishopCuthbert.	
Stephen III. .	757	Pepin, king of France.	Constantinople (754),
Paul . . .	767	John Damascenus.	against Images.
Schism between Paul and Theophylact.		Paul the Deacon, historian of the Lombards.	
Stephen IV. .	772	Charlemagne.	VII. *Nice* (787),
Adrian . . .	795	Alcuin (785—804).	*Seventh General*, for the restoration of Images.
			Aix-la-Chapelle (789), for Reformation.
Leo III. . .	816		Francfort(794),against Image-worship.
			Others at Aix-la-Cha-
Stephen V. . .	817	Benedict of Aniane	pelle (in 797, 799,
Paschal . .	824	(751—821).	802, 809, 816, 817,
		Louis the Meek.	818, 819).
		Dungal.	Five Councils, held in
Eugenius II. .	827	Amalarius.	813, at Arles, May-
		Eginhardt (died 839).	ence, Rheims, Tours,
		Agobardt.	and Chalons.
Valentine . .	827	Claudius, Bp. of Turin.	Paris (824), on Image-worship.

* Neither the fifth nor sixth general council had published any canons respecting ecclesiastical discipline or religious ceremonies. To supply this defect, Justinian II. assembled another in a hall of the Imperial Palace, called *Trullus* (Cupola) ; and it was called Quini-Sextum, as being supplementary to the fifth and sixth. It passed one hundred and two laws, of which six are in opposition to certain rites and opinions of Rome ; on which account the Latins do not hold it general. Mosh., cent. vii., p. 2, ch. 5.

Popes.	Died.	Eminent Persons connected with Ecclesiastical History.	Important Councils.
Gregory IV.	844	Rabanus Maurus. Ansgarius. Walfried Strabo. Paschasius Radbertus.	Mayence (848), against Gotteschalcus.
Sergius II.	847	Ratramn. John Scotus. Gotteschalcus. Rabanus Maurus (776-856)	
Leo IV.	854	Photius raised to see of C. P. Florus. Prudentius. Charles the Bald. Hincmar of Rheims.	
*Benedict III.	858	Lupus of Ferrara.	
Schism.		Petrus Siculus.	
Nicholas	867	St. Ado, A.B. of Vienne.	
Adrian II.	872	Anastasius the Librarian. John the Deacon.	VIII. (*Latin*). *Constantinople* (869, for the condemnation of Photius.
John VIII.	882		Constantinople (879 held by Photius, called by the Latins the False Eighth.
Martin II.	884		
Adrian III.	885	Alfred.	
Stephen VI.	890		
Formosus	897		
Schism.			
Boniface VI.	897		
Stephen VII.	901		
Schism.			
John IX.	903		
Benedict IV.	906		
Leo. V.	906		
Schism.			
Christopher	906		
Schism.			
Sergius III.	910		Trosli (909), on Discipline.
Anastasius III.	912		
Lardo	913		
John X.	927		
Leo VI.	928		
Stephen VIII.	930	St. Odo, abbot of Cluni, (879-942.)	
John XI.	935		
Leo VII.	939		
Stephen IX.	943		
Martin III.	946		

* It is to this place that the fable of the female pope, Joan, seems properly to belong.

Popes.	Died.	Eminent Persons connected with Ecclesiastical History.	Important Councils.
		Frodoard, Canon of Rheims, (894-966)	Augsbourg (952) of French, Italian and
Agapetus II. .	955	Otho the Great.	German Bishops.
John XII. . .	963	Bernhard of Thuringia	On Discipline.
Schism.		Luitprand, Otho's Legate at C. P.	
Benedict V. . .	964		
Leo VIII. . .	965	St. Dunstan.	
John XIII. . .	972		
Domnus II. . .	972		
Benedict VI. .	974		
Boniface VII. .	975		
Benedict VII: .	984		
John XIV. . .	985		
John XV. . .	985		
John XVI. . .	995		
Gregory V. . .	998		
Schism.			
Sylvester II. .	1003		
John XVIII. .	1003		
John XII. . .	1009		
Sergius IV. .	1012		Council at Orleans—
Benedict VIII. .	1024		some Heretics burnt
Schism.			(1017).
John XX. . .	1033		Council of Arras (1025)
Benedict XI. .	1044		
Schism. . .			
Gregory VI. .	1046		
Clement II. .	1048		
Damascus II. .	1049		
Leo IX. . .	1054	Michel Cerularius.	
Victor II. . .	1057		
Stephen X. . .	1058		
Cenedict X. . .	1059		Council of Nich. II.
Nicholas II. . .	1061		(1059) regulating
Schism.			Papal election.
Alexander II. .	1073	Petrus Damiani. Lanfranc.	At Rome, against Berenger.
Gregory VII. .	1086	Berenger. Alexius Comnenus. Hen. IV. of Germany.	At Rome (1074), on the celibacy of the Clergy and Investitures.
Schism.			
Victor III. . .	1087	St. Bruno. Roscellinus. Anselm.	Placentia — Clermont (1095) originates
Urban II. . .	1099	Peter the Hermit.	first crusade.
Paschal II. . .	1118		A Lateran Council (1111), which cancelled Paschal's treaty with Henry V.
Schism.			
Gelasius II. . .	1119	Pierre de Bruis. Peter the Venerable.	At Worms (1122), on question of Investitures. Calixit. II.

Popes.	Died.	Eminent Persons connected with Ecclesiastical History.	Important Councils.
Calixtus II. . .	1124		IX. (*Latin*). *First Lateran Council* (1123), on Investitures. Twenty-two canons.
Honorius II. .	1130	Abelard. Bernard of Clairval.	Council of Pisa (1134).
Innocent II. .	1143	Henri the Heretic.	X. (*Latin*). *Second La-*
Celestine II. .	1144		*teran*(1139), against
Lucius II. . .	1145	Otho Frisingensis.	Heretics; for the ge-
Eugenius III. .	1153	Gratian of Bologna.	neral Reformation
Anastasius IV. .	1154	Peter the Lombard.	of the Church. 30
Adrian IV. . .	1159	Arnold of Brescia.	canons are extant.
Schism. . .		Frederic Barbarossa. Thomas à Becket.	XI. (*Latin*). *Third Lateran* (1179), for
Alexander III. .	1181	Peter Waldus.	the arrangement of
Lucius III. .	1185		Papal Election; a-
Urban III. . .	1187		gainst Heretics; and
Gregory VIII. .	1188		for the Reformation
Clement III. .	1191	Dominic.	of the Church*.
Celestine III. .	1199	Simon de Montfort. Francis d'Assisi.	Council of Paris (1212).
Innocent III. .	1216		XII. (*Latin*). *Fourth*
Honorius III. .	1227	Alexander Hales.	*Lateran* (1215), un-
Gregory IX. .	1241		der Innocent III.
Celestine IV. .	1243	John of Parma. Robert Grossetete.	XIII. (*Latin.*) *First Council of Lyons*
Innocent IV. .	1254	Frederic II. Louis IX. of France.	(1245), under Innocent IV.
Alexander IV. .	1261	Robert of Sorbonne.	Mayence (1261), on
Urban IV. . .	1264		Eccles. Discipline.
Clement IV. · .	1268	Thomas Aquinas.	XIV. (*Latin*). *Second*
Gregory X. .	1276	Bonaventura.	*of Lyons* (1274),
Innocent V. .	1276	Roger Bacon.	under Gregory X.
Adrian V. .	1276		
John XXI. .	1277	Matthew Paris.	
Nicholas III. .	1280		
Martin IV. .	1285		
Honorius IV. .	1288		
Nicholas IV. .	1292		

* The substance of the principal Canons of the *First* Lateran is briefly given at page 310. Of the *Second*, the Ninth Canon prohibited Monks and Canons Regular from practising Civil Law or Medicine; the Thirteenth was directed against usurers; the Fifteenth protected the persons of the Clergy and the right of Asylum. The condemnation of Petrus Leonis and of Arnold of Brescia were separate Acts of Legislation. Of the *Third*, the First Canon ordained, respecting papal election, that if the Cardinals should not be unanimous in their choice, two-thirds of the votes, and not less than two-thirds, should be sufficient. Of the *Fourth*, the most important Canons have been mentioned in various places.

Popes.	Died.	Eminent Persons connected with Ecclesiastical History.	Important Councils.
Celestine V. (abdicated)	1294		
Boniface VIII.	1303	Philip the Fair.	
Benedict XI.	1304	Dante.	
Clement V.	1314	Louis of Bavaria.	XV. (Latin). Council of Vienna (1311), under Clement V.
John XXII.	1334	John Duns Scotus. William Occam.	
Benedict XII.	1341	Marsilius of Padua.	
Clement VI.	1352	Jovanni and Matteo Villani.	
Innocent VI.	1362	Petrarch. St. Brigida	
Urban V.	1370	John Wiclif.	
Gregory IX.	1378	St. Catharine of Sienna.	
Urban VI. (Rome.)	1389	Theodoric of Niem.	
Clement VII. (Avignon.)	1394		
Boniface IX. (Rome.)	1404		
Innocent VII. (Rome.)	1406		
Benedict XIII. (deposed, Avignon.).	1409		
Gregory XII. (deposed, Rome.)	1409	Pierre d'Ailly.	
Alexander V.	1410	Nicholas de Clemangis. John Gerson.	Pisa (1407). XVI. (Latin). Constance (1414).
John XXIII.	1415	John Huss.	
Deposition and Vacancy till 1417.		Jerome of Prague. Sigismond. Poggio of Florence.	
Martin V.	1431	Leonardus Aretinus. Julian Cesarini.	XVII. (Latin). Basle (1431).
Eugenius IV. Schism.	1447	The Cardinal of Arles. Æneas Sylvius. Laurentius Valla.	
Nicholas V.	1455	St. Antoninus, A. B. of Florence.	
Calixtus III.	1458		
Pius II.	1464	John of Wesalia.	
Paul II.	1471	John Wesselus.	
Sixtus IV.	1484	John Laillier.	
Innocent VIII.	1492	Jerome Savonarola.	
Alexander VI.	1503	Cardinal Ximenes.	XVIII. (Latin). Fifth Lateran, by Julius II. (1512.)
Pius III.	1503	Erasmus.	
Julius II.	1513		
Leo X.		Luther.	

GENERAL INDEX.

2 E

delaying to do so, ib.; afterwards forbids the military orders, &c., at Jerusalem to act with him, 283; succeeded by Innocent IV., 284; establishes the Inquisition, 330; his collection of decretals, 366
Gregory X. elected (after three years' vacancy in the holy see) while in Palestine, ii. 296; his zeal for the recovery of Palestine, 297; and his endeavours to reconcile the Guelphs and Ghibellines, ib.; confirms the election of the emperor Rodolph, and endeavours to reconcile the Greek and Latin churches, 298; holds the second Council of Lyons, ib.; dies while preparing to set out on a crusade, 299
———— XI. succeeds Urban V., at Avignon, iii. 24; urged by St. Catharine of Sienna, to fix the papal court at Rome, 25; which he does on hearing that the Romans threaten to have a pope of their own, 26; dies there, ib.
———— XII (Angelo Corrario) elected as successor of Innocent VII., in opposition to the anti-pope Benedict XIII., iii. 80; projected conference between the two popes at Savona, 82; which Gregory shamefully evades, ib.; he and his rival deposed by the Council of Pisa, and Alexander V. elected, 85; he escapes to Gaieta, and obtains the protection of Ladislaus of Hungary, 86; afterwards retires to Rimini, 88; dies shortly after, 106
Guiscard, Robert, created Duke of Apulia, Calabria, and Sicily, by Nicholas II., ii. 64

Hales, Alexander, the "Irrefragable Doctor," ii. 372, note
Hallam, Robert, Bishop of Salisbury, a zealous reformer at the Council of Constance, iii. 128
Henricians, sect of, ii. 177; Eugenius III. sends the legate Alberic to suppress them, ib.
Henry IV., emperor, excommunicated and deposed by Gregory VII., ii. 73; he does penance at Canossa, and is absolved from the sentence of excommunication, 75; deposed again, and his crown bestowed upon Rodolphus, 76; after the defeat and death of Rodolphus, he advances against Rome, 84; makes Clement III. pope instead of Gregory, 85; his misfortunes and death, 105
———— V., son of the preceding, asserts the imperial rights against those of the Romish see, ii. 106; quarrels with, and arrests Pascal II. 108
Heresy, usage of the word, i. 136; variety of early heresies, 138; opposition of the

early fathers, 139; Mosheim's classification of heresies, 141; Burton's classification of heresies, 142; Gnostic heretics, 143; Nicolaites, 145; Cerdo and Marcion, 146; the Encratites, 147; Phantastics or Docetæ, 148; heresies respecting the nature of Christ, 157; Ebionites, ib.; heresy of Theodotus and Artemon, 159; Paul of Samosata, 160; Praxeas, 161; Sabellius, ib.; Montanists, 162; Novatians, 166; the Petrobrussians, ii. 176; Henricians, 177; the Vaudois, 181; Albigenses, 184; persecution of them, 187; zeal of the Fratres Predicatores against heresy, 191; constitutions of Frederic II., against it, ii. 288; Lollards and Beghards, iii. 41; Flagellants, 45; character of the heresies during the thirteenth and fourteenth centuries, 47; distinguished from earlier ones, by opposition to the polity and system of the Romish church, ib.
Heretics, baptism of, i. 163; St. Bernard's sermon against, ii. 144; treatment of, by the church, iii. 375; canon of the fourth Lateran Council against, ib.
Hermes Trismegistus, forgery of doctrine ascribed to him, i. 100, note
Hermits of St. Augustine, account of the order so called, ii. 245
Hesychasts or Quietists, sect of mystics in the Greek church, iii. 213
Hierapolis, bishops of, i. 10; Claudius Apollinaris, ib.
Hilary, Bishop of Poictiers, writer of the fourth century, i. 217
Hildebrand, a monk of Cluni, carried to Rome by Leo IX., ii. 59; his rapid rise, 60; becomes the adviser of Nicholas II., 61; his policy for extending the papal power, by abolishing imperial interference, 63; he secures the election of Alexander II., 64, succeeds him in the papal see, 66. See Gregory VII.
Hincmar, Archbishop of Rheims, defends the claims of Louis the Bald, against the pretensions of Adrian II., ii. 17; defends the church against those of Louis III., 17; his character, 26; his writings, 27, note; he opposes the institution of popes' vicars, 29; his regulations for the discipline of the inferior clergy, 51
Holy Ghost, procession of, discussions relative to, at the Council of Ferrara, iii, 235; common confession of faith between the Latin and Greek churches, 237. See also Double Procession and Procession
Homoousians, i, 205, note
Honorius, emperor, abolishes gladiatorial games, i. 235
———— III., successor of Innocent III.,

428

GENERAL INDEX.

Investiture, origin of the dispute respecting, ii. 70; its termination, 109
Irenæus, Bishop of Lyons, remonstrates with Victor, Bishop of Rome, for his intolerance, i, 20; account of him, 63
Ireland, conversion of, i. 283
Italian clergy, their character and conduct, iii. 131

Jacobellus, a Bohemian preacher, maintains the necessity for administering communion in both kinds, iii. 180
Jacobite heretics of Egypt, their alliance with the Mahometans, i. 286
Jacobites, a name given to the Eutychians, or Monophysites, i. 353, note
James, St., the Just, first Bishop of Jerusalem, i. 2
Jerome, St., account of, i. 277; his vision, ib., note; his prophecy respecting the millenium, 278; his translation of the Bible disapproved of by the church, ib.
——— of Prague, disciple of John Huss, account of, iii. 193; summoned by the Council of Constance, and retracts his opinions after Huss's execution, ib.; his execution, 194
Jerusalem, Church of, i. 1
———, new city at, founded by Adrian under the title of Ælia Capitolina, i. 3; Julian's attempt to rebuild the Temple, i. 225; Ammianus's account of it, 226, note; the phenomenon which defeated the undertaking, attempted to be accounted for naturally, 228; the city taken by the Christians, ii. 340; retaken by Saladin after the second Crusade, 343
Jerusalem, the Latin kingdom of, iii. 221; first establishment of the Latin church in the East, 222; at Constantinople, 223
Jews, decrees against, renewed by the Council of Basle, iii. 151, note
Joan, Pope, story of, ii. 31, note
John the Faster, patriarch of Constantinople, i. 299
———, of England, obliged to submit to Innocent III., ii. 170
——— XXII. (James of Euse) elected, on the death of Clement V., iii. 9; his low origin and character, ib.; he extends the power of the Apostolical Chancery, 10; his immense treasures, ib., note; his dispute with Louis of Bavaria, 11; by whom charges of heresy are brought against him, 13; his opinions as to the intermediate state after death, 14; which he retracts, ib.; his death, 15; his bull against the Fratricelli, iii. 36; asserts the right of the monastic orders to possession of property, 37; his edicts against heresy, 38, note

John XXIII. (Baltazar Cossa) succeeds Alexander V., iii. 87; his unpriestly character, 88; he consents to hold another general council, which the emperor Sigismond determines shall be convoked at Constance, 89; questions as to the relative power of the council and the pope, 93; charges brought against John, 94; his voluntary abdication, 95; he escapes and seeks the protection of Frederic of Austria, 96; further contest in which the rights of the council are asserted to be superior to those of the pope; 96; John is betrayed and kept prisoner at Fribourg, 97; accused, 98; and deposed, 99; promises not to attempt to recover the pontificate, ib.; is imprisoned, 100; released by Martin V., and advanced by him to dignities, 110; his conduct and character, ib.
Jortin, his opinion respecting the council of Nice, i. 196; his severe censure of Gregory the Great, 291, note
Jovinian, account of, i. 337; condemned and banished for attacking monastic asceticism, 338
Jubilee, institution of, ii. 363; its celebration altered to every fiftieth year, by Clement VI., iii. 18; the jubilee of 1350, ib.; a license for holding a jubilee granted by Boniface IX. to Cologne and Magdebourg, 69; jubilee proclaimed by Boniface at Rome, 79; abuse of jubilees, 257; a private jubilee granted to the Poles and Lithuanians, 258
Julian the Apostate, account of, i. 220; contrasted with Constantine, 222; his measures against the Christians, 223; his endeavour to reform paganism, 224. 239; attempts to rebuild the temple of Jerusalem, 225; his literary works, 237; his superstition, 239
Julius II. (see Rovera) succeeds Pius III., iii. 292, promises to convoke a council for reform of the church, ib.; his military character, 293; his military and political successes, 294; his energy, 295; and patronage of the arts, ib.; assembles the fifth Lateran Council, 297, lays France under interdict, ib., note; dies, and is succeeded by Giovanni de' Medici, 299; degeneracy of the Roman see, under Julius, 303
Jurisdiction, ecclesiastical, ii. 154
Justin Martyr, his account of the celebration of the Eucharist, i. 49; praises the morals of the early Christians, 54, 58; account of him, 62; his apologies for Christianity, 63
Justinian, his persecution of heresy, i. 211; account of him, 254; his intolerance,

i. 284; mission to, by Innocent IV., iii. 359

Tatian founds the sect of the Encratites, i. 147

Templars, knights, order of, ii. 234; council held at Vienne, by Clement V. to inquire into their conduct, iii. 4; charges against them, ib.; their probable innocence, 5; enmity of Philip le Bel against them, ib.; the order suppressed, 6

Tertullian, account of, i. 82; his apostacy to Montanism, 83; his treatises written after that change in his opinions, ib. *note*

Tertullianists, sect of, i. 83

Tetzel, copy of the indulgence circulated by, iii. 344

Teutonic order, founded in the twelfth century, ii. 235; they convert Prussia by first subduing it, ib.

Thaborites, sect of Bohemian reformers, iii. 200; massacre of, 201; Æneas Sylvius' account of them, 203, *note*

Theodore of Tarsus, archbishop of Canterbury, his 'Penitential,' iii. 339

Theodoric of Niem, secretary to the Roman court during the schism, account of, iii. 78, *note*

Theodorit, early ecclesiastical writer, i. 216

Theodosius the Great, his opposition to Arianism, i. 208; he assembles the second general council, ib.; his edict against paganism, 231

Theodosius II., consults Simeon the Stylite, i. 250; his severe laws against heretics, 256

Theodotus and Artemon, their heresy, i.159

Theology, scholastic, ii. 134

Thomists and Scotists, ii. 375

'Three Chapters,' the, account of the writings so called, i. 354

Tithes, origin of, i. 433; opinions of some of the early fathers in regard to, 434; not established until the eighth century, 435; the first legislative act for enforcing them passed by Charlemagne, 436; the right universally enforced by Innocent III., 437; not usual in the Greek church, iii. 225

Toledo, councils of, i. 310; canons of, relative to the married clergy, iii. 354, *note*

Tonsure, the, i. 308; immunities conferred by, ii. 155

Toulouse, council of, a system of Inquisition established by, ii. 190

Tradition, importance attached to, ii. 88, *note*

Trajan, persecution of the Christians under, i. 116, 173

Transubstantiation, controversy respecting, ii. 33; opinions of Paschasius Radbert, 35; Johannes Scotus, 35; the doctrine

opposed by Berenger, 92; the doctrine finally established, and the name itself introduced by Innocent III., 173; superstitious practices resulting from it, iii. 345

Trials by ordeal, ii. 9

Trivium and Quadrivium, the two courses of study so named, ii. 135

Ulphilas, a Gothic bishop, disseminates Arianism among his countrymen, i. 210

Umbilicani, sect of mystics in the Greek Church, iii. 214

United Brethren, sect of Bohemian reformers so named, iii. 204

Unity of the church, Cyprian's treatise on, i. 87; the principle of, in the Western church, 309; the unity of the Roman Catholic Church protected by the Inquisition, iii. 376

University of Paris, ii. 366; the four faculties, 367; degrees, ib.; it condemns Aristotle's metaphysical works, 371

Urban II., succeeds Gregory VII., ii. 101; confirms the enactments of his predecessor, 102; exhorts to the undertaking of the Crusades, 104

——— V. succeeds Innocent VI., iii. 23; visits Rome, and returns to Avignon, where he dies soon after, ib.

——— VI. (Bartolomeo Prignano, archbishop of Bari), popular tumults at his election as successor of Gregory XI., iii. 55; his character, 58; he reproaches the prelates for their scandalous conduct, 59; the cardinals declare his election compulsory and void, 61; and proceed to Fondi, where they elect Clement VII.; subsequent schism in the church, 65; St. Catharine of Sienna exerts herself in favour of Urban, 65; he imprisons six cardinals, and afterwards causes five of them to be put to death, 67; his death, ib.; the Roman cardinals elect as his successor Boniface IX., 68

Ursuline nuns, order of, instituted in the sixteenth century, ii. 257

Vacant sees, right of presentation to, first usurped by the Avignon popes, iii. 28

Valens, success of Arianism during his reign, i. 207

Valentinian, his toleration, i. 230; his law prohibiting the clergy from receiving donations, 426, *note*

Valentino, Duke (Cæsar Borgia, second son of Alexander VI.), quitting the church, acts as military commander in Romagna, iii. 288; advises his father to poison Cardinal Corneto, to possess himself of his wealth, 289; they both

CORRIGENDA.

VOLUME I.

PAGE   LINE

16,   last but one, *for* ἐπαίλεις *read* ἐπαύλεις.

19,   30, *for* their *read* his.

81,   Note, for νὺ read νὺν.

103,   6, *for* Næander *read* Neander.

155,   10, *for* even *read* were.

166,   19, *for* them *read* their clergy.

310, last but two, *for* 633 *read* 638.

310, last but one, *after* Gaul *insert* (*aliter* Gallicia.)

355,   27, *for* formerly *read* formally.

384,   *note* †, line 8, *for* γαβοῦσα *read* λαβοῦσα.

VOLUME II.

229, *for* " Council of Paris in 1812" *read* " Council of Paris in 1212."

244,   13, *for* their *read* the.

251,   17, *for* Meronites *read* Maronites.

298,   15, *for* this *read* his.

298,   23, *for* 21st *read* 23rd.

299, 11 and 12, *for* fifteen *read* five.

325,   15, *after* the, *insert* practice of.

330,   17, *for* thus *read* there.

337,   12, *for* II. *read* III.

VOLUME III.

26,   15, *for* impression *read* importance.

45,   8, *for* befell *read* fell out.

57, 5 from bottom, *for* eterim *read* interim.

92,   margin, *for* objections *read* objects.

141,   16, *for* defect *read* defeat.

170, 9 from bottom, *after* 1350 *add* and 1393.

192,   7, *for* those *read* the.

195,   19, *for* bosom *read* bosoms.

259,   22, *for* his *read* the.

321,   29, *for* aggravate *read* irritate.

340,   27, *after* by *add* the suggestion of.

THE END.

LONDON : Printed by WILLIAM CLOWES and SONS, Stamford-Street.

WORKS JUST PUBLISHED

BY

BALDWIN AND CRADOCK, LONDON.

THE LIFE, MINISTRY, AND SELECTIONS FROM THE RE-
MAINS of the Rev. SAMUEL WALKER, B.A., formerly of Truro, Cornwall. By
the Rev, EDWIN SIDNEY, A.M., Author of the " Life of the Rev. Rowland Hill." In
8vo., price 12s. cloth and lettered.

" We recommend this interesting volume to the notice of our readers. The name of Walker of
Truro is justly distinguished among the names of those to whom, under the blessing of God, we are
indebted for the revival of religion in the Church of England during the middle of the last century.
His judicious biographer truly says, that ' no minister has left for the imitation of posterity a more
perfect pattern of parochial administration.' The history of a parish minister is not so full of incident and variety as that of a missionary or an itinerant Evangelist, such as Whitefield, Wesley, or
Rowland Hill ; but Mr. Sidney is entitled to the thanks of the Christian public, for the skill with
which he has arranged so much valuable information concerning one whose purity of life and zeal
in the cause of his Master entitled him to be held in everlasting remembrance."—*The Record*,
May 7.

LIFE OF THE REV. ROWLAND HILL, M.A. ; compiled from
Authentic Documents by the Rev. EDWIN SIDNEY, A.M., of St. John's College, Cam-
bridge. In 8vo., with a fine Portrait, engraved by H. Robinson. Price 12s. cloth boards.

THE LIFE AND LETTERS OF WILLIAM COWPER, ESQ. ;
with Remarks on Epistolary Writers. By WILLIAM HAYLEY, Esq. A new edition,
complete in one volume, with a Portrait, 8vo., price 12s.

LETTERS TO A FRIEND ON THE EVIDENCES, DOCTRINES,
and DUTIES of the CHRISTIAN RELIGION. By OLINTHUS GREGORY, LL.D.
The Fifth Edition, with numerous additions and improvements, in 2 vols. small 8vo.,
price 14s. boards,

NATURAL HISTORY OF RELIGION ; or Youth armed against
Infidelity and Religious Errors. By the Rev. R. TAYLOR, Curate of Hart, in the county
of Durham. In 12mo., price 4s. boards.

MORNING COMMUNINGS WITH GOD; or Devotional Medita-
tions for every Day of the Year, translated from the original German of Christian Chris-
topher Sturm, Author of " Reflections," &c. By WILLIAM JOHNSTON, A.M. In 2 vols.
small 8vo., price 16s. boards.

CONTEMPLATIONS ON THE SUFFERINGS OF JESUS CHRIST,
in a Series of Devotional Exercises, with an explanatory Paraphrase of the Gospel Narrative. By the Same. In one volume, uniform with the preceding, price 8s.

A GRANDMOTHER'S ADVICE TO YOUNG MOTHERS ON
the PHYSICAL EDUCATION of CHILDREN. By the Countess Dowager Mountcashell. Revised and augmented by the Author. Handsomely printed in foolscap 8vo., 7s. in cloth, lettered.

₊ The observations and advice contained in this little work are chiefly the result of the author's own experience; and when they are founded on the information of others, that information has been examined with the strictest attention. The book is the production of many years' study and reflection, and the author cannot help flattering herself that it will be of use to those for whom it is designed—the anxious Mother, the attentive Governess, and the careful Nurse. Long experience and much observation have induced her to believe that a great number of the diseases which afflict the human race, are the effects of imprudence and neglect in the early part of life; and that by constant and judicious attention to the physical education, during the first fifteen years, many of these diseases might be avoided. For this reason, she is anxious to diffuse amongst her own sex a species of knowledge which may enable mothers to educate their children with better prospects of health and happiness; and perhaps occasion them to take a greater interest in the welfare of their offspring, by proving how it depends on their attention.

ELEMENTS OF THE THEORY AND PRACTICE OF MEDICINE.
Designed for the Use of Students and Junior Practitioners. By George Gregory, M.D., Licentiate of the Royal College of Physicians in London; Physician to the Small Pox and Vaccination Hospital, and Consulting Physician to the St. George's and St. James's General Dispensary. Fourth edition, enlarged, revised, and much improved, in a thick volume, 8vo., price 15s.

LECTURES ON THE PRINCIPLES AND PRACTICE OF PHYSIC.
By the late John Armstrong, M.D. Edited by Joseph Rix. In a thick 8vo. volume, of nearly 900 pages, price 16s. boards.

"The substance of these Lectures is so excellent, that we congratulate all our readers on the appearance of the volume before us. To the student it will be invaluable; and we know no one so advanced that he may not derive profit from the instructions of that master of the Art, Dr. Armstrong. Mr. Rix has our hearty thanks for the zeal and ability which he has displayed in enriching medical literature with this excellent text-book."—Medical Quarterly Review, No. III.

MEMOIR OF THE LIFE AMD MEDICAL OPINIONS OF JOHN ARMSTRONG, M.D.
With an Inquiry into the Facts connected with those Forms of Fever attributed to Malaria or Marsh Effluvium. By Francis Boott, M.D. In 8vo., price 13s. cloth boards.

TAXATION, REVENUE, EXPENDITURE, POWER, STATISTICS, and DEBT of the whole BRITISH EMPIRE.
The whole founded on, and illustrated by, Official Tables and Authentic Documents. By Pablo Pebrer. In a large 8vo. volume, with numerous Tables. Price 18s. cloth boards.

LEGENDS AND STORIES OF IRELAND. Second Series. By
Samuel Lover, Esq., R.H.A.

"Here's the best of good spirits."

With fine illustrations by W. Harvey and the Author. In foolscap 8vo. Price 7s. 6d., handsomely bound in cloth, and lettered.

"The great merit of his works is that they are perfectly true to Nature—to Nature as we behold her every day in our streets and fields, mingling shrewd philosophy with caustic satire and brilliant wit, and wild frolic and extravagant whim; but this Nature polished and refined—the offensive suppressed without injury to the force and verisimilitude of the picture."—Irish Monthly Magazine, June, 1834.

Books are to be returned on or before
the last date below